ILLUMINATING SOCIAL LIFE

THIRD EDITION

TITLES OF RELATED INTEREST FROM PINE FORGE PRESS

PETER KIVISTO EDITOR
AUGUSTANA COLLEGE

ILLUMINATING SOCIAL LIFE

CLASSICAL AND CONTEMPORARY THEORY REVISITED

THIRD EDITION

PINE FORGE PRESS
An Imprint of Sage Publications, Inc.
Thousand Oaks • London • New Delhi

For information:

Pine Forge Press
A Sage Publications Company
2455 Teller Road
Thousand Oaks, California 91320
E-mail: order@sagepub.com

Sage Publications Ltd.
1 Oliver's Yard
55 City Road
London EC1Y 1SP
United Kingdom

Sage Publications India Pvt. Ltd.
B-42, Panchsheel Enclave
Post Box 4109
New Delhi 110 017 India

Printed in the United States of America

Library of Congress Cataloging-in-Publication Data

Illuminating social life: classical and contemporary theory revisited / edited by Peter Kivisto.—3rd ed.
    p. cm.
Includes bibliographical references and index.
ISBN 1-4129-0559-1 (pbk.)
   1. Sociology—Philosophy. 2. Sociology—History. 3. Social history—1970-
I. Kivisto, Peter, 1948-

HM585.I44 2005
301′.01—dc22

                                        2004005984

04   05   06   07   08   09   10   9   8   7   6   5   4   3   2   1

Acquiring Editor:	Jerry Westby
Editorial Assistant:	Vonessa Vondera
Production Editor:	Tracy Alpern
Copy Editor:	Dan Hays
Typesetter:	C&M Digitals (P) Ltd.
Indexer:	Karen A. McKenzie
Cover Designer:	Michelle Kenny

To my friend, Mike Kirn.

Contents

About the Editor

Peter Kivisto, PhD (New School for Social Research), is the Richard Swanson Professor of Social Thought and chair of sociology at Augustana College. Among his recent books are *Key Ideas in Sociology* (2nd ed., 2004), *Multiculturalism in a Global Society* (2002), *Social Theory: Roots and Branches* (2nd ed., 2002), and *Sociology of Religion* (2002). His primary scholarly and teaching interests revolve around social theory and ethnic studies. He is serving as secretary-treasurer of the American Sociological Association's International Migration Section and is working on a book on the future of citizenship.

Preface

As the editor of a book with what has proven to be a loyal following, I have been heartened by the very positive responses by my colleagues to its first two editions, both in public forums, such as book reviews and commentaries in professional newsletters, and more informally in numerous conversations and email exchanges. Professors who have adopted *Illuminating Social Life* and students who have been asked to read it have provided all who have been involved in its production—authors, editor, and publisher—with ample testimony that our conviction from the beginning about the need for such a theory reader was on the mark.

Thus, the third edition builds on the strengths of the first two while taking seriously the insights of the many individuals who have offered suggestions, constructive criticisms, and general encouragement. The major difference between this and the earlier editions is that we have added two new chapters devoted to theoretical perspectives that readers have convinced us need to be included or amplified: one employing a symbolic interactionist perspective and the other combining the insights of symbolic interactionism with a postmodern orientation, thereby complementing the other chapter devoted to understanding that notoriously difficult, elusive, and important theoretical orientation. Only one of the original chapters has been eliminated from this edition. Each of the authors was afforded the opportunity to revise his or her chapter, and although most opted for relatively minor changes, two decided to make somewhat more substantive revisions that are intended to amplify and clarify particular points.

The purpose of this book is to illustrate the importance of sociological theory to students attempting to make sense of the world they inhabit. By applying various social theories from the past and the present to selected facets of modern life, the authors who have contributed to this collection of essays share a common purpose: to illustrate how different social theories are capable of providing significant understanding that without theory would not be grasped.

I have taught social theory for more than 25 years and am very aware of the trepidation with which many students approach this seemingly mysterious or irrelevant subject. Indeed, this book is a direct response to the ways that students react to theory. All the contributors are equally aware of this anxiety. Indeed, aside from our one coauthor who is now a lawyer, we have collectively amassed hundreds of years of experience teaching theory to thousands of undergraduates. Over the years, we have worked hard to get students at our respective home institutions to become comfortable with theorizing while at the same time attempting to convince them of the value of theory. From experience, we have learned that one especially effective way to accomplish these goals is by the application of particular theories to concrete examples from everyday life.

Undergraduate students frequently have a difficult time appreciating the relevance of sociological theory. They all too often fail to see the connection of their theory courses to the "substantive" courses in the departmental offerings. Instead, theory courses are seen either as excursions into the history of ideas or as exercises in overly abstract and arcane discourses that, they believe, can only be of interest to sociologists specializing in social theory. In short, students harbor suspicions about the value of social theory for them.

Although we can sympathize with this suspicion, all the contributors to this book are convinced that theory is essential for anybody trying to make sense of the swirling events and perplexing circumstances all of us encounter in our daily lives. In fact, it is fair to say that without realizing it, everyone is a social theorist. The philosopher of science N. R. Hanson thought that this was the case when he wrote that "all observation is a theory-laden activity" (1958, p. 3). By this, he meant that everyone, not merely social theorists, looks at the world through a variety of implicit theoretical lenses. These lenses afford angles of vision that allow us to see and interpret, in novel ways, aspects of the social world.

There are, however, major differences between everyday uses of theory and the sociological uses of theory. By pointing out that in the former case, theories are generally implicit, whereas in the latter they are explicit, I mean to indicate that sociological theories are subjected to examination to determine whether they are coherent, logically consistent, and empirically supported. Everyday theories are simply taken-for-granted assumptions about aspects of the social world that can prove to be more or less helpful in going about the business of our daily lives. They are generally not scrutinized in a critical and reflective way. In contrast, sociological theories are constantly tested to determine if they are actually applicable in any inquiry into aspects of the social world. If they prove to be inapplicable—if they do not further our understanding of whatever it is we are studying—they are discarded. Numerous theories in sociology have proven themselves, over time, to be invaluable tools for advancing the sociological imagination and for helping us to make sense of the social conditions that frame our lives. The essays assembled in this collection testify to this fact.

This book contains 13 chapters devoted to different theories. Part I contains 4 chapters that address aspects of the theories of the four scholars who are seen today as the most influential figures from the formative period in the history of sociology: Karl Marx, Max Weber, Émile Durkheim, and Georg Simmel. Part II examines nine contemporary theoretical orientations or mixes that have had a profound impact on sociology in recent years. We make no claim to have included all the most influential contemporary theories. This would require a multivolume book. The theories we do focus on include neofunctionalism, exchange theory and rational choice, critical theory, feminism, symbolic interactionism, dramaturgy, postmodernism, and globalization theory. Both parts of the book begin with a brief introduction that can serve to outline the general contours of the approaches taken by particular theorists and theory schools.

I stress that this book is not necessarily meant to be a substitute either for reading theorists in their own words or for more conventional social theory texts that survey the discipline in much greater detail. Rather, it is also meant to function as a supplemental text that can be profitably used in conjunction with other readings. All the authors hope that by provoking and stimulating readers with engaging illustrative cases, many students will want to delve more deeply into social theory—and that they will do so without suffering from theory anxiety.

In preparing the manuscript for publication, I benefited from the input of a variety of people. First and foremost, I thank all the scholars who wrote chapters for the book. We have gotten to know one another rather well, despite the fact that a few of us have never met face to face. I suppose it might be said that we are an example of the cyberspace communities that Anne Hornsby writes about in her chapter on surfing the Net. George Ritzer needs to be singled out for thanks because his earlier work on McDonaldization served as a model for the rest of us. Moreover, I thank him for allowing me to pick up a project that he, in fact, had initiated. Thanks to the following reviewers of earlier editions:

Jim Gramlich, University of Illiois at Chicago

Sally Raskoff, University of Southern California

Jay Howard, Indiana University-Purdue University, Columbus

David Williamson, University of North Texas

Lutz Kaelber, University of Vermont

William I. Robinson, New Mexico State University

Ralph Pyle, Michigan State University

Stuart Schoenfeld, York University

Patricia Fanning, Bridgewater State College

Donald Nielsen, University of Wisconsin-Eau Claire

Thomas J. Fararo, University of Pittsburgh

Neil McLaughlin, McMaster University

Glenn A. Goodwin, Pitzer University

The following readers provided valuable commentary and suggestions that inform this edition:

Ione Y. DeOllos, Ball State University

Andrew Perrin, University of North Carolina, Chapel Hill

John Hamlin, University of Minnesota, Duluth

David Brown, Illinois State University

Chien Ju Huang, North Carolina Central University

Stephen Adair, Central Connecticut State University

Stephen Zehr, University of Southern Indiana

Close to home, I thank my secretary, Jean Sottos, for all the work she put into the preparation of several chapters. I also express my delight in having had the opportunity to coauthor a chapter with one of my former students, and a person with a bright future, Dan Pittman. At home, Sarah, Aaron, and Susan read and commented on one or more of the chapters and in other ways encouraged me along the way.

For the first two editions, Steve Rutter proved to be a creative and perceptive publisher. However, for this edition, I extend a huge debt of gratitude to Jerry Westby. Jerry is a consummate pro who knows books and the publishing industry extremely well. I have learned a lot working with him. Moreover, in the few years that I have gotten to know him, I have come to respect his judgment and insights. If this sounds altogether too serious, it is. The truth be told, Jerry is fun to work with! Other folks at Pine Forge assisted me in many ways, large and small, and to them I extend my heartfelt appreciation. I am especially grateful for all the diligent work performed by Tracy Alpern and Vonessa Vondera.

Reference

Hanson, N. R. (1958). *Patterns of discovery*. Cambridge, UK: Cambridge University Press.

PART I

Classical Sociological Theory

Introduction

Peter Kivisto

Of all the many early figures in the history of sociology, four stand out as the most enduringly important: Karl Marx, Max Weber, Émile Durkheim, and Georg Simmel. In different ways, the members of this quartet both shaped the discipline during its formative period and continue to influence sociological thinking today. Although their respective understandings of modern society overlapped in many ways, each of these scholars nonetheless emphasized certain features of contemporary life at the expense of others. Each developed a distinctive theoretical approach that served to provide a novel way of interpreting facets of social life. The course of events since their deaths has proven time and time again that this foursome possessed remarkable insight into the nature and the dynamics of the modern age. Indeed, their insights are crucial to understanding recent social changes associated with the economic transformations brought about by advanced industrial capitalism, the cultural dynamics of modernity and postmodernity, and the political transformations under way as a result of globalization.

None of the essays in Part I pretends to capture the fullness of any of the theorists under consideration. Rather, the authors have attempted to extract from the work important elements that can be treated on their own terms but manage at the same time to reveal something of the overall thrust of the particular theorist's intellectual legacy.

Chapter 1, by John P. Walsh and Anne Zacharias-Walsh, explores the contemporary relevance of a person who historically preceded the other three scholars: Karl Marx (1818-1883). Unlike the others, Marx never held an academic appointment but instead lived his life as a revolutionary outsider. His ideas—or at least particular interpretations of his ideas—had a profound impact on the history of the 20th century, from the success of the Russian Revolution to the collapse of communism in the late 1980s.

Marx, in a unique synthesis of German philosophy, French political ideas, and British economics, sought to understand the dynamics of capitalism. Key to understanding Marx is a realization that he was not concerned with understanding industrial society in general, but rather with revealing the unique dynamics of capitalist industrialization. Indeed, the major sociological question he sought to answer was, how does capitalism work? In addressing this question, Marx also addressed three corollaries: (a) Is capitalism an economic system that necessarily exploits some classes in the interests of another class?; (b) if it is exploitative, is a nonexploitative industrial system possible?; and (c) if a nonexploitative system is possible, how can it come about?

Marx thought that capitalism, being driven by the quest for profits, necessarily placed that quest above the quest for a just, humane, and equitable society. His writings are an attempt not only to claim that capitalism inevitably exploits the working class but also to show why and how this is so. These questions were the ones that most preoccupied him. Marx wrote far less about the alternatives, in part because he had a decided aversion to utopian dreamers. Thus, although Marx thought that a nonexploitative system—which he called socialism or communism—was possible, he had far less to say about what this type of economy would look like and how it would be established than he did about the character of existing capitalism.

What the chapter by Walsh and Zacharias-Walsh illustrates is that today, during a major transformation in the economy, key elements from the core of Marx's analysis of the dynamics of capitalism are as relevant as they were in the 19th century. Specifically, the authors seek to illustrate by using concrete examples of recent labor struggles that contemporary capitalism does not differ from its earlier manifestations insofar as it continues to be based on the systematic exploitation of workers.

In Chapter 2, George Ritzer explores and updates one of the central theoretical concerns of the great German social thinker, Max Weber (1864-1920): his theory of the rationalization of modern life. Weber was one of the most important academics responsible for the development of sociology in Germany. The scope of topics he studied was encyclopedic. Thus, he wrote about economics, politics, culture, and religion. Within these arenas, his interests were equally far-ranging. In economics, for example, he wrote about the agrarian economies of the ancient world as well as about current events, such as the emergence of a socialist economy in revolutionary Russia after World War I. In perhaps his most famous and provocative thesis, on the relationship between what he called the "Protestant ethic" and the "spirit of capitalism," Weber argued that there was an "elective affinity" between Protestant theology and the worldview of capitalism, and this affinity served to account for the fact that capitalism arose in countries where the Protestant Reformation had proven to be successful.

No matter how controversial this thesis would subsequently prove itself to be, what is clear from his argument is that Weber thought that the various institutional spheres that make up society are interconnected. This is certainly the case in his discussion of the topic of central concern to Ritzer: rationalization. Weber thought that a rational, scientific worldview increasingly came to characterize the modern age, with its emphasis on reason. When applied to a capitalist economy, rationalization entailed, as Ritzer notes, such features as predictability, calculability, efficiency, and control. All these are employed by capitalist managers intent on increasing profitability and control over the market.

Weber was one of the great pessimists of his day, and he felt that the progressive advance of rationalization (and its subsidiary, bureaucratization) threatened our freedom. In perhaps the most widely quoted passage from his writings, he contended that our futures would come to resemble an "iron cage." Ritzer's article is an attempt to use this insight by analyzing what is to all of us an altogether familiar and taken-for-granted feature of our social landscape: the fast-food restaurant. The concept of McDonaldization is designed to update and specifically apply the Weberian idea of rationalization to this phenomenon. In the spirit of Weber, Ritzer seeks to explore the darker side of this pervasive phenomenon.

Regarding the third classic theorist, Émile Durkheim (1858-1917), we discover someone with a far more optimistic view of what the modern world holds in store for us. Insofar as he was a pivotal figure in the establishment of sociology in the French university system, Durkheim was the contemporary counterpart of Weber. His ideas had a profound impact on sociology not only in France but also internationally. Indeed, it is fair to say that in the long run, Durkheim's ideas played a larger role in shaping American sociology than did the ideas of the three other people discussed in Part I.

Durkheim was concerned with understanding differing forms of human community and the distinctive bases of solidarity that undergirded them. In rather sweeping fashion, he sought to illustrate how preindustrial, premodern communities were, in significant ways, different from industrial, modern ones. He described earlier societies as being based on mechanical solidarity, whereas contemporary society was predicated on organic solidarity. Central to Durkheim in his attempt to distinguish mechanical from organic societies is the division of labor. In earlier societies, this division was rather minimal because people—or kin units—performed a wide array of tasks necessary to sustain their lives. In stark contrast, in modern industrial society, the division of labor is highly developed. The size and complexity of such societies necessitates the specialization of work. Because people are unable to perform all the tasks associated with sustaining their lives, they are highly dependent on others. Modern society fosters interdependency.

Reviewing these ideas and building on them, Anne M. Hornsby examines the novel phenomenon of "Net communities." She is interested in seeing to what extent these cyberspace communities are merely extensions of modern organic communities or can be seen—because of the lack of physical proximity and the disembodied character of Net social interactions—as a new form of community. In other words, she questions whether Durkheim's ideas can adequately grasp the world of the Net or whether we need to build on, but go beyond, his original contributions to social theory.

The final person discussed in Part I is the German sociologist Georg Simmel (1858-1918). During his lifetime, Simmel's career was consistently stymied because of his Jewish background. German anti-Semitism was chiefly responsible for preventing him from rising to the heights of the German academic world. Nonetheless, his thought was held in high regard by his contemporaries in both Europe and America. Weber was especially impressed by his intellectual achievements. Disturbed by the injustice that befell his colleague, Weber used his considerable influence to try to advance Simmel's career. This proved in the long term to be helpful because, late in life, Simmel finally obtained a professorship that he richly deserved. Simmel had a substantial impact on what was known as the Chicago School of sociology, the most influential center for the development of sociology in the United States during the early part of the 20th century. After his death, Simmel's reputation grew, albeit slowly and somewhat fitfully. Today, his ideas not only are seen as key to sociologists of modernity but also are embraced by theorists who describe themselves as postmodernists.

As a student of contemporary social and cultural life, Simmel's thinking frequently appeared to reflect what he described as a central trait of the modern world: its fragmentary nature. Known as a fine essayist, Simmel provided finely textured descriptions, or snapshots, of social relations and individual types. He was interested in conflict, which he saw as potentially both destructive and creative. Simmel was not a systematic social theorist, but his ideas do reflect a carefully articulated and coherent theoretical framework.

William J. Staudenmeier, Jr., an expert in alcohol studies, reveals the varied ways that Simmel's ideas can be employed to examine the role of alcohol in society. In the spirit of Simmel, Staudenmeier approaches his topic from several different perspectives, showing in the process the many ways that Simmel's ideas can be employed to shed light on various facets of it.

Together, these four chapters reveal the ongoing relevance to us, as we begin the 21st century, of ideas first formulated during the 19th and early 20th centuries. It is for this reason that sociologists continually return to the ideas of their forebears. They do so not simply to understand something about the history of the discipline but also because these ideas still have much to say to us about contemporary society.

CHAPTER 1

Working Longer, Living Less

Understanding Marx Through the Workplace Today

John P. Walsh and Anne Zacharias-Walsh

John P. Walsh *is Associate Professor of Sociology at the University of Illinois at Chicago. His research and teaching interests focus on work, organizations, and new technology. His recent work compares innovation systems in Japan and the U.S., and he has spent several years working in Japanese universities. He has published in journals such as* Science, Research Policy, Work and Occupations, *and* Social Studies of Science. *He has been teaching Marx to undergraduates for over a decade and hopes that the taste of Marx presented here will encourage readers to read* Capital *(Marx, 1867/1977). He encourages students who have questions about Marx or the chapter to email him at jwalsh@uic.edu (the texts of some of the articles cited in this chapter are available on his Web page: www.uic.edu/~jwalsh/soc100.html). Also, he hopes to some day be able to limit his working day to 8 hours.*

Anne Zacharias-Walsh *is an independent writer and labor activist. A former mainstream journalist, Zacharias-Walsh defected from the world of formulaic "news" coverage in search of publications that encourage in-depth reporting on and analysis of current labor and business trends and their effects on working people. Currently she is a visiting researcher at the Social Science Research Institute at International Christian University in Tokyo, where she studies emerging grassroots women's and workers' organizations in Japan. Zacharias-Walsh began studying Marxist theory as an undergraduate in connection with her work in the movement for peace and justice in Central*

America. She began writing about labor while earning a master's degree in cultural theory at Carnegie Mellon University in Pittsburgh.

> We want to feel the sunshine;
> We want to smell the flowers;
> We're sure that God has willed it.
> And we mean to have eight hours.
> We're summoning our forces from
> shipyard, shop and mill;
> Eight hours for work, eight hours
> for rest, eight hours for what we will
>
> —*Hymn of the Eight Hour Movement (1886)*

I n all its handouts, capitalism promises that everyone will benefit from a prosperous economy: What's good for General Motors (GM) is good for the country; a rising tide lifts all boats. The robust business climate of the 1990s in the United States, however, did not lead to increases in workers' standard of living. Instead, soaring corporate profits and business-friendly government resulted in stagnant wages, as well as deteriorating working conditions and job security; union busting; and the worst income disparity since the 1930s. Corporate America increased productivity by decreasing the number of employees, increased profits by holding down workers' wages, and increased working hours while keeping unemployment high. In other words, contrary to "trickle-down" predictions, the corporate world has consolidated power, and workers were, by all indicators, worse off for it.

The Return of the 12-Hour Day

In 1991, the highly profitable A. E. Staley Company, a corn-processing plant based in Decatur, Illinois, offered its employees a contract that called for increasing the regular workday from 8 to 12 hours, mandatory overtime ("If we call you, you will come!"), and pay and benefit take backs. In the same year, Staley was reportedly earning an approximately 22% profit, while its parent company, British conglomerate Tate and Lyle, reaped $400 million in profits on $5.5 billion in sales.

The employees resisted the proposed contract at the bargaining table and in public protests. In June 1993, however, the company locked out its regular employees and brought replacement workers in to run the plant. Although that move launched a 2-year battle that became the rallying point in the struggle to revitalize the American labor movement, in the end the company won out, forcing the workers to accept draconian concessions in the midst of booming business.[1] With its vast financial resources and ever-growing supply of replacement workers, and with state power (in the form of state and local police) stepping in whenever "necessary" to contain the dispute, the company was able to hold out longer than 760 workers who had not received regular paychecks in more than 2 years. In other words, instead of passing along some of its good fortune to workers, Staley used its beefed-up resources as a whip against the employees, taking more and more away from workers merely because it had become strong enough to get away with it.

Although Staley came to symbolize this famine-amid-feast trend, it was by no means unique in its demands or tactics, as the following examples demonstrate:

- Workers at Caterpillar went on strike in June 1994 after the company— widely reported in the business press to be enjoying robust profits— demanded concessions including 12-hour shifts. During the strike, the company posted record profits while operating with replacement workers who received no benefits.
- Bridgestone/Firestone imposed 12-hour shifts and round-the-clock production.
- In 1994, Uniroyal Goodrich threatened to shut down if workers did not go with 12-hour shifts and 24-hour continuous production. Employees capitulated, fearing layoffs.
- The Formica Company in Evendale, Ohio, adopted scheduled overtime in 1992. Employees work seven 12-hour shifts every 14 days.
- Auto manufacturers are also ratcheting up shift lengths. At Ford's plant in Batavia, Ohio, employees work 9-hour shifts, with an additional 8- to 10-hour overtime shift on Saturdays.
- General Motors employees in Flint, Michigan, struck the Buick assembly plant in September 1994 over excessive hours. Management was requiring 12- to 14-hour workdays, often 7 days a week.
- Gates Rubber Company forced workers at its Galesburg, Illinois, plant to accept 12-hour shifts, 7 days a week, after a year-long dispute. During the dispute, management laid off 121 employees, stating that failure to reach an agreement on 12-hour shifts was the cause of many of those layoffs.
- Imperial Wallcoverings in Rhode Island worked to push through a change in state law to allow companies to schedule employees for mandatory Sunday shifts. In addition, the company also instituted 12-hour shifts and a 48-hour workweek. Employees voted to accept the changes because they would bring more work to the plant, which had recently suffered layoffs.

These are but a few examples of what became a nationwide trend, not only recognized by labor sympathizers but also widely referenced in the pages of the business press, including the following:

- The *Chicago Tribune* ("Illinois Jobs," 1995) reported that although the economic recovery was in its fourth year, most indicators show workers across the board are losing ground in real wages, hours worked, and job security.
- The *Christian Science Monitor* ("Middle-Class Labor," 1995) reported that although productivity has gained 2% annually throughout the 1990s, real wages for the average American worker have fallen 11% since 1975.
- According to the *Cincinnati Enquirer* ("Factory OT Shoots Up," 1994), in 1994 the average workweek for factory workers nationwide was the highest on record at 42.2 hours. Average weekly overtime also hit a high of 4.8 hours per week.

- The *Spartanburg Herald-Journal* ("Swing Shifts," 1993) reported that more than one fourth of American workers are on some form of a rotating schedule, under which workers must switch between day and night shifts.

Nor is workday acceleration limited to jobs in the traditional blue-collar sphere. The Economic Policy Institute found that middle-class parents, taken together, work 3,335 hours per year, up from just over 3,000 hours per year in 1979, an increase of 8 workweeks per year in just 20 years (Greenhouse, 1999). A comptroller in a company called ClickAction, for example, reports working a 6-week period without a day off. During that period, the employee said, she had to leave for work at 5 a.m. and didn't return home until 10 p.m., at which time she had to wash dishes and make her family's dinner for the next night (Lardner, 1999).

Proponents of capitalism are hard-pressed to explain this pattern of growing inequality and polarization. Pundits often fall back on "psychologizing" the problems (people are poor or unemployed because of some personal failing: lack of motivation, drug problem, reliance on welfare, etc.) or on "naturalizing" these ills by pronouncing them intransigent facts of human existence. The writings of Karl Marx, however, offer a different interpretation.

More than 125 years ago, Marx (1867/1977) argued that under capitalism, workers must, by definition, lose economic ground as productivity and profits increase. Far from an anomaly or accidental by-product, this pattern is inherent in a capitalist mode of production.

Our point is not to suggest that Marx was a visionary. His writings and theories remain viable today because of the nature of his project: Marx's analysis of capitalism is designed to uncover the dynamics and contradictions inherent in a system that converts all human relations into economic relations. His central work, *Capital*, is a detailed explication of the logic of capitalism (and given that logic, the necessary, albeit often counterintuitive, implications of it). By revealing that logic, Marx is able to write about actual conditions in his time, while also giving future readers tools for analyzing capitalism and its workings in other historical moments. The purpose of this chapter, then, is to take Marx out of 19th-century industrial England and, by analyzing current workplace conditions in Marxist terms, enable the reader to begin to understand Marxism and the cogency of Marxist theory today.

Capital's (Marx, 1867/1977) three volumes contain a multifaceted theory, even a summary of which is beyond the scope of this chapter. We therefore focus our discussion on the cornerstone of Marx's argument: the production of value and surplus value. Following Marx, we then argue that the logic of value production mandates the continuous push to extend the working day. We then examine labor trends in the 1990s, particularly the reemergence of the 12-hour day and rotating shifts, to demonstrate one of the central claims of Marxism: Capitalism by its very nature generates a ceaseless drive to lengthen the working day, with absolute indifference to human needs, abilities, or limitations.

A note before delving into Marxism proper: As is the case with other legendary (if you will) theorists, such as Freud or Einstein, many readers begin to study the material with certain preconceived, "common knowledge" notions about that theorist's work. Unfortunately, these notions are often stereotyped sketches, oversimplified to the point that they bear no useful resemblance to the original.

Worse yet, they can, the authors fear, constrain the way in which a reader approaches the material by setting forth from the outset a frame that is inadequate to the concept. (For example, it is often difficult to convince students to take Freud seriously at first because he is popularly presented as something of a nut who cannot think about anything but penises.) To circumvent this problem, we begin by noting what Marxism is not: Marxism is not the mere conclusion that capitalism is exploitative. That is a critique of capitalism, and it is one with which Marx agrees. That is not Marxism, however. Many theorists before and after Marx have argued that capitalism is exploitative, and modes of production prior to capitalism (slavery and feudalism) were exploitative. Marx's contribution is in explaining how, why, and in precisely what way capitalism, by its own logic, must be so. In other words, the idea that capitalism is exploitative is the beginning, not the end, of Marx's theorizing.

Contemporary Marxist theory contains many strains, some of which dispute the importance of value as a central concept in Marx. In particular, the so-called Analytic Marxists (see Mayer, 1994) emphasize exploitation as the central concept and argue that the concepts of value and surplus value are not analytically useful. In contrast to the Analytic Marxists, the Marxist Humanists (see Dunayevskaya, 1988) argue that alienation is the central concept of Marx and that production of surplus value is the central form of alienation under capitalism. Marx's writings contain much of value and much that can be debated. Our goal in this chapter is to present what Marx wrote and what he emphasized in his writings: that production of value and surplus value are key to understanding capitalism. This presentation, we hope, will help readers form the basis for sifting through contemporary debates (in this book and elsewhere) on how best to develop Marx's theories.

Marx's Theory of Capital

The Concept of Value

According to Marx, the main function of capitalism is not the production of goods (use value), but rather the production of exchange value or, more simply, value.[2] The goal of the capitalist is the production of surplus value. Unlike other modes of production (such as those of hunter and gatherer societies, slave societies, or agrarian feudalism), in which the primary significance of a particular good is its usefulness (use value), the goods produced under capitalism, commodities, are important to capitalists only as bearers of (exchange) value.[3] Marx defines *value* as the total amount of labor time expended in the production of a given commodity.[4]

Value and Commodity Exchange

Because value (as abstract labor time) is the common denominator among all commodities, it allows diverse commodities, such as cotton, steel, hamburgers, and college educations, to be exchanged for each other—or for their objectified equivalent form, money—in the market. When capitalists exchange certain amounts of seemingly diverse types of commodities in the market (one wool coat for two pairs of shoes), they are actually exchanging definite quantities of value, which have been objectified, or embedded, in those diverse commodity forms. Capitalists do not care which commodities they have, or which ones they get, so long as they are able to exchange them in sufficient quantities. This indifference to the kinds of goods that are being produced in turn transforms the entire concept of work. The purpose of working used to be to produce particular goods that have some particular use to people; in other words, to produce use value. Under capitalism, the purpose of work is the production of exchange value.

The shift in focus from use value to exchange value underlies many of the dynamics of capitalism, including the drive toward an endless working day.[5] Also, it is this transformation that fundamentally inverts, or subverts, the notion of a mode of production. No longer a system designed to meet human needs, capitalism becomes a system driven by the desire to generate value, and human concerns are replaced by concerns about maximizing surplus value.

It is important to note that Marx's critique of capitalism does not rest on an assumption of anyone "cheating the system." Instead, he begins with the assumption that all goods are exchanged in the market for their full value. Thus, any exploitation would be inherent to capitalism, independent of any capitalist's will or guile.[6]

Labor as Commodity

The capitalist, then, has a difficult task: Selling a commodity above its value does not count as "capitalism" (i.e., does not create new value); the capitalist must find a way to make the value of his or her commodity greater than the sum of the value of its parts. Labor power is the only commodity that fills that bill because labor power is the only commodity that can create value.

Labor power, or the ability to do a day's labor, is a commodity. It shares the following basic properties of any commodity:

- A day's labor power has a particular amount of value embedded in it.
- A day's labor power is purchased with an equivalent amount of value—in this case, in the form of wages.
- The value of a day's labor power is the quantity of labor time embedded in it.
- The value of a day's labor power is equal to the total amount of socially necessary labor time used to produce the average bundle of (socially necessary) goods a worker must consume each day to be able to come to work again the next day.

Labor: The Secret Behind Surplus Value

Again, it is important to note what Marx is not saying. Marx is not merely saying that capitalists are always trying to make workers work longer so they will have more goods to sell and therefore be richer. Rather, Marx argues that by maximizing the amount of time an individual works in a day, the capitalist will be able to maximize the rate of return he or she gets for the wage he or she has paid. In other words, the capitalist will have maximized the rate of surplus value.

To illustrate the role of labor in the production of surplus value, we arbitrarily assume that 5 hours is the amount of labor time needed to produce a worker's daily subsistence. This means that the value of (or the amount of past labor embedded in) a day's labor is equal to 5 hours. Furthermore, we assume that the quantity of value represented by 5 hours of socially necessary abstract labor time is equal to $100.[7] The capitalist pays the worker $100 for his or her day's labor. Equal values have been exchanged, and everything has been exchanged at its full value. An amazing transformation takes place, however, once we leave the market and enter the realm of production. It is in the realm of production, Marx argues, that the secrets of surplus value, and therefore capitalism, are revealed.

Production of Commodities and Surplus Value

In the market, labor power appeared the same as any other commodity. When we enter the sphere of production, however, the crucial difference emerges: Labor creates value. All other commodities used in the production process add to the new commodity only the set amount of value already embedded in them as a result of their own production. Assume, for example, that 3 pounds of cotton has 3 hours of labor time embedded in it. No matter how the capitalist uses that cotton, the maximum amount of value it can bestow on another commodity in the process of production is 3 hours' worth. That is, it can only transfer the value it has in it. Labor, however, creates value. Therefore, not only can it transfer the value already embedded in it (its current value) but also, by continuing to work, labor can create and add new value. When the capitalist hires a worker, he or she is buying not merely past labor (i.e., labor that has already been expended in the production process) but also the capacity to labor, or labor power. There is no reason to suppose that the amount of value a worker can create (i.e., the amount of labor time the worker can expend in a day) is necessarily the same as the amount of labor time that was necessary to produce his or her daily means of subsistence. Marx (1867/1977) notes,

> But the past labour embodied in the labour-power and the living labour it can perform; the daily cost of maintaining labour-power and its daily expenditure in work, are two totally different things. The former determines the exchange-value of the labour-power, the latter is its use-value. The fact that half a day's labour is necessary to keep the worker alive during 24 hours does not in any way prevent him from working a whole day. (p. 300)

If the worker is hired but left idle all day, that worker produces no value. If the worker works longer (at the socially necessary rate) than the amount of labor time required to reproduce his or her efforts, the worker creates more value than the capitalist paid, thus producing surplus value.

Marx shows us that to understand the secrets of capitalism, it is important that we peer into the details of the production process (details that are hidden from us when we go to the store to buy commodities). We will lay out an extended example of the details of linen production (using hypothetical numbers for simplicity) to illustrate the nature of the production process under capitalism. This section, although somewhat arid, provides the basis for understanding the more dramatic, real-world examples we discuss elsewhere in the chapter. Table 1.1 summarizes all the transactions discussed in this section.

Our capitalist has decided to produce linen. (Because he is a capitalist, his interest is in linen for its exchange value, not its use value.) We make the following assumptions and trace out the first day of production:

- Ten spools of thread are needed to produce 10 yards of linen. The capitalist buys 50 spools of thread (Table 1.1, line 1, column 5) for $50 (Table 1.1, column 6), an amount equal to the value of the labor power embodied in that thread.

- In producing 50 yards of linen, the wear and tear on the loom and all other equipment costs (including rent, light, heat, etc.) equal $50 (Table 1.1, column 7).

- The value of a day's labor (i.e., the cost of reproducing a day's labor) is $100 (Table 1.1, column 3), and this $100 represents 5 hours of socially necessary labor time.

As you can see, in making the purchases necessary to produce linen, our capitalist has exchanged $200 (Table 1.1, column 2) for commodities valued at $200—an even exchange.

We now assume that working at the normal pace, using the average skill and typical equipment, a worker can turn 10 spools of thread into 10 yards of linen in 1 hour. In 5 hours, the worker will have woven 50 yards of linen (Table 1.1, column 9). The following equation summarizes the day's activities:

Labor		Thread		Equipment		Linen
1 day (5 hours)	+	50 spools	+	loom, etc.	=	50 yards
$100		$50		$50		$200

Thus, the linen contains $200 of total labor: $100 of new labor from our worker and $100 worth of old labor contained in the thread and the equipment. Therefore, the 50 yards of linen has a value of $4 per yard (Table 1.1, column 10).

The capitalist now takes the cloth to the market and exchanges his linen at full value—$200. He now has the same $200 he started with; not a very fruitful day (compare Table 1.1, columns 2 and 11). After all his transactions, the capitalist is no better off than before. No surplus value was created (Table 1.1, column 12).

Production of Surplus Value

Despite this early setback, our capitalist quickly sees his mistake and vows to rectify it. The capitalist recognizes that surplus value can only be created by extending the working day beyond the amount of time necessary to produce the means of subsistence for the worker (5 hours in the example).

With this insight, the capitalist goes to the market again. The following day (see Table 1.1, line 2), the capitalist buys 100 spools of thread (Table 1.1, column 5) for $100 (Table 1.1, column 6), $100 worth of looms and lights and such (Table 1.1,

Table 1.1   The Working Day and the Creation of Surplus Value

	Inputs							Outputs				
(1) Day	(2) Money ($) (3 + 6 + 7)	(3) Wage ($)	(4) Hours	(5) Thread (Spools)	(6) Raw Material Costs ($)	(7) Equipment Costs ($)	(8) Labor Power ($)	(9) Cloth (Yards)	(10) Price (per Yard) ($)	(11) Value ($) (9 × 10)	(12) Surplus ($) (11−2)	(13) Profit Rate (%)
1	200	100	5	50	50	50	100	50	4.00	200	0	0
2	300	100	10	100	100	100	200	100	4.00	400	100	33
3	340	100	12	120	120	120	240	120	4.00	480	140	41
4	400	100	150	150	150	150	300	150	4.00	600	200	50

column 7), and hires the worker for another day at $100 (Table 1.1, column 3). The capitalist has exchanged $300 (Table 1.1, column 2) for commodities valued at $300, again, an even exchange. But this time, he makes the worker work 10 hours (Table 1.1, column 4). During this longer day, the worker weaves the 100 spools of thread into 100 yards of linen (Table 1.1, column 9). We now have the following equation:

Labor		Thread		Equipment		Linen
1 day (10 hours)	+	100 spools	+	loom, etc.	=	100 yards
$200		$100		$100		$400

Given that the linen was produced using the same technology and conditions and skill (i.e., contains the same amount of socially necessary labor), it has the same value as yesterday, namely, $4 per yard (Table 1.1, column 10). The value of the linen is $400 (Table 1.1, column 11). The cost of the commodities that went into the linen, however, was only $300 (Table 1.1, column 2). The capitalist has generated surplus value of $100 (Table 1.1, column 12) and a rate of profit (Table 1.1, column 13) of 33% ($100/$300). In other words, money has been used to purchase commodities that were then used to create a new commodity whose value is greater than the original capital outlay, and this new commodity is turned back into an equivalent amount of money. This is the essence of capitalism.

Surplus Value and the Extension of the Working Day

We have seen that surplus value is generated only if the worker works longer than the time required to reproduce his or her labor power for another day.[8] It is therefore in the interest of the capitalist to extend the working day as far as possible beyond the point where the worker is simply reproducing his own labor power.

By following the same process and extending the working day to 12 hours, our capitalist can reap $140 of surplus value, with a profit rate of 41% (see Table 1.1, line 3, columns 12 and 13).

By extending it to a 15-hour day, the capitalist can reap $200 in surplus value, with a profit rate of 50% (see Table 1.1, line 4, columns 12 and 13).

By extending the working day beyond what is necessary for reproducing labor power, the capitalist generates surplus labor, and the more he extends it, the greater his rate of profit.

Surplus Labor

Far from a fixed entity, what constitutes a "working day" is a variable thing, limited by some "natural" boundaries but largely defined through social and political struggle. The minimum length of the working day is the amount of time required to produce the average worker's means of subsistence. If labor as a whole works less than this, society is not reproducing itself and will eventually collapse from starvation. Note that the converse is not true: Even if a society as a whole is extracting surplus value, it may still suffer mass starvation. As Nobel Prize–winning economist Amartya Sen (1999) has shown, in capitalist societies, famines are generally a problem not of too little food but of a lack of buying power among the starving.

Theoretically, the maximum length of the working day is 24 hours. In practice, however, it has to be somewhat less because reproducing the labor power requires some time for sleeping, eating, and procreating.

The history of capitalism has been the history of the struggle to define the length of the working day. Capitalists have often attempted to impose working days of 12, 14, 18, and, if possible, 24 hours to maximize their surplus. Marx (1867/1977, p. 353n) describes a public meeting in Nottingham (home of Robin Hood) to debate whether the working day should be *reduced* to 18 hours. Against the insatiable demand of capital, workers seek to limit the extension of the working day so that they may be able to sell their labor at the same level of intensity the next day and continue to do so over the course of their lives. This leads to the struggle in the workplace over the definition of a fair day's work.

Politics of the Working Day

Although there is constant pressure to increase the working day (and the workweek and weeks worked per year), the length of the working day is a political question (Marx, 1867/1977):

> The capitalist maintains his rights as a purchaser when he tries to make the working day as long as possible, and where possible, to make two working days out of one. On the other hand, the peculiar nature of the commodity sold implies a limit to its consumption by the purchaser, and the worker maintains his right as a seller when he wishes to reduce the working day to a particular normal length. There is here therefore an antinomy, of right against right, both equally bearing the seal of the law of exchange. *Between equal rights, force decides* [italics added]. Hence, in the history of capitalist production, the establishment of a norm for the working day presents itself as a struggle over the limits of that day, a struggle between collective capital, i.e., the class of capitalists, and collective labour, i.e., the working class. (p. 344)

Because the length of the working day is in part a political struggle, labor has some ability to enforce its definition of the "normal" working day. At various points, workers have been successful in their demands for a shorter working day. For example, during the 1990s workers at Volkswagen in Germany negotiated a reduction in their workweek as a way of spreading work to more people. Similarly, workers in France pushed for a reduction of the workweek from 39 hours to 33 hours ("U.S., Europe at Odds," 1993). As the collective power of workers declines, however, capital increasingly has its way, and the working day is extended. Union contracts, for example, have traditionally been one of workers' primary tools for defining and limiting the length of the working day. Union membership in the United States, however, has declined from 23.6% of the labor force in 1960 to 14.1% in 1997. During the same period, the length of the working day has steadily increased. In other words, as union membership has declined, workers are becoming increasingly unable to enforce their definition of a working day.

Table 1.2   Annual Hours Paid Employment for Labor Force Participants

	Year		
Labor Force	1969	1987	Increase
All	1,786	1,949	163
Men	2,054	2,152	98
Women	1,406	1,711	305

SOURCE: Schor (1991).

The Increasing Working Day

In *The Overworked American,* Juliet Schor (1991) documented the increase in the American working day during the prior two decades. As unions have declined, as fixed capital has increased, and as global competition has increased, capital is increasingly attempting to prop up rates of surplus by extending the working day. Schor estimated that the typical American was working approximately 160 hours more per year in 1987 than he or she had in 1969 (Table 1.2). This is the equivalent of working 13 months every year.[9] Furthermore, a 1999 study by the International Labor Organization found that in the bastion of capitalist freedom, the number of hours worked each year was rising at the same time working hours were declining in most other industrialized countries. Americans work more than employees in any industrialized country. On average, Americans work 70 more hours per year than their Japanese counterparts and about 350 more hours—or nearly 9 more weeks—per year than Europeans (Greenhouse, 1999).

Although aggregate figures show a relatively gradual but steady increase, work-weeks and shift lengths in some companies reached hyperbolic levels in the 1990s. Machine operators at Chrysler's Trenton, Michigan, engine plant reportedly work 72-hour weeks. An electrician at the same plant reported working 12-hour shifts 7 days a week ("GM Pact Fallout," 1994). He also reported working 84 consecutive days. Workers in a GM Buick plant clocked in approximately 57 hours per week. Nearly half of the unionized workers at the Dunlop Tire plant in Tonawanda, New York, worked 50 weekends a year and two night shifts during the regular week ("Union Rejects," 1994). In one of the most extreme cases, Thai workers in a garment factory in California were imprisoned and forced to work up to 22 hours per day ("It's Blood," 1996).

Competition and Surplus Value

We have shown that the struggle to increase the working day is driven by a need to produce surplus value. The production of surplus value alone, however, is not enough. Capitalists are driven by competition to produce as much surplus value as possible with a given amount of capital. In other words, firms must, under threat of ruin from their competitors, maximize the ratio of surplus labor to necessary labor. Capital (in the form of investment capital) is constantly on the lookout for a capitalist who is producing surplus value at a greater rate, quickly switching from the laggard capitalist to the capitalist who is most successful at generating surplus value. In a world of global, round-the-clock stock markets and e-trading, capital is more nimble than ever, putting increasing pressure on firms to increase surplus value.

One way firms increase surplus value is by making their workers work faster. By working at above the socially necessary rate, workers can generate extra surplus during the same amount of time. Another way is by extending the working day beyond the amount of time required to reproduce labor power. The *Chicago Tribune* ("9-to-5," 1996) reported that one fourth of U.S. companies were running some form of what is euphemistically called a "compressed workweek," which generally means traditional 8-hour days have been replaced by longer shifts.[10]

The business press is filled with examples of capital's continual demands for an increase in the working day in the name of competition. Prior to implementing its 12-hour rotating shifts, Staley was pulling in substantial profits (one estimate put them at 22% of sales). Those returns were, however, in the words of Staley executive J. P. Mohan, "inadequate" because Archer Daniels Midland, Staley's major competitor in the region, reportedly posted profits of approximately 26%, making it the more attractive site for investment dollars. Mohan said he needed to implement rotating 12-hour shifts for "Staley in Decatur to be competitive" ("Union Stays," 1992).[11] The *Christian Science Monitor* ("Middle-Class Labor," 1995, p. 10) stated, "To the executives at Staley, a subsidiary of London-based Tate & Lyle PLC, the real war is against rival companies. Staley is engaged in a campaign to modernize and streamline production, and blunt a challenge from competing corn millers."

The fact that all three of the companies in the Decatur "war zone" (Caterpillar, Staley, and Bridgestone/Firestone) were willing to wage a battle to the death with long-term employees—in an international media spotlight, while profits for each were robust—reveals the importance of the role of competition. Indeed, few of the companies that we studied used anemic profits to justify moving to longer shifts. As the following examples show, virtually every company pinned the blame on competition:

- With Ford biting at its heels, management at GM's Buick City plant in Flint, Michigan, chose to ride out a strike rather than back off on its demands for 12-hour shifts. "Wall Street is telling GM it must cut payroll before investors will line up behind the company. The possibility that this strike could close the automaker just as the 1995 model year opens is of secondary concern to stock analysts" ("GM Pact Fallout," 1994, p. A1). The fact that GM was profitable did not absolve it of its obligation to decrease the workforce.

- In Baltimore, Poly-Seal Corporation, despite its $60 million to $70 million in annual sales, also withstood a strike rather than concede on 12-hour shifts. Poly-Seal chief executive officer Robert Gillman said the company "remains prosperous" but has suffered a decline in the rate of growth of profits, and because its competitors have gone to longer shifts, it must follow suit or its operations will become "economically unfeasible" ("12-Hour Day," 1994).

• Even the venerable *Encyclopaedia Britannica* bowed to the demands of competition when management announced it was extending employees' workweek by 2 hours without increasing pay. In a memo to less-than-pleased employees, management wrote, "We compete with some of the most aggressive companies in the business. Their employees work hard, and we must match their efforts to compete with them and maintain *Britannica*'s edge."

The demands of competition were also behind innovations at Caterpillar. Because Cat is a producer of means of production for other capitalists, it must, under threat of ruin from its competitors, continually develop innovations that allow its customers to maximize their own surplus value. Caterpillar developed a new earthmover that won an award in Germany for reducing sound pollution ("Award to Caterpillar," 1994). This was a great source of pride at Cat, not because it would ease the burden on those who live near construction sites, but because it allowed firms using Cat equipment to run their construction crews 24 hours a day near residential areas, schools, and hospitals. In other words, Caterpillar's innovation allows Cat's customers to extend their working days to match the continuous working day of the equipment maker.

Investors were very pleased with Caterpillar's actions. In November 1992, Cat stock was selling at $54 per share. By July 1994, Cat's stock was up to $100 per share. Investors had searched among the capitalists and found a firm that was producing substantial surplus value and rushed to join in, driving up the price of Caterpillar's stock.

Again, the pressure on the working day is generated by the logic of capital and does not depend on the wishes of individual capitalists.[12] As such, imposing inhuman shifts is not merely a case of management being antiworker. During the most recent strike, Caterpillar ran its plants with office workers and other replacements. These friends of management were not exempt from the mandates of capital. Instead, they were forced to put in long hours without recourse to a union contract for protection. One worker, normally a business analyst, spent 12 hours each day assembling tractors and then 2 or more hours at his old desk job, thereby giving his employer two jobs each day. A welder brought from Alabama to scab was working 72 hours a week ("Bitter Caterpillar Strike," 1994).

The laws of competition demand these actions. Despite pontifications about "individual will" and "entrepreneurial talent," capitalists recognize that their decisions are often forced by external factors and occasionally call for state power to regulate competition (usually as a response to worker agitation). Marx (1867/1977) quotes a petition by the potteries (including Wedgwood) in 1863:

Much as we deplore the evils before mentioned [extensive workdays for children], it would not be possible to prevent them by any scheme of agreement between the manufacturers. . . . Taking all these points into consideration, we have come to the conviction that some legislative enactment is wanted. (p. 381n)

Thus, it is not capitalists as individuals but rather capitalism that demands that all firms excel at the exploitation of labor power, the production of surplus value. Although individual capitalists may deplore the impact of such logic, they enact these tender feelings under the threat of ruin. All decisions in the workplace are seen through the filter of value production. Even attempts at softening working conditions (such as the Human Relations School, Quality of Work Life Programs, and similar management strategies designed to improve working conditions) are promoted and implemented with arguments that they will increase the productivity of labor and hence increase surplus value.

Mechanisms for Increasing Surplus Labor

Firms are not limiting their strategies for increasing surplus value to lengthening the working day. In their never-ending search for sources of surplus labor, firms have developed a variety of strategies for increasing the working day and squeezing unpaid labor time from employees; these include shaving time, innovation, and the relay system.

Shaving Time

Firms try to increase surplus value in both large and small ways. Extending the working day to 10 or 12 hours is one of the more blatant methods, but firms try other means as well. In an op-ed piece in the *New York Times,* Chicago labor lawyer and author Tom Geoghegan (1999) reported on common ways companies routinely steal time, forcing employees to work for free. Fast-food restaurants often make employees clock out when the restaurant closes, even though the employees have to stay to clean up. The more blatant firms make the employees clock out whenever there are no customers. One Burger King employee in Glasgow was paid the equivalent of $1.55 for a 5-hour shift because he was only "on the clock" for the moments he was serving customers. Hotel employees often worked through their breaks, but the break time was still deducted from their paychecks. Companies hire "part-time supervisors" and "assistant managers," who often do the same work as the people they supervise, but because they are on salary, they don't get paid for overtime hours.

Stealing time is no small trend, Geoghegan (1999) argues. And it's not even one that the corporate world denies. A 1996 Employer Policy foundation study estimated "conservatively" that illegally denied overtime amounts to at least $19 billion every year. Furthermore, Labor Department surveys found that even in jobs supposedly protected by the Fair Labor Standards Act from these kinds of abuses, violations of the act are widespread. In some industries, as many as 60% of employers violate the act (Geoghegan, 1999).

By having workers work off the clock, the capitalist is able to increase unpaid labor and thereby increase the rate of surplus value. Managers are under tremendous pressure to get as much surplus labor as possible from employees and will frequently coerce employees into working off the clock, having them come early, stay late, work through breaks, come in on weekends, take work home—anything that will extend the working day without increasing workers' pay. Workers who accede to such demands are often rewarded with praise and promotions. Those who refuse are badgered, threatened, and occasionally dismissed for not performing up to par.

Innovation

Firms also try to increase surplus labor by innovating to reduce the amount of necessary labor time. Assume our capitalist figures out how to double the productivity of labor (perhaps based on a worker's suggestion during a quality circle meeting). In the simplest form, this can be done by making the workers work twice as fast (under threat of being replaced by unemployed workers). For example, Toyota increases the output quota every quarter. The workers are then expected to work faster to make the new quota—that is, to produce more in the same amount of time—thereby reducing the amount of necessary labor time and increasing the surplus labor time (Kamata, 1983).

As Table 1.3 illustrates, however, there is an interesting twist to the effects of increased productivity, and it is this twist that accounts for the ceaselessness of capitalism's demands on human labor, without reference to human or humane limitations. Assume the same 10-hour working day posited in Table 1.1 (see Table 1.3, line 1). The worker works 10 hours (Table 1.3, column 4), consuming his own labor (worth $100) plus raw materials and tools worth an additional $200, and produces $400 worth of cloth (Table 1.3, column 11), generating a surplus of $100 (Table 1.3, column 12) and a 33% profit rate (Table 1.3, column 13). Now suppose, however, that our capitalist figures out how to get twice as much work from his worker during that same 10 hours (Table 1.3, line 2). The wage ($100) is unchanged (Table 1.3, column 3) because the cost of the means of subsistence is unchanged. Working twice as fast, the worker will use up twice as much thread and put twice as much wear on the loom, so the material costs will double to $400, for a total expenditure of $500 (Table 1.3, column 2). The worker will produce twice as much cloth (Table 1.3, column 9), however, which still has a value of $4 per yard.[13] This 200 yards of cloth is worth $800 (Table 1.3, column 11), yielding a surplus of $300 (Table, 1.3, column 12) and a 60% profit rate (Table 1.3, column 13). Because this capitalist is getting twice as much work out of his workers as is typical in his industry, our capitalist has generated a substantial surplus. Whether this faster rate of productivity is due to new equipment, new techniques, or sweating workers makes no difference. As long as the capitalist can get cloth produced at a pace above that of his competitors—above the socially necessary rate—he can increase the surplus he generates.

After a while, however, other firms will copy his techniques or come up with others of their own, making the pace of 20 yards per hour the new socially necessary rate. As illustrated in Table 1.3 (line 3), our capitalist still buys $100 worth of labor (Table 1.3, column 3) and $400 worth of thread and loom, and the worker produces 20 yards of cloth per hour. Now, however, 20 yards per hour has become the standard rate. All the capitalists are now producing at this rate or have been

Table 1.3   Innovation, the Changing Organic Composition of Capital, and the Declining Rate of Profit

(1) Day	Inputs								Outputs				
	(2) Money ($) (3 + 6 + 7)	(3) Wage ($)	(4) Hours	(5) Thread (Spools)	(6) Raw Material Costs ($)	(7) Equipment Costs ($)	(8) Labor Power ($)	(9) Cloth (Yards)	(10) Price (per Yard) ($)	(11) Value ($) (9 × 10)	(12) Surplus ($) (11−2)	(13) Profit Rate (%)
1	300	100	10	10	100	100	200	100	4.00	400	100	33
2	500	100	10	20	200	200	400	200	4.00	800	300	60
3	500	100	10	20	200	200	200	200	3.00	600	100	20
4	700	100	10	30	300	300	300	300	3.00	900	200	29
5	700	100	10	30	300	300	200	300	2.67	800	100	14

driven out of business. The value of a yard of cloth has now declined (Table 1.3, column 10) to $3 per hour (reflecting the increased "efficiency" with which firms are producing cloth) because there are only $600 of socially necessary labor time (Table 1.3, column 11) in the 200 yards of cloth. The surplus has declined to the previous level of $100 (Table 1.3, column 12) for a 10-hour day. A greater amount of capital was used to generate this surplus, however; thus, the profit rate (Table 1.3, column 13) has declined to 20%.

As a result of what at first appeared to be a profit-enhancing innovation, there is less money to be made in cloth than there was before. Our capitalist, in his search for higher profits and greater markets, and acting from fear of being put out of business in the same way he put others out of business, has in the long run decreased his profit rate. Now, he must find a new technique that makes the worker produce even faster.

The capitalist, constantly on the prowl for new sources of surplus, develops another scheme: a new machine that runs 50% faster than the current model. Table 1.3 (line 4) depicts the result. For his $100 wage (Table 1.3, column 3), the worker uses up $300 worth of thread (Table 1.3, column 6) and $300 worth of this fancy new machine (Table 1.3, column 7) and produces (Table 1.3, column 9) 300 yards of cloth (50% more). Because our capitalist has a jump on his competitors (so the socially necessary rate has not yet been affected), the cloth still has a value of $3 per yard (Table 1.3, column 10), and he can exchange his cloth for $900 (Table 1.3, column 11). He has generated a $200 surplus (Table 1.3, column 12) and raised his profit rate (Table 1.3, column 13) to 29%. Unfortunately, competition again catches up with him. Soon, everyone has this new machine, everyone is producing 30 yards per hour, and the value of cloth drops to $2.67 per yard (Table 1.3, column 10). Thus, he now generates only $800 worth of cloth per day (Table 1.3, column 11) for a surplus of only $100 (Table 1.3, column 12) and a profit rate of 14% (Table 1.3, column 13).

Hence, the contradiction we began with: The capitalist's quest for ever-increasing rates of surplus value is the secret behind increasing demands on workers in the face of rising profits.

The chase for escalating surplus has other effects as well. The capitalist's need to constantly innovate to find new sources of surplus and to stay competitive with other firms means that any particular job or set of skills is likely to become quickly outmoded. Laid-off workers are told to retrain: Capital no longer needs their particular skills, they learn, but might need a different set if only the worker could transform himself or herself. Today's students are training for jobs that are likely to be obsolete within a few years after they graduate. This is all the more true in high-tech fields, in which high levels of skill are demanded and, at the same time, the technology of production is changing so quickly that those skill demands are constantly changing.[14]

This is another of the fundamental contradictions of capitalism, and it plays itself out in the paradox of unemployment coupled with claims that there are jobs going unfilled for lack of qualified workers. It also appears in quality circles and total quality management programs. In these management innovations, workers are driven to constantly find ways of improving productivity to improve the competitive position of the firm. The goal is "continuous improvement," a never-ending stream of innovations that will keep this firm ahead of its competitors. Such programs, however, have the effect of increasing the pace of work for many workers (Banks & Metzgar, 1989). In addition, a very clever worker may be able to uncover an innovation that will eliminate his or her role entirely, and the worker may be rewarded by a layoff, if not of himself or herself, then of a fellow worker. Workers soon recognize this fundamental contradiction and often withhold their contribution by either fighting the introduction of such methods or by giving only token suggestions. Of course, under the conditions of competitive capitalism, such strategies are often doomed by the pressures of competitors who can wheedle or coerce more cooperation from their employees.

Furthermore, in the never-ending search for new sources of surplus, the scale of production is constantly increasing. In the previous example (Table 1.3), at the start, a capitalist could produce at the socially necessary rate by expending only $300 per day (Table 1.3, line 1, column 2). After a series of innovations that temporarily increased the surplus (until they were copied by the competition), however, the capitalist now has to invest $700 per day (Table 1.3, line 5, column 2) to produce at the socially necessary rate. The scale of production has more than doubled. The capitalist now has twice as much equipment and twice the raw materials invested in producing the same amount of surplus (and a substantially smaller profit rate). In other words, capital has grown. Using census of manufacturing data, we can see the growing inorganic composition of capital: Assets per worker in the American manufacturing sector have grown from $9,000 in 1963 to almost $46,000 by 1987. After controlling for inflation, these numbers go from $30,000 per worker in 1963 to $40,000 per worker in 1987, an increase of 33% (Census of Manufactures, 1987, p. 183). In the search for surplus value, capital has expanded to ever greater proportions. With capital's expansion comes a ballooning of its demands.

Demands of Capital

In addition to the demands of competition are the demands of capital itself. Capital, for Marx (1867/1977), is the objectified embodiment of past labor—dead labor—and its value can only be brought to life when living labor is applied to it. An idle factory (idle capital) produces no surplus. Whenever capital sits idle, it represents a loss to the capitalist (what the economist calls "opportunity cost"): "Capital is dead labour which, vampire like, lives only by sucking living labour, and lives the more, the more labour it sucks" (p. 342). As the size of the capital outlay increases over time, the size of the vampire demanding living labor becomes increasingly enormous. Its cries to be fed become increasingly irresistible.[15] The demands on workers to be more productive become more incessant and insistent because the stakes become higher: "Capitalist production therefore drives, by its inherent nature, toward the appropriation of labour throughout the whole of the 24 hours in the day" (p. 366). Capitalists have been very candid about what is driving the trend toward 12-hour days: "Employers like compressed workweeks and continuous production because it is cost-efficient to keep machinery running all the time. [Twelve-hour shifts are more productive because there is] less downtime in two shifts versus three. Overtime or other added labor costs can also be scheduled away" ("Illinois Jobs," 1995). Even more succinctly, to justify a move to 12-hour shifts, managers at Imperial Wallcoverings told the union that "machines aren't making money when they are down" ("Four-on, Four-off," 1996).

Again, business sections in the press were teeming with stories of corporations moving to elongated shifts or so-called compressed workweeks in the name of competition and the need to keep their equipment running. It would be impossible to list all U.S. companies that were on or pushing to adopt 12-hour shifts, but the following partial list serves as an example of how widespread the practice had become: Ford, GM, Chrysler, Fisher-Price Sorrento, Caterpillar, A. E. Staley, Bridgestone/Firestone, Goodrich, Sony, Siltec, Hewlett-Packard, Heinz-Starkist, Formica, Gates Rubber, Imperial Wallcoverings, and Poly-Seal. In virtually every case, workers have protested the longer workday, and in virtually every case, management cited the need for continuous production as the reason for the exorbitant shift lengths.

To facilitate running their plants 24 hours a day, 7 days a week, Caterpillar demanded its employees work 12-hour shifts without overtime for weekend work. In justifying the move to angry workers, an executive at Caterpillar said, "This is about utilization of our multimillion-dollar assets" ("Caterpillar Turns up Pressure," 1992). At Gates Rubber Company, management threatened to shut down the Galesburg, Illinois, plant if employees would not agree to 12-hour shifts—not because the company had to struggle to survive but because business was so good it could not keep pace with demand ("Gates, Union OK Contract," 1996). In other words, even though this is not a case of a company on the verge of collapse, human needs and hardships are eclipsed by the fact that there are even greater profits out there to be made.

Marx (1867/1977) argues that it was capitalism's need for continuous production that gave rise to the shift system in production, under which some portion of the populace is forced to live on a schedule that effectively cuts them out of participation in most aspects of society. Despite the fact that workers in the 1990s were already protesting the move to 12-hour shifts, 12 hours was often the minimum amount of time they were required to work. In Decatur, as well as in many other parts of the United States, workers currently are required to work 12-hour shifts with mandatory overtime on no notice whenever someone is late or absent or when production demands extra hands.

A look at the garment industry reveals that the only limits on shift lengths are those that workers are able to impose through social and political pressure. In the Mandarin textile plant in El Salvador's San Marcos Free Trade Zone, employees (earning approximately 60¢ an hour) were routinely forced to work 18-hour shifts and 7-day workweeks. Once publicized, the plight of these workers sparked international outrage and demands for justice for the Salvadoran workers. Conditions and shift lengths for many garment workers in the United States, however, are not so different. In a particularly dramatic case, a group of Thai workers in El Monte, California, were held in servitude for years, forced to sew garments for up to 22 hours per day for 59¢ per hour. According to an investigation of the case by the U.S. Department of Labor (Rizvi, 1995), the shop was a supplier to some of the largest retailers in the nation, including Nieman Marcus, Filene's, J. C. Penney, Macy's West, and Sears. This case represents the extreme, but garment manufacturers were increasingly moving to sweatshop conditions to cut costs as the glut of manufacturers, consolidation of retailers, and drop-off in sales ratchet up competition to fever pitch ("It's Blood," 1996). At that time the U.S. Labor estimated that 70% of all manufacturers in the United States routinely violated overtime regulations. For capital, the solution to this problem is the elimination of overtime regulations.[16]

Again, no one is exempt. When Allied-Signal's blue-collar workers in Virginia struck in 1993, top management essentially imprisoned white-collar employees inside the plant, forcing them to work 12-hour shifts for 35 straight days. Nearly 1,000 managers-turned-workers were forced to operate dangerous machinery with very little training and to eat, sleep, bathe, and so on in the plant between shifts. The company said it was willing to "take the risk" that some managers would be killed or injured because they had to keep the plant running to keep their customers supplied ("Strike Troops," 1993).[17]

Machines and Continuous Production

Despite the obvious toll continuous production takes on human lives, several factors make it the only "logical" practice under the laws of capitalism. First, machinery must be valorized quickly because it becomes obsolete (no longer producing at the socially necessary rate) quickly, which results in a loss of value for the capitalist. Fear of obsolescence then drives the capitalist to run his or her factories 24 hours a day to get as much use as possible from his or her machines before they no longer produce at the socially necessary rate. Also, continuous production allows the capitalist to take advantage of supersurplus that comes from innovation and to overcome the declining rate of profit that comes from an increase in constant capital (see Table 1.3). Mechanization provides not only the rationale for continuous production but also a built-in defense mechanism against worker opposition. Replacing employees with machines creates a "surplus army" of unemployed workers who stand at the ready to take the jobs of those who resist the capitalist's increasing demands. The mere threat of this shadowy presence is often enough to silence dissatisfied workers.[18]

When the unemployment rate "becomes too low," it generates a frantic search for new sources for the surplus army, including students, housewives, retirees, and, of course, foreign workers. For example, the U.S. government increased the number of visas granted for temporary employment in high-skill jobs, allowing firms to import computer programmers from India, China, and the Philippines. One op-ed commentator from the *New York Times* even called for the repeal of laws preventing firms from using children under age 14, on the grounds that the discipline of work is good for children as young as 9 years old (Brady, 2000).

Marx (1867/1977) argues the insatiable drive to extend the working day is significant beyond the fact of its inhumanity. It reveals a fundamental transformation that takes place under capitalism:

Hence that remarkable phenomenon in the history of modern industry, that machinery sweeps away every moral and natural restriction on the length of the working day. Hence too the economic paradox that the most powerful instrument for reducing labour-time suffers a dialectical inversion and becomes the most unfailing means for turning the whole lifetime of the worker and his family into labour-time at capital's disposal for its own valorization. (p. 532)

Mechanization and technological advances both liberate and enslave workers. Although new production technology might reduce the burden of labor, it also increasingly demands longer days and a faster work pace. Similarly, many recent technological advances designed to make life easier for office workers have had the opposite effect. The cellular phone and the portable computer allow workers to escape the office and work where it might be convenient. This same technology (often provided by the employer) also can be used to require the worker to be available to work any time of day or night. For example, one computer programmer for a retail chain was given a cellular phone and a portable computer with a cellular modem. He was on call day and night and when he got a call, he was expected to be logged on to the company's mainframe within 20 minutes. If he went out to dinner, he brought his equipment with him. The company was able to contact him at any time and convert his leisure time to work hours.

The promise of technological liberation is a common theme in advertising, but one can easily imagine alternate, less idyllic scenarios. An advertisement for one consumer electronics manufacturer shows an office worker jogging serenely on a scenic beach. We hear a mysterious ringing from his pocket, and he pulls out a device that is a cellular phone, hand-held computer, and fax machine in one. He answers: It's his boss asking for a document. With the flick of a finger, he cheerfully forwards the report, averting crisis (and a trip to the office) through the wonders of technology. The boss tells him he needs to get out of the office more, and the worker smiles, signifying that he has played a fast one on his boss. The implication is that this new technology will allow one to go to the beach when one is supposed to be in the office. It is just as likely, however, that the call came while the man was on his vacation, on Sunday, or during his regular off-hours.

Early in the cellular phone boom, researchers conducted experiments to see how this new technology would facilitate geographically dispersed work groups. In one experimental trial, 100 workers in a university, from janitors to high-level administrators, were given cellular phones with free unlimited air time. Several subjects returned the phones and dropped out of the experiment in disgust, saying the phones robbed them of all sense of "off-time." They were at the beck and call of their bosses 24 hours a day, and their leisure time was constantly interrupted by demands from the office. Thus, the same technology that let them wander freely and stay in touch with friends and family also allowed their office to reach out and touch them at any and all times. In other words, the whole world becomes an office, and the whole day one shift.

Relay System

Infiltrating and usurping the whole of a worker's day is nothing new in the annals of labor history. In its attempt to get the most value from its labor power, capital is pressed to take over the entire life of the worker. Arguably the most blatant example is what Marx (1867/1977) described as the relay system:

> During the 15 hours of the factory day, capital dragged in the worker now for 30 minutes, now for an hour, and then pushed him out again, to drag him into the factory and thrust him out afresh, hounding him hither and thither, in scattered shreds of time, without ever letting go until the full 10 hours of work was done. As on the stage, the same person had to appear in turn in the different scenes of the different acts. And just as an actor is committed to the stage throughout the whole course of the play, so the workers were committed to the factory for the whole 15 hours, without reckoning the time taken in coming and going. Thus the hours of rest were turned into hours of enforced idleness, which drove the young men to the taverns and the young girls to the brothels. (p. 403)

Through the use of the relay system, the capitalist can extend the working day to 12 or 15 hours while maintaining the fiction of only using (and therefore only paying for) 10 hours of the worker's time. This practice of extending control over the worker's unpaid time and using workers in scattered fragments has continued in various forms. For example, one major grocery firm would schedule a minimum crew for the week, giving each worker barely enough hours to justify keeping the job. The company would then tell the workers, "If you want more hours, stay by the phone and we will call you in if we get busy." In the days before beepers, this meant sitting at home each day, on the chance that the company might need the worker that day. Today, workers often have cell phones, beepers and/or voice mail, but that means all their personal activities (e.g., eating, playing, and dating) are overlain with the threat of going to work. It also means that the company has access to a whole week's worth of labor power, while only paying for a small fraction of that time.

One of the nation's largest chains of suburban weekly newspapers employs a variant of the relay system. By the nature of their work, reporters tend to work long hours. Morning deadlines, staff meetings, and editors' work ethics often require reporters to come in during the morning, even though their beats may require them to be present to cover events late at night. The union at this company won a contract that called for overtime pay after 37.5 hours per week or 10 hours in a day. To avoid paying overtime, the company put the reporters on a self-regulated relay system. The reporters had to juggle their time so that all meetings would be covered without going over the 10 hours. If a reporter had a morning deadline and a night meeting on the same day, he or she might have to come in at 10 a.m. to meet deadline, work until 5 p.m., leave for a few hours, then return to work at 7 p.m. to cover the meeting that lasts until 10 p.m. This reporter would be paid for 10 hours, but 12 hours were dominated by work. Like the actor waiting backstage until his cue, the reporter's off-time was really just a holding pattern while waiting to come back to work.

Similarly, firms are increasingly using contingent workers—part-time, temporary, contract, or consulting work. In each case, the company can replace full-time employees with a set of workers (often the same workers they used to employ full-time) whose labor power is used in small fragments, with the downtime inherent in most work processes pushed onto the worker's ledger. This is the new "flexibility" that firms are pushing for in their attempt to stay competitive. By reducing the actual "work" time, firms can reduce the amount of paid labor while still getting the same amount of total labor power, thereby increasing surplus value (or, in business jargon, "increasing the productivity of labor").

Approximately 33% of American workers are temporary or contingent employees, according to a 1998-1999 study by the Economic Policy Institute (Cook, 2000). These workers provide their labor as temporaries, consultants, freelancers, and stringers, or in similar positions, and as such, their paid work time is reduced to the minimum required by capital, and many of the fixed costs of work are born by the worker. For example, many workers now must have a home office with computer, phone, fax, printer, and so on to be able to offer their labor power to capital on an as-needed basis. At the same time, contingent workers, most of whom have no union representation, take home on average $100 less per week than permanent employees, and few receive health benefits (20%) or employer pension plans (25%). Also, contingent workers must have a multitude of skills to enable them to meet the constantly changing demands of a production system that itself is constantly innovating to take advantage of new techniques for increasing surplus value. Although capital is constantly looking for ways to replace skilled workers with cheaper, less skilled workers (Braverman, 1974), it also demands that workers are able to be highly productive in any of a number of production processes. This is especially true of contingent workers, who must be able to quickly plug into a wide variety of work settings to supply the ebb and flow of demand in various companies.

Increasing Productivity and Downsizing

One outcome of this increase in the working day and the accompanying increase in productivity (in the sense of getting more surplus value) is the creation of surplus labor. Firms are in a constant search for ways to reduce the number of workers while still increasing output. The popularity of downsizing over the past decade is a reflection of this desire by capital to increase productivity. Downsizing has the added benefit of increasing what Marx termed the surplus army—the set of workers available at any time to be pulled into the production process to supplement, or replace, the existing workforce. An additional 59,000 people would have jobs if the auto industry put a moratorium on overtime, according to the United Auto Workers Union ("Overtime Pressures," 1994). This surplus army of labor keeps pressure on workers to increase their output and be cautious in their demands for an increased share of the output (e.g., through wage increases). Capital is constantly reminding workers that "You can be replaced." News spots of thousands of workers lining up for a few job openings at a factory or hotel or fire department are paraded before the public, reminding them of the surplus army always on call to replace lazy or militant workers.

Capital as Logic

Following Marx (1867/1977), we have argued that the production process, once intended to serve humans' needs, has under capitalism become entirely indifferent to them. Human beings now serve the needs of capital. Indeed, to think otherwise—to argue that an expensive factory should be left idle because workers are tired or that production should be organized using a less efficient but more comfortable process—is considered absurd. Saying that work is taking over our lives and that we should reorganize the economy to put limits on work and reemphasize family and community—while given much lip service—is rarely acknowledged as an argument that should seriously be followed. Indeed, as we have shown, the amount of time Americans spend on the job has increased steadily, and laws limiting the working day have come under attack at the same time "family values" has emerged as the mantra for politicians hoping to take or hold office.

Capital Versus Family

Despite politicians' rhetoric, human and family needs are considered "soft," silly, even childish, whereas the needs of capital—of machines and raw materials—are considered "real-world" issues, and the primacy of such issues is so obvious as to transcend the need for justification: Hence, such discussion-ending clichés as "We have to look at the bottom line" and "This is business." Once capital invokes the "bottom line" argument, the rest of us are supposed to utter "nough said" and walk away completely satisfied that the only reasonable course has been followed. To the extent that we do, Marx (1867/1977) argues, the dialectical inversion of objects holding mastery over human beings is revealed.

When one Staley worker said he could not work overtime one night because of family considerations, his supervisor told him, "I don't care what your outside responsibilities are. Once you come here, I own you and you'll stay as long as I want you to." Another worker, a single mother of two school-aged children, pointed out the antimony of family and capital. She routinely works 50 hours or more a week managing a convenience store (with many of those hours coming between 4 p.m. and 8 a.m.). During those same hours, she needs to be home rearing her children. She voiced her despair as follows: "This is the only job I could get that paid enough for me to take care of them, but it never lets me be home when they need me. I can either feed them or be with them, never both." A worker at Dunlop complained that the longer shifts, although leading to higher pay, did not

SOURCE: Reprinted with special permission of King Features Syndicate. Cartoon drawn by Jim Borgman.

make up for the loss of family time: "We never see our families because we're working every weekend. It's insulting that Dunlop thinks an extra $7 a day is going to compensate for not seeing your kids grow up" ("Union Rejects," 1994, p. C1). Another woman was upset that her children were not able to join family dinners on holidays because they had to be at their jobs in supermarkets, gas stations, restaurants, and so on. Although family gatherings are important, capital is much more concerned with maximizing surplus value and cannot risk the loss that would occur by letting the shops close. This is exacerbated by the ever-present threat from other, less sympathetic capitalists who will be open and will take sales away from the family-friendly capitalists. Laws mandating that stores close on Sundays or preventing 24-hour retailers have become quaint relics of the adolescence of capitalism. In today's unfettered capitalism, it is the more ruthless capitalist who succeeds in the market. Twenty-four-hour groceries, gas stations, and convenience stores provide opportunities for consumers to engage in commodity exchange day and night. This also means that capital demands access to labor power day and night, weekends and holidays included. Although having the grocery open on Thanksgiving to allow you to buy that extra bag of stuffing or case of beer might make your holiday more enjoyable (and the grocer a little richer), it also means that other people have to spend their holiday staffing all those shops instead of relaxing with their families or friends.

Extended shifts and rotating shifts not only decrease the amount of time a worker can spend with family but also diminish the quality of the time families have together. Twelve-hour shifts take a terrible toll on the body, as the manager-workers at Allied Signal pointed out during their stint in the factory (when it was their bodies in question!). Workers on 12-hour shifts commonly suffer an array of signs of exhaustion: headaches, fatigue, soreness, irritability, difficulty concentrating, and insomnia. That means working parents who are lucky enough to be on a shift that allows them to be home before the kids go to bed might still miss out on family activities because they are too tired or do not feel well enough to help with homework, go to a Little League game, or attend a parent-teacher meeting. The situation is even worse for those on rotating shifts because their body rhythms and sleep patterns are continuously being disrupted, leaving them with a sense of perpetual jet lag. A Michelin employee on rotating shifts stated, "You don't function. You can't function. You just exist" ("Swing Shifts," 1993).

Even when employees are paid extra for long shifts or for night work, many say the compensation does not make up for the human costs. Depression, divorce, heart disease, hypertension, drug and alcohol abuse, ulcers, and stress are all common side effects of working long or rotating shifts. A recent study in *Science* found that among couples with children, night-shift workers' marriages are more likely to end in divorce than marriages of day shifters. In the case of male night-shift workers who have been married less than 5 years, the chance of separation or divorce is six times higher than that for men on days (Presser, 1999). Another Michelin man said, "You work swing shifts to make more money for your family, but you end up losing it all anyway. If you lose your family, you lose all that you worked for to begin with" ("Swing Shifts," 1993). Workers at the Buick plant in Flint, Michigan, agreed. Although earning twice their 40-hour pay, hourly employees at Buick City went on strike to protest GM's exorbitant demand for overtime ("GM Hunkers Down," 1994).

Capital Versus Community

A common theme among workers who oppose the longer working day is that it destroyed their participation in community life. Workers in Decatur, Illinois, told us about a city festival (Founders Day) that took place during the height of their struggles over the working day. The workers boycotted the festival in protest of the city's complicity with the companies in this labor dispute. In the end, the festival was a bust because of the central role that working people play in such events, both as participants and as organizers.

As the working day gets longer, workers are increasingly cut off from participation in community life. The increased time spent at work—and the increased time required to recover from a longer working day—constrains participation in activities and voluntary associations such as reading groups, political organizations, social clubs, sports leagues, and churches. One Staley worker stated, "We are the ones who coach the Little League. We organize the town picnics. We are the ones that do all the things that keep this town going. We can't do that now." As workers increasingly become abstract labor power on 24-hour call to the whims of capital, they are no longer able to participate in the intermediate institutions that fill out the structure of society. According to Marx (1867/1977),

It is self-evident that the worker is nothing other than labour-power for the duration of his whole life, and that therefore all his disposable time is by nature and by right labour-time, to be devoted to the self-valorization of capital. Time for education, for intellectual development, for the fulfillment of social functions, for social intercourse, for the free play of the vital forces of his body and his mind, even the rest time of Sunday . . . what foolishness! (p. 375)

That is how capital views workers—as portable labor power. A rubber worker in Decatur, Illinois, echoes this sentiment. Reacting to the 12-hour shifts and 7-day workweeks offered by Bridgestone/Firestone, he said, "You won't have a life. You're not supposed to have any life except work."

Political philosophers such as Robert Putnam noted this declining participation in community life. In his article, "Bowling Alone: America's Declining Social Capital" (Putnam, 1995), he argues that American society has become more isolated and alienated, with people increasingly forgoing participation in community life. He cites statistics such as the nearly 50% drop in Parent-Teacher Association (PTA) participation during the past 30 years, a significant drop in volunteer work in the past 15 years, and 10% to 50% drops in fraternal organization memberships during the past two decades. The title of his article is derived from the observation that, although bowling per se has increased approximately 10% from 1980 to 1993, participation in bowling leagues (a more communal activity) has dropped 40% during that period. Many pundits have long bemoaned the loss of community, blaming it on the selfishness of recent generations or on the alienating effects of television and modern culture. Marx's (1867/1977) analysis more explicitly links the decay of community life with changes in the economic structure. As the data on increasing work hours and more uncertain work shifts show, there has been an increase in time pressure on American workers during the past two decades. Also, as the previous quotes from workers point out (and as the quote from Marx also makes clear), participation in community life suffers as capital extends its reach over ever more of the workers' waking hours. Rotating shifts, unpredictable mandatory overtime, 24-hour on-call responsibilities, weekend and evening work, and elimination of vacation time all remove the space in workers' lives that was used to coach Little League, hang out at the Elks club, attend the PTA, supervise a scout troop, or commit to a Monday night bowling league.

Conclusion

Marx is often (and incorrectly) associated with the political philosophies of countries such as China and the former Soviet Union. The strength of Marx's writings, however, is not in heuristics about a future society; it is in his penetrating analysis of capitalism itself. Marx notes that capitalism is the source of unprecedented wealth and the engine of fantastic innovations, and yet, it is also a system that hinges on exploitation, inequality, and misery. Although the demise of so-called communist governments is used by some to discredit Marx, nowhere can the viability of his theories be more clearly seen than in the strongholds of capitalism.

Although hourly workers are working more, and under increasingly difficult conditions, the number of households earning below $25,000 a year is growing. At the same time, the share of the national income going to the richest 5% of households has increased approximately 25% ("Middle-Class Labor," 1995). What keeps Marx viable nearly a century and a half years after the publication of *Capital* is that his writings offer a structural analysis of why that must be so.

Unlike many who examine the social landscape, Marx does not attribute these outcomes to the greed or lack of feeling of the capitalist nor to the laziness or intemperance of the workers. Instead, he demonstrates how the very nature of a capitalist economy demands such behavior on the part of the owners of capital.

Marx also notes that these contradictions lead to both economic and political struggles, and that the two cannot be separated. At times, workers have been able to gain some political power, through mechanisms such as unions or political parties or in times of labor shortages (brought on by wars, for example), and have been able to increase wages, reduce working hours, and/or put limits on firms' behavior.

The working day is a significant locus of worker resistance throughout the history of capitalism. As Marx notes, the capitalist has bought a full day's labor power from the worker and has the right to the full use of his purchase. The worker has sold the amount of labor that is equivalent to what can be reproduced in a day (so he or she will be able to sell it again tomorrow) and has the right to limit consumption to this amount and no more. "Between equal rights, force decides," Marx wrote, hence, the political struggle over the terms of labor. Marx traces much of the 19th-century struggles in England and the other capitalist countries in Chapter 10 of *Capital*. The struggles in Decatur, Illinois, and elsewhere in the United States echo the themes of Marx's day. The immorality of the overlong workday becomes a rallying cry for worker struggle and worker solidarity. Even in a period of weak unions and little direct action by workers, 12-hour shifts can still get workers to strike and to fight. The dynamics of capital, however, are difficult to resist, and most such struggles have been losing battles for the workers.

Capitalism is more than a long workday, however. It is also a constant search for new ways of generating surplus. Firms push to increase the speed of work. They are constantly innovating to find new ways to beat the competition (or to keep up with innovating competitors). The increased scale of production such innovations produce puts pressure on firms to keep their machines running day and night, 7 days a week, 365 days a year, pushing workers for still more hours.

Finally, capitalism is a production system based on value production. It is this insight that is central to understanding the dynamics of capitalism. Firms exist to produce surplus value. Producing goods is an incidental by-product of that search. Workers exist to provide labor power for the machines and to contribute value and surplus value to the products. Workers serve the firms. Firms do not serve the workers. Society exists as a source of workers to produce commodities and consumers to buy commodities. Needs such as time with family, participation in community life, and time for contemplation and self-development are at best incidental to, and often seen as an impediment to, the demands of capital for constant production.

The Bible asks, "What does it profit a man to gain the world and lose his soul?" Capital replies, "The profit is the ability to compete another day in the hopes of still more profit." Under capitalism, this is sufficient answer to all questions of the purpose of the economy and all the related institutions of society. On the basis of the analysis presented in this chapter, we can see that, although such a system is driven by the impersonal demands of capital, it is, at its roots, still a *social* system, a system of people. Given that, we can then ask, Is this the kind of society we want to reproduce? This is the question that underlies Marx's analyses. It is a question that we should continue to ask.

Notes

1. Decatur, once an anonymous Midwestern industrial town, became known in labor circles throughout the world as the "war zone" after workers at the region's three largest employers, A. E. Staley, Caterpillar, and Bridgestone/Firestone, either went on strike or were locked out of their jobs.

2. Throughout the text, we will follow Marx's usage and use the term *value* to refer to exchange value, not use value.

3. Marx contrasts the terms *use value* and *exchange value*. The *use value* of a good refers to the benefits derived from its consumption. The use value of bread is that it serves as food; the use value of a coat is that it keeps one warm. *Exchange value* refers to the ability of a particular quantity of a good to be traded for some quantity of another good. The exchange value of one coat, for example, may be 100 loaves of bread or two pairs of shoes. Capitalism is characterized by its emphasis on exchange value over use value. Ancient slave societies (Egypt, Greece, and Rome) and feudal societies (medieval Europe and feudal Japan), although still based on class exploitation, utilized modes of production based on use value rather than exchange value.

4. The amount of labor time embedded in a given commodity includes the amount of labor time expended in gathering or producing the materials, tools, or machines used in the production process. When comparing the amount value in given quantities of two commodities (e.g., 20 yards of linen and 100 loaves of bread), what is being compared is the amount of socially necessary abstract labor required to produce that amount of each commodity. By socially necessary, Marx (1867/1977) means "the labour-time required to produce any use-value under the conditions of production normal for a given society and with the average degree of skill and intensity of labour prevalent in that society" (p. 129). A given worker (or workers in a given factory) may work above or below the socially necessary rate and hence contribute more or less socially necessary labor within the same time frame. Abstract labor means undifferentiated labor, abstracted from the particular skills or activities of actual, concrete labor: "working" as opposed to "weaving" or "baking."

5. Marx's theory, which is sometimes incorrectly referred to as the "labor theory of value," can more properly be summarized as the value theory of labor. By converting labor into value production, capitalism fundamentally transforms human activity into a new form—capitalist work.

6. It is certainly the case that individual exchanges can involve one party besting the other, whether through force or through guile. One capitalist may be able to exchange $100 worth of shoes for $110 worth of bread, thereby gaining a $10 "profit." This profit, however, is simply the transfer of value from one person (the dim capitalist) to another (the clever capitalist). No value is created by such exchanges.

7. These numbers are arbitrary. What is key is that there is some time that is needed for what Marx calls "necessary labor" (labor needed to produce a value equal to the value of the means of subsistence).

8. By stating the problem in these terms, we can see that this result is not due to the worker getting paid by the "day" instead of, for example, by the hour. Even if paid by the hour, the worker could potentially produce more in each hour than an hour's share of socially necessary labor time (Marx, 1867/1977, pp. 333-338).

9. Table 1.2 also shows that the increase has affected women substantially more than men.

10. Employers usually argue that compressed schedules actually give employees more time with their families because, in theory, it gives them more days off. In practice, however, those off days get eaten up by mandatory overtime. Employees often end up working five 12-hour shifts instead of five 8-hour shifts. Employees at the Formica plant in Evendale, Ohio, for example, routinely work five 12-hour shifts and 7-day weeks, and even 20-day stretches are not unheard of ("Factory OT Shoots Up," 1994). Managers at Griffin Environmental Company in New York admit that they went to a 4-day week with longer shifts because they rely on overtime to meet demand, and they wanted to leave Friday open for overtime hours ("Griffin Environmental," 1995).

11. Staley even had the gall to invoke the specter of "foreign competition," despite the fact that it is a British-owned company.

12. Marx (1867/1977) stated, "This does not depend on the will, either good or bad, of the individual capitalist. Under free competition, the immanent laws of capitalist production confront the individual capitalist as a coercive force external to him" (p. 381).

13. As in the first example, the cloth's value is $4 per yard, representing the amount of socially necessary labor embedded in the cloth—where socially necessary labor is defined as the labor required to produce the cloth in the usual way, at the usual pace, which was 10 yards per hour.

14. In his chapter on machinery and large-scale industry, Marx (1867/1977) discusses the implications of the constant need for innovation: "Modern industry never views or treats the existing form of a production process as the definitive one. Its technical basis is therefore revolutionary, whereas all earlier modes of production were essentially conservative. By means of machinery, chemical processes and other methods, it is constantly transforming not only the technical basis of production but also the functions of the worker and the social combinations of the labour process. At the same time, it thereby also revolutionizes the division of labour within society, and incessantly throws masses of capital and of workers from one branch of production to another. Thus large-scale industry, by its very nature, necessitates variation of labour, fluidity of functions, and mobility of the worker in all directions" (p. 617).

15. Marx (1867/1977) stated, "Constant capital, the means of production, only exist, considered from the standpoint of the process of valorization, in order to absorb labour and, with every drop of labour, a proportional quantity of surplus labour. In so far as the means of production fail to do this, their mere existence forms a loss for the capitalist, in a negative sense, for while they lie fallow they represent a useless advance of capital. This loss becomes a positive one as soon as the interruption of employment necessitates an additional outlay when the work begins again" (p. 366).

16. A similar sentiment was found in the recent Congress, in which Republican legislators introduced a bill to overturn the 1938 Fair Labor Standards Act. Their goal is to eliminate overtime pay for working more than 40 hours in a week to allow employers to impose longer workweeks without penalty. One proposal would not require employers to pay overtime until a worker worked more than 160 hours in a month, even if those hours were all worked in 2 weeks.

17. Interestingly, one of the reasons the company gave for "sequestering" these managers-turned-workers was that the long shifts would leave them so exhausted they would find it easier just to sleep at the plant. These are the same shifts, however, the company

expects the blue-collar employees to work regularly, while also raising their families, participating in the community, and so on.

18. It is hard to imagine a worker who has not heard a variation of, "If you don't like it, there are 10 people out there who would be glad to take your job right now." As effective as that threat usually is (because how many of us can afford to take the chance?), however, it is not always true. Toy industry giant Fisher-Price recently converted one of its production lines to manufacture new outdoor play equipment. Conditions on that line, however, are so atrocious—12-hour shifts lifting up to 70-pound loads in high heat and bad air—management cannot find enough people to fully staff the line. Regular workers at the plant have agreed to be laid off rather than work under those conditions, so management has had to scramble to keep the line open using temporary workers ("Fisher-Pricers," 1995).

References

Award to Caterpillar for "quieter" machine. (1994, May 5). *Chicago Tribune,* Business section, p. 3.

Banks, A., & Metzgar, J. (1989). Participating in management: Union organizing on a new terrain. *Labor Research Review, 8*(2), 1-55.

Bitter Caterpillar strike grows more corrosive, costly. (1994, September 26). *Chicago Tribune,* p. 4:1.

Brady, M. H. (2000, April 13). Growing in the job. *New York Times,* p. 1.

Braverman, H. (1974). *Labor and monopoly capital.* New York: Monthly Review Press.

Caterpillar turns up pressure on UAW. (1992, November 21). *Chicago Tribune,* p. 2:1.

Census of Manufactures, 1987. (1991). Washington, DC: Department of Commerce, Bureau of the Census.

Cook, C. D. (2000, March 20). Temps demand a new deal. *The Nation* [On-line], http://www .thenation.com/doc.mhtml%3Fi=20000327&s=cook

Dunayevskaya, R. (1988). *Marxism and freedom.* New York: Columbia University Press.

Factory OT shoots up. (1994, December 2). *Cincinnati Enquirer,* p. A1.

Fisher-Pricers rejecting roto-molding jobs. (1995, May 7). *Buffalo News,* p. B13.

Four on, four off. (1996, March 14). *Providence Journal-Bulletin,* p. G1.

Gates, union OK contract. (1996, March 28). *Galesburg (IL) Register-Mail,* p. A1.

GM hunkers down to control costs. (1994, September 28). *Detroit News,* p. B1.

GM pact fallout: Wall Street wary; Workers who like OT will get less. (1994, October 2). *Detroit News,* p. A1.

Geoghegan, T. (1999, January 24). Tampering with the time clock. *New York Times,* Weekend section, p. 15.

Greenhouse, S. (1999, September 5). Running on empty: So much work, so little time. *New York Times* [On-line], www.nytimes.com/library/review/090599work-hours-review.html

Griffin Environmental uses a four day week to build overtime into the system. (1995, June). *Syracuse Business,* p. 1:9.

Illinois jobs grow scarce, pay less. (1995, September 4). *Chicago Tribune,* Business section, p. 1.

It's blood, sweatshops and tears: Legitimate garment makers are being squeezed from both sides. (1996, August 23). *Los Angeles Times,* p. A1.

Kamata, S. (1983). *Japan in the passing lane.* New York: Pantheon.

Lardner, J. (1999, December 20). World-class workaholics: Are crazy hours and takeout dinner the elixir of America's success? *U.S. News Online.* Retrieved from http://tigger.uic .edu/~jwalsh/crazyhours.html

Marx, K. (1977). *Capital: A critique of political economy* (B. Fowkes, Trans.). New York: Vintage. (Original work published 1867)

Mayer, T. (1994). *Analytic Marxism.* Thousand Oaks, CA: Sage.

Middle-class labor in US feels the squeeze as wages decline. (1995, November 29). *Christian Science Monitor,* p. 1:10.

9-to-5 winding down. (1996, January 7). *Chicago Tribune,* p. C1.

Overtime pressures GM to hire more. (1994, August 21). *Fort Wayne (IN) Journal Gazette,* p. F1.

Presser, H. B. (1999, June 11). Toward a 24-hour economy. *Science, 284,* 1778-1779.

Putnam, R. D. (1995). Bowling alone: America's declining social capital. *Journal of Democracy, 6*(1), 65-78.

Rizvi, H. (1995, October). Slaves to fashion. *Multinational Monitor, 16*(10), 6-7.

Schor, J. (1991). *The overworked American.* New York: Basic Books.

Sen, A. (1999). *Development as freedom.* Oxford, UK: Oxford University Press.

Strike troops: 35-day occupation at Allied-Signal. (1993, August 2). *Richmond Times-Dispatch,* p. B1.

Swing shifts may push employees too far: Companies examine employee options. (1993, September 26). *Spartanburg Herald-Journal,* Business section, p. 3.

12-hour day sparks strike at Poly-Seal. (1994, March 3). *Baltimore Sun,* Business section, p. 1.

Union rejects proposed contract with Dunlop. (1994, November 7). *Buffalo News,* p. C1.

Union stays on job, but strikes out at Staley. (1992, December 12). *Chicago Tribune,* p. 1:1.

US, Europe at odds on 4-day workweek. (1993, December 12). *Denver Post,* p. H1.

Discussion Questions

1. Give examples from your own work experience of the company trying to get you to work "off the clock" or work extra time without additional pay. How are such requests justified by your boss? How does Marx explain such requests?

2. It has been said recently that, "The era of lifetime careers is over. Today's workers should expect a multitude of jobs and must constantly be learning new skills." Use Marx to explain the demise of the company man and the rise of the free agent, flexible worker. Discuss your own education strategy in light of this analysis.

3. In the Charlie Chaplin movie, *Modern Times,* Chaplin's boss tries to introduce a machine that feeds workers while they work on the assembly line. Using Marx's analysis, explain why a company might invest in such technology.

CHAPTER 2

The Weberian Theory of Rationalization and the McDonaldization of Contemporary Society

George Ritzer

George Ritzer *is Distinguished Professor of Sociology at the University of Maryland. His major areas of interest are sociological theory and the sociology of consumption. He has served as chair of the American Sociological Association's sections on theory (1989-1990) and organizations and occupations (1980-1981). He has been a distinguished scholar-teacher at the University of Maryland and has been awarded a teaching excellence award. He has held the UNESCO chair in social theory at the Russian Academy of Sciences and a Fulbright-Hays Fellowship. He has been a scholar-in-residence at the Netherlands Institute for Advanced Study and the Swedish Collegium for Advanced Study in the Social Sciences. A new century edition of* The McDonaldization of Society *was published by Pine Forge in 2000. The book has been translated into sixteen different languages, including German, French, Spanish, Italian, Japanese, and Chinese. Several books have been published that are devoted to analyzing the McDonaldization thesis. His most recent book is* The Globalization of Nothing *(Sage, 2004).*

In this chapter, I apply one of the most famous and important theories in the history of sociology, Max Weber's (1864-1920) theory of rationalization, to contemporary society.

In Weber's view, modern society, especially the Western world, is growing increasingly rationalized. As the reader will see, Weber regarded bureaucracy as the ultimate example of rationalization. Thus, Weber can be seen as being focally concerned with the rationalization of society in general and, more specifically, its bureaucratization.

This chapter is premised on the idea that whereas the processes of rationalization and bureaucratization described by Weber have continued, if not accelerated, the bureaucracy has been supplanted by the fast-food restaurant as the best exemplification of this process. Furthermore, we will see that the rational principles that lie at the base of the fast-food restaurant are spreading throughout American society as well as the rest of the world. On the basis of Weber's ideas on the rationalization process, in this chapter I describe the continuation and even acceleration of this process, or what I have termed the "McDonaldization" of society.[1]

Four types of rationality lie at the heart of Weber's theory of rationalization.[2] *Practical rationality* is to be found in people's mundane, day-to-day activities and reflects their worldly interests.[3] In Weber's terms, through practical rationality people seek the "methodical attainment of a definitely given and practical end by means of an increasingly precise calculation of adequate means."[4] Therefore, actors calculate all possible means available to them, choose the alternative that best allows them to reach their ultimate end, and then follow that line of action. All human beings engage in practical rationality in attempting to solve the routine and daily problems of life.[5]

Theoretical rationality involves "an increasingly theoretical mastery of reality by means of increasingly precise and abstract concepts."[6] Among other things, it involves logical deduction, the attribution of causality, and the arrangement of symbolic meanings. It is derived from the inherent need of actors to give some logical meaning to a world that appears haphazard.[7] Whereas practical rationality involves action, theoretical rationality is a cognitive process and has tended to be the province of intellectuals.

Substantive rationality involves value postulates, or clusters of values, that guide people in their daily lives, especially in their choice of means to ends. These clusters of values are rational when they are consistent with specific value postulates preferred by actors.[8] Substantive rationality can be linked more specifically to economic action. To Weber, economic action is substantively rational to "the degree to which the provisioning of given groups of persons with goods is shaped by economically oriented social action under some criterion (past, present, or potential) of ultimate values, regardless of the nature of these ends."[9] Thus, substantive rationality involves a choice of means to ends guided by some larger system of human values.

Formal rationality involves the rational calculation of means to ends based on universally applied rules, regulations, and laws.[10] Formal rationality is institutionalized in such large-scale structures as the bureaucracy, modern law, and the capitalist economy. The choice of means to ends is determined by these larger structures and their rules and laws.

In looking for the best means of attaining a given objective under formal rationality, we are not left to our own devices, but rather we use existing rules, regulations, and structures that either predetermine the optimum methods or help us discover them. This, clearly, is a major development in the history of the world. In the past, people had to discover such mechanisms on their own or with only vague and general guidance from larger value systems. Now, we no longer have to discover for ourselves the optimum means to some given end, because that optimum means has already been discovered: It is incorporated into the rules, regulations, and structures of our social institutions.

Formal rationality often leads to decisions that disregard the needs and values of actors, implying that substantive rationality is unimportant. One example is a formally rational economic system. The needs that come to be emphasized and realized are those for which actors are able to outbid others because they have an abundance of money, not because those needs are of greater importance or of more human value. Profits are the primary focus rather than issues of humanity. Weber stresses this disregard for humanity in a formally rational economic system when he writes, "decisive are the need for competitive survival and the conditions of the labor, money and commodity markets; hence matter-of-fact considerations that are simply nonethical determine individual behavior and interpose impersonal forces between the persons involved."[11] The primary concern of the entrepreneur within a formally rational economic system that is capitalist is such nonethical objectives as continuous profit making. The workers, in turn, are dominated by the entrepreneurs who subject the workers to "masterless slavery" in the formal rational economic system.[12] In other words, the formally economic system robs the workers of their basic humanity by enslaving them in a world denuded of human values.

Unlike the first three types of rationality, formal rationality has not existed at all times and in all places. Rather, it was created in, and came to dominate, the modern, Western, industrialized world. Weber believed that formal rationality was coming to overwhelm and to supplant the other types of rationality within the Western world. He saw a titanic struggle taking place in his time between formal and substantive rationality. Weber anticipated, however, that this struggle would end with the erosion of substantive rationality in the face of the forward march of formal rationality. The fading away of substantive rationality was regretted by Weber because it "embodied Western civilization's highest ideals: The autonomous and free individual whose actions were given continuity by their reference to ultimate values."[13] Instead of people whose actions were guided by these high ideals, we were to be left in the modern world with people who simply followed the rules without regard to larger human values.

Weber saw bureaucracy as the epitome of formally rational domination. Weber links bureaucracies and rationalization as follows:

> Bureaucratic rationalization . . . revolutionizes with *technical means,* in principle, as does every economic reorganization, "from without": It *first* changes the material and social orders, and *through* them the people, by changing the conditions of adaptation, and perhaps the opportunities for adaptation, through a rational determination of means to ends.[14]

The bureaucracy "strongly furthers the development of 'rational matter-of-factness' and the personality type of the professional expert."[15] These "experts" possess a "spirit of formalistic impersonality . . . without hatred or passion, and hence without affection or enthusiasms."[16] The top officials of the bureaucracy develop rules and regulations that lead lower-level officials to choose the best means to ends already chosen at the highest levels. The rules and regulations represent the bureaucracy's institutional memory, which contemporaries need only to use (and not invent and continually reinvent) to attain some end.

The bureaucracies themselves are structured in such a way as to guide or even to force people to choose certain means to ends. Each task is broken up into a number of components, and each office is responsible for a separate portion of the larger task. Employees in each office handle only their own part of the task, usually by following rules and regulations in a predetermined sequence. The goal is attained when each incumbent has completed his or her required task in proper order. The bureaucracy thereby utilizes what its past history has shown to be optimum means to the end in question.

Weber's overall theoretical perspective was that it was largely the unique development of formal rationality that accounted for the distinctive development of the West. Weber suggests that it was key to the development of the Western world, that it came into conflict with the other types of rationality, especially substantive rationality, and that it acted to reduce them in importance and ultimately to subordinate, if not totally eliminate, them in terms of their importance to Western society.

For Weber, the bureaucracy was the height of (formal) rationality, which he defined in terms of the five elements of efficiency, predictability, quantifiability (or calculability), control through substituting nonhuman technology for human judgment, and the irrationality of rationality.

Bureaucracies operate in a highly predictable manner. Incumbents in one office understand very well how the incumbents of other offices will behave. They know what they will be provided with and when they will receive it. Recipients of the service bureaucracies know with a high degree of assurance what they will receive and when they will receive it. Because bureaucracies quantify as many activities as possible, employees perform their duties as a series of specified steps at quantifiable rates of speed. As with all rationalized systems that focus exclusively on quantity, however, the handling of large numbers of things is equated with excellence, and little or no evaluation is made of the actual quality of what is done in each case. Bureaucracies control people by replacing human judgment with nonhuman technology. Indeed, bureaucracy itself may be seen as one huge nonhuman technology that functions more or less automatically. The adaptability of human decisions vanishes into the dictates of rules, regulations, and institutional structures. The work to be done is divided up so that each office is allocated a limited number of well-defined tasks. Incumbents must do those tasks and no others. The tasks must be done in the manner prescribed by the organization; idiosyncratic performance will get one demoted or even fired. The idea is to get the job done in a certain way by a certain time without mistakes. The bureaucracy's clients are also controlled. The organization provides only certain services, and not others; one must apply for the services on a specific form by a specific date, and one will receive those services only in a certain way.

Weber praised bureaucracies for their advantages over other mechanisms for discovering and implementing optimum means to ends, but at the same time he was painfully aware of the irrationalities of formally rational systems. Instead of being efficient systems, bureaucracies often become inefficient as the regulations that are used to make them rational degenerate into "red tape." Bureaucracies often become unpredictable as employees grow unclear about what they are supposed to do and clients do not get the services they expect. The emphasis on quantifiability often leads to large amounts of poor quality work. Anger at the nonhuman technologies that are replacing them often leads employees to undercut or sabotage the operation of these technologies. By then, bureaucracies have begun to lose control over their workers as well as their constituents, and what was designed to be a highly rational operation often ends up irrational and quite out of control.

Although Weber was concerned about the irrationalities of formally rational systems, he was even more deeply disturbed by what he called the "iron cage of rationality." Weber saw the bureaucracy as a rationalized cage that encased increasing numbers of human beings. He described bureaucracies as "escape proof," "practically unshatterable," and among the hardest institutions to destroy once they are created. The individual bureaucrat is seen as "harnessed" into this bureaucratic cage and unable to "squirm out" of it. Given its strength, and our inability to escape, Weber concludes resignedly and with considerable unease, to put it mildly, that "the future belongs to bureaucratization."[17] He feared that more sectors of society would come to be dominated by rationalized principles so that people would be locked into a series of rationalized workplaces, rationalized recreational settings, and rationalized homes. Society would become nothing more that a seamless web of rationalized structures.

Weber has a highly pessimistic view of the future. He saw no hope in the socialistic movements of his day, which he felt (and time has borne him out) would only succeed in increasing the spread of bureaucratization and formal rationality.

There is little question that the process of rationalization has spread further and become even more firmly entrenched than it was in Weber's day. The fast-food restaurant, of which McDonald's is the best-known chain, has employed all the rational principles pioneered by the bureaucracy and is part of the bureaucratic system because huge conglomerates now own many of the fast-food chains. McDonald's utilized bureaucratic principles and combined them with others, and the outcome is the process of McDonaldization.

Several years ago, I wrote a paper titled "The McDonaldization of Society." The main thesis of that essay was that Max Weber was right about the inexorable march of formal rationality but that his paradigm case of that type of rationality and the spearhead in its expansion, the bureaucracy, have been superseded in contemporary American society by the fast-food restaurant. It is the fast-food restaurant that today best represents and leads the process of formal rationalization and its basic components—efficiency, predictability, quantification, control through the substitution of nonhuman for human technology,[18] and the ultimate irrationality of formal rationality. A decade after the original essay, as we had begun progressing through the 1990s, I once again examined the process of McDonaldization. I was astounded by the forward progress of McDonaldization during the previous decade and the degree to which it has spread its tentacles ever farther into contemporary society.

The most obvious, and perhaps least important, extension is that fast-food restaurants themselves have grown and expanded. The McDonald's chain, which began operation in 1955, opened its 12,000th branch in 1991; the leading 100 restaurant chains operate more than 110,000 outlets in the United States alone.[19] No longer restricted to the good old American hamburger, fast-food chains now traffic in pizza and Italian, Mexican, Chinese, and Cajun food, among others. Nor are the fast-food chains limited any longer to low-priced restaurants—now there are "upscale" chains, such as Sizzler (steaks), Red Lobster (seafood), and Fuddruckers (gourmet burgers), as well as trendy saloons such as Bennigan's and TGI Fridays. There is also the geographic expansion of American fast-food restaurants throughout the world, with the most notable examples being the world's largest McDonald's in Beijing and the slightly smaller, but hugely successful McDonald's in Moscow. While America expands its chains, many other countries are developing their own, most notably the fast-food croissanteries spreading throughout one of the most unlikely of locations for such a phenomenon, the center of gourmet dining: Paris.

Instead of being content to surround college campuses, fast-food chains are increasingly found on those campuses. There is also more involvement by the chains in the food served at the nation's high schools and grade schools.[20] Once characterized by an odd and unpredictable mix of restaurants, the nation's interstate highways are coming to be increasingly populated by fast-food chains. A similar thing is happening at the nation's airports, and United Airlines has begun serving McDonald's meals on some of its flights. The military has been forced to serve fast food at its bases and on its ships. Fast-food outlets are turning up increasingly in hospitals, despite the innumerable attacks on the nutritional value of the food. The latest, but undoubtedly not the last incursion of the fast-food chains is into the nation's baseball parks and other sports venues.

Still another element involves the degree to which a wide array of other kinds of businesses are coming to be operated on the basis of the principles pioneered by the fast-food chains. For example, the vice chairman of one of these chains, Toys"R"Us, said, "We want to be thought of as a sort of McDonald's of toys."[21] Other chains with a similar model and similar ambitions include Jiffy-Lube, AAMCO Transmissions, Midas Muffler, Hair Plus, H&R Block, Pearle Vision Centers, Kampgrounds of America (KOA), KinderCare (dubbed "Kentucky Fried Children"), Nutri/System, Jenny Craig, and many more.

McDonald's influence is also felt in the number of social phenomena that have come to be prefaced by "Mc." Examples include McDentists, McDoctors, McChild care centers, McStables (for the nationwide racehorse training operation of Wayne Lucas), and McPaper[22] (for *USA Today;* its short news articles are sometimes called "News McNuggets"). When *USA Today* began an aborted television program modeled after the newspaper, it was immediately dubbed "News McRather."[23] With the latter kinds of extensions, we get to the real core of the expansion of McDonaldization and the real reason for revisiting the process. In the past decade, McDonaldization has extended its reach into more and more regions of society, and those areas are increasingly remote from the heart of the process in the fast-food business. As the previous examples make clear, dentistry, medicine, child care, the training of racehorses, newspapers, and television news have come to be modeled after food chains. Thus, *McDonaldization* is the process by which the principles of the fast-food restaurant are coming to dominate more and more sectors of society.

Even the derivatives of McDonald's are, in turn, having their own influence. The success of *USA Today* ("McPaper") has led to changes (shorter stories and color weather maps) in many newspapers across the nation. One *USA Today* editor stated, "The same newspaper editors who call us McPaper have been stealing our McNuggets."[24] The influence of *USA Today* is manifest most blatantly in the *Boca Raton News,* a Knight-Ridder newspaper. This newspaper is described as "a sort of smorgasbord of snippets, a newspaper that slices and dices the news into even smaller portions than does *USA Today,* spicing it with color graphics and fun facts and cute features like 'Today's Hero' and 'Critter Watch.'[25] As in *USA Today,* stories in the *Boca Raton News* do not usually "jump" from one page to another; they start and finish on the same page. To meet this need, long and complex stories often have to be reduced to a few paragraphs. Much of a story's context, and much of what the principals have to say, are severely cut back or omitted entirely. The main function of the newspaper seems to be to entertain, with its emphasis on light and celebrity news, color maps, and graphics.

The objective of the remainder of this chapter is to demonstrate the continued relevance of Weberian theory by attempting to get at the full reach of McDonald's influence throughout society. I will do this by breaking McDonaldization down into its key elements (Weber's five dimensions of rationalization) and then demonstrating how each of these elements is being manifest in more and more sectors of society.

Efficiency

The first element of McDonaldization is efficiency, or the choice of the optimum means to an end. Many aspects of the fast-food restaurant illustrate efficiency, especially from the viewpoint of the restaurant, but none better than the degree to which the customer is turned into an unpaid laborer. The fast-food restaurant did not create the idea of imposing work on the consumer, getting the consumer to be what is, in effect, an unpaid employee, but it institutionalized and expedited this development. Customers are expected to stand in line and order their own food (rather than having a waiter do it) and to "bus" their own paper, plastic, and styrofoam (rather than having it done by a busperson). Fast-food chains have also pioneered the movement toward handing the consumer little more than the basics of the meal. The consumer is expected to take the naked burger to the "fixin bar" and there turn it into the desired sandwich by adding such things as lettuce, tomatoes, and onions. We all are expected to log a few minutes a week as sandwich makers. In a recent innovation, we are now handed an empty cup and expected to go to the fountain and fill our glasses with ice and a soft drink, thereby spending a few moments as what used to be called a "soda jerk." In some ultramodern fast-food restaurants, customers are met by a computer screen when they enter and they must punch in their own order. In these and other ways, the fast-food restaurant has grown more efficient.

The salad bar, also popularized if not pioneered by the fast-food restaurant, is a classic example of putting the consumer to work. The customer buys an empty plate and then loads up on the array of vegetables (and other foods) available. Quickly seeing the merit in all this, many supermarkets have now instituted their own salad bars with a more elaborate array of alternative foods available to the consumer. The salad lover can now work as a salad chef at lunch hour in the fast-food restaurant and then do it all over again in the evening at the supermarket by making the salad for the evening meal. All this is very efficient from the perspective of the fast-food restaurant and the supermarket because only a very small number of employees are needed to keep the various compartments well stocked.

There are many other examples of this process of imposing work on the consumer. Virtually gone are gas station attendants who filled gas tanks, checked oil, and cleaned windows. We now put in a few minutes a week as unpaid gas station attendants pumping gas, checking oil, and cleaning windows. Instead of having a readily available attendant to pay for gasoline, we must trek into the station to pay for our gas. In the latest "advance" in this realm, customers put their own credit cards in a slot, they pump the gas, their account is automatically charged the correct (we hope) amount for the gas pumped, and finally the receipt and the card are retrieved with no contact with, or work done by, anyone working in the gas station.

The latter development was pioneered in the banking industry with the advent of the cash machine, which allows us all to work for at least a few moments as unpaid bank tellers.

When calling many businesses these days, instead of dealing with a human operator who makes the desired connection for us, we must deal with "voice mail" and follow a series of instructions from a computer voice by pushing a bewildering array of numbers and codes before we get, it is hoped, to the desired extension.[26]

Efficiency has been extended to the booming diet industry, which encompasses diet drugs, diet books, exercise videotapes, diet meals, diet drinks, weight loss clinics, and "fat farms."[27] Diet books promising all kinds of efficient shortcuts to weight loss are often at the top of the best-seller lists. Losing weight is normally difficult and time-consuming. Hence the lure of various diet books that promise to make weight loss easier and quicker—that is, more efficient. For those on a diet—and many people are on more or less perpetual diets—the preparation of low-calorie food has been made more efficient. Instead of cooking diet foods from scratch, an array of pre-prepared diet foods is available in frozen or microwavable form. For those who do not wish to go through the inefficient process of eating these diet meals, there are diet shakes such as Slimfast that can be mixed and consumed in a matter of seconds.

In addition, there is the growth of diet centers such as Nutri/System and Jenny Craig.[28] Dieters at Nutri/System are provided (at substantial cost) with prepackaged freeze-dried food. The dieter needs only to add water when it is time for the next meal. Freeze-dried foods are efficient not only for the dieter but also for Nutri/System because they can be efficiently packaged, transported, and stored. Furthermore, the dieter's periodic visit to a Nutri/System center is efficiently organized. A counselor is allotted 10 minutes with each client. During that brief time period, weight, blood pressure, and measurements are taken, routine questions are asked, a chart is filled out, and some time is devoted to "problem solving." If the session extends beyond the allotted 10 minutes, and other clients are waiting, the receptionist will buzz the room. Counselors learn their techniques at Nutri/System University (NSU), where, after a week of training (no inefficient years of matriculation here), they earn certification and an NSU diploma.[29]

Calculability

The second dimension of McDonaldization is calculability. McDonaldization involves an emphasis on things that can be calculated, counted, and quantified. In terms of the latter, it means a tendency to emphasize quantity rather than quality. This leads to a sense that quality is equal to certain, usually large, quantities of things.

As in many other aspects of its operation, McDonald's emphasis on quantity (as reflected in the Big Mac) is mirrored by the other fast-food restaurants. The most notable is Burger King, which stresses the quantity of the meat in its hamburger, called the "Whopper," and of the fish in its sandwich called the "Whaler." At Wendy's, we are offered a variety of "Biggies." Similarly, 7-Eleven offers its customers a hot dog called the "Big Bite" and a large soft drink called the "Big Gulp" and now, the even larger, "Super Big Gulp." This emphasis on quantity in a McDonaldized society is not restricted to fast-food restaurants. United Airlines boasts that is serves more cities than any other airline.

What is particularly interesting about all this emphasis on quantity is the seeming absence of interest in communicating anything about quality. Thus, United Airlines does not tell us anything about the quality (passenger comfort) of its numerous flights. The result is a growing concern about the decline or even the absence of quality in society as a whole.[30]

As with efficiency, calculability has been extended from eating in food chains to many settings, including dieting. Given its very nature, the diet industry is obsessed with things that can be quantified. Weight, weight loss (or gain), and time periods are measured precisely. Food intake is carefully measured and monitored. Diet foods detail number of ounces of food, number of calories, and many other things.

Another interesting extension of the emphasis on quantity rather than quality is found in *USA Today*. This newspaper is noted for its "junk-food journalism"— the lack of substance in its stories.[31] Instead of offering detailed stories, *USA Today* offers a large number of short, easily and quickly read stories. One executive stated, "*USA Today* must sell news/info at a fast, hard pace."[32] One observer underscored the newspaper's corresponding lack of concern for quality and, in the process, its relationship to the fast-food restaurant: "Like parents who take their children to a different fast-food every night and keep the refrigerator stocked with ice cream, *USA Today* gives its readers only what they want, no spinach, no bran, no liver."[33]

There is a growing emphasis on the number of credentials one possesses. For example, people in various occupations are increasingly using long lists of initials after their names to convince prospective clients of their competence. Said one insurance appraiser with ASA, FSVA, FAS, CRA, and CRE after his name, "the more [initials] you tend to put after your name, the more impressed they [potential clients] become."[34] The sheer number of credentials, however, tells us little about the competence of the person sporting them.

The emphasis on quantity rather than quality of publications among academics led to an announcement not too long ago by the president (since departed) of Stanford University, Donald Kennedy, that there would be a change in the university's emphasis on the quantity of publications in the decision to hire, promote, or grant tenure to faculty members. He was disturbed by a report that indicated "that nearly half of faculty members believe that their scholarly writings are merely counted—not evaluated—when personnel decisions are made."[35] Kennedy stated,

> First, I hope we can agree that the quantitative use of research output as a criterion for appointment or promotion is a bankrupt idea. . . . The overproduction of routine scholarship is one of the most egregious aspects of contemporary academic life: It tends to conceal really important work by sheer volume; it wastes time and valuable resources.[36]

To deal with this problem, Kennedy proposed to limit the number of publications used in making personnel decisions. He hoped that the proposed limits would "reverse the appalling belief that counting and weighing are the important means of evaluating faculty research."[37] It remains to be seen whether Stanford, to say nothing of the rest of American academia, will be able to limit the emphasis on quantity rather than quality.

Predictability

Rationalization involves the increasing effort to ensure predictability from one time or place to another. In a rational society, people want to know what to expect in all settings and at all times. They neither want nor expect surprises. They want to know that when they order their Big Mac today it is going to be identical to the one they ate yesterday and the one they will eat tomorrow.

The movie industry is increasingly characterized by predictability. One manifestation of this is the growing reliance on sequels to successful movies rather than producing completely new movies based on new concepts, ideas, and characters. The Hitchcock classic *Psycho*, for example, was followed by several sequels (of course, not made by Hitchcock), as were other less artistically successful horror films such as *Halloween* and *Nightmare on Elm Street*. Outside of the horror movie genre, a range of other movies have been succeeded by one or more sequels, including *Star Wars, Godfather, Back to the Future, Terminator,* and many more.

The routine use of sequels is a relatively new phenomenon in Hollywood. Its development parallels, and is part of, the McDonaldization of society. The attraction of sequels is their predictability. From the point of view of the studios, the same characters, actors, and basic plot lines can be used over and over. Furthermore, there seems to be a greater likelihood that sequels will be successful at the box office than completely original movies; profit levels are more predictable. From the viewer's perspective, there is great comfort in knowing that they will once again encounter favorite characters played by familiar actors who find themselves in accustomed settings. Moviegoers seem more willing to shell out money for a safe and familiar movie than for a movie that is completely new to them. Like a McDonald's meal, these sequels are typically not as high quality as the originals, but at least the consumers know what they are getting.

One of the early manifestations of predictability, the TV dinner, has now been joined, and in some cases superseded, by even more rational meals eaten at home. The microwavable dinner is more efficient to store and cook. To this list of advances, we can now add the freeze-dried foods that blossom into predictable dishes merely through the addition of water.

A similar process can be seen in camping. Although some people still "rough it," many others have sought to eliminate most, if not all, of the unpredictability from camping. We have witnessed the development of "country-club campgrounds," spearheaded by such franchises as KOA.[38] Instead of simple tents, modern campers might venture forth in an RV to protect them from the unexpected thunderstorms, tick bites, and snakes. Of course, "camping" in an RV also tends to reduce the likelihood of catching sight of the wandering deer or bear.[39] Furthermore, the Winnebago carries within it the predictable video recorder, stereo, and so on. One camper, relaxing in his air-conditioned 32-foot trailer, stated, "We've got everything right here. . . . It doesn't matter how hard it rains or how the wind blows."[40]

Much of the attraction of the shopping mall is traceable to its predictability. The unpredictabilities of weather are eliminated:

> One kid who works here told me why he likes the mall. . . . It's because no matter what the weather is outside, it's always the same in here. He likes that. He doesn't want to know it's raining—it would depress him.[41]

The malls, like fast-food restaurants, are virtually the same from one place or time to another. One finds the same chains represented in malls throughout the country. Finally, those who spend their days wandering through malls are relatively free from the unpredictabilities of crime that beset them when they wander through city streets.

Part of the success of *USA Today* is traceable to its predictability. Because it is a national newspaper, travelers are reassured by the fact that the familiar masthead and contents will be available wherever they go. The structure and makeup of the newspaper is highly predictable from one day to another. The stories are all predictably short and easily digestible. There are as few surprises in one's daily *USA Today* as in one's nightly Big Mac; in fact, they are best consumed together.

I close this discussion of predictability in a McDonaldized society with the example of modern, suburban housing. Many of Steven Spielberg's movies take place in these rationalized and highly predictable suburbs. Spielberg's strategy is to lure the viewer into this highly predictable world and then to have a highly unpredictable event occur. For example, in *ET* the extraterrestrial wanders into a suburban development of tract houses and is discovered by a child who lives in one of those houses and who, up to that point, has lived a highly predictable suburban existence. The unpredictable ET eventually disrupts not only the lives of the child and his family but also those of the entire community. Similarly, *Poltergeist* takes place in a suburban household, and the evil spirits ultimately disrupt its predictable tranquility. The great success of Spielberg's movies may be traceable to our longing for some unpredictability, even if it is frightening and menacing, in our increasingly predictable lives.

Replacing People With Nonhuman Technologies

I combine the discussion of two elements of McDonaldization—increased control and the replacement of human by nonhuman technology. The reason for the combination is that these two elements are closely linked. Specifically, replacement of human by nonhuman technology is often oriented toward greater control. The great sources of uncertainty and unpredictability in any rationalizing system are people—either the people who work within those systems or the people who are served by them. McDonald's seeks to exert increasing control over both its employees and its customers. It is most likely to do this by steadily replacing people with nonhuman technologies. After all, technologies like robots and computers are far easier to control than humans. In addition to eliminating some people by replacing them with technologies, those who continue to labor within McDonald's are better controlled by these new technologies. These nonhuman technologies also exert increasing control over people served by the system.

As in the production and consumption of food in the fast-food restaurant, the production of some of the raw materials required by such restaurants—bread, fish, meat, and eggs—has also come to be characterized by increasing control through replacing people with nonhuman technologies. In the case of raising animals for food, relatively small, humanized family-run farms are being rapidly replaced by "factory farms," in which people and animals are controlled by nonhuman technologies.[42] One of the first animals to find its way into the factory farm was the chicken. Among its other advantages, chicken farms allow one person to manage more than 50,000 chickens. Raising chickens in this way involves a series of highly predictable steps. The chickens themselves will be far more predictable in size and weight than free-ranging chickens. It is also obviously far more efficient to "harvest" chickens confined in this way than it is to catch chickens that are free to roam over large areas.

Confining chickens in such crowded quarters, however, creates such unpredictabilities as violence and even cannibalism. These irrational "vices" are dealt with in a variety of ways, such as dimming the light as the chickens approach full size and the "debeaking" of chickens so that they cannot harm one another.

The replacement of people with nonhuman technology, and the consequent increase in control, is found not only in food production and the fast-food restaurant but also in home cooking. Technologies such as the microwave or conventional oven with a temperature probe "decide" when food is done rather than leaving that judgment to the cook. Ovens, coffee makers, and other appliances are now able to turn themselves on and off. The instructions on all kinds of packaged foods dictate precisely how the food is to be prepared and cooked. Even the now old-fashioned cookbook was designed to take creativity away from the cook, who would be inclined to flavor to taste, and put it in the hands of the rigid guidelines laid down by the cookbook.

A very similar development has taken place in supermarkets. In the past, prices were marked on food products, and the supermarket checker had to read the price and enter it into the cash register. As with all human activities, there was a chance for human error. In recent years, to counter this problem, many supermarkets have installed optical scanners. Instead of the human checker reading the price, the mechanical scanner "reads" the code and the price for a given code number that has been entered into the computer, which is the heart of the modern cash register. This nonhuman technology has eliminated some of the human uncertainty from the job of supermarket checker. It has also reduced the number and level of sophistication of the tasks performed by the checker. The checker no longer needs to read the amount and enter it in the cash register. Left are less skilled tasks such as scanning the food and bagging it. In other words, the supermarket checker has undergone *deskilling*—a decline in the amount of skill required on the job.

The next step in this development is to have the customer do the scanning, thereby eliminating the need for a checkout person. In fact, a nearby Safeway recently instituted such a system. To make things easier, Safeway is providing its customers with a brochure titled "Checkout for Yourself Just How Easy It Is." (Of course, one might ask, easy for whom?) The following are three "easy" steps as described in the brochure:

1. Pass the item's barcode over the scanner. Wait for beep. Place item on conveyor belt.

2. When you are finished scanning all items, touch END ORDER button on screen.

3. Pick up receipt at the end of the lane. Proceed to the pay station.

Such military-like orders exert great control over the customer, and they allow for the elimination of the checkout person. The next "advance" may be a technology that permits the insertion of the customer's credit card in the scanning system, thereby avoiding the need to move on to a human cashier and pay for the food.

The supermarket scanners permit other kinds of control over customers. Prior to the scanner, customers could examine their purchases and see how much each cost; they could also check to be sure that they were not being overcharged at the cash register. With the advent of the scanner, prices no longer appear on goods, only bar codes. This change has given the supermarket greater control over customers; it is almost impossible for the consumer to keep tabs on the checkers. When the scanners were instituted at my local market, management announced that it was issuing markers to customers who were interested in writing the price on each item. This, again, is consistent with the trend toward getting the consumer to do work historically done by others, in this case by grocery clerks who worked deep into the night to mark each item. In any case, the supermarkets did not keep the markers very long because few hurried shoppers had the desire to spend several additional minutes a day as grocery clerks.

Telemarketing is increasingly ubiquitous in modern society. Many of us are called several times a day in efforts to get us to buy something. Those who work in these telemarketing "factories" are rigidly controlled. They often have scripts that they follow mindlessly. Furthermore, there are a range of alternative scripts designed to handle most foreseeable contingencies. Those doing the phoning are often listened in on by supervisors to be sure the correct procedures are followed. There are rigid demands for numbers of calls and sales required in a given time period. If employees fail to meet the quotas, they are summarily fired. Following the usual progression, instead of having people solicit us over the phone, some companies are now using computer calls. Computer voices are far more predictable than even the most rigidly controlled human operator. Not only do we have computer calls but also we are now seeing the utilization of computers that respond to the human voice. A person receiving a long-distance collect call might be asked whether he or she will accept the charges. The computer voice demands, "Say yes or no" or "Press one for no, zero for yes." Although efficient and cost saving, such a system is anonymous and dehumanizing:

> The person senses that he cannot use free-flowing speech. He's being constrained. The computer is controlling him. It can be simply frustrating. . . . People adapt to it, but only by filing it away subconsciously as another annoyance of living in our technological world.[43]

An even more extreme version of this is found in the educational variant of the fast-food restaurant, KinderCare. KinderCare tends to hire short-term employees with little or no training in education. What these employees do in the "classroom" is determined by a uniform "instruction book" that includes a preset, ready-made curriculum. All that is required is that the staff member open up the manual to the appropriate place where all activities are spelled out in detail on a day-by-day basis. Clearly, a skilled, experienced, and creative teacher is not the kind of person McChild care centers seek to hire. Rather, relatively untrained employees are more easily controlled by the nonhuman technology of the omnipresent instruction book.

The modern, computerized airplane, such as Boeing's 757 and 767, represents an interesting case of substituting nonhuman for human control. Instead of flying "by the seat of their pants" or using old-fashioned autopilots for simple maneuvers, modern pilots "can push a few buttons and lean back while the plane flies to its destination and lands on a predetermined runway."[44]

Said one Federal Aviation Administration official, "We're taking more and more of these functions out of human control and giving them to machines."[45] The new, automated airplanes are in many ways safer and more reliable than older, less technologically advanced models. There is a fear, however, that pilots dependent on these technologies will lose the ability to find creative ways of handling emergency situations. An airline manager stated, "If we have human operators subordinated to technology, then we're going to lose that creativity. I don't have computers that will do that [be creative]; I just don't."[46]

The Irrationality of Rationality

There are great gains involved in increasing rationalization, resulting from increases in efficiency, predictability, calculability, and control through the substitution of nonhuman for human technology. I enumerate some of the advantages of the fast-food restaurant and, more generally, of other elements of McDonaldized society. The fast-food restaurant has expanded the alternatives available to consumers: More people now have ready access to Italian, Mexican, Chinese, and Cajun foods; the salad bar enables people to make salads exactly the way they want them; microwave ovens and microwavable foods allow us to have dinner in minutes or even seconds; for those with a wide range of shopping needs, supermarkets and shopping malls are efficient sites, and home shopping networks allow us to shop even more efficiently without ever leaving home; today's high-tech, for-profit hospitals are likely to provide higher quality medical care than their predecessors; we can get almost instantaneous medical attention at our local, drive-in McDoctors; computerized phone systems allow people to do things (like getting a bank balance in the middle of the night) that were impossible before and automated bank teller machines allow people to obtain money any time of the day or night; package tours permit large numbers of people to visit countries that they would otherwise be unable to see; diet centers such as Nutri/System allow people to lose weight in a carefully regulated and controlled system; Winnebagos let the modern camper avoid excessive heat, rain, insects, and the like; and suburban tract houses have permitted large numbers of people to afford single-family homes.

The rational systems also allow us to avoid the problems created by nonrational systems in other societies. The following is a description of a recent visit to a pizzeria in Havana, Cuba:

> The pizza's not much to rave about—they scrimp on tomato sauce, and the dough is mushy.
>
> It was about 7:30 p.m., and as usual the place was standing-room only, with people two deep jostling for a stool to come open and a waiting line spilling out onto the sidewalk.
>
> The menu is similarly Spartan. . . . To drink, there is tap water. That's it—no toppings, no soda, no beer, no coffee, no salt, no pepper. And no special orders. The waiter wears a watch around his belt loop, but he hardly needs it; time is evidently not his chief concern. After a while, tempers begin to fray.
>
> But right now, it's 8:45 p.m. at the pizzeria, I've been waiting an hour and a quarter for two small pies.[47]

Few would prefer such irrational systems to the rationalized elements of our society.

Although there are many advantages to a McDonaldized society, there are also great costs associated with McDonaldization that can be dealt with largely under the heading of the irrationality of rationality. In other words, it is my thesis, following Weber, that rational systems inevitably spawn a series of irrationalities that serve to limit, ultimately compromise, and perhaps even defeat, their rationality.

We can conceive of the irrationality of rationality in several ways. At the most general level, it is simply the overarching label for all the negative aspects and effects of McDonaldization. More specifically, it can be seen as the opposite of rationality and its several dimensions. That is, McDonaldization can be viewed as leading to inefficiency, unpredictability, incalculability, and loss of control. Most specifically, irrationality means that rational systems are unreasonable systems. By that, I mean they serve to deny the basic humanity, the human reason, of the people who work within or are served by them. Rational systems are dehumanizing systems. Although in other contexts rationality and reason are often used interchangeably, here they are employed to mean antithetical phenomena.

The most obvious manifestation of the inefficiency of the fast-food restaurant is the long lines of people that are often found at the counters or the long lines of people that are often found at the drive-through windows. What is purported to be an efficient way of obtaining a meal turns out to be quite inefficient. The fast-food restaurant is far from the only aspect of the McDonaldization society that operates inefficiently. Columnist Richard Cohen described the inefficiencies of the automated teller machines (ATMs) as follows:

> Oh Lord, with each advance of the computer age, I was told I would benefit. But with each "benefit," I wind up doing more work. This is the ATM rule of life. . . . I was told—nay promised—that I could avoid lines at the bank and make deposits or withdrawals any time of the day. Now, there are lines at the ATMs, the bank seems to take a percentage of whatever I withdraw or deposit, and of course, I'm doing what tellers (remember them?) used to do. Probably, with the new phone, I'll have to climb telephone poles in the suburbs during ice storms.[48]

At least three different irrationalities are being underscored in the previous quotation: Rational systems are not less expensive, they force us to do a range of unpaid work, and, most important from the point of view of this discussion, they are often inefficient. It might be more efficient to deal with a human teller, either in the bank or drive-through window, than to wait in line at an ATM machine, perhaps on a cold, snowy night. For many, it would be far more efficient to prepare a meal at home than to load the family in the car, drive to McDonald's, fill up on food, and then drive home again. This may not be true of some meals cooked at home from scratch, but it is certainly true of TV dinners, microwave meals, or full-course meals brought in from the supermarket. Many people, however, persist in the belief, fueled by endless propaganda from the fast-food restaurants, that it is more efficient to eat there than to eat at home.

The main reason that we think of McDonaldization as irrational, and ultimately unreasonable, is that it tends to become a dehumanizing system that may become antihuman or even destructive of human beings. In terms of the latter, there are a number of ways in which the health, and perhaps the lives, of people have been threatened by progressive rationalization.[49] One example is the high calorie, fat, cholesterol, salt, and sugar content of the food served at fast-food restaurants. Such meals are the last things the vast majority of Americans need.

Many suffer from being overweight or have high cholesterol levels, high blood pressure, and perhaps diabetes. The kinds of meals typically served at fast-food restaurants only serve to make these health problems much worse. Even more worrisome, they help to create eating habits in children that contribute to the development of these and other health problems later in life. It can be argued that, with their appeal to children, fast-food restaurants are creating not only lifelong devotees of fast food but also people who will grow addicted to diets high in salt, sugar, and fat.

The fast-food industry has run afoul of not only nutritionists but also environmentalists. It produces an enormous amount of trash, some of which is non-biodegradable. Many people have been critical of the public eyesore created by litter from innumerable fast-food meals strewn across the countryside. Almost two decades ago, prior to much of its enormous expansion, it was estimated that it took 315 square miles of forest to provide the paper needed by McDonald's.[50] That figure must be far greater today than it was in 1972, even though some paper containers have been replaced by styrofoam and other products. Even greater criticism has been leveled at the widespread use of virtually indestructible styrofoam. Styrofoam debris piles up in landfills, creating mountains of waste that simply remain there for years, if not forever.

McDonaldized institutions have a negative effect not only on our health and on the environment but also on some of our most cherished institutions, most notably the family. A key technology in the destruction of the family meal is the microwave oven and the vast array of microwavable foods it helped generate.[51] A recent *Wall Street Journal* poll indicated that Americans consider the microwave their favorite household product.[52] In fact, the microwave in a McDonaldizing society is seen as an advance over the fast-food restaurant. One consumer researcher stated, "It has made even fast-food restaurants not seem fast because at home you don't have to wait in line."[53] Consumers are demanding meals that take no more than 10 minutes to microwave, whereas in the late 1970s people were more willing to spend a half hour cooking dinner, and in the early 1970s they were more willing to spend as much as an hour on dinner. This emphasis on speed has, of course, brought with it poorer taste and lower quality, but people do not seem to mind this loss: "We're just not as critical of food as we used to be."[54]

The speed of microwave cooking, as well as the wide variety of foods available in that form, makes it possible for family members to eat at different times and places. To give even children independence, companies are marketing products such as Kid's Kitchen, Kid Cuisine, and My Own Meals. As a result, "Those qualities of the family meal, the ones that imparted feelings of security and well-being, might be lost forever where food is 'zapped' or 'nuked' instead of cooked."[55]

The advances in microwave cooking continue. There are already plastic strips on some foods that turn blue when the food is done. The industry is promising strips that communicate cooking information directly to the microwave oven:

> With cooking reduced to pushing a button, the kitchen may wind up as a sort of filling station. Family members will pull in, push a few buttons, fill up and leave. To clean up, all we need do is throw away plastic plates.[56]

What is lost, of course, is the family meal, and we must decide whether we can afford the loss:

> The communal meal is our primary ritual for encouraging the family to gather together every day. If it is lost to us, we shall have to invent new ways to be a family. It is worth considering whether the shared joy that food can provide is worth giving up.[57]

Thus, it is my argument that contrary to McDonald's propaganda, and the widespread belief in it, fast-food restaurants, as well as the innumerable other McDonaldized institutions, are not truly rational systems. They spawn all kinds of problems for the health of their customers and the well-being of the environment, they tend to be dehumanizing and therefore unreasonable in various ways, and they often lead to the opposite of what they are supposed to create—for example, they lead to inefficiency rather than increased efficiency. All this is not to deny the many advantages of McDonald's mentioned previously, but it is to point to the fact that there are counterbalancing and perhaps even overwhelming problems associated with the fast-food society.

Perhaps the ultimate irrationality of McDonaldization is the possibility that people could ultimately lose control over the system, and it would come to control us. Already, many aspects of the lives of most of us are controlled by these rational systems. It at least appears, however, that these systems are ultimately controlled by people. These rational systems, however, can spin beyond the control of even the people who occupy the highest level positions within those systems. This is one of the senses in which we can, following Weber, talk of an "iron cage of McDonaldization." It can become a system that comes to control all of us.

There is another fear: that these interlocking rational systems can fall into the hands of a small number of leaders who, through them, can exercise enormous control over all society. Thus, there are authoritarian and totalitarian possibilities associated with the process of McDonaldization. We may come to be increasingly controlled by the rational systems themselves or by a few leaders who master those systems.

This kind of fear has animated many science fiction writers and is manifest in such sci-fi classics as *1984, Brave New World,* and *Fahrenheit 451.* The problem is that these novels described a feared and fearsome future world, whereas McDonaldization is with us now, has been with us for awhile, and is extending its reach throughout society.

Conclusion

The objective in this chapter has been to show the continued, if not increasing, relevance of Max Weber's theory of rationalization to the modern world. Although the bureaucracy may have been replaced by the fast-food restaurant as the ultimate example of a rational structure, and bureaucratization by McDonaldization as the heart of the process, the rationalization that undergirds both sets of structures and processes remains at least as powerful a force today as it was in Weber's day. In fact, the old sites remain rationalized while new ones are coming under the sway of the rationalization process. In this sense, we seem closer to the iron cage of rationalization today than was the case in Weber's day.

Notes

1. Ritzer, G. (1983). The McDonaldization of society. *Journal of American Culture, 6,* 100-107; (1993). *The McDonaldization of society.* Newbury Park, CA: Pine Forge Press.

2. Kalberg, S. (1980). Max Weber's types of rationality: Cornerstones for the analysis of rationalization processes in history. *American Journal of Sociology, 85,* 1145-1179; Levine, D. (1981). Rationality and freedom: Weber and beyond. *Sociological Inquiry, 51,* 5-25; Brubaker, R. (1984). *The limits of rationality: An essay on the social and moral thought of Max Weber.* London: Allen & Unwin; Habermas, J. (1984). *The theory of communicative action: Vol. 1. Reason and rationalization of society.* Boston: Beacon.

3. Weber, M. (1958). *The Protestant ethic and the spirit of capitalism* (p. 77). New York: Scribner's. (Original work published 1904-1905)

4. Weber (1958), *The Protestant ethic and the spirit of capitalism,* p. 293.

5. Levine (1981), *Sociological Inquiry, 51,* 12.

6. Weber (1958), *The Protestant ethic and the spirit of capitalism,* p. 293.

7. Kalberg (1980), *American Journal of Sociology, 85,* 1151-1154.

8. Kalberg (1980), *American Journal of Sociology, 85,* 1155-1156.

9. Weber, M. (1978). *Economy and society* (p. 85). Berkeley: University of California Press. (Original work published 1921)

10. Kalberg (1980), *American Journal of Sociology, 85,* 1158.

11. Weber (1978), *Economy and society,* p. 1186.

12. Weber, M. (1975). *Roscher and Knies: The logical problems of historical economics* (p. 1186). New York: Free Press. (Original work published 1903-1906)

13. Kalberg (1980), *American Journal of Sociology, 85,* 1176.

14. Weber, M. (1968). *Economy and society* (3 Vols., p. 1116). Totwa, NJ: Bedminster Press. (Original work published 1921)

15. Weber, M. (1946). In H. H. Gerth & C. Wright Mills (Eds.), *From Max Weber: Essays in sociology* (p. 240). New York: Oxford University Press.

16. Brubaker (1984), *The limits of rationality: An essay on the social and moral thought of Max Weber,* p. 21.

17. Weber (1968), *Economy and society,* p. 1401.

18. In this essay, I combine control and nonhuman for human technology, whereas in the previous essay they were differentiated.

19. Ramirez, A. (1990, October 30). In the orchid room . . . Big Macs. *New York Times,* pp. D1, D5.

20. Farhi, P. (1990, September 21). Domino's is going to school. *Washington Post,* p. F3.

21. Egan, T. (1990, December 8). Big chains are joining Manhattan's toy wars. *New York Times,* p. 29.

22. Prichard, P. (1987). *The making of McPaper: The inside story of USA Today.* Kansas City, MO: Andrews, McMeel, & Parker.

23. Zoglin, R. (1988, April 11). Get ready for McRather. *Time,* pp. 32-33.

24. Zoglin (1988, April 11), *Time,* pp. 32-33.

25. Zoglin (1988, April 11), *Time,* p. 33.

26. Barron, J. (1989, February 17). Please press 2 for service; Press? for an actual human. *New York Times,* pp. A1, B2.

27. Kleinfeld, N. R. (1986, September 7). The ever-fatter business of thinness. *New York Times,* p. 1ff.

28. Big people, big business: The overweight numbers rising, try Nutri/System. (1988, October 10). *Washington Post,* Health section, p. 8.

29. I thank Dora Giemza for these and other insights into Nutri/System.

30. Tuchman, B. W. (1980, November 2). The decline of quality. *New York Times Magazine,* p. 38ff.

31. Prichard (1987), *The making of McPaper: The inside story of USA Today,* p. 8.

32. Prichard (1987), *The making of McPaper: The inside story of USA Today,* p. 113.

33. Prichard (1987), *The making of McPaper: The inside story of USA Today,* p. 196.

34. Gervasi, S. (1990, August 30). The credentials epidemic. *Washington Post,* p. D5.

35. Cooper, K. J. (1991, March 3). Stanford president sets initiative on teaching. *Washington Post,* p. A12.

36. Cooper (1991, March 3), *Washington Post,* p. A12.

37. Cooper (1991, March 3), *Washington Post,* p. A12.

38. Johnson, D. (1986, August 28). Vacationing at campgrounds is now hardly roughing it. *New York Times,* p. B1.

39. Country-club campgrounds. (1984, September 24). *Newsweek,* p. 90.

40. Johnson, D. (1986, August 28). *New York Times,* p. B1.

41. Kowinski, W. S. (1985). *The malling of America: An inside look at the great consumer paradise* (p. 27). New York: William Morrow.

42. Singer, P. (1975). *Animal liberation: A new ethics for our treatment of animals.* New York: Avon.

43. Langer, G. (1990, February 11). Computers reach out, respond to human voice. *Washington Post,* p. H3.

44. Lavin, C. H. (1989, August 12). Automated planes raising concerns. *New York Times,* p. 1.

45. Lavin (1989, August 12), *New York Times,* p. 1.

46. Lavin (1989, August 12), *New York Times,* p. 1.

47. Hockstader, L. (1991, August 5). No service, no smile, little sauce. *Washington Post,* p. A12. Reprinted with permission.

48. Cohen, R. (1990, August 5). Take a message—please! *Washington Post Magazine,* p. 5.

49. Spencer, M. (1983). Can Mama Mac get them to eat spinach? In M. Fishwick (Ed.), *Ronald revisited: The world of Ronald McDonald* (pp. 85-93). Bowling Green, OH: Bowling Green University Press.

50. Boas, M., & Chain, S. (1976). *Big Mac: The unauthorized story of McDonald's.* New York: NAL.

51. Visser, M. (1989, December). A meditation on the microwave. *Psychology Today,* pp. 38ff.

52. The microwave cooks up a new way of life (1989, September 19). *Wall Street Journal,* p. B1.

53. The microwave cooks up a new way of life (1989, September 19). *Wall Street Journal,* p. B1.

54. The microwave cooks up a new way of life (1989, September 19). *Wall Street Journal,* p. B1.

55. Visser (1989, December), *Psychology Today,* p. 40.

56. Visser (1989, December), *Psychology Today,* p. 42.

57. Visser (1989, December), *Psychology Today,* p. 42.

Discussion Questions

1. Weber thought that the overly bureaucratized, overrationalized world was, to use his image, a huge "iron cage" from which it appeared we could not escape. In what ways do you see yourself and your peers trapped in a McDonaldized world? Do young people perceive such a world to be something like a prison? What are the chances of resisting this trend—of escaping from the new iron cage?

2. One of the key elements of McDonaldization is predictability. Why do consumers place such a high premium on predictability? What are some of the social consequences of an increasingly predictable world?

3. This chapter identifies some of the negative consequences of McDonaldization. What do you think the main positive consequences of such a process are? Do the positives outweigh the negatives, or is the reverse the case? Defend your argument.

CHAPTER 3

Surfing the Net for Community

A Durkheimian Analysis of Electronic Gatherings

Anne M. Hornsby

Anne M. Hornsby has turned to sociological theory for a critical lens on understanding and changing society for more than a decade. She finds theory both inspirational and useful, not only as a professor teaching theory but also as a sociologist in other work settings. Her first realization of the practical power of sociological theory occurred while working for Boston's public health department. She was assigned to investigate organizational dysfunction in neighborhood health clinics, and while searching for a framework that made sense of her findings, she remembered Max Weber's argument about the tension between bureaucracy and democracy. Drawing on Weber's ideas, she effectively communicated her findings to decision makers. She has served as a consultant on health care reform in Latin America. In 1991, she received a PhD in sociology from Harvard University. She has taught at Tulane University and Loyola University in New Orleans. Currently she is employed as a policy analyst at the Center for Medicare and Medicaid Services.

The global and multilayered network of electronic networks known as the Net offers access to an astonishing diversity of information, relationships, and social rituals. Through connections among computers around the world, friends in Egypt and Japan can send each other birthday messages; scholars in the United States can retrieve a new book manuscript in seconds from a university in Australia; a public health worker in Fiji can receive the latest World Bank memo on clean water projects by fax from a laptop in the airspace over South Africa; rock music fans in India can listen to selections from their favorite American pop star's latest CD; and a Chilean journalist can listen to replays of U.S. National Public Radio broadcasts.

In addition to retrieving and sending information and messages, there also has emerged an astonishing range of social activities in Net gatherings. On-line participants carry out virtual sex, weddings, funerals, and the on-line equivalent of murder (deleting someone's persona from an on-line milieu through clever but unacceptable programming wizardry). People pursue hobbies, seek friends, compose music, and conduct political activism electronically. For example, experimenting with new forms of democratic participation in local government is growing through the creation of municipal systems such as Santa Monica's Public Electronic Network and Seattle's Community Network.

We can also enter on-line communities known as multiuser domains or dungeons (MUDs), in which dozens of people can simultaneously play adventure games or hang out in worlds they have created just for the purpose of being sociable. In some MUDs, we can engage in conversation with someone we think is another person when in fact we are talking with a "bot" (derived from robot), a computer program that presents itself as a person by generating conversation (including humorous retorts) and physical self-description when asked. One variant of MUDs that has emerged recently is MUSH, which stands for multiuser shared hallucination, games that involve role playing in "another" world.

An excerpt from a transcript of a chat between Julia (a bot residing in a computer in Pittsburgh) and Ace (a human) provides a flavor of how our social boundaries between human and machine are being reworked in life on-line (Turkle, 1995):

> Ace says, "So why won't you kiss me, Julia?"
> Julia says, "Sorry, I'm not into geeks, Ace."
> Ace says, "Julia, I'm not a geek."
> Julia says, "Then lose the pocket protector, Ace." (p. 89)

What do these new developments mean for the social organization of human societies? The emergence of computer-mediated communications (CMCs) has raised a set of entirely new questions about the late 20th-century phenomenon of virtual relationships and the nature of their connections to community life off-line. Hints of change are reflected in the increasing use of the prefix *cyber* to create new words describing CMCs, such as cyberspace, cybernauts, cybersex, and cyberculture.

We know that the Net is not just a cyberplace where people pursue information through solitary surfing or browsing. Thousands of people also seek conversation, affiliation, support, and affirmation as social beings (Sproull & Faraj, 1995). Almost as soon as the distinction between "real life" and life on-line emerged, when the Net became familiar to larger numbers of people in the 1980s, the boundaries between real and virtual became oddly blurred. In the following, Turkle quotes Doug, a Midwestern college junior, who describes a typical evening of life in four windows:

I'm in some kind of argument in one window and trying to come on to a girl in a MUD in another, and another window might be running a spreadsheet program or some other technical thing for school. . . . And then I'll get a real-time message [that flashes on the screen as soon as it is sent from another system user], and I guess that is RL [real life]. . . . *RL is just one more window . . . and it's not usually my best one* [italics added]. (p. 13)

How many others like Doug think life on-line can be an equivalent experience to real-life interactions? For the first time in human history, many people seriously pose the question of whether we can have intimate relationships of emotional depth and substance with people we know only through a computer-mediated social tie, without face-to-face contact. What impact will there be on our sense of social order and connectedness to other people? After all, surfing the Net usually involves an individual sitting alone in front of a computer terminal. If approximately 10 to 40 million individuals access Net services today (most of whom are in the United States), what impact will such large-scale attachment to computer terminals have on our communities?

Chapter Organization

This chapter will analyze virtual social organization on the Net by applying the ideas of French sociologist Émile Durkheim, one of the founders of sociology in the late 19th century. There is a shortage of systematic research on the social organization and social uses of the Net. Most of the rigorous research is conducted on use of computers for work. The focus here is to analyze social uses; the available evidence is largely anecdotal and descriptive. This relatively new literature does, however, provide a rich guide to understanding the texture of the people's experiences on-line in the 1990s.

This chapter has three goals. This first goal is to explain the Net. Because the Net continues to increase in social, economic, and political importance, this section offers a thorough overview of the history and organization of the Net. I describe both the types of Net services (electronic mail [email], MUDs, and chat channels) and types of electronic gatherings (discussion groups, fantasy worlds, and civic networks). Second, the core of the chapter educates readers about the sociological theories of a great thinker. To do this, I analyze in what ways electronic gatherings are similar to Durkheimian societies. I present Durkheim's argument about what ingredients are necessary for stable and cohesive societies—which he calls regulation and integration. Next, I apply Durkheim's ideas on regulation and integration to analyze electronic gatherings as Durkheimian "Net societies."

The third goal of the chapter is to demonstrate how Durkheim's ideas can be applied to understand how CMCs are affecting human societies. I discuss Durkheim's ideas about two different ways in which societies can be organized—which he calls mechanical and organic societies. Next, I draw on his ideas to develop a hypothesis about the emergence of a third, new type of society in the 21st century, which I call "cyborg society." This section attempts to illustrate how sociological theory can be used to better understand our rapidly changing world.

I present Durkheim's arguments in some depth to acquaint the reader with the original ideas of a great sociologist and also to demonstrate how an argument can be presented as a sequence of concepts and reasoning. I also quote him throughout the chapter. Too often, people believe that the classic works of a discipline are stuffy, out of date, and incomprehensible. By letting Durkheim speak for himself, I hope to show that his ideas are clear, still fresh, and exciting and that they can help us better understand our world today.

Background on the Net and Electronic Gatherings

What Is the Internet?

The Internet is only one of a number of computer networks throughout the world. Because it is the world's largest collection of interconnected computer networks, however, the Internet is often confused with the entire matrix of global networks. In this chapter, I will distinguish between these two by calling the global matrix of all networks by the popular term, "the Net." This section discusses both the Internet and the larger Net.

The term *Internet* refers to the experimental system that was designed and built in the 1970s under the auspices of a U.S. Department of Defense agency, the Advanced Research Projects Agency (ARPA). By 1982, the initial version of the Internet (ARPANET) was in operation at a few academic and industrial research locations, including approximately 200 computers. By 1983, the U.S. military had selected the ARPANET as its main computer communication system, which doubled the number of interconnected computers (Batty & Barr, 1994; Comer, 1995; Kahin, 1995).

The Internet grew from a small, U.S.-based experimental research network to an international network (Comer, 1995). It is difficult to determine the actual number of Internet users, but a recent estimate concluded that in 2000 there were more than 400 million users worldwide, with over two-thirds of them located in the United States, Canada, and Western Europe (Ishaq, 2001). As indicated by Figure 3.1, the wealthy nations of the North have far more people on-line than do the nations of the South. This is part of what Pippa Norris (2001) refers to as the "digital divide," a divide that differentiates wealthy nations from poor ones in terms of Internet access, and likewise within nations it distinguishes the ease of access on the part of the wealthier members of the society in contrast to the lack of access by the poor.

Essentially, the Internet consists of thousands of computer networks linked by dedicated, special-purpose computers called *routers*. Routers can be interconnected to link incompatible networks because of the invention of a special package of software protocols called TCP/IP. Creation and diffusion of TCP/IP software was a major breakthrough because it can break messages into "packets" in a way that allows them to travel across a multitude of computer networks using incompatible

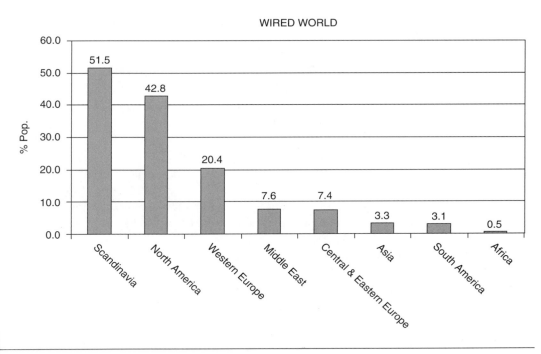

Figure 3.1   The Percentage of the Population Online by Major Region, 2000

SOURCE: Norris, P. (2001). From *Digital divide: Civic engagement, information poverty, and the Internet world-wide.* Reprinted with permission of Cambridge University Press.

technologies (e.g., between IBM and UNIX-based Digital systems). Thus, the Internet appears to users as one large network, when in reality it consists of multiple layers of many different types of computer networks scattered across the United States and throughout the world (Comer, 1995).

If all the computers linked by high-speed lines, TCP/IP software, and routers were shut down (the Internet), millions of people would still be able to send email to each other by using telephone lines, modems, and special software for their personal computers (PCs). (To use phone lines, you must use a modem to translate the electronic impulses coming out of the computer into the audible tone that carries the data over the telephone wires and vice versa.) For example, America OnLine and similar companies are commercial organizations that sell network services that mostly travel by wires leased from telephone companies, although these organizations did establish gateways to the Internet in the 1990s.

Types of Electronic Gatherings on the Net

Electronic gathering is a name that highlights the core social activity on the Net— conversation about shared interests for the sheer pleasure of it (Sproull & Faraj, 1995).

The Net literature suggests, however, that people can have a wide range of needs met (to varying degrees) by on-line groups, including the following:

- Feelings of affiliation and emotional support
- Contact with others who share similar interests
- Access to information, technical advice, and expert opinion
- Access to educational opportunities and job leads
- Entertainment, role-playing, and identity experiments
- Opportunities for political and social activism
- Access to the informal economy, such as swap shops (e.g., ebay.com)

Informal Net histories invariably remark on the pleasure and emotional support people get just from the sheer sociability of gathering and chatting on-line. Computer system administrators and government officials are often described as surprised at the depth of people's interest in all kinds of conversations with all types of people all over the world (Rheingold, 1993).

It is helpful to think of social life on the Net as consisting of three main types of electronic gatherings: (a) discussion groups, (b) fantasy worlds, and (c) civic networks. My typology is based on the main activity that occurs in a gathering. Probably the most familiar Net service is email. Originally, email was designed for communication between two people. Today, we can use email to communicate with large groups of friends and colleagues by creating personally tailored public or private email mailing lists. After creating a mailing list and a group name, you send a message to all members of your list by addressing it to the group name.

In the United States and internationally, Usenet is the most well-known bulletin board service. Indeed, many people equate the Net with Usenet newsgroups ("netnews") (Rheingold, 1993):

> Usenet is . . . like a giant coffeehouse with a thousand rooms; it is also a worldwide digital version of the Speaker's Corner in London's Hyde Park, an unedited collection of letters to the editor, a floating flea market, a huge vanity publisher, and a coalition of every odd special-interest group in the world. (p. 130)

Usenet newsgroups constitute the largest system of interconnected message centers on the Net. Usenet has developed its own language. *Newsgroup* is the name for a discussion group, and *article* is the name for a message. Note that the Usenet service is itself not a computer network; "it is a network of bilateral agreements among system administrators to cooperate in managing bulletin boards" (Sproull & Faraj, 1995, p. 68). Netnews is posted to an estimated 90,000 sites on five continents, with an estimated 3 million participants (Baym, 1995). Each Usenet discussion category has dozens of division topics, and each division is subdivided into layers, analogous to the branching of logic trees.

A recent entry into the discussion category is the *blog*, a slang term for *weblog*, which refers to personal journals that individuals post, usually in chronological order. Some bloggers, such as the humorist Dave Berry, have a lively blog that elicits considerable reader reaction. This is not the case with many blog sites. Blogs are oftentimes essentially an individual's private diary made public for any and all to read.

Fantasy Worlds

Fantasy worlds are real-time interactive programs that allow people to create one or many alternative identities and build computational objects representing rooms in houses, objects to furnish these rooms, gardens, tools, and so on. Created personae interact in these fantasy environments. Fantasy world activities, such as role-play and maneuvering in utopian worlds, go on in MUDs and chat rooms.

MUDs

MUDs originally stood for multiuser dungeons, in reference to the popular Dungeons and Dragons game of the 1970s. Today, it also stands for multiuser domains because many people can log into the program as a created identity (e.g., Xena, the Warrior Princess) and then interact by typing text and commands to each other. Invented personae interact by having (typing) conversations and by moving from place to place in a conceptual building or environment.

People join fantasy worlds for different reasons (Turkle, 1995), including the following:

- Simple escape
- A psychological adjunct to real life (e.g., picking a fight in a MUD or chat room as an escape valve for anxiety and anger)
- Experimenting with real-life roles (e.g., parenting)
- Having experiences you cannot imagine for yourself (e.g., disabled people acting on-line as athletes)

Some MUDs have been created to give players the experience of constructing and inhabiting virtual social worlds from scratch. Players in some of these social worlds are designing innovative institutions, such as legal systems and economies (e.g., LambdaMoo in the United States and Habitat in Japan).

Often, the main activity in a MUD is creating and displaying an identity for the sole purpose of being sociable (e.g., presenting as a bear who is trying to kiss another on-line persona, such as an elf). In other MUDs, the main activity is participating in fantastic activity such as slaying dragons, launching a military invasion of another galaxy, or designing an innovative municipal transportation system.

Chat Rooms

Chat rooms are interactive services that can support both discussion groups and fantasy worlds. I discuss chat rooms in the section on fantasy worlds because of what they have in common with MUDs—people experiment with alternate identities in real time. Users join rooms by entering a nickname, and people typically choose names that disguise their identity (e.g., a woman chooses "wildman" or people choose animal names). Because of this feature, chat rooms are very popular for carrying on *Tinysex* (also known as *netsex* and *cybersex*), that is, text-based erotic encounters among two, three, or many.

Chat rooms allow people to communicate in real time about any subject, either by joining an open room with many others or by agreeing with someone to enter a private talk mode. Internet Relay Chat (IRC), a popular chat service, is a multiuser chat system; not all chat systems support multiple users. On IRC, anyone can review the list of rooms currently open, join one of these, or choose to open his or her own. A room creator selects a topic name and indicates whether the room is public or restricted to people identified by the operator. Commercial services also offer chat services.

Chat rooms lack the community memory available in discussion groups or MUDs because there is no mechanism in the software for storing conversations centrally. Also unlike MUDs, communication does not occur in the context of a collectively created virtual background, such as cities, mansions, or enchanted forests. Conversation scrolls down the computer screen as people fast and furiously type their "two cents." (Individual users can capture a dialogue at a given time by downloading a portion of the conversation.)

Whereas most MUDS are organized around fantasy identities, no one can know whether identities presented in chat rooms are real or fictional. In the early years of chat rooms, many participants assumed that when you entered private talk mode, people were exchanging real information about themselves. In the mid-1980s, however, aficionados of CompuServe's CB chat service were outraged to discover that a prominent New York psychiatrist in his early fifties had been carrying on intimate friendships with many women using the false persona of Joan, a neuropsychologist in her late twenties who was mute and confined to a wheelchair. This betrayal was one of the first such scandals to shake up cyberculture. One woman described his deceit as "mind rape" (Van Gelder, 1996, p. 534). Debates emerged about the ethical and legal status of hidden role-play and virtual rape.

Many participants feel that role-play in real-time gives a special intensity to social experiences in a MUD or chat room (Curtis, 1992). Of course, people may also join discussion groups using a false identity; this can be accomplished by using a pseudonym to log on remotely through one of the anonymous servers throughout the world (Shade, 1996). Despite this technical option of using pseudonyms, however, such behavior is highly discouraged in many discussion groups. Participants are not allowed to use aliases to role-play. For this reason, I categorize discussion groups and fantasy worlds as separate types of electronic gatherings.

Civic Networks

Civic networks are electronic gatherings for organizing civic and political activities, such as recruiting participants for a citywide cleanup campaign or a regional environmental conference. The purpose of the civic network is to promote citizen participation in the activities of governance (Anderson, Bikson, Law, & Mitchell, 1995; Schuler, 1996).

This use of the Net was envisioned at the outset by many of the early programmers. They designed computer networking systems to support the development of communities oriented to social justice and democracy. It was hoped that networked computers would offer "a rich array of options to alternative political movements and grass-roots groups concerned with labor, ecology, feminism, peace, civil rights, [and] homelessness" (Downing, 1989, p. 154). One of the best-known organizations backing the community networking movement is the Institute for Global Communications (IGC). With subscribers in more than 70 countries, IGC supports PeaceNet, EcoNet, ConflictNet, and LaborNet (Schuler, 1996).

Mobilizing people for political activism can be done with different goals in mind. For example, extreme right-wing and allegedly paramilitary groups, such as The Order and the National White Patriots Party, have set up their own computers to provide email mailing lists, discussion groups, and pages on the World Wide Web to communicate their ideas and recruit members.

One of the burning issues today is how to provide equal opportunity for access to the Net. Who will pay the costs of Net connectivity? In the world of civic networks, several models for community access have emerged (Keller, 1995; Miller, 1996; Odasz, 1995; Schuler, 1996):

- Big Sky Telegraph, founded in 1988, is a model for a rural cooperative network that is being emulated around the country. Rural networks are used for activities such as teaching at a distance in rural schools, increasing people's access to public libraries and art through on-line galleries, informing citizens about government activities and crucial votes, and enhancing communication through email.

- Freenets operate as discussion groups that provide free dial-up access to local and national information and to email services. They exist in approximately 20 communities in the United States, Canada, and New Zealand. This model relies on voluntary labor and donations of equipment and operating funds, and it is not clear whether the increasing demand for freenets can be met by volunteers and philanthropists.

- Cities are also initiating municipal network systems using tax dollars—for example, Public Electronic Network in Santa Monica, the Seattle Community Network, and COARA and Biwa-Neto in Japan. Residents can log on to these civic networks to chat, to learn about garage sales, volunteer opportunities, local political issues, and community events, and to find what they need in city hall.

In addition to routine civic activities, the Net also has been used for organizing episodes of protest, ongoing social movement organizations and activities, and even antigovernment activities. The following are examples:

- Students at Taiwanese universities who had Usenet access and telephone links to relatives in China formed a network of correspondents during the 1989 Tiananmen Square pro-democracy movement, forwarding the latest information from Peking to the rest of the world (Rheingold, 1993).

- The March 1996 Third National Citizens Conference on Dioxins recruited participants through Net networks such as the Futurework electronic mailing list.

- Each of the protests against the World Trade Organization that began with the 1999 demonstration in Seattle.

The astonishing growth of the Net has been encouraged, in part, by the decision of the U.S. government to make the Internet an open system (unlike the closed network systems in many private corporations, which define their technical specifications as private property not to be disclosed). Thus, from the 1960s to the 1980s, when scientists developed new software programs, they uploaded their creations onto the Internet, making them publicly available to the few hundred computers that were linked.

Sharing software (*shareware*) not only increased the speed of invention and development but also became an important feature of the emerging Net culture, a feature receiving considerable attention in both the social scientific and popular literatures. In a society dominated by an ethos of individualism, analysts are endlessly fascinated by why people on-line are so helpful to strangers. Keller (1995) stated, "The question of what has promoted the cooperative nature of the Internet is an important one for planners and policy-makers. . . . [T]here may be a potential model for community development or organizational design" (p. 41). Next, I analyze the communal character of the Net by introducing Durkheim's ideas on solidarity in society.

Electronic Gatherings as Durkheimian Societies

What Is a Society for Durkheim?

When we ask someone with an accent what society he or she comes from, he or she might say, "China," "Argentina," or "Here, the United States." In everyday language, we tend to use the word *society* to refer to nations. Durkheim means something different by the concept of society. He uses the term to refer to any form of ongoing and patterned interactions in groups: "Every aggregate of individuals who are in continuous contact form a society" (Durkheim, 1893/1933, p. 276).

Why is regular and continuous contact the crucial ingredient defining a society? Through interacting with others and forming patterns of regular social relationships, we are reminded again and again that there is some purpose to life larger than just our individual self-interests. This larger purpose is society or life in groups. The more we interact with others, the greater emotional arousal we have and the greater draw we feel to group life. Durkheim says that our recurrent social relationships with others remind us about the collective interests of the groups in which we live, group goals, and shared ways of acting to reach these goals. This is a challenge, however, because Durkheim (1957) assumes that our basic animal nature is forever in a struggle against the collective interests of the group we live in:

The interests of the individual are not those of the group he belongs to and, indeed, there is often a real antagonism between one and the other.... [T]here should be ... a code of rules that lays down for the individual what he should do so as not to damage collective interests and so as not to disorganize the society of which he forms a part. (p. 14)

Durkheim has a very concrete concept of society. It refers to the groups in which we live our lives and also to larger collectivities such as nations. We cannot interact directly with the United States. Instead, we interact "only with its concrete manifestations, its groups, communities, and associations" (Nisbett, 1974, p. 201). For this reason, *society* and *group* will be used interchangeably in this chapter.

What Is Social Solidarity?

Having defined the concept of society, Durkheim turns to his central question, which is one of the great questions of sociology: How are societies created and sustained over time? In other words, where does social order come from? Durkheim uses the term *social solidarity* instead of *social order,* and by *solidarity,* he means a state of unity, cohesion, or social harmony that exists when members of a group or society at large share the same moral rules and practices. For social solidarity to exist, all the parts (individuals, groups, or institutions) somehow must be "glued together." Durkheim wants to discover what it is that glues together the parts of society into a cohesive, solidaristic whole.

Social solidarity is not an abstract essence. It takes different forms in different historical periods and varies in strength from group to group in the same society. "It [social solidarity] is not the same in the family and in political societies; we are not attached to our country in the same fashion as the Roman was to his city or the German to his tribe" (Durkheim, 1893/1933, p. 66). Only through empirical research can we discover the nature and strength of social solidarity in any group or society at large.

Because the United States is a society that celebrates individualism, many of us would approach Durkheim's question about the sources of social solidarity from the viewpoint of the individual. We would ask, why and how do individuals choose to get involved in group life in all its different forms—from marriages, neighborhoods, and networks of friends and coworkers to municipal or state voluntary associations, national political parties, and international religious organizations?

Durkheim establishes a different approach. Instead of asking how individuals choose different forms of social interaction and group life, he frames the question from the opposite point of view. He asks, how do societies create and sustain social solidarity by attracting people to the pleasures of group life and by controlling them to conform with societal ways of acting, thinking, and feeling?

Durkheim does not start from the viewpoint that individual choices create and sustain society. Society "creates" people. Societal "ways of acting, thinking, and feeling ... are not only external to the individual, but are, moreover, endowed with coercive power, by virtue of which they impose themselves upon him, independent of his individual will" (Durkheim, 1895/1938, p. 2). He points out the following two ways in which society is prior to the individual (Giddens, 1971, pp. 65-71; Lukes, 1973, pp. 19-22):

1. We are all born into preexisting societies. To get along with others in their daily lives, individuals must learn how to consistently act, think, and feel in ways that support societal values (desired ideal states and goals for what "ought" to be) and norms (guidelines for how to behave that help them realize values and attain these social goals).

2. At any one moment in time, a society's ways of acting, thinking, and feeling exist independently of any one person. A pattern of behavior that expresses values and norms will continue if some or even many members of a society are ignorant about how to act or are rebelling by purposely acting in a deviant way.

For example, if a society or group shares the value that democracy is the best form of government plus the norm that voting is a very important means of upholding democracy, the fact that many people do not vote does not erase the existence of this value and norm. It means instead that the people have been weakly socialized into this behavioral pattern. (If everyone ceases to vote over a long period of time, however, the norm can disappear from lack of use, and the value of democracy can be threatened if other norms do not support it adequately.)

The process of learning how to act, think, and feel in ways that support the shared rules and practices of a group or society at large is called *socialization*. Socialization will not happen unless individuals come into regular contact with others. Ongoing interaction with other group members helps individuals learn and remember the moral rules of their societies.

We can learn what "glues together" societies by analyzing socialization. There are two levels of socialization, which Durkheim calls "regulation" and "integration" (Lehmann, 1993). Socialization is a lifelong process, not just something that children must undergo. *Regulation* refers to the institutional level of socialization; society controls our animal appetites by giving us a sense of duty and clear guidance about what goals to seek and the proper means to follow in seeking our goals.

Individuals experience regulation as knowing their duties to the group and having feelings of obligation. This guidance provided by society takes a variety of forms, from the informal constraints of public opinion to formally institutionalized rules such as laws. The more numerous and more effective that rules are in constraining individual behavior, the more regulated is a society.

Different institutions in modern societies regulate individuals through one or more of the following mechanisms: (a) defining moral rules, (b) communicating and clarifying them, and (c) enforcing them. Legislatures and parliaments define new laws. Governmental agencies must communicate, clarify, and enforce rules. Families also instill sentiments of duty and attraction to parental authority and other relatives by defining, communicating, and enforcing rules of conduct. All societal institutions are involved in some way in regulation. Durkheim is especially interested in how educational institutions can reinforce democracy by teaching civic morals to children.

Integration refers to the level of socialization that occurs in the everyday life experience of interacting in groups. All societies offer individuals opportunities for collective activity. The more regular are these opportunities for group activity and the more intense the experiences of acting together in a group, the more integrated and thus solidaristic is the group. Collective activity reinforces over and over again strong social ties, shared beliefs, values and norms, and shared emotions that let members feel duty and attachment to the group.

Unlike many sociological theorists, Durkheim pays attention to the importance of emotions in human life. Knowing your duty and having respect for authority are not enough for social solidarity. Individuals must also desire regular participation in groups, so they must feel that collective life is pleasurable and that it provides a sense of goodness and reward (Durkheim, 1893/1933):

> When individuals who are found to have common interests associate, it is not only to defend these interests, it is . . . to have the pleasure of communing, to make one out of many, which is to say, finally, to lead the same moral life together. (p. 15)

Hence, Durkheim emphasizes the importance of being regularly moved by feelings of excitement and warmth just from the sheer energy generated by doing things with other people. Durkheim (1912/1995) uses phrases such as "rush of energy" (p. 213) to describe the pleasurable feelings that keep us coming back for more connections to group life. He emphasizes that only at the level of everyday group life can society generate feelings of "warmth which animates its members, making them intensely human, destroying their egotisms" (Durkheim, 1893/1933, p. 26). Integration cannot happen if groups are not "close" enough to individuals to awaken strong feelings and "drag them"—like a magnet—into social life.

For example, Durkheim is critical of societies that have strong national governments without also having a well-developed sector of secondary associations, such as interest groups and voluntary associations. Durkheim fears that a strong state that is not counterbalanced by a strong civil society of voluntary associations could result in unstable government or even dictatorship (Durkheim, 1893/1933):

> The State is *too remote* from individuals; its relations with them too external and intermittent to penetrate deeply into individual consciences and socialize them within. . . . A nation can be maintained only if . . . there is a series of secondary groups *near enough* to the individuals to attract them strongly in their sphere of action and *drag them, in this way, into the general torrent of social life* [italics added]. (p. 28)

Integration is best reinforced through interpersonal contact in face-to-face gatherings. When there is "active interchange of views and impressions . . . [and] the circulation of these views and impressions from one person to another" (p. 28), an intensely vital collective life emerges that makes groups solidaristic. In *The Elementary Forms of the Religious Life* (1912/1995), Durkheim states,

> There can be no society that does not experience the need at regular intervals to maintain and strengthen the collective feelings and ideas that provide its coherence and its distinct individuality. *This moral remaking can be achieved only through meetings, assemblies, and congregations in which the individuals, pressing close to one another* [italics added], reaffirm in common their common sentiments. (p. 429)

Vital and solidaristic group life is especially enhanced by participation in rituals. Rituals are a special type of collective activity in which people meet face to face to carry out nonpractical actions for symbolic ends (Collins, 1994, p. 206). During moments of ritual, we experience thoughts and feelings that remind us of the moral power of society. Durkheim (1912/1995) says we actually feel this power as a type of pressure—we "feel the weight" (p. 214) of "something in us that is other than ourselves" (p. 213). For example, we use the common phrase "carrying the weight of the world on her shoulders" to describe this moral power of society from the viewpoint of someone who has too many duties or has an overdeveloped sense of obligations to others.

Although we often think of rituals as religious, Durkheim argues that social rituals are moments of great emotional intensity that are crucial to all types of nonreligious integration of societies. Rituals make it possible to control and attach individuals to groups even when people are not in each other's presence. During the moments of jointly repeating common gestures, ideas and emotions circulate among group members like a kind of mental current flowing through everyone; this current attaches special "moral charges" to these ideas and feelings (Collins, 1994). This current (which we can experience as goose bumps, hair rising on our neck, or a full and aching heart) helps focus individual attention intensely on others and on the life of the group.

Normal Versus Pathological States of Integration and Regulation

What happens when regulation and integration are weak or missing in group life? All societies have different levels of integration and regulation, and they can change with time. Therefore, Durkheim provides another set of concepts for analyzing societies: the absence of integration is *egoism,* and the absence of regulation is *anomie.* Table 3.1 summarizes his typology and shows that, for Durkheim, weak integration or regulation create "pathological" states. (Durkheim fails to adequately address the question of what constitutes "normal" levels of solidarity.)

Egoism and one of its consequences, egoistic suicide, emerge when the group's collective activities (meetings, ceremonies, projects, etc.) have declined in number and intensity to the point where individual members are isolated from the "stimulating action of society" that gives them a "rush of energy" (Durkheim, 1912/1995,

Table 3.1   Durkheim's Typology of Normal Versus Pathological States of Social Groups

	Pathologically ◄──► weak	Normal (in equilibrium)	◄──► Pathologically strong
Integration (first aspect of social solidarity)	*Egoism:* excessive individuation and withdrawal due to insufficient degree of collective activity in society	High degree of collective activity in a group or society at large → large number of social bonds that keep attracting individuals into group life (especially if the bonds are based on strongly shared values and norms)	*Altruism:* overidentification with a group to the extent that the individual will is eclipsed by social values and norms (e.g., Kamikazi pilots in Japan who commit suicide for national honor)
Regulation (second aspect of social solidarity)	*Anomie:* normlessness due to sudden rupture of society's control over individual passions or unregulated capitalist activity	Well-developed guidelines for action (values about proper desires and ideal goals and norms about the "right" way to attain goals) that are widely spread through a group or society → effective control over individual behavior	*Fatalism:* extreme oppression of individual action (e.g., slavery or people persecuted under brutal military dictatorships)

SOURCE: Durkheim (1897/1951).

NOTE: Each of the four pathological states refers to the quality of the individual connection to society. For Durkheim, societies can change states from normal to pathological and back to normal, depending on the conditions that exist in a given historical period.

p. 213). In conditions of isolation, our attachment to social ties and our obligations to others wither away; we can become excessively individualistic and withdraw from group life. This is why later in his life, Durkheim (1912/1995) decided that rituals are fundamental to group integration: The very acts of jointly repeating gestures such as prayers, chants, songs, and dances strongly charge participants' moral batteries because "a sort of electricity is generated from their closeness" (p. 217).

Anomie develops when society fails to instill in its members a sufficient spirit of discipline that regulates our animal appetites. Anomie is a state of normlessness (Lukes, 1973). Durkheim talks of two main sources of anomie: (a) experience of a crisis and (b) the lack of regulation in capitalist economies. First, in crisis situations, the values and norms that used to make sense no longer have meaning because the conditions of life have drastically changed. For example, suicide rates often increase after severe economic shocks such as massive depressions, when people lose the material security they have worked their entire lives to acquire.

Second, the lack of regulation of capitalist economies produces chronic anomie. For Durkheim, the "free market" of late 19th-century capitalism follows only one rule: the endless pursuit of self-interest. Anarchy is the inevitable result, which leads to a chronic state of normlessness or anomie. There are no shared beliefs in who has what rights and duties relative to whom. Instead, there is constant pressure to consume ever greater quantities of goods to "keep up with the Joneses" and feed insatiable appetites for material well-being. Moreover, there is ruthless competition replete with industrial monopolies, constant bankruptcies, pressures to fire workers and reduce their wages, and consequent pressures for workers to engage in strikes or even industrial sabotage. Constant conflict and anarchy prevail.

For Durkheim, the "ever-recurring conflicts" symptomatic of chronic anomie are a sign of sickness and lack of moral development that will hold back civilization. To redress this sad state of affairs, the capitalist economy should be regulated in two ways: (a) by the development of state regulations (e.g., Federal Drug Administration and the Securities and Exchange Commission) and (b) through the development of intermediary associations in which citizens define systems of rights, duties, and professional ethics that are appropriate to their spheres of economic activity (e.g., the American Bar Association and arbitration councils for labor-management disputes).

We are now ready to examine evidence on the Net to assess whether regulation and integration have emerged in electronic gatherings. Are any solidaristic Durkheimian societies forming or are regulation and integration absent in electronic gatherings, thus making the Net a new and powerful source of anomie and egoism?

Do Electronic Gatherings Have Any Characteristics of Durkheimian Societies?

Have electronic gatherings generated continuous interaction among a regular core of people to the extent that there is evidence of regulation and integration? There are a few ethnographic studies of Net groups, but there is no systematic survey research and no time-budget studies to tell us what type of people spend how much time in virtual reality (Wellman & Gulia, 1995). Thus, popular ideas about community on the Net—both utopian and dystopian—remain somewhat speculative.

Electronic gatherings "rich in social information, prominent personalities, valued relationships, and behavioral norms" are widely described in the literature on computer networks (Baym, 1995, p. 141). The ethnographic and anecdotal studies do include extensive evidence that regulation and integration have developed in many electronic gatherings (Harasim, 1993; Jones, 1995; Odasz, 1995; Shields, 1996; Sproull & Faraj, 1995). I discuss mechanisms of regulation, followed by integration.

Mechanisms of Regulation in Electronic Gatherings

As mentioned previously, there are three mechanisms of regulation in the Net: (a) defining rules of conduct, (b) communicating and clarifying rules of conduct, and (c) enforcing rules of conduct. Each of these is discussed in the following sections.

Mechanism 1: Defining Rules of Conduct

There are several layers of moral rules or norms for Net conduct. By developing what is commonly referred to as Netiquette, "each particular networld has its own culture and norms. . . . Standards vary as to what is considered legal, tasteful, and manageable communication" (Harasim, 1993, p. 31). Group moderators or fantasy world system operators usually establish the netiquette for their Net society, often in collaboration with active participants.

As in real life, some norms for Net conduct are vague and "diffuse," and others are more precisely "crystallized." Diffuse rules typically are modeled by the moderator, group organizers, and core group members, whereas crystallized rules often take the form of written guidelines.

Examples of diffuse rules include the following:

- "Keeping logs of conversations in which you participate for your own purposes is socially acceptable on MUDs. Sharing them publicly without permission is considered bad manners" (Turkle, 1995, p. 312).
- "Thou shall not offend; thou shall not be easily offended" (Rheingold, 1993, p. 137).
- "You own your own words" (also known as YOYOW) (Figallo, 1995, p. 53).
- "Do not violate the sanctity of nicknames by adopting someone else's nickname" (Rheingold, 1993, p. 181).

There also are rules of conduct that point to specific behaviors as appropriate or inappropriate. Some of these rules have sanctions attached to them, such as blocking log-on access, which can be applied by system administrators, chanops, sysops, or discussion group moderators. Many rules, of course, have no sanctions except verbal reprimands. Those with sanctions usually are communicated in a written form that newcomers encounter upon joining.

Table 3.2 presents a detailed list of behaviors considered inappropriate. McLaughlin et al. (1995) analyzed messages posted to a sample of five Usenet newsgroups during a three week period, to identify rules of conduct. *Comp.sys.ibm. pc.games, rec.sport.hockey, soc.motss, rec.arts.tv.soaps,* and *soc.singles* were selected because they were available at many host sites and had a high volume of messages.

Finally, there are precise behavioral norms that are widely used in the Net to compensate for the lack of physical and emotional context on-line. Examples of these communication conventions include the following (Argyle & Shields, 1996):

- Emoticons (CONventions for expressing EMOTIons): Because most Netizens cannot yet see or hear each other, they have created a variety of icons or pictorial expressions to represent emotions in textual communication. For example, when read sideways, :-) is a smile, and ;-) is a winking face that can

Table 3.2 A Taxonomy of Reproachable Conduct on Usenet

Violation of networkwide conventions

Failing to encrypt offensive materials
Failing to include a signature
Posting commercial announcements
Demonstrating lack of familiarity with recent threads; lack of regular reading
Reproaching others for minor violations (e.g., typos and spelling errors)

Ethical violations

Reposting or forwarding private email without permission
Posting personal information about others (phone number, sexual orientation, etc.)
Playing pranks; intentional disruption
Posting "how-to" articles on illegal activities

Inappropriate language

Flaming (except where encouraged, e.g., *alt.flame*)
Coarse or vulgar language
Personal attacks and insults
Ridicule

Incorrect or novice use of technology

Confusing the "reply privately" and "reply to group" options
Posting multiple copies of same article to group
Attributing quotes incorrectly
Word wrap errors

Bandwidth waste

Posting answers to (individual) questions rather than using private email
Posting a question that is covered in the FAQs
Indiscriminate cross-posting
Posting excessively long articles

SOURCE: From McLaughlin et al. (1995, pp. 97-98). Reprinted with permission from Sage Publications, Inc.

indicate sarcasm or humor. Typing your message in capital letters indicates shouting. Members of electronic gatherings often compile lists of emoticons, which are easily available to new users seeking to learn group norms of communication.

• Generic actions: In many Net services, commands to the system produce output on the screen to other participants that represents social gestures using the body. For example, if Evita is logged into a MUD or chat channel in real time and she types "handshake Anne," all other participants would see on their screens "Evita is shaking hands with Anne." If I want to respond to Evita's greeting, I type "handshake Evita," and the system outputs "shake shake" to everyone's screen. (The words vary from one conferencing system to another.)

Mechanism 2: Communicating and Clarifying Rules of Conduct

For many Net veterans, there is a libertarian orientation to the notion of rules of conduct: People believe there should not be any overarching moral framework that covers the Net. Instead, electronic gatherings should be self-policing. In Durkheim's terms, regulation should exist at the level of the individual discussion group, MUD, or civic network and not at any higher level in the system. For example, discussion groups often post frequently asked questions (FAQs) to socialize newcomers to the community standards that have evolved. FAQs are usually edited by a volunteer, and newcomers can read them to get a sense of the Net group culture and activities and learn about more practical matters such as common problems newcomers have in using system commands.

Acrimonious debate is another form of communicating to participants that norms have been violated or that they need to be changed. For example, members of discussion groups in the whole earth 'lectronic link (WELL) understand that there is a diffuse rule of "what you post you have a right to scribble." *Scribbling*—erasing all your contributions from the community archives—is rarely done, however, because it can destroy the threads of conversation. Rheingold (1993) describes an occasion when a core member scribbled his texts, and there were weeks of debate about whether the norm should change to keep any one individual from destroying a collective product. This is a classic conflict between individual rights and group rights—the very stuff of Durkheimian solidarity.

Mechanism 3: Enforcing Rules of Conduct

What authorities exist in the Net to enforce rules? In real life, the authority to enforce rules is vested in organizations such as courts (criminal and civil law) and administrative agencies (regulatory law), such as the Environmental Protection Agency. Although electronic gatherings have developed internal rules for governance, to date there is no organized central authority for Net governance that is analogous to the federal judicial system of a country.

For example, Usenet used to have a type of limited ruling council that was called the "backbone cabal" (Jones, 1995; Kling, 1996; Shields, 1996). Members of the cabal were the system administrators of sites that carried most of the traffic for Usenet and also absorbed the costs (e.g, AT&T, Apple, Digital, and Bell Labs). This changed when Usenet began using the Internet as well as the UUCP net to pass along news, and system administrators from the original set of organizations no longer had control.

Today, most of Usenet is ruled by internal group-specific norms and the practice of participant voting. Usenet newsgroups have defined rules for creating new groups: A call for discussion is posted, a discussion period is held, followed by a vote. The convention is that a new newsgroup is created if there are 100 people more who voted for its creation than who voted against it.

It is remarkable that the Internet—as the largest of the Net's linked network systems—is not owned nor managed by any one central authority or administrative hierarchy. Instead, segments of the infrastructure are owned and managed by a variety of firms, governmental units, and universities. Private firms sell gateways to the Net, but they can only enforce rules for their customers (e.g., America OnLine and CompuServe).

By the late 1980s, the Internet had surpassed the U.S. government's ability to manage it, and in 1987, the first private-sector contracts were awarded to Merit Network, Inc., IBM, and MCI to upgrade and manage the central network (backbone). This first step at privatization has been very unpopular with many Internet veterans. Because the research that created the technologies supporting the Internet had been funded by U.S. tax dollars, policies defining "acceptable use" of the network once excluded commercial activity. Not until 1990 were there any commercial networks linked to the Internet. Privatization continued in 1993, with the award of an additional $12 million of contracts for Internet management to private-sector firms, including the giant AT&T. For many Net veterans, this has raised the specter of increased prices and thus increased inequality in access to Internet services, a topic that currently is being debated on Capitol Hill and in electronic gatherings throughout the United States (Branscomb, 1995).

The Search for Integration in Electronic Gatherings

This section presents evidence on Net experiments in creating social integration. Although many observers see CMC as a solitary activity in which individuals sit alone in front of computers, for many folks, meeting in cyberspace has generated a strong sense of emotional attachment to electronic groups. According to Durkheim, emotional attachment to a society comes from and is best sustained by high levels of collective activity, which reinforce members' social ties and their sense of shared worldviews and shared commitments to each other. That is, integration depends on the level and quality of group activity.

Just as in real life, the experience of powerful community can wax and wane. Perhaps it is because of this challenge of creating and sustaining the feeling of community that anecdotal studies of Net life reveal a fascinating feature. Many people desire a sense of strong attachment to their electronic gatherings. This desire for integration is manifest in the following ways:

- Participants in electronic gatherings try to ground physically their on-line relationships by creating a sense of embodiment in cyberspace. People construct and interact with reference to images of physical spaces and bodies in their shared virtual spaces.
- Group members agree to take their relationships "off-line" and meet socially in real life.

One study found that "members of electronic virtual communities act as if the community met in a physical public space" (Stone, 1991, p. 104). For example, members refer to the discussion group as a physical public space when saying (typing) remarks such as "This is a convenient place to meet." Net users also create descriptions—some quite elaborate—of the physical place they are meeting. You can hang out at Larry's Bar on The Sierra Net or Roger's Bar on Big Sky Telegraph (Sproull & Faraj, 1995). Finally, members often invest considerable energy developing descriptions of their bodies or the bodies of their on-line personae. Cyberspace is more real when participants are embodied.

The second manifestation of desire for feelings of attachment is taking Net relationships off-line. One well-known example in Net lore is the WELL. The WELL was created in 1985 as one of the first commercial computer-conferencing networks, and it was located in Sausalito, California. Founders Stewart Brand and Larry Brilliant envisioned the WELL as a prototype for regionally based electronic communities. As Brand once remarked, "Let a thousand CompuServes bloom" (Figallo, 1995, p. 51).

At first, most WELL members lived in the San Francisco Bay Area because access was available only by direct-dial modem, which was much cheaper for local callers. Consequently, many members thought of the WELL as an on-line community with a geographical base. In fact, in 1986, the WELL organization began holding monthly face-to-face gatherings open to anyone, not just WELL users. WELL members also have initiated real-life contact among participants through an annual summer picnic and annual December Pickle Family Circus benefit and potluck in the Bay Area (Rheingold, 1993).

In my travels through various Usenet discussion groups, I have often noticed messages about real-life gatherings organized by a subset of group members who live in the same city. The following is another example: During a public, real-life meeting of people interested in the National Capital Freenet in Ottawa, facilitator David Sutherland announced, "We will hold a meeting the first Tuesday of every month, so we can keep in contact with each other." When asked afterward whether he meant a physical meeting, he replied, "People seem to come out for face-to-face things, though we shouldn't need them, given the media" (Argyle & Shields, 1996, p. 68). Currently, however, we do not know how common this penchant is to integrate on-line relationships into real life.

The WELL offers an example in which the Net is only one of several "places" in which the same networks of people may interact. Sociologists Wellman and Gulia (1995) make the important point that we cannot assume that the Net is a completely compartmentalized sphere in people's lives. We need to study how life in Net groups is connected to other areas of people's lives to understand what is the sociopolitical impact of having a portion of social life ongoing in cyberspace.

Mechanisms of Integration in Electronic Gatherings

Having established that a desire for integration within electronic gatherings is often strong, I have identified three mechanisms that help generate and sustain high levels of collective activity: (a) celebrating rituals, (b) engaging in gift exchange, and (c) building what Durkheimian scholars Bellah, Madsen, Sullivan, Swidler, and Tipton (1985) call "communities of memory."

Mechanism 1: Celebrating Rituals

One longtime participant in the WELL remarked, "You aren't a real community until you have a funeral" (Rheingold, 1993, p. 37). Durkheim would agree that rituals help create and sustain moral community. Rituals produce two important outcomes: social ties and symbols. Durkheim's nephew, the anthropologist Marcel Mauss, who collaborated with his uncle for years, suggests that some symbolic objects can be so powerful that they can tie together people who "are far apart and . . . may never actually see each other face to face" (Collins, 1994, p. 232). There is evidence that members of electronic gatherings draw on symbolic objects that are very powerful in our culture to create rituals that can bond people who never physically meet.

In electronic gatherings, several types of rituals are found, especially in fantasy worlds but also in discussion groups, such as rituals of mating (flirting, having Tinysex, dating, and marrying), rituals of death (on-line funerals), and rites of passage (creating status hierarchies through which members advance, often based on programming skill). Here, I present one example of mating rituals to represent the types of symbols created and the fanciful but realistic flavor of these occasions, which often seem to be taken quite seriously by participants. Although there are no data on how widespread Net rituals are, there is abundant description of mating rituals. (The following descriptions are taken from Turkle, 1995, pp. 194-196.)

For example, Stewart, a 23-year-old physics graduate student in the Boston area interviewed by Turkle (1995), joined a MUD based in Germany, presenting himself as the persona Achilles. There, he met Winterlight and eventually asked her on a first date. Through text-based dialogue and place description, he simulated a romantic evening with various MUD commands, including picking her up in a limousine at the airport and taking her to dinner at an Italian restaurant (which exists in real life), where he described the menu to her and ordered. This first date led to a courtship and a formal engagement ceremony on the MUD.

The following is an excerpt from his speech at the community engagement ceremony (from his log of their on-line dialogue):

> I have traveled far and wide across these lands. . . . I thank the people of Gargoyle for their support. . . . I searched far and near for a maiden of beauty with hair of sunshine gold and lips red as the rose. With intelligence to match her beauty. . . . Winterlight, will you marry me?

Winterlight gives Achilles a rose, and he gives her a thousand paper stars, two symbols that connote thoughts and feelings of love. The ceremony fills 12 single-spaced pages of text!

The wedding was more elaborate: Achilles created a "sacred clearing in cyberspace, a niche carved out of rock, with fifty seats intricately carved with animal motifs." The ceremony, which was conducted by the persona of a priest, Tarniwoof, included wedding vows that followed the traditional ritual format: "Do you promise to take Silver Shimmering Winterlight as your mudly wedded wife, in sickness and in health, through time-outs and updates, for richer or poorer, until linkdeath do you part?" During the wedding rites, Stewart was in the United States alone in his room; but across the Atlantic, 25 wedding guests traveled to a city in Germany from Sweden, Norway, Finland, The Netherlands, and other regions of Germany to be with Winterlight at a real-life celebration that coincided with the on-line ceremonies. Everyone dressed for a wedding and shared food and champagne.

Mechanism 2: Engaging in Gift Exchange

Electronic gatherings have developed practices that support the Net norms of building community together and advancing the pursuit of knowledge by sharing expertise. Users often talk of reciprocity or gift exchange: If you give something, you will receive something sometime in the future. The exchange is both self-interested and altruistic. Even if only a small proportion of Net group members respond regularly to requests for assistance and information, "a small number of small acts can sustain a large community because each act is seen by the entire community" (Sproull & Faraj, 1995, p. 75).

I notice three common practices that support the norm of reciprocal exchange on the Net: helping strangers, sharing tools, and creating directories accessible by anonymous file transfer protocol (FTP). Perhaps the Net practice most widely commented on is helping strangers (Wellman & Gulia, 1995)—for example, helping newcomers maneuver through different types of electronic environments and answering requests for information from strangers. *Sharing tools* means uploading programs you have written that others may find useful.

Anonymous FTP is a service that allows people to share their written work. For example, while doing research for this chapter, I "went" to California to retrieve several papers by Pavel Curtis on MUDs from his workplace computer site, Xerox Palo Alto Research Center (PARC), using anonymous FTP (part of the Internet's communications capabilities). As an outsider, I do not have the password to enter the PARC computer system, but I can use the log-in ID *anonymous* and the password *guest* to get access to special directories that the PARC system administrator made accessible to the public. Anyone at PARC who wishes to share a document can upload it to this special part of the system. Many Net citizens see this capability as one of the most important parts of the Net, where anyone on the continuum of familiarity—from strangers to acquaintances to friends—can share with others.

Mechanism 3: Building "Communities of Memory"

Sociologists Bellah et al. (1985) take a Durkheimian perspective on requisites for solidaristic community. They emphasize that solidaristic groups have histories that are not forgotten. They have community traditions. That is, to sustain itself as a community, any society must organize ways to retell its story. An important part of retelling the story is adding to a repertoire of community exemplars—people and practices that have given the group a special flavor; examples of the "good and virtuous" member; stories of pain, suffering, and threats the group has experienced and inflicted on others; and stories of achievements.

Some members of electronic gatherings are very conscious of the need for tradition. A WELL system administrator believes in the importance for the quality of WELL life of the "keeping of a historical record of its environs, its people, their works, and the relationships and organizations that define the direction of the collective entity" (Figallo, 1995, p. 55). The WELL keeps a great deal of past discussion texts archived on tape and placed in the system on disks that users can access.

Usenet has created another form of community of memory. Statistics describing Usenet are collected and published in the newsgroup called *news.lists*. Usenet newsgroups also regularly update and direct newcomers to the group's FAQs. (FAQs thus fill both functions of regulation and integration.) FAQs present a Net society as a coherent group with traditions that newcomers should assimilate. They also serve the practical purpose of keeping newcomers from repeating discussion threads that have already occurred, which prevents social splits between newcomers and old-timers. As Durkheim would argue, in the process of jointly acting with others, ideas are created about who "we" are, what we are doing, and why we are doing it—ingredients crucial to solidaristic societies.

Of course, practices that regulate and integrate Net users do not emerge in all discussion groups, MUDs, chat channels, or civic networks. Nor does solidarity last forever within any group. When the evidence on mechanisms of regulation and integration is considered, however, it supports the conclusion that electronic gatherings can and do develop characteristics of a Durkheimian society. We need further research to learn how often and to what extent this happens.

Do Electronic Gatherings Represent the Emergence of a Third Type of Durkheimian Society?

The previous section presented Durkheim's argument about the ingredients of social solidarity that are necessary for any society (regulation and integration). This section discusses another important issue he analyzes: How are modern Western societies with capitalist economies organized differently from premodern societies with noncapitalist economies? In other words, after establishing what creates a solidaristic society, Durkheim then seeks to discover the different types of solidaristic societies that have emerged historically.

Durkheim reduces the great variety of human societies to two basic types, which he calls *mechanical* and *organic societies*. Today, sociologists recognize that this simple typology presents a problem because the broad contrast between traditional and modern societies covers an extremely wide range of social organization. For example, the category of traditional society includes both the largely rural societies of early modern Europe, dominated by small, isolated farming villages, and the medieval city-states of Italy, which were densely populated and embedded in a complex web of international trade. Thus, before discussing Durkheim's two types of societies, it is important to understand why he simplified his analysis in this way.

Like many intellectuals of his generation, Durkheim was influenced by organicist thinking: He turns to analogies with biological organisms to analyze human societies. In organicist thinking, individuals are analogous to the cells of an organism, and societies are analogous to the human body. For example, as the fetus grows and develops, clusters of embryonic cells (which were originally identical in structure and function) change and specialize, such that some become kidney cells, whereas others become blood cells or form the lungs. Durkheim (1893/1933) suggests, for example, that the modern state becomes the "social brain" because it has "directive power" in a society (p. 84).

This process of specialization into distinct functions or roles is called *differentiation.* Sociologists often analyze processes of institutional differentiation. For example, differentiation in educational institutions around the world meant that the one-room schoolhouse gradually developed into a complex system of kindergartens, elementary schools, middle schools, and high schools.

Durkheim uses the term *division of labor* to discuss differentiation. Generally speaking, the division of labor refers to the system of work specialization that exists in all societies, such as the division of economic production into *jobs* and *occupations* and into higher levels of specialization, such as branches of industry or the separation of household production from factory production (Sayer & Walker, 1992). Durkheim (1893/1933) extends the concept, however: "the division of labor is not peculiar to the economic world; we can observe its growing influence" in all institutional realms, including political system, religious institutions, the arts, science, and educational systems (p. 40).

Durkheim's Two Types of Society

The influence of organicist thinking leads Durkheim to conceptualize only two basic types of societal organisms—simple and complex:

Mechanical societies are small, simple organisms with no specialized parts. For example, traditional villages are composed of households organized in a similar manner; each household fulfills the same wide range of economic, educational, familial, and religious functions as do the other households. That is, each "part" of the organism fulfills the same functions as all the other parts.

Organic societies are complex organisms because they are composed of specialized parts, each of which performs distinct functions to support the whole society. In a complex, modern society, no one household, neighborhood, town, or company can produce everything its members need to survive. Moreover, the economy depends on the family and educational institutions to produce dependable workers with a range of needed skills.

In mechanical societies, social relations are based on the fact that everyone is similar to each other because there is little or no division of labor and little diversity in people's ideas. Everyone shares the same values, norms, and beliefs—even the same religion. In contrast, in organic societies, a complex division of labor has developed. Consequently, people and groups become different from each other—with many different occupations, a great diversity in racial and ethnic backgrounds, and a wide range of religious beliefs and political views.

From organicist thinking, Durkheim also takes the idea that in the long term, organisms tend to stability and harmony. Although he admits that conflict and disharmony do exist, he sees these as temporary social problems. In the long term, societies will reach states of equilibrium and harmony (perfect coordination) among their parts. For example, the educational system may produce more lawyers than the economy can absorb for a number of years, but then these two institutions will adjust themselves into a state of balance.

Basically, Durkheim was more interested in understanding the bases of social order and solidarity than he was in analyzing conflict. For this reason, Durkheim is often depicted as a conservative thinker who fails to emphasize the role of power and inequality in social life and the inevitability of struggles among groups with competing interests, unlike two other founding figures of sociology, Karl Marx and Max Weber.

What Causes the Differences Between Mechanical and Organic Societies?

In his well-known statement, "Social life comes from a double source, the likeness of consciences and the division of social labor" (p. 226), Durkheim (1893/1933) identifies the following two factors, which continue to be important variables in sociology today, determining whether a society is mechanical or organic: (a) the extent (degree of complexity) of the division of labor and (b) the extent to which members of a society share a collective consciousness, by which Durkheim means all the ways of thinking, feeling, and acting that are common to a group or society. (The extent of collective consciousness means the number and intensity of the values, beliefs, norms, emotions, and ways of acting that are shared.) Durkheim adds that when the division of labor becomes more complex, the collective conscience changes. Together, both changes produce a different type of society. Table 3.3 summarizes Durkheim's argument.

In societies with complex divisions of labor and great diversity of people, the collective consciousness becomes very "stretched" and abstract in an attempt to include only values and norms that are meaningful to everybody. As a result, the values and norms that are strongly shared are far fewer in number and are more ambiguous. Thus, society is less able to regulate all behavior, and social solidarity is threatened. Durkheim notes that maybe the only value remaining in modern Western societies in which everyone believes very strongly is *individualism*— protecting the inherent dignity, worth, and freedom of the individual.

Exactly how does the division of labor become more complex? Durkheim's argument flows as follows:

1. Population size increases.

2. There are changes in how the population is physically distributed across a territory. Improvements in transportation and communication link people

Table 3.3   Two Types of Societies

Type of Society	Division of Labor	Collective Consciousness	Basis of Social Ties
Mechanical	Absent or weak	Large number of clear, powerful ideas and feelings shared by all members in very homogeneous societies	Likeness; value consensus grounded in religiously based common culture
Organic	Present or complex	Smaller number of more ambiguous and less constraining ideas and feelings shared by all members; great diversity of people and ideas	Difference; functional interdependence and a few abstract values such as individualism and patriotism

SOURCES: Durkheim (1893/1933), Collins (1994), Giddens (1971), and Lukes (1973).

and villages more easily. Villages and towns grow together and become new entities called cities. Several cities grow together and become a new entity called a metropolis (the central urban area of a country or region, such as a capital).

3. As urbanization increases, each person has more social contact with a great many more people. This results in competition for jobs and other resources.

4. From this competition, an increasingly complex division of labor emerges. For example, people find their occupational niches, companies find their market niches, and different zones of a city specialize in different functions (e.g., the warehouse district, the red-light district, the shopping malls, and the residential sections).

Recall from the description of organicist thinking that the division of labor becomes more complex in two stages. First, association occurs, in which separate organisms (e.g., villages or small towns) grow in size and become linked together through improved transportation and communication systems; that is, they combine and form a new whole. Second, differentiation occurs, in which the parts within the new whole specialize by taking on different functions. The more complex division of labor plus a weaker, more ambiguous collective consciousness comprise a new type of society. Social ties are based on difference instead of likeness.

Electronic gatherings can be seen as examples of organic societies. The thousands of discussion groups, fantasy worlds, and civic networks attest to a complex division of labor and a wide diversity of beliefs. Could social activities on the Net also represent the emergence of a third type of society? Although he could not have anticipated the development of computer technology, I use Durkheim's ideas to guide creative thinking about the future impact of the Net on how we live. In this chapter, I can only begin the process of developing a hypothesis about a new, third kind of Durkheimian society. I hope to illustrate how great ideas from the past can still be applied to make sense of our world today.

Cyborg Societies: A Third Durkheimian Type?

Following Durkheim's argument, I should look for evidence of change in the division of labor and in the collective consciousness. If I find some evidence, then I can hypothesize that a third type of Durkheimian society is emerging. Future researchers studying the Net could then test this hypothesis.

My hypothesis is that (a) technological advances (such as computer science and telecommunications systems, including the creation of the Net) are contributing to the consolidation of a new international division of labor and (b) technological advances are also contributing to changes in the collective consciousness—brand new ways of thinking and feeling about the relationship between humans and machines are appearing. Together, these changes suggest the emergence of a new type of society—a cyborg society.

We usually use the term *cyborg* to refer to an individual who is part human and part machine. Here, I extend the term to refer to human-machine interactions (also see Haraway, 1991). Because our relations with machines are becoming social in many ways, future societies may have to create new mechanisms of regulation and integration—not only for human-human interactions but also for cyborg interactions. What evidence is there that a cyborg society is developing?

Changing Division of Labor

The globalization of the economy means that increasingly firms operate independently of nation-state boundaries (Rubin, 1996). Partly related to economic globalization is a second change: an increase in the number and influence of international political organizations, such as the United Nations, World Trade Federation, European Economic Union, General Accord on Trade and Tariffs, and World Bank.

In Durkheimian terms, this is evidence of a change in the division of labor:

1. Improvements in transportation and telecommunication systems have allowed people from different nation-states to increase the frequency of contact with each other. This has stimulated the growth of new entities—global corporations and international political organizations.

2. One result of this is a new form of competition at the international level—such as among global corporations for better positions in world markets. From this competition come new forms of flexible specialization (Rubin, 1996). For example, different regions of the world fill different functions for a firm selling women's clothing: Thread and cloth might be made in China, whereas dress patterns are created in Italy, and dress assembly occurs in Mexico; sales and

distribution, however, might be organized from corporate headquarters in the United States.

Technological developments have changed the frequency of contact and the locus and intensity of global competition, resulting in a new division of labor. We are also in the very early stages of changes in the nature of our relationships with machines and technology. In her research, Turkle (1995) finds that some people are developing intense relationships with their computers; moreover, "these relationships are changing the way we think and feel" (p. 22).

Changing Collective Consciousness

Changes in the way on-line aficionados think, feel, and act are based, in part, on the following two contemporary ideas:

1. The world is composed of coded messages circulating in networks.

2. Machines and humans are both made of coded messages, so our centuries-old distinction between humans and machines no longer makes any sense.

In today's digital world, vast quantities of information exist only in the form of bits (the *bi*nary dig*its* 0 and 1) that constitute computer code and circulate through computer networks. Computer software exists as bits; every message we send by email travels as bits. People surf the Net and work hard to think of it as a place. At one level, however, the entire social world of the Net is nothing more than code.

Moreover, many scientists today think of both machines and biological organisms—including humans—as essentially complex systems of coded messages (bits of 1s and 0s) that circulate in networks. For example, one of the most ambitious scientific projects of the late 20th century is the Human Genome Project, whose purpose is to identify and map all the genes in human DNA. From the perspective of this project, human beings are DNA code, and the challenge is to decipher that code. Once we unlock the secret of the code, perhaps we can clone humans just as we manufacture machines.

Norbert Weiner, often called the father of cybernetic science, said in 1964 that "it is conceptually possible for a human being to be sent over a telegraph line" (Keller, 1994, p. 315). Fans of *Star Trek* will recognize this image: turning humans and their machines into sparkling particles (of code?) and "beaming them up." At the other end, the particles or code regenerate the humans and machines into the form of embodied organisms. What humans and machines would share is their common basis of existence as code.

Until recent decades, everyone took for granted the absolute distinction between machine and human. Today, research indicates that this element of the collective consciousness is changing due to the proliferation of computers that act like people in some ways. With regard to the bot Julia, which was quoted in the beginning of this chapter in a conversation with the human Ace, Turkle (1995) questions,

How does one treat machines that perform roles previously reserved for people [like having conversations]? In other words, once you have made a pass at an on-line robot, it is hard to look at computers in the same old way. (p. 88)

Turkle's (1995) research suggests that we can find evidence of a new collective consciousness by analyzing the beliefs and practices of kids interacting with computers in play and in school. From interviews with children in the United States and England and from observing these children using computers, she finds that they are comfortable with a new idea—that machines do have personalities, intentions, and ideas.

Computers can sing, talk interactively, and do math with children. Also, more children are beginning to see these machine activities as signs of consciousness. At te same time, however, they do not believe that the computer machinery is alive like humans, because being alive means breathing, having blood, being born, and having real skin. Humans have real bodies, whereas reality in cyberspace does not.

When this idea that machines are inanimate organisms—with consciousness but not alive—becomes part of the Durkheimian collective consciousness, what new mechanisms of regulation and integration will develop? One consequence of our changing ideas about machine-human relations is already emerging: People are beginning to raise the issue of what rules of conduct to follow with computers. Computers do things for us and can do things to us, whether in the form of bots like Julia or in other forms such as self-help programs, which users know are code but at the same time they respond as if there is a psychotherapist inside the machine. (For example, you can purchase "technotherapy" software for help with depression, eating disorders, and stress management.)

Turkle (1995) suggests that we increasingly treat our computers as "intimate machines," and we thus seek rules of conduct for dealing with this situation. For example, she finds growing numbers of people who think that if a computer took on the role of judge in the court system, it might be less racist than a human judge (p. 292). What rules should we evolve about what, how, and when computers can do things with us and to us? Should there be limits on where bots can appear in the Net and what they can do? Is virtual rape actionable in real-life courts of law?

In a cyborg society, advanced technologies could invert the way that societies create and maintain themselves—the Durkheimian question with which this chapter began. Neighborhoods, corporations, and governments could become "just another part of an informational network, now machine, now message, always ready for exchange, each for the other" (Keller, 1994, p. 302). If societal organisms are designed and organized as codes and networks, this will change the ways that humans experience social life.

As Durkheim might say, cyborg social solidarity thus would depend on creating (a) effective regulation for machine-human interactions and (b) new forms of collective activity among machines and humans to ensure integration. Will we create a new species of social rituals whose participants are humans, computers, and other forms of artificial life, such as those seen today by TV viewers on the space station *Babylon 5?* Will we enter an era in which we talk about the human rights of robots like Data on *Star Trek?*

Conclusion

Although the scenario of cyborg solidarity may seem far-fetched, some of these changes are already happening. Children are already creating new ideas about human-machine relations. Many people are already cyborgs, given 20th-century advances such as prosthetic limbs and pacemakers for hearts. This raises the important Durkheimian question of what societies should begin to do about regulating human use of the new technologies of telecommunications, artificial life, and biological cloning.

Today, kids play with transformer toys that "morph" (metamorphize) back and forth between machine, animal, and human, such as the popular Power Rangers. Tomorrow, societies will probably have to concern themselves with the legal regulation of morphing and cloning—who and what get to switch states from body to code to body and under what conditions?

By giving us critical lenses through which to study, understand, and organize our worlds, sociological theory can help us prepare for the changes cascading on us with tremendous velocity at the start of the 21st century. I hope that this chapter illustrates this potential of sociological theory, through the application of Durkheim's theoretical framework to an analysis of the Net as a social phenomenon.

As sociologist C. Wright Mills (1959) notes, the rapid pace of change outstrips our ability to act in accord with our cherished values. Today, we often "sense that older ways of feeling and thinking have collapsed and that newer beginnings are ambiguous to the point of moral stasis" (p. 4). What we need, Mills argues, is a *sociological imagination*. This is a quality of mind that enables us to use our skills of reasoning plus the vast amounts of information available to discover a central insight about social life—that our personal troubles are often not just personal but are also public issues affecting many people and even an entire society.

Mills and Durkheim share elements of a vision: When individuals develop sociological imaginations, societal anomie and egoism can be transformed into societal regulation and integration through greater citizen involvement in the collective activities of public life. I share the vision and hope that sociological theory can help build a sociological imagination meaningful to ordinary citizens, thus contributing to the invigoration of our communities and democracies.

References

Anderson, R., Bikson, T., Law, S., & Mitchell, B. (1995). *Universal access to email: Feasibility and social implications*. Santa Monica, CA: RAND.

Argyle, K., & Shields, R. (1996). Is there a body in the Net? In R. Shields (Ed.), *Cultures of Internet: Virtual spaces, real histories, living bodies* (pp. 58-69). London: Sage.

Batty, M., & Barr, B. (1994). The electronic frontier: Exploring and mapping cyberspace. *Futures, 26*(7), 699-712.

Baym, N. (1995). The emergence of community in computer-mediated communication. In S. Jones (Ed.), *Cybersociety: Computer-mediated communication and community*. Thousand Oaks, CA: Sage.

Bellah, R., Madsen, R., Sullivan, W., Swidler, A., & Tipton, S. (1985). *Habits of the heart: Individualism and commitment in American life*. New York: Harper & Row.

Branscomb, L. (1995). Balancing the commercial and public interest visions of the NII. In B. Kahin & J. Keller (Eds.), *Public access to the Internet*. Cambridge, MA: MIT Press.

Collins, R. (1994). *Four sociological traditions*. Oxford, UK: Oxford University Press.

Comer, D. (1995). *The Internet book*. Englewood Cliffs, NJ: Prentice Hall.

Curtis, P. (1992). *Mudding: Social Phenomena in Text-Based Virtual Realities*, Proceedings of DIAC 1992 [Online]. Retrieved from http://www.zacha.net/articles/mudding.html

Downing, J. (1989, Summer). Computers for political change: PeaceNet and public access data. *Journal of Communication, 39*(3), 154-162.

Durkheim, É. (1933). *The division of labor in society* (G. Simpson, Trans.). New York: Free Press. (Original work published 1893)

Durkheim, É. (1938). *The rules of sociological method* (S. Solovay & J. Mueller, Trans.). New York: Free Press. (Original work published 1895)

Durkheim, É. (1951). *Suicide: A study in sociology* (J. Spaulding & G. Simpson, Trans.). New York: Free Press. (Original work published 1897)

Durkheim, É. (1957). *Professional ethics and civic morals* (C. Brookfield, Trans.). London: Routledge Kegan Paul.

Durkheim, É. (1995). *The elementary forms of the religious life* (K. Fields, Trans.). New York: Free Press. (Original work published 1912)

Figallo, C. (1995). The WELL: A regionally based on-line community on the Internet. In B. Kahin & J. Keller (Eds.), *Public access to the Internet*. Cambridge, MA: MIT Press.

Giddens, A. (1971). *Capitalism and modern social theory*. Cambridge, UK: Cambridge University Press.

Harasim, L. (1993). Global networks: An introduction. In L. Harasim (Ed.), *Global networks*. Cambridge, MA: MIT Press.

Haraway, D. (1991). *Simians, cyborgs, and women: The reinvention of nature*. New York: Routledge.

Ishaq, A. (2001). On the global digital divide. *Finance & Development,* 38(3), 44-47.

Jones, S. (1995). Understanding community in the information age. In S. Jones (Ed.), *Cybersociety: Computer-mediated communication and community*. Thousand Oaks, CA: Sage.

Kahin, B. (1995). The Internet and the national information infrastructure. In B. Kahin & J. Keller (Eds.), *Public access to the Internet*. Cambridge, MA: MIT Press.

Keller, E. F. (1994). The body of a new machine: Situating the organism between telegraphs and computers. *Perspectives on Science, 2*(3), 311-320.

Keller, J. (1995). Public access issues: An introduction. In B. Kahin & J. Keller (Eds.), *Public access to the Internet*. Cambridge, MA: MIT Press.

Kling, R. (1996). Social relationships in electronic forums: Hangouts, salons, workplaces, and communities. In R. Kling (Ed.), *Computerization and controversy: Values conflicts and social choices*. San Diego, CA: Academic Press.

Lehmann, J. (1993). *Deconstructing Durkheim*. New York: Routledge.

Lukes, S. (1973). *Emile Durkheim*. Middlesex, UK: Penguin.

McLaughlin, M., Osborne, K., & Smith, C. (1995). Standards of conduct on Usenet. In S. Jones (Ed.), *Cybersociety: Computer-mediated communication and community*. Thousand Oaks, CA: Sage.

Miller, S. (1996). *Civilizing cyberspace: Policy, power, and the information superhighway*. Reading, MA: Addison-Wesley.

Mills, C. W. (1959). *The sociological imagination*. London: Oxford University Press.

Nisbet, R. (1974). *The sociology of Emile Durkheim.* New York: Oxford University Press.

Norris, P. (2001). *Digital divide: Civic engagement, information poverty, and the Internet worldwide.* Cambridge, UK: Cambridge University Press.

Odasz, F. (1995). Issues in the development of community cooperative networks. In B. Kahin & J. Keller (Eds.), *Public access to the Internet* (pp. 115-137). Cambridge, MA: MIT Press.

Rheingold, H. (1993). *The virtual community: Homesteading on the electronic frontier.* New York: HarperCollins.

Rubin, B. (1996). *Shifts in the social contract.* Thousand Oaks, CA: Pine Forge Press.

Sayer, A., & Walker, R. (1992). *The new social economy: Reworking the division of labor.* Cambridge, MA: Basil Blackwell.

Schuler, D. (1996). *New community networks: Wired for change.* Reading, MA: Addison-Wesley.

Shade, L. (1996). Is there free speech on the Net? Censorship in the global information infrastructure. In R. Shields (Ed.), *Cultures of Internet: Virtual spaces, real histories, living bodies.* Thousand Oaks, CA: Sage.

Shields, R. (1996). Introduction: Virtual spaces, real histories, and living bodies. In R. Shields (Ed.), *Cultures of Internet: Virtual spaces, real histories, living bodies.* Thousand Oaks, CA: Sage.

Sproull, L., & Faraj, S. (1995). Atheism, sex, and databases: The Net as a social technology. In B. Kahin & J. Keller (Eds.), *Public access to the Internet.* Cambridge, MA: MIT Press.

Stone, A. (1991). Will the real body please stand up: Boundary stories about virtual cultures. In M. Benedikt (Ed.), *Cyberspace: First steps.* Cambridge, MA: MIT Press.

Turkle, S. (1995). *Life on the screen: Identity in the age of the Internet.* New York: Simon & Schuster.

Van Gelder, L. (1996). The strange case of the electronic lover. In R. Kling (Ed.), *Computerization and controversy: Values conflicts and social choices.* San Diego, CA: Academic Press.

Wellman, B., & Gulia, M. (1995, August). Net surfers don't ride alone: Virtual communities as communities. Paper presented at the American Sociological Association session on "Reinventing Community," Washington, DC.

Discussion Questions

1. Which of the mechanisms of regulation and integration discussed in the chapter have you noticed in the electronic gatherings you have joined?

2. What if there were no college classes in the first 2 years of a 4-year program? What if all courses were offered only as education at a distance: multimedia lectures on CD-ROMs available in the library and bookstore; all assignments computer-based; and all interactions with professors conducted by email? Which of his concepts would Durkheim use to explain the impact of this change on college life? What would Durkheim say about the impact on our sense of social order and our connectedness to other people?

3. Are computers and computer networks neutral vehicles for communication among people or are they "intimate machines" because they can talk and sing to us and can play the role of "human" (like the bot Julia)?

CHAPTER 4

Alcohol-Related Windows on Simmel's Social World

William J. Staudenmeier, Jr.

William J. Staudenmeier, Jr. was educated in engineering at West Point, graduating in 1972. Professor Staudenmeier worked in Air Force Social Actions, which emerged from his concern with racial injustice and his volunteer work with heroin addicts while at West Point. Helping to pioneer workplace treatment programs for military addicts and alcoholics, he was also involved with equal opportunity and treatment, race relations education, and promoting cross-cultural understanding at overseas bases. He received a PhD from Washington University in St. Louis, and he has taught at Drake University and now teaches as Professor of Sociology at Eureka College, where he has been awarded the college's highest teaching honor. Also recognized for his scholarly work on the social response to alcohol and other drugs, he was a visiting fellow at Cornell University and a visiting scientist at the University of Edinburgh, Scotland.

The German sociologist and philosopher Georg Simmel (1858-1918) was born in Berlin, the son of a successful businessman. Simmel lost his father while still young and became financially independent from the inheritance of his guardian's estate. At the University of Berlin, he was the student of some of the leading historians, philosophers, anthropologists, and psychologists of his time. This broad education and the lively intellectual interest it showed were reflected across Simmel's career. In 1881 he received his doctorate in philosophy with a somber-sounding thesis on "The Nature of Matter According to Kant's Physical Monadology" after having had his first dissertation, "Psychological and Ethnographic Studies on Music" (complete with a section on yodeling), rejected the year before.[1]

Upon graduation, Simmel became a private lecturer (Privatdozent) at the University of Berlin, compensated only by student fees between 1885 and 1900. He remained uncompensated by the university for the next 14 years while receiving the honorific title of "professor extraordinary" owing to his international reputation, the fame of his entertaining lectures, and his important position in Berlin intellectual life. In the prestige-conscious world of academia, however, Simmel had not made it; he did not have a permanent academic position, and despite his title, he did not get to participate in university governance. The prevalent anti-Semitism of the time (his father had converted to Christianity from Judaism), Simmel's welcome to otherwise unwanted students (e.g., women, dissidents, and Eastern Europeans), and Simmel's intellectual rebelliousness may all have played a role in his rejection despite the patronage of famous senior academics such as Max Weber and Edmund Husserl. Sadly, in 1914, when he finally was named a full professor at the University of Strasbourg, World War I interfered with his ability to fulfill the duties of the position. He died of liver cancer in 1918 before the end of the Great War.[2]

In contrast to some of the other social theorists covered in this book, who left behind comprehensive theories where the conceptual parts were clearly connected and consistent, Simmel seems more like a butterfly or a bee, flitting from subject to subject pollinating different intellectual blossoms. To read much of Simmel is an intellectual wonder, a dizzying ride as he moves from topic to topic and from one perspective to another within each topic. Simmel crosses time and place, disciplinary boundaries melt away, and the everyday is mixed with the profound as insights follow quickly one after another. For some cautious scholars, all of this is suspect. When confronted with breadth, intellectuals often question depth; when diverse interpretations are made of the same body of work, theoretical critics wonder if the readers are wishfully seeing their own preferred ideas in a shallow, murky reflecting pool. Speaking for the critics of Simmel, Émile Durkheim called his most magisterial work, *The Philosophy of Money,* more ingenious than valuable. But Schmoller, Goldscheid, and Lukács compared the same work to some of the greatest sociological books of the time. Reflecting the difficulty of classifying Simmel, however, each of them compared it to a vastly different work.[3]

But what of Simmel's influence, his legacy beyond his time? Simmel is considered by some a philosopher, a cultural theorist, a social psychologist, and a sociologist. If we include as his students those who traveled to attend his lectures, our list will encompass several major figures who went on to make a mark in diverse fields of study: Georg Lukács, Siegfried Kracauer, Robert E. Park, Richard Kroner, and George Santayana, to name a few.[4] But Peter Kivisto notes, "He did not create a school of thought that could be inherited by subsequent generations of sociologists. Thus, there is no Simmelian sociology in the same way that there is a Marxist sociology, a Weberian sociology, or a Durkheimian sociology."[5] Reflecting on his own intellectual estate, Simmel wrote, "I know that I shall die without spiritual heirs (and this is good). The estate I leave is like cash distributed among many heirs, each of whom puts his share to use in some trade that is compatible with his nature but which can no longer be recognized as coming from that estate."[6]

For much of the rest of the 20th century, Simmel would remain underappreciated by sociologists. Today, however, his early influence on American sociology is generally accepted and his self-described "cash" can be seen today in conflict theory, exchange theory, symbolic interactionism, and postmodern social theory.[7]

Simmel argued during his professional life for "the conception that society consists of a web of patterned interactions, and that it is the task of sociology to study the forms of these interactions as they occur and reoccur in diverse historical periods and cultural settings."[8] The particular contents—that is, concrete historical cases or examples—were of interest to the sociologist only as a way of determining the more general patterns and forms of interaction or types of interactants. The noted sociologist Lewis Coser described Simmel's focus as follows:

> In his view, society consists of an intricate web of multiple relations between individuals who are in constant interaction with one another. . . . The larger superindividual structures—the state, the clan, the family, the city, or the trade union—are only crystallizations of this interaction, even though they may attain autonomy and permanency and confront the individual as if they were alien powers. The major field of study for the student of society is, therefore, sociation, that is, the particular patterns and forms in which men associate and interact with one another.[9]

His ambition in doing this, according to German sociologist Richard Münch, was to assert "a distinctive place for sociology in the family of sciences."[10]

When we study a particular aspect of society, such as the human use of alcoholic beverages, it provides us a window on a much larger world. This chapter explores some of Simmel's major and minor ideas using examples that are alcohol related. Like Simmel's writings, coverage in this chapter will include examples from different places and times, ranging from the macro to the micro, and it will assuredly be incomplete in its treatment of alcohol-related content and in its coverage of Simmelian forms and ideas. Although we cannot climb the whole mountain, however, the view from the foothills is inspiring, the fresh air is exhilarating, and the exercise is good for us. Let us start with one of Simmel's best-known areas—conflict and change.

Alcohol, Conflict, and Change in America

Conflict Over Alcoholic Beverages

The history of the United States has been marked by considerable conflict over alcoholic beverages. David Pittman has gone so far as to say that, relative to alcoholic beverage use, "in America one finds the prototype of the ambivalent culture." For Pittman, the ambivalent culture is one characterized by "conflict between co-existing value structures."[11] Traditionally, in American society alcoholic beverages were the dietary beverages of choice, integrated with work, home life, and play. The temperance and prohibition movements of the 19th and 20th centuries, however, combined with successive waves of immigrants with their own distinctive beliefs and practices, led to conflict over the nature of alcohol and alcohol problems and the appropriate social response. Was alcohol necessary for health or destructive of health? Did alcohol promote vigorous work or prevent it? Was alcohol the social lubricant that helped facilitate social relations or the addicting drug that destroyed families and friendships? Each contrasting set of beliefs carried vastly different implications for an enlightened social response. This conflict became political as Prohibitionists and their opponents fought over local, state, and then national legislation or constitutional amendments to prohibit the manufacture, sale, and transportation of alcoholic beverages.

For Simmel, such conflict is an intensive form of interaction that at least temporarily binds the two parties together. People and groups that do not normally interact, often separated by culture and social class, are suddenly arguing, debating, paying close attention to each other's words and actions, and trying to counteract the effect of those words and actions.

The political conflict over Prohibition also enhanced the centralization (i.e., solidarity) of the group and the group identity within the competing parties. Simmel noted the following:

This need for centralization, for the tight pulling together of all elements, which alone guarantees their use, without loss of energy and time, for whatever the requirements of the moment may be, is obvious in the case of conflict.[12]

He also noted,

The group as a whole may enter into an antagonistic relation with a power outside of it, and it is because of this that the tightening of the relations among its members and the intensification of its unity, in consciousness and in action, occur.[13]

Conflict related to alcoholic beverages, however, has not always been just two-sided.

The Third Party and Conflict

For Simmel, social interaction could not be explained by merely looking at the attributes of the individuals or groups in the interaction. Rather, he put forward a social geometry in which the numbers, distance, and symmetry of the interactants (to name a few of the geometric influences) created different possibilities for interaction that could not be explained by reductionism.[14] This social geometry can be seen in the example of alcohol-related conflict in which a third party is added.

Often, a third party becomes involved, and this can be viewed using Simmel's concepts of the dyad and triad. Simmel's ideas about the difference between a group of two (a dyad) and a group of three (a triad) were applied to groups, for instance, when two groups (a dyad of groups) are joined by a third group (a triad of groups), as well as to individuals (e.g., a dyad of two individuals). According to Simmel, there are three typical interactional functions of the third added element: the divide et impera, the *tertius gaudens,* and the nonpartisan and mediator. The historical examples in the following paragraphs will illustrate each type in situations of alcohol-related group conflict drawn from different periods of American history.

The first example is from the late 1800s and early 1900s and regards the contentious issue of African Americans and alcohol. Reform-oriented blacks and whites came together in the South on issues of alcohol reform in the 1880s and economic reform with the Populist Party of the 1890s. African Americans were divided on their beliefs about drinking and its social control, just as were Southern whites. Although the available evidence indicated a greater sobriety among African Americans, racist stereotypes raised fears about drunken freed slaves terrorizing good people. Elites, however, were concerned that if the white vote split, the black vote would decide major political contests. Denise Herd writes about how major political leaders used the race and alcohol cards to drive a wedge between the Southern white and black farmers and laborers who had united on economic reform.[15] African Americans were blamed by politicians for the failure of several anti-alcohol votes throughout the South. Their vote was seen as corruptible, anti-reform, and decidedly wet (proalcohol).[16] This was only part of a broader concern about the negative effects of black political power, and the solution was seen as taking away the black vote (disfranchisement). White laborers and farmers supported these measures even though these politically successful disfranchisement measures also reduced the numbers of lower-class white voters. Herd wrote, "Prohibition played an important role in the wave of repression which stifled political dissent and maintained reactionary economic policies."[17]

This first case study can also be seen as an example of Simmel's concept of *divide et impera* (divide and rule), one of the three typical interactions with a third party. In this case, the third element is the politically conservative major political leaders, who used the Prohibition issue, among others, to divide the coalition of white and black farmers and laborers who had been seeking economic reform and threatening their political power. *Divide et impera* worked, and they removed the threat of a lower-class black and white political coalition.

The second case regards the early 1930s battle to repeal the Eighteenth Amendment to the U.S. Constitution, the amendment passed in 1919 that had outlawed the manufacture, sale, and transportation of alcoholic beverages since 1920. The anti-Prohibitionist movement gained popularity and support by the end of the 1920s, leading historians Mark Lender and James Martin to conclude that after 1930, "repeal was clearly an idea whose time had come." The rise of organized crime funded by the profits of illegal booze was seen as a threat to the social order and was tied to corruption in law enforcement. The scale of law violation and the ineptitude of some of the enforcers helped make Prohibition enforcement visibly ineffective. The dry leaders, however, who were out of touch with changing popular opinion, called for harsher and harsher enforcement, thus leading to more public opposition to unpopular criminal justice actions and inconsistent, seemingly arbitrary harshness. At the same time that the leadership effectiveness of the drys diminished, so did the number of their active members and supporters. By 1930, the growing unemployment and decrease in tax revenue associated with the Great Depression provided two more economic reasons for repeal: jobs and tax revenue. The Association Against the Prohibition Amendment made effective use of these rationales during their public relations campaigns, and even such prominent dry supporters as John D. Rockefeller, Jr., and the DuPonts switched sides and favored repeal by the 1930s.[18]

The public conflict between the Prohibitionists and the anti-Prohibitionists was very heated. In the 1932 election, both groups were contesting for the support of the Democratic Party. The anti-Prohibitionists wanted the Democratic candidate, Franklin Delano Roosevelt, to come out as a wet candidate in favor of repeal as one of the measures to fight the Depression by creating jobs and gaining new tax revenue. Roosevelt eventually campaigned for repeal.[19]

This second case is an example of Simmel's concept of *tertius gaudens* (the rejoicing third party). The Democrats, sensing a good issue, were the *tertius gaudens,* the rejoicing third party that benefits from the conflict between the two other parties but does not cause it. By coming out in favor of the wet cause, the Democrats gained the strong support of the anti-Prohibitionists and a popular economic campaign issue during the Great Depression. Also, their candidate, Roosevelt, won; and the Twenty-first Amendment to the Constitution of the United States was passed, repealing the Eighteenth Amendment and ending "the Great Experiment"—national Prohibition.

The third case is from the recent past. The dismissal or serious disciplining of an employee in a unionized work organization is often a cause for conflict between management and the union. Management tries to maintain labor discipline, whereas the union tries to protect the right of workers not to be treated unfairly. Two major areas of conflict over the disciplining of employees for alcohol-related offenses have been the following: (a) Under what circumstances can an employee be disciplined for possessing alcohol at the workplace, drinking, or being under the influence of alcohol during working hours if there is no written alcohol policy? and (b) if an employee has a drinking problem, can he or she be dismissed without first attempting voluntary treatment? To prevent or reduce conflict, management and labor use binding arbitration to resolve such questions. The arbitrator hears the case and then renders a decision, which is normally published for other arbitrators to see. Although the arbitrator has the Solomon-like discretion to rule as he or she sees fit, the publishing of cases encourages arbitrators to rule alike, creating a nonbinding, informal type of case law.

Arbitrators have generally ruled that in the absence of a written policy, employers must show that there was just cause to discipline the employee and that other employees in the same circumstances have consistently been disciplined. Clearly, however, case rulings act to encourage employers to develop written alcohol policies. The second area of conflict, dismissing employees with drinking problems, did not result in as uniform a result. In a review of arbitration cases published between 1963 and 1980, Michael Marmo found that in slightly more than half of the cases in which alcohol rehabilitation was considered, arbitrators required employers to offer it as a chance for the employee with a drinking problem to avoid dismissal.[20]

Arbitrators used different rationales for their decisions. Different cultural positions on alcohol in American society partially explain this inconsistent result.[21]

This third example illustrates Simmel's concept of a third party that is nonpartisan and provides a mediating role to avoid or reduce conflict between the two parties—in this case, labor and management. When arbitrators are consistent, the results are more predictable, and the two parties can better avoid conflict. Where arbitrators are inconsistent, uncertainty is greater and conflict more difficult to avoid. In some cases, arbitrators stick with custom, but in others they are moved by the fashions of their time.

Custom and Fashion

To follow custom is to be accepted by your group. Customary behavior provides the security of knowing what is right without the social risk associated with individual choice. Previous to the 20th century, most American drinking behavior was customary and traditional, although because America was heterogeneous, there were different customs and traditions to be followed. Also, new groups would bring new traditions. Italian Americans would drink wine at meals, German Americans would drink beer at urban beer gardens, and Irish American miners would bring whiskey down into the coal mines to make the work easier and prevent "coal consumption" (black lung disease). In the 20th century, however, the disruptive effects of the rise and fall of national Prohibition, the marketing and sale of individually packaged units of alcohol for at-home consumption, and the introduction and commercial promotion of new beverages and drinks at an unprecedented pace were witnessed.

Simmel thought that in his time, fashion was escaping the bounds of mere personal accouterments to encompass more of social life and that the rise of the middle classes, with their emphasis on fast-paced change, was one of the causes. Although customary group drinking still persists, the rise and fall of fashions in drinking and drinking places have become more pronounced today than in the past. In the past two decades, for example, wine coolers and liquor coolers emerged as a significant, new category of drink. Although wine coolers had existed as a bar mixed drink for a long time, the individual-portion packaging and commercial promotion of, for instance, Bartles & Jaymes coolers, were remarkably successful. Different flavors of these coolers rose and fell in fashion. New mixed drinks became fashionable, such as fuzzy navels, a concoction of orange juice and peach schnapps. Specialty beers and ales brewed in small, regional breweries have lately become fashionable, and large brewers are now imitating these products. Fashion remains unpredictable, however.

Simmel wrote, "There seem to be two tendencies in the individual soul as well as in society." This dualism can be seen as the "adaptation to society and individual departure from its demands." Imitation serves the former, and the effort to change and distinguish oneself from the pack serves the latter.[22] With custom, the emphasis is on the adaptation to society. Fashion, however, combines both tendencies:

Fashion is the imitation of a given example and satisfies the demand for social adaptation; it leads the individual upon the road which all travel, it furnishes a general condition, which resolves the conduct of every individual into a mere example. At the same time it satisfies in no less degree the need of differentiation, the tendency towards dissimilarity, the desire for change and contrast.[23]

Fashion also has another dualistic aspect to it; it joins us to the group in fashion and separates us from all others. Thus, it both joins us and separates us from others.[24] In part, this is possible with fashion because "in its very nature it represents a standard that can never be accepted by all."[25] For instance, the change in fashion in large drinking and dance places in urban areas in the past 30 years includes go-go dancers, light shows, discos, and urban cowboys. Ironically, the success of any fashion signals its death:

As fashion spreads, it gradually goes to its doom. The distinctiveness that in the early stages of a set fashion assures for it a certain distribution is destroyed as the fashion spreads, and as this element wanes, the fashion also is bound to die.[26]

Therefore, writes Simmel, "From an objective standpoint, life according to fashion consists of a balancing of destruction and upbuilding."[27] Because we will do things in the name of fashion that we would otherwise not do (the group frees us from carrying the burden of choice), we may be happier to see some fashions die than others.

Drinking Places

Both custom and fashion influence the choice of drinking places because people drink in many different settings. Some examples include one's home, a friend's home, a dormitory, a park, a car, a restaurant, a sporting venue, a tavern, and a private club. Whereas drinking alone often occurs in one's own home, it is less common in public places. The need to be with others is a basic human one and motivates much of the interaction that occurs in the commercial drinking establishments called taverns.

Types of Taverns

Different types of taverns both constitute and are constituted by different types of patrons. Marshall Clinard, in his classic work on public drinking houses, divides public taverns into five types: the Skid Row tavern, the downtown bar and cocktail lounge, the drink and dine tavern, the night club, and the neighborhood tavern.[28] Mary Ann Campbell, in her review of the literature on tavern types and based on her own fieldwork, found different types of patrons across the various types of taverns. Neighborhood taverns, for instance, tended to have large groups of regulars. Skid Row taverns, however, had many strangers. Nightclubs had many of that special category of dyad: the couple.[29]

Sometimes, the characteristics of different types of taverns can be found in one place. Clinard describes the three rooms commonly found in the British pub:

> The vault has a bar or counter where an exclusively male patronage drink standing. Most men come singly, and some are total strangers. In the taproom, drinking is a male group affair, and they are seated around plain wooden tables and benches. It is like a clubroom and strangers are not welcome. While games are played in both the vault and the taproom, most are in the latter. The lounge . . . is well decorated and comfortably furnished with tables, chairs and a piano; it attracts women and couples. There are no games.[30]

Exchange in Taverns

Clearly, economic exchange is a core element of the interaction in commercial drinking establishments. We pay our money, and in exchange we get a drink. For Simmel, however, "It is the object of exchange to increase the sum of value; each party offers to the other more than he possesses before."[31] This occurs because each person in the exchange desired what the other had more than what he or she had. That, after all, is why they engaged in the economic exchange in the first place. The end result, in Simmel's colorful prose, is "a surplus of satisfaction." The bar owner wanted the customer's money more than the drink he sold, and the customer wanted the drink more than the money! It is also the peculiar characteristic of economic exchange, however, that it "always signifies the sacrifice of an otherwise useful good"—in this case, our money, which is no longer available to us to purchase, for instance, tickets to the theater or soup for supper.[32]

Because of the commercial nature of taverns, all drinking in these places has some element of economic exchange governed by formal rules. Individuals in groups, however, also practice another form of exchange in these settings that follows custom: the practice known as treating or buying rounds. In this case, one person buys drinks for all the others in the group, and eventually, everyone will have a chance to reciprocate and buy a round, although the reciprocity is delayed, normally until most people are ready for another drink. As with other forms of delayed reciprocity, it is considered bad manners not to complete the exchange, follow custom, stay, and buy a round. If a member of the group leaves early before buying a round, the faux pas can be made up in part by insisting on being the first to treat the next time the group gets together. It would not normally be acceptable, however, if the individual departing early gave the others money to compensate for their expenditure. Why? Simmel sees money as unique in this regard: "The relationship is more completely dissolved and more radically terminated by payment of money than by the gift of a specific object . . . . Money is never an adequate mediator of personal relationships."[33] Treating, then, has to do with personal relationships, and it is not strictly an economic exchange.

Treating has some of the elements of the aforementioned economic exchange in that there is a loss of the purchasing value of the money used to treat, but if we look closer, what is normally exchanged within the group is identical: a drink. Where, then, is the "surplus of satisfaction?" It comes from the value of giving and receiving in a group in which such actions and the thought of such actions make us feel good and make us feel a part of the group. This is outside the narrow cash nexus of economic exchange because what is calculated here is not mere profit and loss.

Simmel, however, never intended the concept of exchange to be limited to economic exchange. For Simmel, exchange is "an original form and function of social life."[34] He writes that "most relationships between people can be interpreted as forms of exchange."[35] Thus, examples of exchange to be found in taverns include buying and selling drinks and treating, as discussed previously, but also include conversation and even love.

Conversation is at the center of what takes place in many traditional taverns. For Ray Oldenburg, a good tavern

> combines drinking with conversation such that each improves the other. . . . Tempered drinking "scatters devouring cares" as Horace observed and dispels "all unkindness" as Shakespeare knew. In a relaxed and socially conducive setting, drinking becomes the servant of those assembled by easing tensions, dissolving inhibitions, and inclining people toward their latent sense of humanity. The art of drinking subordinates that activity to its senior partner in the synergism, that of talking. It is a telling truth that the abuse of the synergism, excessive drinking, is first signaled by impairment of the power of speech.[36]

When we exchange this kind of conversation in a tavern, we gain without loss, unlike the case with economic exchange, which always involves elements of lost utility as well as gain.

What Oldenburg describes is an excellent example of what Simmel termed *sociability*—"the play-form of association." Simmel comments,

> This world of sociability, the only one in which a democracy of equals is possible without friction, is an artificial world made up of beings who have renounced both the objective and the purely personal features of the intensity and extensiveness of life in order to bring about among themselves a pure interaction, free of any disturbing material accent. . . . Sociability creates . . . an ideal sociological world, for in it . . . the pleasure of the individual is always contingent upon the joy of others.[37]

Strangers and Regulars

In contrast to a more sociable view, however, not all people who enter a tavern enter with others, form a group, or join a group already there. Some enter, stay, and leave as strangers. For Simmel, "being a stranger is . . . a completely positive relation; it is a specific form of interaction." The stranger is not "the wanderer who comes today and goes tomorrow, but rather . . . the man who comes today and stays tomorrow."[38] The stranger is both close and distant to others in the tavern. By remaining a stranger, and by remaining outside of the personal attachments forged in the tavern, the individual maintains an objectivity and freedom that others do not have.

Unlike the stranger, however, others find that the rewards of group membership in gathering places outweigh the loss of their freedom of coming and going. In *The Great Good Place,* Oldenburg describes the often unappreciated human need for gathering places. For Oldenburg, the home is our first place, work our second place, and "the core settings of informal public life" our third place—the place that serves "the human need for communion."[39] Beauty parlors, coffee shops, general stores, and taverns are examples of traditional third places in American society. Some of the common characteristics of third places include the following:

> Third places exist on neutral ground and serve to level their guests to a condition of equality. Within these places, conversation is the primary activity. . . . The character of a third place is determined most of all by its regular clientele and is marked by a playful mood.[40]

Oldenburg also notes the "comfort and support" of third places.

Although the social types of strangers and regulars persist as part of society, real individuals may leave the stranger type behind and become a regular at third places by establishing trust over time. Oldenburg writes,

> The third place gang need only know that the newcomer is a decent sort, capable of giving and taking in conversation according to the modes of civility and mutual respect that hold sway among them, and the group needs some assurance that the new face is going to become a familiar one. This kind of trust grows with each visit.[41]

This atmosphere is captured in the theme song for the television show *Cheers;* Cheers is truly a place "where everybody knows your name."

Strangers, however, are no longer just a few. Zygmunt Bauman writes,

> The world we live in seems to be populated mostly by strangers; it looks like the world of universal strangerhood. We live among strangers, among whom we are strangers ourselves. In such a world, strangers cannot be confined or kept at bay. Strangers must be lived with.[42]

The bars inhabited by strangers can be contrasted with the third-place taverns discussed previously. Oldenburg describes one bar as having small, private groups talking quietly, separated by everything but their common dress (in this case, the dress of "fledgling attorney and career-woman-after-hours") and protecting their privacy.[43] These people have dealt with the problems of universal strangerhood by selecting a place where "the uncertainty entailed in being in the presence of persons who can be anybody' has been thereby considerably, though only locally and temporarily, reduced."[44] They bring with them the only company they will keep. Their strategy, however, still leaves them among strangers. This is in stark contrast with the third-place tavern (or coffee shop) in which they could have joined a larger community group.

Among strangers, we find ourselves in "the company of people who are physically close yet spiritually distant." Among strangers in a tavern, we have physical proximity but little moral proximity—"the feeling of responsibility for the welfare and well-being" of the others around us.[45] Oldenburg also describes a type of tavern he calls the deadly place, where everyone is a stranger and thunderous silence prevails.[46] Bauman characterizes our interaction in this world of strangers as follows:

> There is a wall of reserve, perhaps even antipathy, inevitably rising between you and them—a wall which one cannot hope to scale, a distance one has little chance to bridge. People are tantalizingly close physically, and yet spiritually— mentally, morally—they manage to remain infinitely remote from each other. The silence which separates them, and the distance which is used as a clever and indispensable weapon against the danger sensed in the presence of strangers, feel like a threat. Lost in the crowd, one feels abandoned to one's own resources; one feels unimportant, lonely and disposable.[47]

In stark contrast, E. E. LeMasters describes the situation he found in a working-class tavern he studied as follows:

> One night I stopped in at the tavern and found the people at the bar talking about a man in his forties who had been a regular patron of The Oasis and was reported to be dying of cancer. One of the men brought a glass jar over and asked me to contribute to a fund for the man's family. "Lee," he said, "put something in this jar. That poor sonofabitch is up there in that hospital tonight dying of cancer and his four little kids are sitting down in that damn house crying."[48]

LeMasters concludes that

> In a very real sense the inner core of the tavern's patrons functions as a mutual aid society: Psychological support is provided in times of crisis; material help is available if needed; children are cared for; cars are loaned; and so on.[49]

The number of these places, however, has been shrinking as Americans drink more at home, drink at bars among strangers, live in communities without walking access to a neighborhood tavern (or coffee shop) due to zoning restrictions and developers' ideas about contemporary American living spaces, or all three.[50]

This decline is an excellent example of what Simmel feared: That the rapidly growing objective culture of modern life, although created by people, had taken on an autonomy of its own and would not help and may even hinder subjective culture—that is, the development of people, their improvement, "cultivation," and "heightened existence." Simmel noted that, "Things become more perfected, more intellectual, and to some degree more controlled by an internal, objective logic tied to their instrumentality; but the supreme cultivation, that of subjects, does not increase proportionately." [51]

Interaction in Taverns

Waitresses: Subordination and Superordination

Within tavern life there is a hierarchy. Simmel begins his discussion of superordination and subordination with the point that domination is a form of interaction, albeit an often unrecognized form of interaction; it is not merely the one-sided action of the dominant person giving orders. Simmel writes, "Interaction, that is, action which is mutually determined, action which stems exclusively from personal origins, prevails even where it often is not noted," such as in the case of superordination and subordination.[52] He emphasizes the personal freedom that we have in such a relationship:

> Within a relationship of subordination, the exclusion of all spontaneity whatever is actually rarer than is suggested by such widely used popular expressions as "coercion," "having no choice," "absolute necessity," etc. Even in the most oppressive and cruel cases of subordination, there is still a considerable measure of personal freedom. We merely do not become aware of it, because its manifestation would entail sacrifices which we usually never think of taking upon ourselves.[53]

A common example of this would be when an employer requires an employee, as a condition of employment, to do something that he or she would prefer not to do. Waitresses and waiters in some bars may be required to engage in deceptive practices with customers. Some examples are serving bar brands when a customer orders and pays for an expensive brand, serving liquor that is diluted or not a full measure, and serving single shots in mixed drinks when a customer has ordered and paid for double shots. Simmel would emphasize, however, that the employees retain their freedom to leave that employment.

In the interaction between superordinate and subordinate, the subordinate also influences the superordinate.[54] In the example mentioned previously, waiters and waitresses who are engaged in such deceptive practices will often pursue hustles that directly benefit themselves, such as saving unconsumed drinks for resale.[55]

Today, it is common for women to wait on customers who order a drink. Following the repeal of national Prohibition in the United States in 1932, however, which brought back the legal service of alcoholic beverages, a campaign was fought to ban women from serving alcoholic beverages. Both state legislative and union bans were sought by waiters' unions with limited success. Many waitresses agreed at the time, however, that women should not work in establishments that only served alcoholic beverages without any food service, and some waitresses' local unions enforced this provision. The broader attempt to prohibit female serving of alcoholic beverages fizzled, however, by the end of the 1930s. Although there had been little success in keeping women from serving alcoholic beverages as waitresses where food was also served, a similar campaign to ban them from bartending met with greater success after World War II. By 1948, 17 states prohibited female bartenders, and that same year the Supreme Court upheld the constitutionality of the relevant Michigan state law. It was not until the success in the 1970s of sex discrimination lawsuits using Title 7 of the 1964 Civil Rights Act that bartending was opened to women.[56]

One way of viewing these historical cases is as an example of the conflict between two strata (levels) that are next to each other—for example, male and female waiters—but are gradated (unequal), with males having the higher position at that time. Simmel found that conflict often occurred between strata that were next to each other in a hierarchical pyramid rather than just between the top (the superordinate) and those below (the subordinate).[57]

Within the tavern setting, bartenders are usually considered superordinate to waitresses, just as cooks are considered superordinate to waitresses in restaurants. Waitresses, being in a service occupation, are also often considered subordinate to their customers. Ann-Mari Sellerberg was interested in investigating "typical contradictory features in the service jobs done by women, focusing on conditions that entail subordination and superordination." Her study examined Swedish waitresses and alcohol as a clear example of these contradictory features. Clearly, these waitresses were given responsibility for controlling customers' alcohol consumption and alcohol- related behavior. This control "from below . . . produces a particular reciprocity." Customers will use such devices as foul language, crude behavior, sexual innuendo, and antagonistic behavior "to undermine technical/practical superordination" from the subordinate waitress.[58] Sellerberg concluded,

> The analyses put forward in this study are based on Simmel's specific understanding of the nature of social relations: they are dialectical, that is, they consist of opposing tendencies. . . . The waitress's control of the guest's liquor consumption gains its particular significance from being practised by a subordinate.[59]

Just Business

Certain types of taverns can also be sites for another, very different type of relationship—the pairing of a prostitute and her client. Clinard, for example, notes that the Skid Row tavern is often frequented by prostitutes attempting to solicit customers. Furthermore, Robert Prus and Styllianoss Irini describe the importance of prostitution in some hotel cocktail lounges to the economic well-being of these hotels and their staff.[60] Normally, these taverns have extensive rules and procedures for managing the interaction among the bar staff, hookers, "johns," and other tavern-goers.

Simmel was interested in the general form the interaction took, and for him the role of money was crucial; in fact, he uses prostitution as a clarifying example of the special nature of a monetary relationship. He wrote,

Money best serves, both objectively and symbolically, that purchasable satisfaction which rejects any relationship that continues beyond the momentary sexual impulse, because it is absolutely detached from the person and completely cuts off from the outset any further consequences.[61]

Money concludes the deal and releases the customer from further obligation. Although some johns will become regular customers of certain prostitutes, this does not usually create the same ties one would expect in a normal extended relationship. The regular john may at any time choose a new prostitute for a variety of reasons, including cost. One prostitute reports, "You know he's not going to go out with you again for 40 when he can get her for 35." [62]

Time of service concludes the deal and releases the prostitute from further obligation. One of the prostitutes in the hotel bar study reported about the interaction with customers in the hotel room:

Usually they take about fifteen minutes in the room, and if they take longer, well it's more money. Sometimes you have problems with guys not wanting you to leave, but when their time is up, you just tell them, "Well, I've got other customers waiting for me. I have to go do my work, I'm a business girl."[63]

The interaction is reduced to payment for service. Another prostitute commented, "You think of it as work. They're strangers and you're providing a service . . . You think in terms of the $40 or whatever it is that the trick might be giving you."[64] Such monetary relationships are seen in stark contrast with other relationships that these prostitutes have with hotel staff, friends, family, pimps, and other lovers.

Clearly, there is something disturbing about this. Simmel wrote,

Kant's moral imperative never to use human beings as a mere means but to accept and treat them always, at the same time, as ends in themselves is blatantly disregarded by both parties in the case of prostitution. Of all human relationships, prostitution is perhaps the most striking instance of mutual degradation to a mere means.[65]

The means, says Simmel, are virtually interchangeable. A john with money is just a john. A willing prostitute is just another prostitute.

Such interaction may change the boundaries of what is considered personal. For example, the hotel bar prostitutes usually will not kiss their customers. One prostitute explains that sex "becomes regular, that it's not personal anymore, so what's left that is? Kissing. So then they treat kissing as something they really care about. It's the only thing left, right?"[66]

Simmel recognized, however, that there are always other factors, such as individual personality, that influence the content of social life in the real world. Therefore, some prostitutes may become personally involved with clients, and some prostitutes may view kissing in the same impersonal way they view sex. Clearly, it is also the case that a third party, such as a pimp, the police, or hotel staff, may affect the interaction between the prostitute and the client in the hotel bar. As the interaction changes from that of a dyad to a triad, Simmel would have us once again look for the role of the third party in the triad, the influence of group size.

Group Size

Simmel drew attention to the influence of group size on group dynamics in his classic work, *Sociology, Studies of the Forms of Societalization*. This section will first examine the influence of group size on group control and then return to the structural question of how a change in the specific number in a group influences interaction within it. In this section, a reconsideration of the dyad and the triad will focus on interacting individuals rather than interacting groups.

When we wish to host a group of friends at a tavern, how many do we need to have to make a party? Two or three casual business acquaintances would probably not make a party, but a dozen good friends would. Clearly, the size of the group matters, but we cannot set a specific number and say that, for instance, six always make a party, but five does not. Although size is the most important factor in determining whether or not there is a party, Simmel offers the following factors that also have an influence:

> Three circumstances—the host's relations to each of the guests, the relations among the guests, and the way in which each participant interprets these relations—form the basis upon which the number of members decides whether there occurs a "party" or a mere togetherness of a friendly or of an objective- utilitarian sort.[67]

Furthermore, although small numbers of friends may content themselves with good conversation, larger numbers mean different requirements for food, dress, behavior, and alcoholic beverages. Interestingly, Simmel explains this by saying,

> A "party," therefore, merely because of its emphasis on number, which excludes a common interaction of more refined and intellectual moods, must all the more strongly make use of these sensuous joys, that are shared by all with incomparably greater certainty.[68]

Thus, to illustrate, comfortable intimacy, honest companionship, and good conversation are replaced by the "sensuous joys" of eating, drinking, and mating behavior—joys that are more likely to be a sure hit with a larger, less intimate group.

Simmel also found that for large groups, it was impossible to determine generally the influence of one more person. For instance, by what logic or evidence could we hope to determine the difference between a group of 50 and a group of 51 at any time in any tavern? By dealing with the simplest groups, however, he attempted to determine the influence of a specific group number. His classic formulation was investigating the smallest group, the dyad or group of two, and then exploring the difference that adding one, forming a triad or group of three, would make. Simmel thought that the differences between a dyad and a triad were large and significant. Also, because these differences were due to the numerical structure, they were also general rather than situational.

When there are two people sitting together in a tavern having a drink and talking, individuals who walk in and see them may perceive them as a group—that is, as something more than just two individuals. Each of the drinkers in the dyad, however, perceives only the other—another single individual. According to Simmel, the pair of drinkers would not perceive themselves "as an autonomous, super-individual unit." If either of the two drinkers leaves the other, then the dyad is destroyed. Simmel wrote,

> This dependence of the dyad upon its two individual members causes the thought of its existence to be accompanied by the thought of its termination much more closely and impressively than in any other group, where every member knows that even after his retirement or death, the group can continue to exist.[69]

The structural change of the addition of a third member to the group, now a triad, alters that sense of mortality and the role of the members in the group.

When there is a group of three friends drinking in a bar, the departure of one does not destroy the group. The three also do not have to agree on a course of action; two can create a coalition against the third and decide what the group will do. The group thus possesses a position above the individual not subject to every individual's will. The result may be paying for drinks we do not want, staying longer than desired, or leaving the group prematurely. The spatial boundaries of the tavern setting, however, also create a group of sorts—a group that includes all those within the tavern. Clinard stated that all drinking in taverns is group drinking.[70] Even the isolated stranger in a tavern is influenced by the social nature of the drinking, aware of and responding to those in the same tavern space.

Some Contemporary Drinking Problems

This discussion ends where most formal public discussions of alcohol begin—with a few examples from the area of drinking problems and the social response to them.

Alcoholism and Its Treatment

Clearly, Simmel was concerned with the identification and description of social types (such as the stranger discussed previously) as part of his effort to understand the general forms of social life. On the basis of empirical observation, Simmel would identify the more general social type in terms of its social relationships.[71] Over the years, several names have been given to those individuals in society who drink way too much and experience serious problems over time because of this drinking behavior. The reaction to them has varied as well. In America, these labels include habitual drunkards, inebriates, alcoholics, alcohol addicts, alcohol abusers, problem drinkers, alcohol dependents, substance abusers, chemically dependents, and so on. Although there have been some clear distinctions with practitioners distinguishing definitionally among these labels, for most Americans today the term *alcoholism* is the operative one, and its definition for them is often vague. Among clinicians and researchers, there have been a series of attempts to operationally and clinically define these problems under two levels of problem definition: (a) alcohol abuse, the less serious form, and (b) alcohol dependence, the more serious form. With alcohol dependence, the individual has alcohol-related social problems as well as signs of tolerance (can drink more over time), withdrawal ("a maladaptive behavioral change with physiological and cognitive concomitants"), or compulsive alcohol-related behavior. *Alcohol abuse* is the label used when the individual has not met the criteria for alcohol dependence but shows "a maladaptive pattern of substance [alcohol] use leading to clinically significant impairment or distress."[72] An example of this would be an individual who is doing poorly at work because of patterns of heavy drinking.

The Epidemiologic Catchment Area Study provides some interesting information about "the structure of alcoholism in the general population." In the study, the researchers use the term *alcoholism* to refer to the condition of anyone who has exhibited alcohol abuse or alcohol dependence or both. On the basis of their results, they estimated "4.5% to 7% of the population being actively symptomatic in the past year" for alcoholism. Alcoholism, they found, "is a disorder of youthful onset," with almost 40% of the cases having their first symptom by age 20 and more than 80% by age 30. Fifty-three percent of the people who had ever had lifetime symptoms for alcohol abuse or alcohol dependence or both were currently in remission; that is, they had experienced no symptoms in the past 12 months. Some of these, unfortunately, may be expected to relapse and have future problems. More than half of the cases in remission (54%) had alcoholism symptoms for a relatively short duration, with less than 5 years between the dates of their first and last symptom. The authors conclude that "it is those who try [to stop their symptomatic drinking] and fail that appear for treatment." [73]

Historically, there was a significant decline in the help available for the alcoholic by the time national Prohibition was repealed in 1932. This was the milieu in which Alcoholics Anonymous (AA) emerged in 1935 to become "the best known and most popular therapy for alcoholism." At its core, AA "is a voluntary fellowship of problem drinkers, both men and women, who join with one another in an effort to refrain from drinking alcohol." The now-famous 12 steps are the program that the alcoholic follows in interaction with other alcoholics. The organization has no dues, no hierarchy, and no formal officers and is self-supporting, not accepting donations from other sources.[74]

A key part of AA is the 12th step—the obligation of its members to help other alcoholics by encouraging them to affiliate with AA and helping them to become and stay sober. William Madsen describes the experience of becoming a new AA member as follows:

The alcoholic person finds that he is merely a "normal" member of the group rather than an idiosyncratic misfit in society. . . . One person said, "I'd always been a stranger on earth, yearning to find someone who understood me. When I found AA, it felt like coming home to a loving family I'd never known."[75]

In his classic studies of affiliation with AA, Harry Trice found that those who joined AA "showed a stronger need to establish and maintain close emotional ties with others than did alcoholics not affiliated with AA."[76] Madsen talked further about the transformation that group membership wrought:

The very alcoholism that had alienated him from society becomes the bond linking him to this loving primary group. Thus, his alcoholism is metamorphosed from a destructive force to perhaps the most positive identity he has ever had.[77]

On the basis of his affiliation studies, Trice concluded that "despite AA's effectiveness, many alcoholics are unable to affiliate."[78] Therefore, in those cases, other approaches might be required.

In 1966, when Trice published his book, *Alcoholism in America,* inpatient alcoholism treatment was so infrequent that it received little coverage in his book. The 28-day, inpatient hospital-based or affiliated treatment program with aftercare as an outpatient (following completion of the 28 days), however, became widespread during the next two decades. The dominant treatment approach in these centers is "multimodality"—the use of several different approaches together—and using the 12 steps of AA. Group therapy is a core approach in these settings, emphasizing open communication, disclosure, and insight. The German theorist, Jürgen Habermas, optimistically sees group therapy as an "example of the 'ideal speech community,' in which everything can be said without inhibition, and dialogue can go on until consensus is finally reached without any coercion." He sees the number of these freed individuals and groups using ideal speech growing and improving the world.[79] Perhaps this evolution will occur, but the case of alcoholism treatment is an interesting example of the factors influencing the growth and possible decline of this social form as well—because money is involved.

Historically, the growth of inpatient treatment in the United States is linked with the growth of employer-based programs to identify and rehabilitate alcoholic employees (often called employee assistance programs) and the increasing percentage of employees' insurance plans that cover alcoholism treatment. The triumvirate was (a) employers identify them and make the referral, (b) treatment centers treat them, and (c) the insurance pays for the treatment. For a variety of interesting, seemingly rational reasons at the time, a one-size-fits-all approach emerged, with insurance companies commonly providing benefits for inpatient 28-day treatment but not for outpatient treatment.

Due to the rising cost of health care, managed care emerged as a way to control the health care costs of employers and their insurers. The contribution of alcoholism, drug abuse, and mental health treatment to these escalating costs was widely publicized, and managed care organizations started to restrict the use of inpatient facilities for alcoholics. Managed care led to a precipitous decline in the number and percentage of employer referrals to inpatient alcoholism treatment, and treatment centers were closed across the United States in the early 1990s. For example, one of the industry leaders had a decline in treatment beds from 1,876 in 1989 to 385 in 1993.[80] During congressional hearings, Betty Ford testified, "Today, the real money is to be made in setting up systems to deny and prevent treatment."[81] Currently, there is a tendency toward managed care requiring brief therapy, usually six visits or less, to replace the more expensive alternatives of intensive outpatient, day-patient, and inpatient treatment. Cost accountants' decisions based on monetary criteria using selected social science findings to legitimize these decisions won the day in lieu of the more flexible matching of patients to treatment that some of the early proponents of more flexible care had hoped would replace the rigid 28-day approach. One key informant who had hoped for this told me that instead, it was "cost, cost, cost," and they are "doing everything they can not to provide good treatment."[82] Money became the ultimate arbiter of value—and treatment became a shadow of its former self.

Violence and Vandalism

All groups try to control interaction within their group to make group life more predictable. Due to the wide range of human alcohol-related behaviors, special issues of control are always present in drinking groups. The bases for control of unpredictable and undesirable alcohol-related interaction, however, vary with group size. The German social theorist Richard Münch described Simmel's ideas regarding control:

> A small group can rely on trust in the personal morality of its members, because they know each other completely. A medium-sized group has outgrown that complete knowledge of each other and needs closer control of actions by the group and a binding definition of its group morality in mores and conventions. A large group cannot even rely on such informal standards embedded in group solidarity but needs much more formal establishment of control by positive law and a legal system. The large group will contain all three levels of regulation but with a growing importance attached to positive law.[83]

An example of a small drinking group relying on trust and associated with few problems of violence or vandalism would be a family or group of friends drinking wine with a meal.

An example of a very large drinking group would be the group at a European soccer game, a beer festival, or a campuswide party. Because of predictable problems of control, there is usually a visible presence of police, private security, or bouncers. Positive law, a reliance on formal laws and rules and their enforcement, becomes much more important with the increase in size. Formal alcohol controls, however, are often less effective than informal group controls, and these venues are often associated with riotous behavior and a breakdown of controls. For instance, in 1988, one Midwestern university campus party of approximately 1,000 people was closed by the police following neighborhood complaints. Bricks and bottles were thrown at the police, and a fire was started using a stage and other flammable materials. On the second night of the party, a police car was overturned, and on the third night of the party, to which 5,000 people showed up, another bonfire was started using furniture looted from neighborhood houses, telephone poles, and so on. Neighbors and police were threatened, including one threat to throw a student who was trying to protect her property into the fire; students and one policeman were treated for minor injuries; and 50 arrests occurred during the third night, which lasted from Saturday night to Sunday morning. Pointing to a change in controls, Brent Bruton and Robert Schafer observed, "The legal drinking age change has resulted in restrictive alcohol policies in college residence units which have in turn shifted drinking from legitimate contexts with adequate control mechanisms to illegitimate contexts without adequate mechanisms of social control."[84]

The size of the party was clearly of major importance in this case as well. The discussion of medium-sized groups will illustrate some of the variation in alcohol-related aggressive behavior.

For medium-sized groups that rely on closer group control and mores and conventions, we return to the setting of the tavern. The first obvious point is that the mores and conventions that a group enforces vary widely among different taverns. In some American bars, the bar fight is normative, a regular part of the weekend entertainment not to be avoided but to be sought, either as a participant or as an entertained bystander. In these bars, drinking is tied inextricably with aggression, which is normative.

This situation contrasts sharply with that described by John Honigmann in his study of village taverns in an Austrian village. What the villagers seek out in their taverns is "an evening filled with wit and laughter," sociability, and what the villagers call *lustigkeit* (gaiety).[85] Honigmann observed,

> Drunkenness itself earns men no disapproval; in fact moderate intoxication is the very basis for gaiety. . . . Immoderate drunkenness—intoxication that can no longer be called tipsy, in which a man loses his ability to evaluate and control his acts, and wherein he becomes aggressive—arouses annoyance and even repugnance. Drinking to this extreme occurs uncommonly.[86]

A similar contrast can be found in two examples of drinking situations in settings other than taverns.

In his classic study of the drinking patterns of the Bolivian Camba tribe, Dwight Heath observes, "Both drinking and drunkenness are the norm on these occasions [ritualized social gatherings] and an integral part of their social ritual." He adds, however, that "aggression and sexual license are conspicuously absent on these sole occasions when beverage alcohol is used."[87] What occurs in the Camba's behavior as they drink and sit in a circle is at first an increase in sociability and then a quiet "retreat inward" as they get more drunk. In stark contrast, Mac Marshall describes the common drunken battles on the weekends of young men in the streets of the Micronesian island of Truk: "The positively valued personal attributes of bravery, respectfulness, and strong thought are achieved and validated in large part through drunken fighting, which has substituted for the major traditional avenue available for establishing a positive masculine image: warfare."[88]

In a society in which the suppression of aggression is the norm, Marshall notes, drunkenness allows the young men to be aggressive and demonstrate their masculinity while "they are looked upon as crazy and therefore not responsible for their words and deeds."[89]

In their influential book, *Drunken Comportment, A Social Explanation,* Craig MacAndrew and Robert Edgerton help to explain this wide variation in drunken behavior:

> Rather than viewing drunken comportment as a function of toxically disinhibited brains operating in impulse-driven bodies, we have recommended that what is fundamentally at issue are the learned relations that exist among men living together in a society. More specifically, we have contended that the way people comport themselves when they are drunk is determined not by alcohol's toxic assault upon the seat of moral judgment, conscience, or the like, but by what their society makes of and imparts to them concerning the state of drunkenness.[90]

MacAndrew and Edgerton conclude, "Since societies, like individuals, get the sorts of drunken comportment that they allow, they deserve what they get."[91]

Conclusion

In G. K. Chesterton's famous obituary of George Bernard Shaw, he reflected on his impressions of Shaw during their one meeting: "He did not talk about the books he had written; he was far too much alive for that. He talked about the books he had not written. . . . I went out of that garden with a blurred sensation of the million possibilities of creative literature.[92]

And so it is that Georg Simmel leaves us feeling the same way, with a sense of the "million possibilities" of sociological inquiry. For some, like Jürgen Habermas, Simmel is "a different type" and "a creative although not systematic thinker." For Habermas, "Simmel's pieces vacillate between essay and scientific treatise; they roam around the crystallizing thought."[93] Simmel is criticized for his lack of coherence across his work, his undeveloped ideas, and his lack of unifying theory. But what of Simmel's ambition and intent? Lawrence Scaff observes:

> Critical synthesis of contradictory viewpoints, system building, or reconciliation between opposing forces in the world was not Simmel's ambition, however. For again and again he presents himself to us as a man of ideas having an uncommon will to originality, adopting an "experimental" stance, a mode of

writing, and a "style" that reveals the unique grammar of his thinking. His emphasis is on maintaining the dualisms, the dyadic tensions, rather than imposing a new synthesis or schematic "master narrative."[94]

And what of us; can we appreciate and enjoy the original, creative gifts of "this different type"? Can we learn from his view of modern life?[95]

For Simmel, life was full of conflicts, contradictions, and dualisms,[96] and the case of alcohol-related social phenomena illustrates well the accuracy of his observation. Alcoholic beverages remain a major object of conflict in American society. Conflicts over the drinking age, warning labels, drunk driving, alcohol advertising, the price of alcohol, the nature of alcohol problems, and the appropriate response to alcoholism are just some of the political conflicts of the past decade. Also, alcohol-related social life is full of contradictions and dualisms (good and bad, permissions and controls, intimate and distant, etc.), which were discovered as we explored this aspect of the social world and illuminated "the general" pointed to by Simmel in forms and types that could be found in our particular alcohol-related cases.

Being a student is part of the quest for improving your subjective culture—your own development—using the material and nonmaterial cultural objects found in society. Part of your challenge may be to find an answer to the social (and individual) quandary posed by Simmel, a quandary clearly including alcoholic beverages for today's college student but certainly not limited to alcohol-related content: "The dissonance of modern life . . . is caused in large part by the fact that things are becoming more and more cultivated, while men are less able to gain from the perfection of objects a perfection of the subjective life."[97]

How do we create a delightful life in a world of artificial delights? How do we master the material world if we do not keep our distance from it? How do we live a good life in a world full of more and more cultivated goods? Finally, returning to our case, how do we keep good drinks from destroying the good drinker?

Notes

1. Coser, L. (1977) *Masters of sociological thought* (pp. 194-195). New York: Harcourt Brace Jovanovich; Levine, D. N. (Trans., Ed.). (1971). *On individuality and social forms* (pp. ix-xv). Chicago: University of Chicago Press (Original work published in 1910); Wolff, K. H. (Trans., Ed.). (1964). *The sociology of Georg Simmel* (pp. xvii-xxv). New York: Free Press (Original work published in 1908); Kivisto, P. (1998). *Key ideas in sociology* (pp. 123-125). Thousand Oaks, CA: Pine Forge Press.

2. Coser (1977), *Masters of sociological thought,* pp. 194-197; Levine (1971), *On individuality and social forms,* pp. ix-xv; Kivisto (1998), *Key ideas in sociology,* pp. 123-125.

3. Frisby, D. (1990). Preface to the second edition. In G. Simmel, *The philosophy of money* (D. Frisby, Ed.; T. Bottomore & D. Frisby, Trans.; 2nd enlarged ed., pp. xvi-xvii). New York: Routledge. (Original work published in 1907)

4. Frisby, D., & Featherstone, M. (Trans., Eds.). (1997). Introduction to the texts. In *Simmel on culture* (pp. 2, 23-24). Thousand Oaks, CA: Sage.

5. Kivisto (1998), *Key ideas in sociology,* p. 123.

6. Simmel, G. (1990), quoted in Introduction to the translation, *The philosophy of money*, p. 4.

7. Ritzer, G. (2000). *Sociological theory* (5th ed., p. 151). New York: McGraw-Hill.

8. Coser (1977), *Masters of sociological thought*, p. 177.

9. Coser (1977), *Masters of sociological thought*, p. 178.

10. Münch, R. (1994). *Sociological theory* (Vol. 1, pp. 95-96). Chicago: Nelson-Hall.

11. Pittman, D. J. (1967). International overview: Social and cultural factors in drinking patterns, pathological and nonpathological. In D. J. Pittman (Ed.), *Alcoholism* (pp. 8-10). New York: Harper & Row.

12. Simmel, G. (1955). In K. H. Wolff & R. Bendix (Trans.), *Conflict & the web of group affiliations* (p. 88). New York: Free Press. (Original work published 1923)

13. Simmel (1955), *Conflict & the web of group affiliations*, p. 91.

14. Ritzer (1992), *Sociological theory*, pp. 166-167; Coser (1971), *Masters of sociological thought*, pp. 186-189.

15. Staudenmeier, W. J., Jr. (1985). *Race and deviance: Blacks and alcohol in the age of temperance*. Paper presented at the meeting of the Midwest Sociological Society, St. Louis, MO; Herd, D. A. (1983). Prohibition, racism, and class politics in the post-Reconstruction South. *Journal of Drug Issues, 13*, 77-94.

16. Ironically, African Americans were also blamed or given credit for the passage of local Prohibition in several cases. For example, for a description of their role in passing local option in Alexandria, Virginia, see Women's Christian Temperance Union. (1883). *Temperance and prohibition papers* (Series 3, roll 1, p. xxii) [Microfilm].

17. Herd (1983), *Journal of Drug Issues, 13*, 77-94.

18. Lender, M., & Martin, J. (1982). *Drinking in America, a history* (pp. 164-168). New York: Free Press.

19. Lender & Martin (1982), *Drinking in America, a history*, pp. 164-168; Gusfield, J. R. (1976). *Symbolic crusade* (pp. 127-128). Urbana: University of Illinois Press.

20. Marmo, M. (1983). Arbitrators view problem employees: Discipline or rehabilitation? *Journal of Contemporary Law, 9*, 41-79.

21. Staudenmeier, W. J., Jr. (1987). Context and variation in employer policies on alcohol. *Journal of Drug Issues, 17*, 255-271.

22. Simmel, G. (1957, May). Fashion. *American Journal of Sociology, 62*(6), 542-543.

23. Simmel (1957, May), *American Journal of Sociology, 62*(6), 543.

24. Simmel (1957, May), *American Journal of Sociology, 62*(6), 544.

25. Simmel (1957, May), *American Journal of Sociology, 62*(6), 549.

26. Simmel (1957, May), *American Journal of Sociology, 62*(6), 547.

27. Simmel (1957, May), *American Journal of Sociology, 62*(6), 549.

28. Clinard, M. B. (1962). The public drinking house and society. In D. J. Pittman & C. R. Snyder (Eds.), *Society, culture, and drinking patterns* (pp. 270-292). New York: John Wiley.

29. Campbell, M. A. (1991). Public drinking places and society. In D. J. Pittman & H. Raskin White (Eds.), *Society, culture, and drinking patterns reexamined* (pp. 361-380). New Brunswick, NJ: Rutgers Center of Alcohol Studies.

30. Clinard (1962), in *Society, culture, and drinking patterns*, pp. 278-279.

31. Simmel, G. (1990). *The philosophy of money*, p. 82.

32. Simmel (1990), *The philosophy of money*, pp. 83-84.

33. Simmel (1990), *The philosophy of money*, p. 376.

34. Simmel (1990), *The philosophy of money*, p. 100.

35. Simmel (1990), *The philosophy of money*, p. 82.

36. Oldenburg, R. (1991). *The great good place* (pp. 167-168). New York: Paragon House.

37. Simmel, G. (1971). Sociability. In D. N. Levine (Trans., Ed.), *On individuality and social forms* (pp. 132-133). Chicago: University of Chicago Press. (Original work published 1910). For an interesting application of Simmel's ideas on sociability to alcohol, see J. Partanen (1991). *Sociability and intoxication, alcohol and drinking in Kenya, Africa, and the modern world.* Helsinki: The Finnish Foundation for Alcohol Studies. Thanks are due to Robin Room at the University of Stockholm for making me aware of this source.

38. Simmel, G. (1971). The stranger. In D. N. Levine (Trans., Ed.), *On individuality and social forms* (p. 143). Chicago: University of Chicago Press. (Original work published 1908)

39. Oldenburg (1991), *The great good place*, pp. 16-20.

40. Oldenburg (1991), *The great good place*, p. 42.

41. Oldenburg (1991), *The great good place*, p. 35.

42. Bauman, Z. (1990). *Thinking sociologically* (p. 63). Cambridge, UK: Basil Blackwell.

43. Oldenburg (1991), *The great good place*, pp. 172-173.

44. Bauman (1990), *Thinking sociologically*, p. 65.

45. Bauman (1990), *Thinking sociologically*, pp. 66, 69.

46. Oldenburg (1991), *The great good place*, pp. 169-170.

47. Bauman (1990), *Thinking sociologically*, p. 68.

48. LeMasters, E. E. (1975). *Blue-collar aristocrats: Life-styles at a working-class tavern* (pp. 141-142). Madison: University of Wisconsin Press.

49. LeMasters (1975), *Blue-collar aristocrats*, pp. 141-142.

50. Oldenburg (1991), *The great good place*, pp. 167-168.

51. Simmel, G. (1971). Subjective culture. In D. N. Levine (Trans., Ed.), *On individuality and social forms* (pp. 233-234). Chicago: University of Chicago Press. (Original work published 1908)

52. Simmel, G. (1964). Superordination and subordination. In K. H. Wolff (Trans., Ed.), *The sociology of Georg Simmel* (pp. 181-183). New York: Free Press. (Original work published 1908)

53. Simmel (1964), in *The sociology of Georg Simmel*, pp. 181-183.

54. Simmel (1964), in *The sociology of Georg Simmel*, pp. 185-186.

55. Prus, R., & Irini, S. (1988). *Hookers, rounders, & desk clerks* (pp. 144-157). Salem, WI: Sheffield.

56. Cobble, D. S. (1991). Drawing the line: The construction of a gendered work force in the food service industry. In A. Baron (Ed.), *Work engendered: Toward a new history of American labor* (pp. 216-242). Ithaca, NY: Cornell University Press.

57. Münch (1994), *Sociological theory*, pp. 105-107.

58. Sellerberg, A.-M. (1994). *A blend of contradictions, Georg Simmel in theory and practice* (pp. 25-31). New Brunswick, NJ: Transaction.

59. Sellerberg (1994), *A blend of contradictions*, pp. 30-31.

60. Clinard (1962), in *Society, culture, and drinking patterns*, p. 276; Prus & Irini (1988), *Hookers, rounders, & desk clerks*, pp. 144-157.

61. Simmel (1990), *The philosophy of money*, p. 376.

62. Prus & Irini (1988), *Hookers, rounders, & desk clerks*, p. 21.

63. Prus & Irini (1988), *Hookers, rounders, & desk clerks*, p. 16.

64. Prus & Irini (1988), *Hookers, rounders, & desk clerks*, p. 19.

65. Simmel (1990), *The philosophy of money*, p. 377.

66. Prus & Irini (1988), *Hookers, rounders, & desk clerks*, p. 17.

67. Simmel, G. (1964). The quantitative determination of group divisions and of certain groups. In K. H. Wolff (Trans., Ed.), *The sociology of Georg Simmel* (pp. 111-114). New York: Free Press. (Original work published 1908)

68. Simmel (1964), in *The sociology of Georg Simmel,* pp. 111-114.

69. Simmel, G. (1964). The isolated individual and the dyad. In K. H. Wolff (Trans. & Ed.), *The sociology of Georg Simmel* (pp. 123-124). New York: Free Press. (Original work published 1908)

70. Clinard (1962), in *Society, culture, and drinking patterns,* p. 271.

71. Ritzer (1992), *Sociological theory,* pp. 165-169.

72. American Psychiatric Association. (1994). *Diagnostic and statistical manual of mental disorders* (4th ed.). Washington, DC: Author.

73. Helzer, J., Burnam, A., & McEvoy, L. (1991). Alcohol abuse and dependence. In L. N. Robins & D. A. Regier (Eds.), *Psychiatric disorders in America* (pp. 81-98). New York: Free Press.

74. Trice, H. M., & Staudenmeier, W. J., Jr. (1989). A sociocultural history of Alcoholics Anonymous. In M. Galanter (Ed.), *Recent developments in alcoholism* (pp. 11-35). New York: Plenum.

75. Madsen, W. (1979). Alcoholics Anonymous as a crisis cult. In M. Marshall (Ed.), *Beliefs, behaviors, & alcoholic beverages* (p. 385). Ann Arbor: University of Michigan Press.

76. Trice, H. M. (1966). *Alcoholism in America* (pp. 106-107). New York: McGraw-Hill.

77. Madsen (1979), in *Beliefs, behaviors, & alcoholic beverages,* p. 385.

78. Trice (1966), *Alcoholism in America,* pp. 106-107.

79. Collins, R. (1988). *Theoretical sociology* (pp. 36-38). New York: Harcourt Brace Jovanovich.

80. Staudenmeier, W. J., Jr. (1994, October). *From moral entrepreneurs to economic entrepreneurs: Rationalization and disenchantment in the American social movement against alcoholism.* Paper presented at the 38th Scottish Alcohol Problems Research Symposium, Pitlochry, Scotland.

81. Schmidt, L., & Weisner, C. (1993). Developments in alcoholism treatment. In M. Galanter (Ed.), *Recent developments in alcoholism* (Vol. 11). New York: Plenum.

82. Staudenmeier (1994), *From moral entrepreneurs to economic entrepreneurs,* p. 10.

83. Münch (1994), *Sociological theory,* p. 102.

84. Bruton, B. T., & Schafer, R. B. (1989). *Social control and student drinking behavior: An exploratory case study of an issueless riot.* Paper presented at the meeting of the Midwest Sociological Society, St. Louis, MO.

85. Honigmann, J. (1979). Dynamics of drinking in an Austrian village. In M. Marshall (Ed.), *Beliefs, behaviors, & alcoholic beverages* (pp. 418-419). Ann Arbor: University of Michigan Press.

86. Honigmann (1979), in *Beliefs, behaviors, & alcoholic beverages,* pp. 427-428.

87. Heath, D. B. (1962). Drinking patterns of the Bolivian Camba. In D. J. Pittman & C. R. Snyder (Eds.), *Society, culture, and drinking patterns* (pp. 25-26). New York: John Wiley.

88. Marshall, M. (1979). *Weekend warriors: Alcohol in a Micronesian culture* (p. 130). Palo Alto, CA: Mayfield.

89. Marshall (1979), *Weekend warriors,* p. 130.

90. MacAndrew, C., & Edgerton, R. (1969). *Drunken comportment: A social explanation* (p. 165). New York: Aldine. I am not sure, however, that Simmel would agree with this statement because he saw the pernicious, unwanted effects of the realm of objective culture on subjective culture. If objective culture creates conditions that lead to drunken comportment that is unwanted, can the individual change it or can he or she only at best avoid it?

91. MacAndrew & Edgerton (1969), *Drunken comportment: A social explanation,* p. 173.

92. Chesterton, G. K. (1925), *Tremendous Trifles* (pp. 166-167). New York: Dodd, Mead and Company.

93. Habermas, J. (1996). M. Deflem (Trans.) Georg Simmel on Philosophy and Culture: Postscript to a Collection of Essays. *Critical Inquiry, 22,* 1.

94. Scaff, L. (2000). Georg Simmel. In G. Ritzer (Ed.), *The Blackwell Companion to Major Social Theorists* (p. 253). Malden, MA: Blackwell.

95. David Frisby calls Simmel "the first sociologist of modernity." Frisby, D. (1997). Georg Simmel: First Sociologist of Modernity. In R. Boudon, M Cherkaoui, and J. Alexander (Eds.), *The Classical Tradition in Sociology, The European Tradition,* Volume II (pp. 323-349). Thousand Oaks, CA: Sage.

96. Ritzer (1992), *Sociological theory,* pp. 160-161.

97. Simmel (1971), in *On individuality and social forms,* p. 234.

Discussion Questions

1. Think about the friendship dyads of which you have been a part. Apply Simmel's ideas about the dyad and triad from this chapter to one of your examples. What changes took place when a third person joined the group?

2. What are some of the current conflicts in American society over alcohol or other drugs or both? Do these conflicts, as Simmel suggests, temporarily bind the two parties together in intensive interaction? Does the conflict lead to greater centralization and unity within each party to the conflict? What other effects does the conflict seem to have on each of the groups? Defend your position.

3. Like clothes, academic majors and ideas come into and go out of fashion. What changes in fashion have occurred in the recent past on your campus? (Hint: Ask librarians and professors for their insights and get the registrar's list of majors.) Choose one example and apply Simmel's ideas on fashion to that case.

PART II

Contemporary Theories and Their Connections to the Classics

Introduction

Peter Kivisto

The sociological imagination today is informed by numerous theoretical perspectives. A by no means inclusive list of some of the most influential theories in the discipline would include structural functionalism, systems theory, exchange theory, rational choice theory, poststructuralism, structuration theory, symbolic interactionism, ethnomethodology, dramaturgy, phenomenology, neo-Marxism, critical theory, feminist theory, globalization theory, and postmodernism.

Thus, unless I wanted to produce a multivolume collection, I was forced to make decisions about which theories would be included. All the previously noted theories have had a significant influence on contemporary sociology, and by making the decision to include particular theories while excluding others, I am not implicitly arguing that the ones selected for inclusion are somehow more important than the others. The main reason for selecting the particular theories represented in Part II is that, taken together, they afford the student reader the opportunity to get a sense of the range and variability of social theory.

If one were to divide all theories into two categories, it would be possible to do so by looking to see if the theories emphasize the role of humans (typically referred to as actors or agents) in creating their social conditions or if the theories emphasize the influence of social conditions (often called structures or forces) on individual attitudes and behaviors. The chapters included herein are equally divided between these two foci.

Chapter 5, coauthored by Paul Colomy and Laura Ross Greiner, is devoted to a neofunctionalist examination of institutional responses to adolescents and crime. Their theoretical perspective is a recent development that has arisen as an effort to both build on and revise older functionalist tradition in sociology. Functionalism was the dominant theoretical paradigm in sociology during the 1950s and 1960s, a period during which Harvard sociologist Talcott Parsons emerged as the most influential social theorist of his generation. However, by the 1970s, critics of functionalism had become increasingly vocal and dismissive. While many were prepared to claim that functionalism was dead, a younger group of theorists associated with UCLA sociologist Jeffrey Alexander concluded that although functionalism needed to be substantially revised, it would be a serious mistake to reject it. Instead, they argued on behalf of what has become known as "neofunctionalism." Colomy is one of the theorists responsible for the promotion of this perspective. After providing an overview of the key strengths and weaknesses of functionalism, the authors present a discussion of neofunctionalism's efforts to retain what was valuable about functionalism, while simultaneously showing how it has attempted to redress the problematic features of the tradition.

Colomy and Greiner employ a neofunctionalist perspective in their examination of the ways American society has responded to adolescents who are chronic criminals or who have committed serious crimes. They seek to understand the circumstances in which the public and lawmakers have shifted from a perspective that treats youth as capable of rehabilitation to a viewpoint that increasingly wants to get tough by punishing them as adults. The particular case study that serves to highlight this topic focuses on the Youth Offender System that was passed into law in Colorado in 1993, after what was described—inaccurately, as it turns out—as an unprecedented "summer of violence." The chapter assesses the factors, from the cultural to the institutional, that put into motion and shaped the political response to these perceptions.

Christopher Prendergast, in Chapter 6, offers what he refers to as a structuralist explanation of why African Americans pay more for new cars than white people do. His theoretical perspective makes use of various interconnected theoretical strands, the most important of which include the exchange theory most closely associated with the work of the late Richard Emerson and the rational choice theory developed by the late James Coleman. In addition, he uses elements from a range of other theoretical perspectives, including those of French theorist Pierre Bourdieu, phenomenological theorist Alfred Schutz, and action theorist Carl Menger.

The reason for all this theory becomes evident in his presentation. Prendergast wants to show why we need an alternative to the most obvious explanation we are likely to offer for the answer to the above posited question: prejudice and discrimination. Given the racism of American society, this layperson's theoretical account would appear to be more than plausible. However, a closer examination of the process of car buying, from both the salesperson's and the customer's perspectives, reveals the shortcomings of this explanation and the need to look for an alternative. In the process of weaving together his structuralist explanation of the car price mystery, Prendergast makes a powerful case for the singular significance of this particular kind of theorizing for the sociological enterprise.

Chapter 7, by Steven P. Dandaneau, examines the critical theory of Jürgen Habermas. As will be evident immediately, the issues addressed in this article bear a close resemblance to those discussed in the chapter on Marx. This is not surprising because critical theory has been profoundly influenced by Marx's thought. Perhaps less obviously, critical theory has also been shaped by Weber's ideas. Critical theory was developed, beginning in the 1920s, by a number of German scholars who came to be identified as the Frankfurt School. Habermas is the most important inheritor of this tradition of social theory, and he is widely regarded as one of the three or four most important theorists in contemporary sociology.

Critical theorists have been particularly interested in the changing character of capitalist industrial society and in the struggle between democratic and authoritarian political systems. Critical theory often operates at a high level of abstraction that is difficult for students both to comprehend and to connect to concrete events. Dandaneau, having studied the devastating impact of deindustrialization on his hometown of Flint, Michigan (the city featured in *Roger & Me,* the highly acclaimed first film by Michael Moore, who more recently directed *Bowling for Columbine* and *Fahrenheit 9/11*), has found that the insights from critical theory can be employed to make sense of the factors that have contributed to Flint's problems and to offer some sense of future possibilities. Thus, in this chapter, the focus is on social structural forces shaping the community.

In contrast, Chapter 8 is concerned with the role of actors in social construction, in this case with the social construction of the body. Two eminent feminist scholars, Judith Lorber and Patricia Yancey Martin, have used various strands of contemporary feminist theory to explore such everyday life issues as gender and sport as well as problems associated with eating disorders.

Feminist theory (or more appropriately, perhaps, theories) appeared on the sociological scene in the past three decades, emerging out of the women's movement of the 1960s and closely associated with the establishment of programs of women's studies on college and university campuses. Given these origins, there are several unique features to feminist theory. First, it links efforts to better understand gender issues with political activism aimed at ending the various forms of patriarchal domination that have resulted in the subordination of women. Second, feminist theory is inherently interdisciplinary—reaching out not only to other social sciences but also to the arts and humanities. Third, because the classics tended to ignore or downplay the significance of gender relations, feminist theory is less indebted to the founders than are other theories (it should be noted in fairness to them, however, that both Simmel and Weber wrote rather perceptively on gender topics).

Lorber and Martin show how gender permeates social life. Gender definitions and distinctions tend to be taken for granted and are generally seen as universal and unchanging. Feminist theory is a powerful antidote to these views, having proven itself to be an effective tool in the process of making the invisible visible.

Chapters 9 and 10 are also actor, rather than structure, focused. Gary Alan Fine and Kent Sandstrom provide an overview of a distinctly American version of interpretive sociology known as symbolic interaction. The label of this school of thought was coined by Herbert Blumer, who taught at the University of Chicago and the University of California at Berkeley. This theory school is rooted in American pragmatist thought as developed by such philosophers as William James, Charles Pierce, John Dewey, and especially George Herbert Mead, as well as in the sociological approach advanced by Robert E. Park and others at the Chicago School of Sociology. According to Blumer, symbolic interaction theory begins with the assumption that people act in the social world on the basis of the meaning imputed to various situations and contexts. However, meaning is not simply an individual construct, but rather emerges out of interaction and via ongoing interpretive processes. The use of the word *symbol* in the label is significant insofar as it emphasizes the fact that humans rely on symbols as tools in the process of meaning creation.

Fine and Sandstrom illustrate the theoretical advantages of this perspective in their examination of the ways that people who view themselves as environmentalists construct the meaning of nature and utilize ideologies to frame their particular relationship with "nature" and with social concerns, practices, and policies that impact the environment. One of the tasks that the authors set out to accomplish is to articulate a distinctly symbolic interactionist perspective on the nature and the role of ideology. In presenting their case, they make use of field work done by Fine on mushroomers in Minnesota—in the process revealing that symbolic interactionists tend to prefer research strategies that are variously referred to as qualitative, ethnographic, or participant observation methods.

In Chapter 10, Peter Kivisto and Dan Pittman examine the dramaturgical sociology of Erving Goffman. There are clear similarities between this orientation and the approach in the preceding chapter. This is not surprising because Goffman was trained at the University of Chicago, which was a key center of symbolic interaction theory. Temperamentally, Goffman bears a decided resemblance to Simmel because both wrote with a unique ironic style. Somewhat surprisingly, however, given the fact that Durkheim is usually seen as a structuralist sociologist, Goffman has indicated his affinity with Durkheimian sociology. Essentially, Goffman is concerned with the ways people manage to act within the constraints imposed by preexisting social structures.

Thus, although interpretive sociology examines how people, individually and collectively, construct their social realities, the dramaturgical sociology advanced by Goffman examines how people fashion and act out various roles in what turns out to be a rather constricted set of options. Often interpretive theorists tend to downplay the constraints of social structure by concentrating on the creative ability of people to shape and modify structures. In stark contrast, Goffman thinks that people operate within circumscribed social conditions: Their freedom of action appears much more limited.

For this reason, Kivisto and Pittman find his work particularly useful in exploring the highly scripted world of sales and service. Rather than emphasizing how actors freely create their roles, this chapter, in Goffmanesque fashion, explores how people manage and manipulate the roles they play in the interactional realm of consumer culture. Dramaturgical sociology highlights some of the dilemmas and tensions inherent in people's identification with or distance from the roles they play as well as some of the difficulties that arise as they attempt to effectively and convincingly embrace certain identities and perform various roles.

In Chapter 11, George Ritzer picks up on topics related to both the preceding chapter and his contribution on McDonaldization. In this chapter, however, he addresses a recent development in social theory: postmodernism. Unlike some theorists, who view postmodernism as a theory that chronologically comes after modernist theories and therefore should be seen as reflecting a qualitatively new type of society, Ritzer thinks that postmodernism should best be viewed as complementing other theories.

Moreover, as this chapter indicates, Ritzer thinks that although Marxist-inspired theories remain particularly useful in understanding productive processes (e.g., topics such as those addressed by Walsh and Zacharias-Walsh in Chapter 1), the distinctive value of postmodern theory can best be appreciated when looking at what Ritzer refers to as the " 'new' means of consumption," which involves the growing prevalence and significance of such phenomena as large chain restaurants and stores, shopping malls, home shopping on television or over the Internet, infomercials, and telemarketing. Although there is a clear parallel in topics to the preceding chapter, postmodern theory opens up for inquiry issues related to the pervasiveness of simulations of reality in postmodern consumer culture and to the advent of what is called "hyperreality." As with his chapter on McDonaldization, Ritzer is particularly interested in the more problematic features of the new means of consumption. He concludes the chapter with suggestions about how people might go about both coping with and also, at times, subverting disturbing features of consumer culture.

Turning to Chapter 12, Norman Denzin's essay on "cinematic society" is intended to complement Ritzer's essay on postmodernism. Denzin comes out of the symbolic interactionist tradition, but without abandoning it, he has made what can be called the "postmodern turn." Much of his recent research has focused on the powerful impact that the mass media, and in particular television and film, have had on contemporary societies, wherein the boundaries between the real and the hyperreal become blurred. Since symbol interaction offers theoretical insights into social psychology, it is not surprising that Denzin is particularly concerned with the impact that postmodern "cinematic society" has had on conceptions of the self. In this regard, his concerns also dovetail with those of Goffman, though with a difference due to his conviction that the mediated nature of perceptions of the self and of social relations is qualitatively different in the postmodern epoch.

One of the features that makes Denzin's essay distinctive is that he seeks to locate what he defines as the "reflexive interview" as a methodological tool appropriate to this new historical conjuncture. In particular, he explores the significance of reflexivity in conducting ethnographic research, raising the prospect that such an approach can allow us to move beyond media mediation to something that people might dare call truth. Ironically, he finds clues to this approach in the cinema itself, particularly in the documentary film by Trinh T. Minh-ha, *Surname Viet Given Name Nam.*

In Chapter 13, William H. Swatos, Jr., examines another recent development in social theory: globalization. That people around the globe are more interconnected and interdependent than ever before is one of the hallmarks of our age. Globalization theory is an attempt to make sense of these developments. It attempts to provide a way of examining, for instance, the workings of the global economy, in which multinational corporations not only compete internationally but also appear to be severing the attachments they once had to the nations where they originally operated. Flint, Michigan, cannot be fully understood without also understanding what is happening in developing nations. Likewise, penetration into new markets is a characteristic feature of the global economy, as in the introduction of McDonald's and other fast-food restaurants into Russia and the rest of the former communist bloc.

Globalization, as Swatos indicates in his study of the impact of fundamentalist religious beliefs on world politics, is also having an impact on politics and culture. As a reaction to many aspects of modernity, religious fundamentalisms emanating from all of the major world religions have had an impact on politics, both nationally and transnationally. As Swatos reveals, this is nowhere more evident than in the contemporary Middle East, where the fundamentalist ideals of the three historical Occidental religions—Judaism, Christianity, and Islam—are engaged in a conflict of worldviews that has in recent years produced global political consequences.

Collectively, these nine chapters provide students with an appreciation of the diversity, adaptability, and value of a cross section of major contemporary theoretical orientations. They reveal continuities with the topics and theoretical approaches of the classics. Building on them, but going beyond them, both in terms of what they study and in terms of the particular theoretical lenses that they have crafted, we see theorists today influenced by the same sociological imagination that inspired the founders of the discipline.

CHAPTER 5

Criminalizing Transgressing Youth

A Neofunctionalist Analysis of Institution Building

Paul Colomy and Laura Ross Greiner

Paul Colomy *is Professor and Chair of Sociology at the University of Denver, where he teaches classic and contemporary theory. His research uses neofunctionalism and other theoretical traditions to examine the creation of new institutions and roles. He is particularly interested in understanding the origins and transformation of the juvenile justice system. This chapter is part of a book,* Beyond Delinquency: The Summer of Violence and the Construction of the Youthful Offender System, *which he is coauthoring with Laura Ross Greiner.*

Laura Ross Greiner *is an independent writer and consultant working primarily for the Center for the Study and Prevention of Violence at the University of Colorado, Boulder. She helped establish the Center in 1992, and her institution-building efforts included assembling a national information house on youth violence. She received her MA from the University of Colorado and her PhD from the University of Denver. Her major research interests are youth violence, juvenile justice, and the sociology of mass media.*

The last decade has witnessed a virtual sea change in the way American society responds to juveniles who commit chronic or serious crimes.[1] For most of the 20th century, law-breaking youth were sent to juvenile courts and, if found delinquent, received relatively mild sanctions (compared to the punishments meted out to adults guilty of the same offense). Convinced that adolescents were malleable and could be redeemed, juvenile justice officials aspired to rehabilitate delinquent youth. Dubious about a youngster's ability to form criminal intent and explicitly rejecting the language of punishment and retribution, these officials were principally concerned with the child's best interests. These notions justified a separate system of justice in which adolescents were adjudicated (not tried) and were liable for no more than a 2-year term in a reform school where, in theory, they were treated (not punished). A cumbersome waiver hearing was reserved for the most extreme cases, which were sometimes transferred to adult criminal court. The very cumbersomeness of these hearings discouraged prosecutors and judges from requesting transfers and reaffirmed the presumption that juvenile court was the most appropriate forum for transgressing youth.

Today, that presumption has been largely discredited as soft-minded sentimentalism. Reacting to an apparently growing legion of really bad kids who commit shocking crimes and are reputedly contemptuous toward the juvenile justice system's ministrations, lawmakers across the country have approved, at breathtaking speed, a spate of far-reaching statutes. From 1992 to 1995, 48 of 51 state legislatures (including the District of Columbia), enacted laws targeting serious juvenile offenders.[2] In all but 10 states, these laws make "it easier to prosecute juveniles in criminal courts."[3] In 25 states, new legislation gives judges additional sentencing options to incarcerate young people for longer periods of time. Openly espousing the language of punishment and retribution, 23 states now impose more severe penalties, including confinement in adult prisons, to sanction youth convicted in criminal courts.[4] Taken together, these innovations reflect a pattern of institutional and legal change that has been called "(re)criminalization," a process of relinquishing elements of the juvenile justice system (and certain categories of transgressing adolescents) to the adult criminal justice system.[5]

This chapter analyzes how this process unfolded in a single state. On September 13, 1993, Colorado Governor Roy Romer signed a law establishing the Youth Offender System. This legislation, along with several other measures, was introduced, debated, and amended during a 5-day special session of the Colorado General Assembly convened to address the problem of youth violence. Two elements of this measure are particularly noteworthy. First, the bill gives considerable discretion to district attorneys, who now decide whether to direct-file on young lawbreakers. (The direct-file provision effectively circumvents cumbersome judicial waiver hearings and makes it much easier to charge and try juveniles in adult court.) Second, the bill authorized construction of a new tier in the correctional apparatus. The 14- to 18-year-olds sent to the Youthful Offender System (YOS) are prosecuted as adults for crimes ranging from theft to manslaughter and, if convicted, are sentenced to the adult prison system. That sentence is suspended, conditional on completing a term ranging from 2 to 6 years in YOS. Those failing the program are returned to court for imposition of the original sentence and remanded to an adult correctional facility. With its no-nonsense, military-like regimen, stringent discipline, and succeed-or-perish philosophy, YOS represents "the hammer" Colorado lawmakers said was necessary to combat serious juvenile crime. At the same time, legislators envisioned this new tier as a "second last chance" for youthful offenders, and the teens housed at YOS are provided with treatment and a variety of educational, vocational, cognitive-behavioral, life-skills, and mentoring programs. Believing that youth violence had become a critical problem requiring a forceful response, Colorado policymakers allocated substantial sums to this 480-bed facility: Over $37 million was spent to construct YOS; operating costs run another $10.2 million annually.

Although many other states have approved legislation similar to Colorado's YOS law, the passage of this bill was hardly inevitable. To the contrary, when initially proposed, the YOS statute was regarded as a dubious proposition. During its regular session, which concluded in mid-May 1993, the Colorado General Assembly rejected several bills that were moderate versions of the YOS measure approved 4 months later. Writing in early August, shortly after the special session on youth violence had been announced but a month before it opened, and distressed by the dismal prospect of a fruitless repeat performance, a reporter predicted that "lawmakers will have a sense deja vu, already having considered—and killed—many of the issues expected to come before them again in the special session."[6] In the regular session, the legislature had rebuffed a provision that would have asked voters to consider a one-quarter-cent increase in the state's sales tax to generate additional revenue for prison construction. Another proposal recommended expanding "the seriously overcrowded Colorado Division of Youth Services [the agency responsible for the state's reform schools]," but while lawmakers approved this plan, they refused to fund it, thereby rendering the legislation an empty gesture.[7] Ironically, a cost-cutting statute approved in the regular session reduced sentences for some crimes to slow the growth of prisons. The governor, however, was not dissuaded by the seemingly long odds. Intuiting a fateful change, he sensed that similar, and even more costly and controversial renditions of measures rejected in May were "more likely to pass" in September.[8] "There is a different atmosphere now than there was in the spring when the session was here," the governor assured the worried journalist, and in this altered environment, there was "a much more radical need for action."[9]

The governor was right. Between May and August 1993, a significant transformation had occurred, and there was mounting pressure on local and state officials to "do something" about street violence. From May 2, when a baby at the Denver Zoo was wounded by a stray bullet, to August 2, when an elementary school teacher was murdered in a suburban parking lot, print and electronic media gave extensive coverage to several "high-profile" violent crimes, a number of which were allegedly committed by gang-affiliated juveniles. These incidents became the centerpiece of an unfolding media event, eventually dubbed "the Summer of Violence" by the local press, which continued until mid-September when lawmakers concluded their deliberations. The unremitting coverage of this putative crime wave heightened fear of violence, prompting some residents to flee the supposedly deadly environs of Denver for the alluring (but ultimately elusive) safety of the suburbs, while others organized marches to "take back the streets" or badgered public officials to "crack down" on violent youth. This was the "different atmosphere" in which the governor divined "a much more radical need for action" and convened the special session.

Employing the neofunctionalist perspective, this chapter explains how new institutions, such as the Colorado YOS, are created. The founding of YOS is one instance of a general process known as "institution building," and neofunctionalists maintain that this process is profoundly shaped by both the encompassing social and cultural context and the efforts of institutional entrepreneurs, the individuals, groups, and/or organizations who assume leadership roles in episodes of institutional change. After outlining neofunctionalism's fundamental principles, the empirical part of this chapter uses content analysis and a qualitative assessment of the print media's coverage of the Summer of Violence to indicate how street crime became a visible social problem. We then discuss the crystallization of a new category of transgressing adolescents and the complementary claim that the existing juvenile justice system had failed to respond adequately to this novel "breed" of offender. Finally, we examine how a prominent institutional entrepreneur, Governor Roy Romer, mobilized support for a new institution (YOS) designed to control and treat serious juvenile lawbreakers.

Neofunctionalism

Neofunctionalism's central concepts are most effectively presented as a critical response to the functionalist tradition. The latter is a macrosociological perspective that examines the creation, maintenance, and alteration of enduring social practices, institutions, and entire societies. Émile Durkheim, a French sociologist who published several provocative books between 1890 and 1915, is often regarded as the classic founder of functionalism. This approach was articulated most forcefully, however, by a group of American sociologists, including Talcott Parsons, Robert K. Merton, Wilbert Moore, Bernard Barber, and Robin Williams, during the 25 years following World War II. Although functionalism dominated the sociological imagination from 1945 to 1970, it also spawned considerable controversy and critique. Acknowledging the merit of many (but not all) of these criticisms, a younger generation of scholars led by Jeffrey Alexander began (in the early 1980s) responding to the critics' legitimate objections by revising the postwar version of functionalism in significant ways.[10] Bringing together the valuable elements of orthodox functionalism with the insights of several other sociological traditions, these revisions have culminated in a substantially modified rendition of functionalism, a rendition its proponents call neofunctionalism. We discuss neofunctionalism in terms of four key notions: problem solving, structural differentiation, systems, and culture.

Problem solving. Traditional functionalism likens societies (and all types of social units, stretching from dyads to world systems) to problem-solving entities. If a society is to persist, functionalists assert, it must address certain vital problems in a reasonably satisfactory way. (Several terms were coined to characterize these vital problems, including *requirements, functions, needs, prerequisites, exigencies,* and *functional prerequisites.*) An enduring society must, for example, socialize its youngest members, produce and distribute food and other essential goods and services, and devise mechanisms to control deviance and contain conflict. If a society does not satisfactorily address these (and other) prerequisites, it will experience considerable strain, and if its failure to address these problems continues, it will collapse.

A definitive catalog of the essential exigencies confronting all societies has never been compiled. Nevertheless, both proponents and critics of functionalism agree that Parsons offers the most incisive statement of functional requirements now available.[11] Pitched at a high level of abstraction, Parsons's model identifies four universal problems confronting every social unit. *Adaptation*, the first function, refers to how a social system supports itself in relationship to an external environment. When societies are the unit of analysis, adaptation refers to the production and distribution of the basic necessities of life. *Goal attainment*, the second prerequisite, is concerned with the collective definition of goals and the mobilizing and coordinating processes associated with reaching these goals. *Integration* underscores the necessity of sustaining a minimal level of cohesion among members of the social unit. Finally, *latency* (or pattern maintenance) highlights the problem of maintaining basic value patterns. (An acronym, AGIL, is shorthand frequently used when discussing Parsons's analysis of *a*daptation, *g*oal *a*ttainment, *i*ntegration, and *l*atency.) Parsons believed that social organizations of every size and type are built around these exigencies and claimed that the AGIL grid supplied an indispensable tool for comparative and historical studies of social life.

Extending the metaphor that likens societies to problem-solving entities, functionalists portray ongoing social practices and structures as provisional answers or solutions to fundamental prerequisites. Families and schools, for instance, are institutions that emerge to answer the problem of socializing and educating the young. (In Parsons's terminology, these institutions are organized around the problems of latency and integration.) Economic institutions such as the free market, however, address the problem of producing and distributing the basic necessities of life (the problem of adaptation). Political systems, whether democratic or totalitarian, attempt to articulate collective goals and mobilize citizens in support of shared objectives (the problem of goal attainment).

Neofunctionalists have recast the notion of problem solving. First, they suggest that the prerequisites discussed by Parsons identify only very broad, open-ended parameters, and these generalized exigencies alone cannot fully explain the particular practices and structures that emerge in a given society. Second, they supplement functionalism's characterization of institutions as problem-solving entities with the observation that problem solving is also a cognitive framework and a powerful rhetoric deeply rooted in modern societies. A pervasive, problem-solving schema, in other words, shapes the way many elites—reformers, citizens, and social scientists— think about and evaluate institutions. The rhetoric of problem solving is often used to justify existing practices, with supporters of the status quo insisting that established institutions serve vital functions. But the very same problem-solving rhetoric is also employed to assail current arrangements for their failure to fulfill essential tasks. Moreover, the perception that important needs are not being met effectively frequently fuels calls to reform existing institutions or to create new ones.

Third, neofunctionalists suggest that citizens and officials usually assess practices and institutions not by reference to abstract, universal functions (e.g., adaptation or latency) but in light of more specific concerns (e.g., an apparent rise in crime or a decline in students' test scores). These concrete problems are socially constructed, and episodes of institutional change cannot be considered apart from the processes by which such problems are identified and made publicly visible. Salient social problems that appear to exceed the problem-solving capacities of existing structures are a potent impetus to alter the established institutional order. And the socially defined character and scope of these unresolved problems vitally affect the types of alterations proposed and approved.

Structural differentiation. Over the course of human history, societies have devised many different institutional arrangements to address the exigencies of social life. These variable institutional arrangements are not equally effective, however. In the long run, functionalists hypothesize, more specialized or differentiated institutions have responded more efficiently and effectively to functional perquisites than have multifunctional (or multipurpose) institutions. In an important sense, the proliferation of increasingly specialized structures represents a master trend of modern social change. Two hundred years ago, the family was a multifunctional institution, in that it fulfilled many different tasks, such as economic production, procreation, socialization, care for the infirm elderly, and social control. Today, many of these chores have been delegated to specialized institutions. Economic production, for instance, is no longer addressed by the family but by business enterprises legally and institutionally separated from family life, whereas crime control is increasingly delegated to differentiated social control agents such as police and courts. The family, too, has become a more specialized institution, one whose primary tasks include procreation, socialization of the very young, and emotional support for family members.

Functionalists attribute the growth of differentiated institutions to an imperative toward greater efficiency and effectiveness built into the very fabric of modern societies. The dissatisfaction that arises when functional requirements are not met effectively generates innumerable reform proposals.[12] Because more specialized institutions enable societies to operate more effectively and efficiently, reform programs advocating higher levels of differentiation tend to be, in the terms of neoevolutionary theory, "selected out" and "stabilized"[13] Structural differentiation can be understood, then, as an unconsciously evolved device modern societies have "hit upon" to increase their overall effectiveness and efficiency.

Neofunctionalists agree that differentiation accurately describes something fundamental about the structure of modern societies. But they also argue that a satisfactory explanation of this master trend of social change must supplement allusions to increased efficiency and effectiveness with a consideration of how individuals and groups affect the course of institutional change. New institutional arrangements are due in part to the efforts of institutional entrepreneurs, the individuals, groups, and organizations that assume leadership roles in episodes of institutional change.[14] These movers and shakers are not, moreover, altruistic agents of greater societal effectiveness or efficiency. To the contrary, their proposed reforms are impossible to separate from their own particular material and ideal interests. Not surprisingly, resource-rich elites and secondary elites, including powerful state actors and various professional groups, are disproportionately represented among successful entrepreneurial groups.[15] But few elite groups possess the resources, power, and legitimation necessary to impose their institutional vision on the larger society unilaterally. Consequently, the success of many institution-building projects depends largely on entrepreneurial groups' ability to cultivate allies and defuse resistance. Coalitions, compromises, entreaties for public support, and recurring struggles with opponents are staples of institution building. And as a result, the course of institutional change is shaped by political dynamics as much (or more) than it is by concerns for greater efficiency and effectiveness.[16]

Systems. Functionalism conceptualizes societies (and other social units) as systems comprising autonomous-but-interdependent institutions (or subsystems).[17] This approach rejects reductionist theories, which claim that one subsystem (e.g., the economy or the state) dictates what transpires in other subsystems (e.g., law or religion). Each institution is guided, in large measure, by its own internal logic. Science, for example, is organized around distinctive premises and procedures, just as religion, politics, and the military are. These distinctive logics impart considerable (but not unlimited) autonomy to each institution. At the same time, these partially autonomous subsystems are interrelated in complex ways. Parsons's interchange model uses the terms outputs and inputs to describe the interdependent relations between different institutions.[18] In essence, this model suggests that the operation of any single institution (e.g., schools) depends on the inputs it receives from other institutions (e.g., families, business, and government), while that institution, in turn, produces (part of) what the other subsystems require to perform effectively.

Neofunctionalists have extended the concept of systems in three ways. First, they caution that the notion of institutions regulated by a distinctive logic must not obscure the fact that different positions within the same institution frequently spawn disparate perceptions and interests.[19] For example, although the child's best interests and the preservation of public safety are the principal concerns of contemporary juvenile justice, this overarching institutional logic does not preclude chronic conflicts from arising between judges, probation officers, reform schools, residential care providers, parole officers, and other participants in this subsystem.[20]

Second, noting that the interchange model is intended to describe the interworkings of a perfectly integrated social system—a conceptual ideal type that no actual society has ever approximated—neofunctionalists have supplemented Parsons's analysis of the mutually rewarding, interinstitutional exchanges with examinations of the tensions within and between institutions. When one subsystem fails to fulfill its particular exigencies, for example, other subsystems dependent on its outputs will be pressed to perform its functions, even though they often lack the necessary resources. Elementary school instructors, for instance, sometimes complain that they must devote inordinate time attending to a few unruly pupils. Believing that these children's emotional, psychological, and/or medical needs are the responsibility of families and health care providers, these educators claim that when these unmet needs are displaced onto teachers (in the form of disruptive classroom conduct), it is nearly impossible to provide a quality education for all their students.

The lead-and-lag principle identifies another common source of institutional strain. Presuming a social system composed of several parts (or subsystems), the idea of leads and lags maintains that rapid alterations in any single subsystem can outstrip the responsive capacity of other (interdependent) subsystems. In the classic statement of this principle, William Ogburn wrote,

> Not all parts of our [society] are changing at the same speed or at the same time. Some are rapidly moving forward while others are lagging. These unequal rates of change in economic life, in government, in education, in science, and religion, make zones of danger and points of tension.[21]

Third, neofunctionalists recommend treating the notion of system (and subsystems) as "environments of action" that shape the change-oriented activities of institutional entrepreneurs.[22] Entrepreneurs' projects are not articulated in a sociological vacuum: Their indictment of the existing institutional order, their proposed alterations of that order, and their strategies for attracting allies and overcoming opponents are influenced by the environing systems in which they pursue their reforms. From the standpoint of entrepreneurs, these encompassing systems comprise a constellation of opportunities and constraints that render some reforms and some mobilizing strategies more feasible than others.

Culture. How do modern societies containing scores of specialized institutions and hundreds of heterogeneous subgroups manage to sustain themselves without dissolving into an anarchic "war of all against all?" Recognizing that coercion, artifice, and domination are indelible features of social life, functionalists nevertheless insist that these dynamics alone do not adequately account for the coherence of complex social orders. They attribute the modicum of social integration characteristic of many modern societies to two main mechanisms. First, an important product of increasing structural differentiation is the emergence of specialized, integrative institutions and processes—for example, inclusive citizenship rights, religious ceremonies, athletic contests, media events, and nationally celebrated holidays—that affirm some solidarity among people who otherwise might have little in common.[23] Second, as modern societies differentiate and as their populations (and the heterogeneity of these populations) expand, the values they espouse are generalized and universalized.[24] The prevailing value commitments of contemporary postindustrial societies, in other words, are abstract and are formulated in an inclusive way so that, in principle, they apply equally to every citizen. For example, some social scientists suggest that much of the continuity and change evident throughout American history is due to the fairly high level of agreement on the country's core values (values that are sometimes referred to as the American Creed), including individualism, freedom, equality, democracy, achievement, and work.[25] Incorporated into different institutions and internalized by individuals (during the course of their early socialization), these shared values enable the diverse components of a large, differentiated society to coexist and bond rather than disintegrate into chronic chaos.[26]

Neofunctionalists have rounded out the functionalist conception of culture in three ways. First, they supplement the analysis of consensus on core values with discussions of the cultural roots of conflict and change. They note, for example, that many cultural systems contain strikingly inconsistent elements. In American society, the inclusive values of freedom and equal opportunity for all are opposed by a potent exclusive tradition of sexism, homophobia, and racism, which historically has supported the privileged position of white, Anglo-Saxon, Protestant (WASP) males over women, gays and lesbians, and racial, ethnic, and religious minorities.[27] Another source of contention and change is the wide gap between cherished cultural ideals (e.g., equality and freedom) and the actual realities of social life (e.g., marked inequalities and repression). When these cultural ideals are taken seriously, they can produce significant instability, fueling attacks on the way things are in the name of the way things should be.[28]

Neofunctionalists also contend that cultural systems are no less preoccupied with the negative than they are with the positive. Functionalist theories of culture focus on values, which are commonly defined as socially shared ideas about what is good, right, and desirable. But this equation of culture with positive, idealized imagery omits a critically important consideration: The bad, evil, and undesirable are key elements of every cultural system, and they are "symbolized every bit as elaborately as the good."[29] Inspired by Durkheim's classic analysis of religious systems, neofunctionalists suggest that the meanings and symbols most central to social life are frequently imbued with religious-like properties, frequently assuming a sacred or profane cast. Sacred symbols "provide images of purity and they charge those who are committed to them with protecting their referents from harm. Profane symbols embody this harm; they provide images of pollution, identifying actions, groups, and processes that must be defended against."[30] The sacred and profane are "highly charged" emotional symbols, and when they are used to classify particular acts as transgressions against the community's conception of the sacred and to portray the transgressors as embodiments of the profane, these highly charged symbols are likely to trigger a dramatic community response.

Third, neofunctionalists direct attention to the cultural dimensions of entrepreneurs' projects. When identifying crucial public problems or unmet social needs, criticizing current arrangements, and proposing alterations in the institutional order, entrepreneurs invoke, often in innovative ways, shared cultural traditions and symbol systems. In doing so, they treat culture as a tool kit, adroitly wielding its elements to construct persuasive rhetorical appeals.[31] But it must be recognized that symbol systems have an internal logic of their own, one whose tacit assumptions and taken-for-granted status render culture partially opaque, even to those who use it competently.[32] Consequently, explicating what can be called entrepreneurs' signifying or interpretive work[33] requires consideration of the meanings they consciously articulate, as well as an analysis that pushes below the surface, from intended meanings to the deeper, symbolic codes infusing their projects.[34]

Identifying a Problem: Making Street Violence Visible

The criminalization of transgressing youth is not the handiwork of a single individual, group, or organization. Rather, it evolves within the context of a complex division of labor, and several different institutions, entrepreneurial groups, and the general public contribute to this process. In Colorado, the news media—particularly the Denver news media (which are the largest and most influential news agencies in the state)—played an important part in this division of labor. Through continuous and prominent coverage of violent crime (particularly violent crime allegedly committed by juveniles) and the construction of an ongoing narrative that forged links between several isolated, "high-profile" incidents, journalists helped to make street crime much more salient than it had been only 3 or 4 months earlier. These news reports—which, in neofunctionalist terminology, can be construed as outputs of the media subsystem—established a new significatory context (or environment of action), one that supplied officials and reformers with compelling justifications for taking, in Governor Romer's words, "radical action" against serious young offenders.

There is little evidence that the press's voluminous reports reflected a sharp jump in the amount of street crime. The journalistic standard of newsworthiness, a standard central to the news media's unique institutional logic, provides a more persuasive explanation of the coverage. This criterion, which sets a premium on the novel and dramatic, occasionally fosters (factually) unwarranted inferences: A succession of atypical (and hence newsworthy) cases is depicted as an alarming crime wave, even when there is little or no change in the overall rate of offending. News organizations also have material interests: As privately (and often corporately) owned, profit-oriented ventures, the media are well aware that crime news is an appealing commodity. In addition, in medium-size markets like Denver (as compared to the much larger markets in New York, Chicago, and Los Angeles), competition among media outlets—evident in both journalists' ambition to break newsworthy stories and owners' interest in circulation, audience shares, and advertising dollars—fosters exhaustive coverage of the same events. This produces an amplification effect as print journalists, television anchors, and radio announcers inundate audiences with reports of the same crimes.

Our substantive discussion of the Denver media's accounts of the Summer of Violence is divided into two parts. First, we review the findings from a quantitative content analysis that documents the prominent and continuous newspaper coverage of youth and violent crime in the summer of 1993. Then, we discuss the general themes reporters devised to tell the story of that summer's violence.

Continuous and prominent coverage of youth and violent crime. Newspapers are divided into sections and pages, and placing a story on a specific page in a specific section—like the decisions about a story's appropriate length and whether it should be accompanied by a photograph and, if so, how large a photograph—reflects a professional judgment about the story's newsworthiness. And because journalists place a premium on novelty, frequent reports about the same issue—particularly when they appear on the paper's front page and in its editorial section—also signal an assessment about that issue's significance. When the press plays, in effect, an initiating role in identifying a pressing public problem, it typically does so by devoting continuous and prominent coverage to a particular issue. This was clearly the case in Denver (and Colorado) during the summer of 1993, when both the print and electronic media gave extensive coverage to the problem of juvenile and violent crime.

Table 5.1 Number, Placement, and Length of Youth and Violent Crime Stories and Accompanying Photographs Appearing in the *Denver Post* by Summer

	Summer/Year		
	1992	*1993*	*1994*
Stories			
Total stories	73	196	61
Front-page stories	2	44	6
Section A stories	2	73	10
Editorial page stories	3	48	5
Length of all stories[a]	1512.65	5606.87	1615.98
Photographs			
Total photographs	29	106	32
Front-page photographs	0	32	3
Length of all photographs[b]	177.89	1153	495.89

a. Length of all stories is measured in column inches.
b. Length of all photographs is measured in column inches.

Table 5.1 presents data generated from a content analysis of the *Denver Post*, the newspaper with the largest circulation in Denver (and Colorado.) These data indicate that, depending on the particular indicator employed, juvenile and violent crime[35] received from 2 to over 10 times more coverage in the *Post* during summer 1993 than in either the previous or subsequent summer. For example, with 196 stories on youth and violent crime,[36] the 1993 summer clearly outpaced both the 1992 summer, during which 73 such articles were published, and the 1994 summer's publication of 61 stories. In addition, 44 *front-page* stories on juvenile and violent crime were published during the summer of 1993, whereas in the summers of 1992 and 1994, only 2 and 6 such stories, respectively, made the front page. Editorials about youth and violent crime were also much more common during the 1993 summer; similarly, the juvenile and violent crime articles printed in the 1993 summer were more likely to be accompanied by photographs, and these photographs were much more likely to appear on the front page.

As noted earlier, the extensive news coverage of youth and violent crime in the summer of 1993 was not due to a dramatic rise in the incidence of serious offenses. We consulted the official monthly reports of the Denver metro area's two largest police departments (Denver and Aurora), which are forwarded to the Federal Bureau of Investigation and summarized in its annually published *Crime in the United States: The Uniform Crime Report*. We used these monthly reports to calculate the amount of violent crime and the number of juvenile arrests for violent offenses in these two cities during the summer months of 1992, 1993, and 1994. The reports disclose a small but unspectacular upturn in violence during the summer of 1993. In the 1993 summer, Denver and Aurora police recorded two more homicides than they did in the summer of 1992 and three more than in the summer of 1994. The number of nonlethal violent offenses (i.e., forcible rape, robbery, and aggravated assault) in the summer of 1993 was about 3.5% higher than in the 1992 summer and roughly 5% to 10% higher than in the 1994 summer.[37] It appears highly improbable, however, that this modest increase in serious crime (including the slight increment in homicides) during the 1993 summer can fully account for the remarkable surge in media coverage that occurred then.

The available data on juvenile arrests (which both the Denver and Aurora police departments define as arrests of youth under 18 years old) belie the notion that the metro area experienced an explosion of youth crime in the 1993 summer. The monthly reports indicate that 5 juveniles were arrested by the two departments for homicide in the 1992 summer, 2 in the 1993 summer, and 1 in the 1994 summer. During the summer of 1992, Denver and Aurora police arrested 128 juveniles for other serious, nonlethal violent offenses; 159 juvenile arrests were made for these offenses in the 1993 summer, whereas in 1994's summer, 186 juveniles were arrested for these crimes. This steady increase in juveniles arrested for serious, nonlethal crimes coupled with the steady decline in juveniles apprehended for homicide over the three summers stands in stark contrast to the undulating pattern of media coverage, with the relatively small number (and low priority) of news articles published in the summers of 1992 and 1994 interrupted by the dramatic spike of prominent juvenile crime stories in the 1993 summer.

Narrating the Summer of Violence.[38] Like the sheer volume and salience of media coverage, the actual content of reports written and broadcast during the 1993 summer heightened the visibility of juvenile violence. Journalists narrated an unfolding story, drawing meaningful, gestalt-like links between what could easily have been construed as unrelated or merely coincidental crimes and articulating overarching themes that offered a persuasive interpretation of the summer's violence. Four themes were central to the media's narration of the Summer of Violence: innocent victims, unprecedented violence, encroaching violence, and random violence.

Innocent victims. The perceived innocence of select victims injured or killed by gun-toting assailants, many of them allegedly juveniles, was the anchoring theme in the media's coverage. Seven high-profile violent crimes, which received front-page coverage immediately after they occurred and, subsequently, were frequently mentioned and briefly recapitulated in reporters,' columnists,' and editorial writers' summary characterizations of the summer's violence, figured prominently in the elaboration of this theme. In four of these incidents, children, ranging in age from 10 months to 6 years, were victimized. In the other cases, four "exemplary adults" were killed or seriously injured.

The Denver press presented these crimes in graphic detail, conveying, to the extent that words, photographs, and videotape can, their destructive immediacy. Reporters described how a woman stood by helplessly as her husband was murdered and, moments later, after "falling to her knees," suffered a "savage beating" that caused her head to swell to twice its normal size.[39] They described how a bullet struck a 4-year-old in the cheek and traveled to the back of his throat[40] and how a man shot in the side three times while driving home in the early morning hours bled to death as his car came to rest on a corner lawn.[41] Journalists offered their descriptions of these crimes and of the other high-profile incidents and victims as eye-grabbing and gut-wrenching examples of the general problem of street crime.

The victims' cultural-moral status made the violence appear even more ominous. Unequivocally innocent victims of street crime are rare. Many victims act in a manner that contributes, unwittingly or not, to the sequence of events that results in their injury or death, and they are not easily distinguished from those who attack or kill them.[42] Reporters are keenly attuned to moral character, and estimates about a victim's moral standing figure into their calculations about a crime's newsworthiness. In journalists' eyes, the children and adults attacked in the high-profile cases closely approximated the folk concept of the "ideal victim"[43]: These victims were innocent not merely in a technical, legal sense but in a morally and sociologically compelling way. The media were particularly sympathetic to the child victims, whom they regarded as morally pure and whose victimization qualified as eminently newsworthy. As one reporter[44] told us,

> The children. That was why there was so much coverage [of violent crime in the summer of 1993]. Little kids getting shot and killed. That put it [violence] on an entirely different level. Innocent blood. That's a tabloid statement, but it's true. . . . Children and animals are innocent. It brings outrage when this type of thing is done to innocents.

Given the reigning (Western) cultural conception of childhood,[45] the young child victims' moral innocence could simply be assumed, both by the press and the public. The moral standing of the adult victims, however, could not be taken for granted, and journalists offered some interpretive work to affirm these men's and women's innocence. Quoting liberally from testimonials offered by these victims' families, friends, and colleagues, reporters constructed idealized mini-narratives attesting to these adults' exemplary character. For example, neighbors described an adult victim, Richard Prentice [pseudonyms are used for all victims], as "easygoing" and "as nice as can be."[46] He had volunteered as a Big Brother, and a friend recollected an occasion when the victim had taken "one of his charges to buy fishing equipment. The kid swiped some items. [Prentice] forced him to go back into the store and return the stolen goods and apologize. Then he bought the kid the stuff he stole."[47] The victim's boss described him as a man, who despite his imposing, 6-foot, 4-inch stature, was "a gentle guy who was very dependable and was the most likable cable marketer he ever had."[48] Prentice had graduated from a local college with a bachelor's degree in fine arts and often sold tickets to the Colorado Ballet, a company in which his wife was a well-known dancer. He recommended "works of Shelley and Keats that were [an] inspiration" for her performances.[49] "He'd always be standing in the wings," his wife said. "I would never go on stage without a hug and a kiss." Richard was, she added, "My best friend. My confidant. My biggest supporter."[50]

The press portrayed the high-profile incidents as "typifying examples"[51] of the summer's violence. In fact, the child and exemplary adult victims were, socially and demographically, strikingly different from the majority of those injured or killed by youth (or adult) violence in Denver (and Colorado) that summer. Statistically, the "average victim" was a "Hispanic male, 17.7 years old," who was also a gang member, "a high school drop-out, and [himself] a perpetrator of youth violence."[52] The four child victims' ethnicity and race—three were Latino, the other African American—were similar to the average victim (73% of those victimized by juvenile violence were either Latino or African American), but the children differed markedly along nearly every other meaningful social attribute. The four exemplary adults, who ranged in age from 27 to 43 and who were all white, middle-class, and college-educated, were also starkly unrepresentative of those most likely to be victimized by street violence. The criterion of newsworthiness (which stipulates that typical crimes and victims merit minimal coverage) in conjunction with remnants of America's exclusive cultural tradition (which valorizes middle-class WASPs over people of color) prompted the media to give little attention to the statistically average victims while granting exhaustive coverage to the ideal victims. Consequently, despite their singular character, the high-profile incidents powerfully shaped the community's and officials' "perception of the problem" of youth violence.[53]

Unprecedented violence. Although lacking corroborating, statistical data from law enforcement agencies (or other sources), the local media claimed that juvenile (and adult) violence in Denver (and Colorado) was rising at an alarming rate during the 1993 summer. In the place of credible numeric evidence, journalists buttressed this claim by turning to presumably knowledgeable public officials and, uncritically quoting and paraphrasing their remarks, passed off their rough approximations and gut-level impressions as fact. In the wake of the first high-profile crime (which occurred in early May 1993), the Denver police chief, while conceding that he did not "have the statistics yet to prove it," nonetheless told reporters that "he believes violence is on the rise in Denver."[54] Drawing on interviews with several officers and gang-intervention workers, a front-page article titled "Police: Violence Escalating" indicated that the number of guns possessed by juveniles, the number of drive-by shootings, and the number of homicides were all on the rise.[55]

Reporters kept a running tabulation of the high-profile cases, a form of counting that, unlike a single summary statement of the crime rate, justified meticulous accounts of each new incident. Explicitly connecting each high-profile event to the others preceding it, this running tab also implied that the crimes cohered into a meaningful pattern and that the summer's violence represented something greater than the sum of its individual crimes. For instance, an article reporting the shooting of a 6-year-old began, "Yet another young child was fighting for his life last night."[56] Similarly, a story about the killing of an elementary school teacher opened with the line, "In what has become a deadly ritual in the metro area, yet another innocent victim was fatally shot."[57]

Using disquieting imagery and analogies, reporters dramatized the threat violence posed to the city and state. For example, medical personnel interviewed by the press frequently made analogies connecting the city's (and state's) street crime with international and civil wars. A Denver trauma surgeon compared "the recent sharp increase in [violent] incidents" to "a battle zone," adding that, "This is like Korea or something."[58] Other reports insinuated that Denver was a city under siege. One appeared beneath the heading, "City a Hostage to Violence?"[59] A full-page (Sunday) editorial column about Denver's street violence was entitled, "Under Siege: Living with Barbarians at the Gate."[60] Other journalists characterized the summer's violence with such emotionally charged images as "urban terrorism,"[61] "a seemingly endless, senseless plague of wanton violence,"[62] and, in a column titled "Where Are Our Leaders as Denver Dies?" a "city teetering on the edge of a murderous abyss."[63]

Characterizing the high-profile victims not only as individuals but also as symbols of collective life, the press alluded to another dimension of the summer's ostensibly unprecedented violence. Durkheim's classic analysis of Aboriginal totems and other religious objects notes that they are "among the most preeminently sacred things" and, as a result, are bound up with "the collective fate of the entire clan."[64] In the summer of 1993, the local media transfigured the child and exemplary adult victims, in their injuries and deaths, into symbolic emblems of Denver's (and Colorado's) communal life. For instance, after applauding the "overwhelming" public response to "the bounty fund" he had established to "persuade someone to turn in the punks who shot a 6-year-old boy," a columnist explained the child's totemic status:

> You [those who contributed to the fund] understood that the moment that bullet penetrated [the boy's] brain he became all of our sons, all our children, brown and yellow, pink and red, rich and poor.
>
> He was our hope for a better tomorrow, our dreams and our aspirations for a better world. And you understood we couldn't sit by passively while the thugs stole that from us.[65]

With the media spotlight brightly focused on the high-profile cases, reporters suggested that a distinguishing feature of the Summer of Violence was a succession of assaults against cherished icons. These desecrations, the media intimated, constituted "a disaster, the greatest misfortune that can befall a group."[66] Amplifying the language of communal crisis, disorder, and dissolution—for example, "a city teetering on the edge of a murderous abyss"—journalists effectively conveyed the notion that transgressions against a community's quintessentially sacred objects represent symbolically "a retrogression to chaos."[67]

Encroaching violence. During the summer of 1993, news agencies regularly remarked on the apparent movement of violence from the "streets" to purportedly idyllic social space. This media-conveyed sense of encroaching violence was frequently joined to the distinction many make between ostensibly "good" and "bad" parts of town, and the complementary expectation that serious, violent crime will be concentrated in a community's less reputable areas. Journalists hold a similar folk concept, tending to regard as commonplace the violence that occurs in what is regarded as the "socially disorganized, inner city" (or its analogues in smaller communities). More novel and newsworthy is street crime erupting in presumably "nice" residential neighborhoods or sacrosanct public space.

The notion of violence invading safe, inviolate space was elaborated in reports suggesting that violent crime had escaped its traditional confines and was trespassing on urban enclaves and into suburban areas that heretofore had been relatively unscathed by street violence. A state legislator, reflecting on the summer's shootings, succinctly summarized this sentiment: "I think we assumed for a long time that some neighborhoods are safe and some aren't. We can't assume that any more."[68] This invidious differentiation of (inner) city and suburban space infused newspaper (and television) coverage of several high-profile cases, while the more generalized motif of violence radiating from corrupt centers to pristine peripheries appeared in stories decrying the spread of street violence from Denver and its immediate environs (including its suburbs) to smaller cities and towns—for example, Colorado Springs, Durango, Grand Junction, and Pueblo—throughout the state.[69]

The theme of violence encroaching on sacrosanct social space was redeployed in other ways. Several articles deplored the spread of street violence to revered social institutions, including churches and schools, once regarded as sanctuaries sequestered from the tumult and dangers of the profane world. The Denver Zoo is not itself a sacred place, but its representational value as an emblem of civic pride and its powerful association with weekend family outings, often with young children in tow, renders it a potent symbol of public space. An editorial characterized the shooting of an infant, who was sitting in front of the zoo's celebrated polar bear exhibit, as a riveting reminder that no institution or public (or private) space is inviolate:

> The bullet that sent the youngster to Denver General Hospital . . . could serve as a metaphor for how violence robs this city's soul of its collective peace. . . . No citizen is safe anywhere as long as a predilection to violence remains prevalent. Drive-by shootings can happen anywhere an automobile can travel, and that includes any street in the core city or its suburbs. Gangs, drugs, and guns can infest any school, whether it is located in the inner city or in an upscale enclave. The failure of the city, the state, and the nation to cope with violence has come to haunt every corner of society—even the polar bear exhibit at the local zoo.[70]

Random violence. Continually pointing to the seemingly unpredictable character of the seven high-profile incidents, reporters suggested that random violence threatened the entire community. Underscoring this theme, one article observed, "With tiny children shot, men murdered, [and] women beaten . . . the specter of random violence [is] taking center stage this summer."[71] Several distinct meanings were attached to the theme of random violence, but perhaps the most salient was its unpredictable character, the unnerving sense that "anyone could be the next victim."[72] A local talk-radio host we spoke with emphasized this element of random violence:

> It [the violence occurring the summer of 1993] wasn't predictable. It could happen anywhere for no apparent reason, all of a sudden, out of the blue. People don't like that. If you've got a problem that people can identify and isolate, then they can adjust to it. You can't adjust to random violence.

The threat of random violence becomes psychologically salient only when the perception that "anyone could be the next victim" is interpreted as meaning "the next victim could be me or someone I care about." Personal identification with recent, actual victims of apparently random violence fostered this heightened sense of vulnerability. The print media suggested that many citizens identified strongly with one or more of the victims described in the high-profile cases. For example, shortly after the shooting at the zoo, a reporter interviewed a 14-year-old relaxing in City Park, which is immediately adjacent to the Denver Zoo. The boy said, "My mom's starting to worry about me. She's real hyper about this, real hesitant since the gunshots. She says that little kid [who was shot at the zoo] coulda been me."[73]

Several of the journalists we interviewed remarked that the high-profile incidents, with their detailed, dramatic descriptions, supplied readers with abundant opportunities for intuiting connections between themselves, or their immediate social circle, and the victims. Proximity, for example, whether calculated in terms of physical space or social networks, frequently elicits identification with a victim of crime. As one reporter said, "When it's somebody that your mother knows or it's two blocks from your home and he got shot in your neighborhood, suddenly it could be said, 'That could be me.'"

Common social and demographic attributes (e.g., age, class, ethnicity, race, gender, marital status) can spark a vivid recognition of the self-in-the-other. The Coles (Bob Cole was murdered while Mary Cole survived a severe beating)—portrayed in news accounts as a dynamic, popular, loving, handsome young couple; recently married, with a newly acquired apartment of their own; and working hard to launch a successful business venture—embodied a social identity and trajectory that, several reporters speculated, mirrored the aspirations of many young adults in Denver (and Colorado) while eliciting the nodding approval of older residents.

It can be hypothesized, as many journalists did in their interviews with us, that the print media's idealized representations of victims, which emphasized their impeccable character and moral innocence, resonated with the way many people like to think about themselves and encouraged members of the public to see a critical similarity between themselves and the high-profile victims. The following conjecture, ventured by a reporter, describes the folk reasoning that may have connected readers to Ann Temple, the slain elementary school teacher:

A teacher, who is from Eagle [a small mountain town, roughly 75 miles west of Denver], comes down to take a job in Denver. And it's her dream to teach in the school and everything. And she is staying with a girlfriend. She goes out to dinner and then drives to Safeway and gets something. And some gang members scope her and kill her in a parking lot as they try to rob her pocketbook. So here is another innocent victim, *like you and I,* [emphasis in original] killed in quote our safe neighborhoods of Denver.

In brief, through their continuous and prominent coverage and their (melo)dramatic narrative of the Summer of Violence, the Denver media took the lead in identifying an apparently urgent problem. In effect, news reports democratized the risk of street violence, suggesting that anyone—regardless of class rank, moral standing, or demographic profile—could be violently assaulted. In addition, these reports intimated that the attacks on innocent children and good adults represented nothing less than transgressions against the community's conception of the sacred. But acknowledging the media's leadership role in focusing public and policymaker attention on an issue does not imply that news agencies, by themselves, can simply mandate the existence of a serious social problem. Press accounts of problematic behaviors or harmful social arrangements are more accurately conceptualized as claims, which can be accepted, revised, or rejected, by citizens, public officials, and other institutional elites. When media claims about allegedly troublesome conditions are broadly affirmed by significant segments of the public and by elites in other institutional sectors, a social problem is effectively ratified. This is exactly what occurred during the Summer of Violence.

In response to news reports about the Summer of Violence, local and state officials, as well as Colorado's congressional representatives, issued calls for forceful measures against street crime.[74] An array of opinion leaders, including luminaries in the business and professional communities, the archbishop of Denver, and Pope John Paul II (who traveled to the Mile High City to celebrate World Youth Day), confirmed that it was "time to take action."[75] At the grassroots level, frightened residents altered the routes they drove to and from work, suspended their daily jog, mowed their lawns in the early morning hours, refrained from sitting on the porch after dark, installed bars across the windows of their homes, put their young children to sleep in the bathtub to avoid stray bullets, imposed what their teenage children regarded as outrageously restrictive curfews, considered moving to safer locales, or took more precautions about locking car doors and looking over their shoulders while walking city streets.[76] Street violence became a prominent issue in a burgeoning public debate, with many concerned citizens sending letters to newspapers, calling local talk-radio programs, participating in town meetings, organizing protest marches to decry the violence, and contacting city and state officials, urging them to "do something."[77] The net and mutually reinforcing effect of these reactions, which themselves were circulated back into the media's unfolding narrative about the Summer of Violence, was to magnify the visibility of violent crime and reaffirm the perception that it constituted a vitally serious problem requiring immediate action.

Attributing Blame for the Problem: A New "Breed" of Transgressing Adolescent and the Juvenile Justice System

When pressing problems are identified and ratified, the problem-solving paradigm hardwired into modern societies supplies a powerful impetus to devise suitable remedies. These solutions take many forms, one of which is simply expanding the institutional sector whose purview of responsibility encompasses the problem that has been identified. When communities confront crime waves, for example, they often expand their social control agencies: They assign more police to troubled neighborhoods, pay officers to work overtime, and/or hire additional recruits. This kind of response, which can be called institutional expansion, was clearly evident during the Summer of Violence. The Denver mayor, for example, provided up $1.1 million in overtime pay as incentive for police officers to work "around the clock."[78]

Institutional differentiation is a second type of response, and it involves devising specialized organizational arrangements and practices to address what is regarded as a significant and distinctive problem. Differentiation usually occurs when existing institutions (or the simple expansion of existing institutions) are deemed incapable of addressing the problem in a satisfactory way. The presumed incapacity of established institutions, in turn, becomes a warrant for proposing new arrangements that are typically heralded as much more efficient and effective than the structures they replace. In this vein, one of the most important legacies of the Summer of Violence was the crystallization of a new category of transgressing adolescent who, many believed, exceeded the problem-solving capacities of the existing juvenile justice system.

Denver journalists asserted that an "unholy trinity" of guns, gangs, and juvenile offenders was responsible for the Summer of Violence.[79] Reporters repeatedly insisted that the principal culprit was a gun-toting, gang-affiliated adolescent. The press did not arrive at this conclusion on its own. After focusing public and policymaker attention on a riveting issue (such as an apparent surge in street violence), the media typically turn to other respected institutions and groups (rather than to insurgents, radicals, and outsiders) for definitive characterizations of the sources of the problem.[80] Relying heavily on interviews with select state legislators, juvenile court judges, public defenders, police, gang-intervention workers, and district attorneys, the press sharply distinguished the juveniles blamed for the summer's violence from conventional delinquents. In fact, reporters rarely used the word *delinquent:* In the more than 500 youth and crime stories published by the *Denver Post* and *Rocky Mountain News* from May through mid-September 1993, the terms *delinquent* and *delinquency* appear less than two dozen times. And when employed, these words were dubbed anachronisms: "delinquent" and "delinquency," reporters implied, conjured up forms of adolescent transgression characteristic of an earlier and more innocent time and place. Playing cultural entrepreneur, reporters coined dozens of clever catchwords to characterize an allegedly new "breed" of juvenile lawbreaker— for example, "criminal kids," "kid gangsters," "hard-core juvenile offenders," "scary and dangerous youths," "young thugs preying on their fellow citizens," "the state's nastiest young felons," "kids doing the criminal work of adults," "greedy, self-serving, predatory street punks," "an infestation of teenage evil," and "tiny terrorists."

A rough sketch differentiating this hyperthreatening teen from the traditional delinquent complemented the slogans. This invidious comparison held, first, that the "new breed of youthful offender" committed more serious crimes and engaged in more chronic law-breaking: Whereas delinquents filched cars and played mailbox baseball, youthful offenders "swagger out to kill motorists, passers-by, neighbors, each other. What isn't targeted for dead is fair game for robberies, rapes, carjackings, and drug dealing."[81]

A second contrast underscored the contemporary youthful offender's debased moral character. In the early decades of the 20th century, Denver had been the site of a remarkably compassionate characterization of the delinquent.[82] Consistently affirming delinquents' basic humanity and fundamental, childlike innocence, Judge Ben B. Lindsey, the leading figure of the early Denver juvenile court, passionately proclaimed (in articles, books, and speeches) that the sins of young lawbreakers paled in significance when compared to the sins committed against them by negligent parents and/or a corrupt, hypocritical social order. In the summer of 1993, the Denver media, leaning on insights supplied by elected officials and professionals in the juvenile and criminal justice systems, repudiated this sympathetic conception of transgressing youth as sentimental, mushy-headed nostalgia. As an influential state representative observed, "We have a tendency to believe the Father Flanagan/ Spencer Tracy *Boys' Town* thing, that there's no such thing as a bad boy. But that's a movie. Our reality today is that Spencer Tracy wasn't right."[83] Today, there are, added the governor's chief legal counsel, "really bad kids."[84]

Lacking essential moral attitudes and emotions, these bad kids struck journalists and public officials as not quite fully human. Denver's chief juvenile court judge told a reporter, "I see, in the youths who are appearing in court, a lack of valuation of life, a lack of respect for life . . . some scary, scary kids."[85] Others elaborated this observation, adding that contemporary young offenders are incapable of empathy or compassion. A former public defender said, "There is just a different attitude among the kids now. It's not just that they have no social conscience. It's almost like there is no morality. There is not any feeling toward other people."[86]

Elements of a powerful cultural code informed this burgeoning portrait of contemporary youthful offenders. Accounts of the high-profile cases assigned religious-like features to the juveniles suspected of injuring or killing ideal child and adult victims. Modern Western societies, according to Durkheim, are permeated by a "religion of humanity," which constitutes the "human person" as "sacred in the ritual sense of the word" and imbues the individual in general with "the transcendent majesty that churches of all time lend to their gods."[87] Like more orthodox forms of religiosity, however, the religion of humanity actually gravitates around two poles, the sacred and the antisacred, with the latter viewed as "evil and impure powers, bringers of disorder, causes of death and sickness, instigators of sacrilege."[88] It is in this quasi-religious sense that Christie portrays ideal victims and ideal offenders as two sides of the same symbolic coin: "Ideal victims need—and create—ideal offenders . . . . The more ideal the victim is, the more ideal becomes the offender."[89] Ideal victims personify innocence, and so ideal offenders embody evil; the ideal offender "is, morally speaking, black against the white victim."[90] Ideal victims are symbolic icons of community life; ideal offenders are symbolic outsiders, strangers, foreigners, aliens, and intruders. "The more foreign the better," according to Christie, who adds that the ideal offender "is a dangerous man coming from far away."[91] Ideal offenders, moreover, lack qualities essential for being regarded as fully human: The ideal offender "is a human being close to not being one."[92] The religion of humanity implies, in other words, that those who desecrate innocent children and morally upstanding adults are something less than human beings, a sentiment aptly conveyed in the evocative phrases some Denver reporters used to describe violent youth: for example, "ugly, creepy, putrid cockroaches," "predators," "wolves out looking for prey," and "wild animals."

In addition to the religious-like contrast between ideal victims and ideal offenders, the exclusive tradition in American culture permeated the media's sociomoral profile of these dangerous teens. There is abundant evidence suggesting that "mainstream America," particularly white mainstream America, associates (and has long associated) African American and Latino male adolescents and young adults with violence, danger, and disorder.[93] There can be little doubt that this association, powerfully reinforced by continuous coverage of the high-profile attacks on children and exemplary (white) adults—assaults the media attributed explicitly and exclusively to young Latinos and African American males—figured significantly in the construction of a more ominous category of transgressing adolescent. This association, it is reasonable to surmise, also served as potent cultural subtext for key themes in the media's account of the Summer of Violence, with the themes of unprecedented, encroaching, and random violence animated by the frightening specter of African American and Latino youth wreaking havoc on middle-class, Anglo lives and neighborhoods, in the public space Anglos share with other groups.

Although they incorporated the symbolic opposition between the ideal victim and the ideal offender and the exclusive tradition's stereotype linking minority males to street crime, media accounts did not depict juvenile offenders as unequivocal embodiments of evil. Rather, these accounts were infused with considerable ambivalence: Although assuredly a more forbidding figure than the joyriding, hubcap-stealing delinquent of yesteryear, the contemporary young offender was not (yet) a "hardened adult criminal." Journalists, like the officials and experts they interviewed, were unwilling to abandon completely the cultural precept that youthfulness mitigates, to an extent, the culpability of young offenders. Nor were they inclined to jettison entirely belief in the presumed malleability of youth, a conviction that sustains hope that juvenile lawbreakers, even violent ones, can be redeemed. The youthfulness of the new type of transgressing adolescent did not prevent some columnists and reporters from likening violent juveniles to "bringers of disorder," but it also generated a nearly equal number of columns and reports that counterbalanced this demonology by describing the conditions—largely of familial, social, economic, and moral breakdown[94]—that purportedly propel "our young people" to act "with so little regard for human life." As portrayed by the *Denver Post* and the *Rocky Mountain News* during the Summer of Violence, youthful offenders were not, as a group, completely credible icons of "dangerous men coming from far away."

If reporters and their sources expressed some ambivalence in their characterization of this new type of youthful offender, they displayed little equivocation in indicting the juvenile justice system for its inability to respond effectively to these hyperthreatening teens. Fashioning a commonsense version of the lead-and-lag principle, the press, along with several others (e.g., the governor, state legislators, social control agents, and gang intervention workers), observed that the system of juvenile justice had, in the words of a *Rocky Mountain News* editorial, originated back in "the palmier days when serious juvenile rebellion . . . meant filching a car and the term delinquent suggested only a temporary pause from civilized behavior."[95] At that time, it was widely acknowledged "that kids make mistakes" but ought not to be severely punished for their lack of judgment. Juvenile justice's firm-but-compassionate stance toward delinquents made perfect "sense so long as the offenses themselves were relatively minor."[96]

But as the Summer of Violence seemed to demonstrate all too clearly, yesterday's delinquent had been eclipsed by a new brand of juvenile offender who commits heinous crimes and exhibits viciousness unknown to adolescents of an earlier era. As a Denver assistant district attorney noted, "The type of kid we're talking about isn't your next-door neighbor. This is the kid who is robbing, raping, killing and shooting."[97] No less important was the fact that the juvenile justice system had proved incapable of responding effectively to this exceedingly dangerous youthful offender. Governor Romer's opening remarks to the special legislative session on youth violence zeroed in on this key point:

> The fact is, the [traditional juvenile justice] system never contemplated and is totally unprepared to handle the problems we see today—kids shooting kids, kids raping kids, kids terrorizing neighborhoods, kids running sophisticated criminal organizations that deal in drugs.[98]

Legislators, police, prosecutors, and many others elaborated the governor's claims. They noted, for example, that many teens confined in the Colorado Division of Youth Services (DYS) reform schools were much tougher than the facilities in which they were incarcerated and, consequently, were unfazed by the experience. In this vein, a state senator said,

> I went and talked to a bunch of kids . . . who have been in and out of DYS facilities. . . . They said if they are sent back to Montview [a reform school], it's like old home week and they go back and see their friends. There is no fear. . . . It doesn't bother them if they go in and out of this revolving door at DYS because they know they are not going to stay very long.[99]

A representative of the county sheriffs of Colorado made a similar claim: "Many of these kids, and we've seen some of the profiles on them, have been in and out of the Division of Youth Services five and six times. DYS for these kids is a joke."[100]

This endlessly reiterated version of the lead-and-lag principle—that young people had become more dangerous, deadly, and disdainful, while the juvenile justice system had utterly failed to keep pace with this new type of offender—led, inexorably, to a painfully obvious conclusion: "We can't keep doing things the same way because it's different than it was in the '50s. It's different than it was in the '70s. There's a new breed of kid out there that is not afraid of anything."

Fixing the Problem: Creating and Mobilizing Support for the Youthful Offender System

The institutional logic of newsworthiness discourages news agencies from assuming political responsibility for the deleterious conditions their coverage highlights.[101] Instead of assuming an obligation to ameliorate problems, the media's tack more commonly revolves around identifying "the responsible office or person" and assigning that party the chore of doing something about the problem, often using follow-up reports to hold the designated authority accountable for fulfilling that charge.[102] Practicing a "trickle-up principle," journalists generally assign responsibility to individuals holding high-ranking positions in the pertinent public or private institution, especially when a serious problem allegedly occurs "during their watch."[103]

In a complex polity with multiple levels of governance, an abundance of civic groups, and numerous opportunities for activist citizens to voice their concerns and recommendations, a socially ratified problem commonly elicits a host of proposed remedies. The Summer of Violence proved no exception to this generalization. Providing seemingly incontrovertible evidence that the function of controlling juvenile crime was not being fulfilled effectively, the Summer of Violence generated dozens of "plans of action" aimed at fortifying social control institutions and stemming the apparent surge of youth violence.[104]

The deeply felt urge to "do something" prompted Denver-area teens to form a group, Helping Young People Educate (HYPE), to assist adolescents and their families in coping with youth violence.[105] A charismatic community activist and former gang member, a city councilman, and several gang leaders attempted to negotiate a truce between rival gangs, an effort they called Operation Reconstruction.[106] Metro-area educators took steps—for example, closing off streets bordering a school during lunch periods to prevent drive-by shootings and encouraging school administrators to accompany students as they went to lunch off campus—to protect students from violent crime.[107] A 30-member committee, appointed by the Denver mayor and the Denver city council president, was asked to devise a plan to combat youth violence.[108] Aurora assigned 20 additional officers to its police gang unit,[109] whereas Adams County instituted a "zero tolerance policy" requiring that any juvenile committing a crime with a gun be jailed immediately[110] and the city councils of Denver and Westminster approved ordinances "forbidding the possession of firearms by juveniles and imposing penalties upon adults who furnish minors with guns."[111] District attorneys representing Denver and seven nearby counties announced plans to "make violent crimes involving weapons our highest priority."[112] Congressman Bill Armstrong (from Colorado) argued that fighting juvenile and gang violence would require more money to hire additional police officers.[113] Congresswoman Pat Schroeder (also from Colorado) sought $4.4 million from Congress to fund a military-style program aimed at "reclaim[ing] America's youth."[114] Announcing that violent crime was the number one priority of the city police department, Denver Mayor Wellington Webb outlined a six-point plan, heavy on increased law enforcement, to combat gang and youth violence.

The summer's most ambitious (and successful) institutional entrepreneur, however, was Governor Roy Romer, whose 14-point strategy to curtail violent youth crime received the greatest attention from policymakers, news organizations, and the public. Promoting his plan as "an 'iron fist' against outlaw gangs and a 'helping hand' for Coloradans fighting to take back their neighborhoods," Romer urged the swift prosecution of gangs and of youth charged with violent offenses, targeted juveniles with guns, and recommended building a new youthful offender system.[115] He characterized YOS as a "middle tier" in the correctional apparatus, a tier carefully crafted to fit between the existing criminal and juvenile justice systems. Envisioned as a differentiated structure targeting a distinctive group of juvenile lawbreakers, YOS did not simply replicate existing adult prisons or juvenile reform schools. Rather, YOS is an instance of institution building, involving the creation of a new set of arrangements and practices aimed at controlling and treating a group of offenders who are neither hardened adult criminals nor malleable juvenile delinquents.

Devised as a response to an allegedly new type of transgressing adolescent, Romer's YOS mirrored the ambivalence permeating the youthful offender category itself. Just as juvenile offenders purportedly differ from traditional delinquents by posing a more ominous threat to public safety, so YOS differs from conventional (juvenile) reform schools in its more explicit commitment to punishment. Romer and other advocates of YOS asserted that juveniles committing serious, adultlike crimes forfeit any legitimate claim to be recognized and treated as juveniles by the community and courts. As one district attorney put it, "Let's differentiate juveniles [from adults] on the basis of their conduct, not on the basis of their age."[116] According to Romer, YOS originated, in part, "to impose the kind of punishment such [adultlike] crimes deserve."[117] Some of YOS's punitive elements were outlined earlier—for example, the direct-file provision and the sentencing of (convicted) juveniles to adult prisons, a sentence suspended conditional on completing a 2- to 6-year term in YOS. The institution's explicitly punitive components are also manifest in the decision to place YOS under the administrative (and symbolic) purview of the (adult) Department of Corrections, not the (juvenile) Division of Youth Services. Programmatically, YOS includes a rigorous boot camp that tests inmates' physical and psychological limits. Chronically recalcitrant youth are sent to "readjustment centers," where they are locked up for 23 hours a day. Those who continually flout the institution's rules can be returned to court for imposition of the original sentence to adult prison.

Despite having committed a serious, violent offense and posing a genuine threat to public safety, the juvenile offender still possesses some of the cultural attributes ascribed to youth, attributes that entitle her or him to a "second last chance at rehabilitation." Thus, one proponent of YOS argued that youthful offenders

> are still children and so in that regard . . . we still have to hope that given as young as some of these kids are, that we can with some intensive programming and a very big stick over their heads, turn some of them around.[118]

Sounding a similar note, the bill's cosponsor, Senator Wham, said,

> We have to treat youngsters who are doing adult crimes with some punishment that is meaningful. At the same time, I think the [youthful offender] system says we're not giving up on you completely and maybe it's the second and last chance.[119]

The bill's other cosponsor, Representative Berry, maintained,

We do recognize that young offenders are entitled, in many cases under constitutional provisions, and just in good common sense ought to have
treatment and try to get them to change their attitude. . . . Hopefully, we can
change the behavior. We can get their attention. We can in fact have it sink into
their minds the seriousness of the conduct and of the attitude they have. Turn
that around. And I think it is all of our hopes that when they come out they
will not re-offend.[120]

To help ensure that YOS would not become merely a "prison for punks," the
enabling legislation mandated that its staff must have at least a bachelor's degree, a
requirement that effectively ruled out many correctional officers already employed
by the (adult) Department of Corrections, officers who the YOS architects believed
would be too preoccupied with custody and too little concerned with treatment.
Advocates of YOS also believed that requiring a college degree would be more likely
to attract staff wholeheartedly committed to rehabilitating young people. Moreover,
the three phases of the YOS program following the boot camp induction are, in
theory, structured around an intensive form of compulsory resocialization. In
Phase 1, inmates receive academic instruction, vocational training, and various
forms of individual and group counseling. In Phase 2, they are moved to a community facility and prepared for reentry to community life. In the final phase, a parole
officer provides YOS youth with intensive community supervision and support.

Romer championed YOS in large part because he sincerely believed that this new
institution represented a potent antidote to serious juvenile crime. He was also
convinced that by reacting forcefully to the Summer of Violence, he would restore
credibility in government, demonstrating that public officials were attuned to the
populace's concerns and were willing to take drastic action in response to a crisis.
But like other institutional entrepreneurs, Romer did not act solely as an altruistic
agent of greater societal effectiveness or democratic governance. By presenting his
14-point plan, convening the special legislative session, and successfully securing
passage of YOS and other initiatives, Governor Romer's public visibility and approval ratings soared. Throughout his tenure, Romer had been an enormously
popular governor. However, some of his political capital had been depleted the previous year (1992), when he lobbied heavily on behalf of higher taxes for schools
(a measure the public rejected decisively) and when he vehemently opposed an
amendment to the state's constitution limiting government spending (a bill voters
overwhelmingly approved).

Since 1994 was an election year, it is reasonable to suppose that Romer and his
staff were fully aware that decisive action against street crime in the summer of 1993
would improve the governor's prospects for reelection. Moreover, the juvenile crime
problem presented Romer, a Democrat, with an opportunity to seize an issue—law
and order—that heretofore had been the preserve of conservative Republicans. By
embracing a tough-on-crime stance, Romer enriched not only his own political fortunes but those of his party as well. Finally, in their interviews with us, several Romer

staff members conceded that the governor relished the publicity and acclaim he received while leading the fight against youth crime. In the words of one respondent, "Roy Romer liked the spotlight, there's no question about that. . . . No man ever got more press than he did and no man ever wanted what he got more."

Proposing a new institution as a remedy to a socially ratified problem is one thing; mobilizing support for that proposal is another. Romer and his staff confronted several obstacles to winning approval for the YOS initiative. First, the Colorado governor is, in important respects, a constitutionally weak chief executive, with limited appointive powers, little authority over important state programs, and a lack of control over the state budget. Second, Romer had to ensure that the public's and policymakers' attention remained focused on youth violence. A third impediment involved defining youth violence as a credible, statewide issue and not just a problem confined to Denver. Fourth, both houses of the General Assembly were controlled by Republicans, and up until 1993, Colorado Republicans had "owned" the crime issue. Finally, YOS raised potentially divisive racial and ethnic issues, with some activist citizen groups predicting (correctly as it turned out) that young Latinos and African Americans would be statistically overrepresented in the YOS population.

Romer's adroit use of the media and the bully pulpit of the governorship amply compensated for the constitutional infirmities of his office and enabled him to sustain citizens' and officials' focus on the issue of serious juvenile crime. In this regard, an expert on the state's politics notes that Colorado governors are well-positioned to serve as leaders of public opinion:

> The governor of Colorado is usually the best known public official in the state other than the president of the United States. The governor is frequently in the news and becomes a celebrity. He has only to notify the press that he intends to give a pint of blood to the Red Cross or pay his personal respects to a one-hundred-year-old grandmother and his performance will be broadcast across the state. This ability to reach the public with his message exceeds that of all other politicians in the state. . . . What the governor says is important if for no other reason than that it is heard far and wide. The legislature, on the other hand, speaks with a hundred voices, none of which begins to match the governor's command of public attention. This fact affects legislators, who understand very well that the governor is better equipped than they to reach the voters.[121]

During the summer of 1993, the governor spoke frequently about youth violence, and his remarks almost always made news. By late June 1993, he announced that serious juvenile crime was "the highest thing on my agenda now."[122] He met with family members of victims struck down by street crime and walked in protest marches denouncing the summer's violence. He convened "town meetings" with citizens across the state to discuss the problem of youth violence, soliciting participants' feedback and enlisting their support for his proposals. (His staff alerted news agencies to these meetings, which invariably received extensive coverage.) He spent a night in a jail cell where he spoke to print and television reporters about the need for a tough, no-nonsense response to serious young offenders. An evening ride-along with the Aurora and Denver police netted a juvenile suspect packing two-loaded firearms and front-page coverage in both Denver newspapers. His rhetorical hyperbole underscored both the seriousness of youth crime and the urgent need for a solution. He claimed, for example, that Colorado confronted a crisis unlike anything the state had seen and that absent dramatic, forceful action, "society's not going to hold together."[123]

While traveling across the state to speak to various groups about juvenile crime and other issues, Romer continually reiterated his belief that far from being confined to Denver, youth violence had erupted in every corner of Colorado and constituted a statewide problem. At a press conference, for example, the governor pulled out a recent newspaper article from the *Pueblo Chieftain* that he had been carrying. The article described a teen (living in the city of Pueblo) who was shot in the back while he slept, a murder police characterized as a retaliatory strike for the boy's reporting of another drive-by shooting to the authorities.[124] And, in his opening remarks to the special legislative session, Romer repeated this point: "This [youth violence] is not just a Denver problem. It's a problem throughout the state—in Colorado Springs, in Pueblo. We even had a drive-by shooting this summer in Lamar [a very small town in southeastern Colorado]."[125]

Romer used the pressure of public opinion, the goodwill he had cultivated earlier with legislators on both sides of the aisle, and traditional political horse-trading to garner cooperation from the Republican-controlled General Assembly. More than any other policymaker, Romer propelled youth violence to the top of the policy agenda while periodically entertaining the possibility of calling a special legislative session to address the issue. Legislators, particularly Republican legislators, were reticent about convening such a session and questioned whether anything significant could be accomplished in a 4- or 5-day session. In response, Romer continued to use his bully pulpit and the media to highlight the problem of juvenile crime while promising to consult Republican leaders before making a final decision about the special session. But during the last week of July, when four high-profile incidents occurred in rapid succession (and were extensively covered by the media), and while several Republican lawmakers were in San Diego attending the National Conference of State Legislators, Romer announced that a special session would be held. Romer's failure to contact legislators before making this announcement angered Republicans, but the public clamor about juvenile violence and widespread calls to "do something" effectively precluded objections or organized resistance to the session. In the weeks leading up to the session, Romer aggressively pursued a bipartisan approach to win approval of his initiatives. He persuaded Dottie Wham, the powerful and highly respected Republican chairwoman of the Senate Judiciary Committee, and Chuck Berry, the Republican speaker of the house, to cosponsor the YOS bill. With their help (given in exchange for future political rewards, including the prospect of augmenting their political capital by cosponsoring an important piece of legislation), in conjunction with the pressure he applied to members of his own political party, Romer successfully piloted the bill through the legislature.

Finally, some civil rights activists publicly predicted that minority youth would be disproportionately incarcerated in YOS. These predictions sounded a note of dissent within the Democratic coalition, a group Romer was counting on to deliver votes in support of YOS. Romer addressed this potentially divisive issue in three ways. First, Romer proclaimed that the problem of youth violence cut across racial, ethnic, and class lines and that violent young people existed in every community. In his opening address to the special session, Romer said, "This [youth violence] is not just a problem for any particular ethnic group. We are all in this together. Rural, urban, Black, Latino, Asian-American, and Anglo—our whole community is victimized by violence."[126]

Second, Romer met privately with leading representatives (political, social, and civic) of the African American and Latino communities. According to Romer's staff members, these leaders expressed concerns not only about the violence in their neighborhoods but also about police harassment. Romer assured these leaders that his legislative initiatives neither singled out minority youth nor gave police (or other social control agents) license to mistreat Latino or African American youth. He reiterated this point publicly in his opening remarks to the special session:

> Let me say this right up front—this is a tough package we are about to discuss, and I hear and understand the concerns of parents and others in the communities of color that what we do here not be an excuse for the police to harass kids because of the color of their skin. We're not here to do that. We're trying to get the guns out of the hands of children so that they don't hurt one another, no matter what their color. I will work with you and with law enforcement agencies to ensure these laws are applied fairly. What we want to do is stop the violence, not harass innocent kids.[127]

Third, although Romer's role in this decision is not entirely clear, it is worth noting that the person appointed as the first director of YOS, Regis Groff, was a highly respected, liberal, African American state senator who, during the special session, delivered the single most powerful speech in support of the YOS measure. Groff's appointment provided YOS with a battle-tested leader, one whose strong ties to the legislature enhanced appreciably the new institution's prospects for future funding. This appointment also signaled that YOS would be keenly attuned to racial and ethnic disparities among its inmate population and that discrimination would not be tolerated.

Conclusion

This chapter has indicated how the recent trend toward criminalizing a subset of youth can be understood from a neofunctionalist perspective. This perspective maintains that new, differentiated institutions are often justified as a remedy to pressing problems and that successful episodes of institution building depend, in part, on the ability of entrepreneurs to mobilize support for new and purportedly more effective problem-solving structures. While successful entrepreneurs make institutional history, they do not, to paraphrase Marx, make it in circumstances of their own choosing. Accordingly, understanding entrepreneurs' institution-building efforts requires situating their change-oriented projects and mobilization strategies in a broader institutional and cultural context. Through a detailed examination of the Summer of Violence and the creation of the Colorado YOS, we have attempted to illustrate these general ideas.

Neofunctionalism's interest in the creation of new institutions can be profitably joined to traditional functionalism's concern with the consequences of long-standing structures and practices. It was, after all, a functionalist who first formulated "the law of unintended consequences" and pointed out that institutions, once established, operate in ways their originators never intended or anticipated.[128] This chapter is not the place to present a comprehensive treatment of YOS's unintended consequences, but three issues pertinent to that type of analysis can be briefly considered. First, although YOS was touted as better equipped to address the problem of serious juvenile offenders, little systematic evidence has been generated to support this claim. A performance audit of YOS (published in August 1999) conducted by the Office of the Colorado State Auditor offered this observation:

> More than five years have passed since the Youthful Offender System began accepting offenders. . . . Yet the Department [of Corrections] has not evaluated the effectiveness of the program or measured its outcomes. Consequently, the overall effectiveness of the program is unknown. This is particularly troubling because YOS was intended to be an innovative approach to turning youthful offenders around before it was too late—a second last chance. . . . However, the Department can provide no real evidence that YOS has been successful in achieving the goals for which it was created.[129]

The absence of a rigorous evaluation—despite the fact that the legislation creating YOS explicitly mandated such an evaluation—is not surprising. During the early stages of institution building, entrepreneurial groups and their allies herald newly proposed structures as much more effective and efficient problem solvers than the existing structures they are designed to replace. But once the new structures are in place, their management and staff resist systematic assessments of the institution's performance. With regard to YOS, the consequence of this "assessment avoidance" is that few people, and certainly not the general public, know whether the YOS program succeeds in resocializing its inmates and significantly reducing their rates of reoffending.

Second, the ambivalence built into YOS—the uneasy balance between punishment and treatment—seems to be inherently unstable and, in the long run, may be unsustainable. Like scores of previous correctional programs, YOS appears to be subordinating its commitment to treatment and rehabilitation while elevating its concern for control and custody.[130] This development may overlap with the pattern of assessment avoidance described in the previous paragraph: So long as YOS succeeds in controlling and incapacitating its inmates, little public or policy-maker attention is likely to be given to whether the institution successfully treats young offenders.

Third, the continuing decline of violent juvenile crime in Colorado (and across the nation) raises an obvious question about the future of institutions like YOS that emerged in response to an apparent surge in the number of gang-affiliated, violent youth. Proponents of YOS presumed that high rates of violent juvenile offending would continue indefinitely and that the institution's 480 beds would be filled with dangerous young felons. What is likely to happen if there are not enough violent adolescents to occupy those beds? The sociology of prisons provides an answer: The beds will be filled, and if not by hyparviolent gang members, then by some other type of transgressing adolescent, albeit not the "new breed of youthful offender" who was invoked to justify the construction of YOS in the first place.

Notes

1. Feld, B. C. (1999). *Bad kids: Race and the transformation of the juvenile court* (p. 225). New York: Oxford University Press.

2. Torbet, P., Gable, R., Hurst, H., IV, Montgomery, I., Szymanski, L., & Thomas, D. (1996). *State responses to serious and violent juvenile crime* (p. xv). Washington, DC: Office of Juvenile Justice and Delinquency Prevention.

3. Torbet et al. (1996), *States responses to serious and violent juvenile crime*, p. xii.

4. Torbet et al. (1996), *State responses to serious and violent juvenile crime*, p. 13.

5. Singer, S. I. (1996). *Recriminalizing delinquency: Violent juvenile crime and juvenile justice reform* (pp. 1-2). Cambridge, UK: Cambridge University Press.

6. *Denver Post*, August 8, 1993, p. 16A.

7. *Rocky Mountain News*, May 31, 1993, pp. 8A, 10A.

8. *Denver Post*, August 8, 1993, p. 16A.

9. *Denver Post*, August 8, 1993, p. 16A.

10. Alexander, J. C. (Ed.). (1985). *Neofunctionalism*. Beverly Hills, CA: Sage.

11. Parsons, T., & Smelser, N. J. (1956). *Economy and society*. New York: Free Press.

12. Smelser, N. (1959). *Social change in the industrial revolution*. Chicago: University of Chicago Press.

13. Parsons, T. (1966). *Societies: Evolutionary and comparative perspectives*. New York: Free Press.

14. Eisenstadt, S. N. (1964). Social change, differentiation, and evolution. *American Sociological Review, 29*, 235-247; (1995). *Power, trust, and meaning*. Chicago: University of Chicago Press.

15. Colomy, P. (1998). Neofunctionalism and neoinstitutionalism: Human agency and interest in institutional change. *Sociological Forum, 13*, 265-300.

16. Smelser, N. (1985). Evaluation the model of structural differentiation. In J. C. Alexander (Ed.), *Neofuntionalism* (pp. 113-129). Beverly Hills, CA: Sage.

17. Parsons, T. (1971). *The system of modern societies*. Englewood Cliffs, NJ: Prentice Hall.

18. Parsons, T., & Smelser, N. J. (1956). *Economy and society*. New York: Free Press.

19. Smelser, N. (1974). Growth, structural change, and conflict in California higher education, 1950-1970. In N. Smelser & G. Almond (Eds.), *Public higher education in California* (pp. 9-141). Berkeley: University of California Press.

20. Jacobs, M. D. (1990). *Screwing the system and making it work: Juvenile justice in the no-fault society*. Chicago: University of Chicago Press.

21. Ogburn, W. F. (1922). *Social change: With respect to culture and original nature* (p. xiii). New York: B. W. Huebsch.

22. Alexander, J. C. (1988). *Action and its environments: Toward a new synthesis*. New York: Columbia University Press; Colomy, P., & Rhoades, G. (1994). Toward a micro corrective of structural differentiation theory. *Sociological Perspectives, 37*, 547-583.

23. Etzioni, A. (2000). Toward a theory of public ritual. *Sociological Theory, 18,* 44-59; Marshall, T. H. (1964). *Class, citizenship, and social development.* Chicago: University of Chicago Press.

24. Durkheim, É. (1984). *The division of labor in society.* New York: Free Press. (Original work published 1893)

25. Lipset, S. M. (1996). *American exceptionalism: A double-edged sword.* New York: Norton.

26. Parsons, T., & Bales, R. F. (1955). *Family, socialization, and interaction process.* New York: Free Press.

27. Alexander, J. C. (1990). Core solidarity, ethnic out-groups, and social differentiation. In J. C. Alexander & Paul Colomy (Eds.), *Differentiation theory and social change: Comparative and historical perspectives.* New York: Columbia University Press; Glazer, N. (1975). *Affirmative discrimination.* New York: Basic Books.

28. Huntington, S. (1981). *American politics: The promise of disharmony.* Cambridge, MA: Harvard University Press.

29. Alexander, J. C., & Smith, P. (1993). The discourse of American civil society: A new proposal for cultural studies. *Theory and Society, 22,* 158.

30. Alexander & Smith (1993), *Theory and Society,* p. 157.

31. Swidler, A. (1986). Culture in action: Symbols and strategies. *American Sociological Review, 51,* 273-286.

32. Williams, R. H. (1995). Constructing the public good: Social movements and cultural resources. *Social Problems, 42,* 124-144.

33. Snow, D. A., & Benford, R. D. (1988). Ideology, frame resonance, and participant mobilization. *International Social Movement Research, 1,* 197-217.

34. Bellah, R. (1999, April 6). *Protestants, Catholics, and the common good.* Chester Alter Lecture delivered at Regis University, Denver, CO.

35. Youth and violent crime articles were identified through the *Denver Post Index* using several topical categories: crime, crime prevention, criminal law, criminal sentences, detention centers, gangs, juvenile delinquency, murder and murder attempts, victims of crime, violent crime, and violence. Every story in the category of juvenile delinquency was included in the sample. For the category gangs, every story was included with the exception of articles describing adult, mobster gangs. Stories for all other categories were included only if the Index indicated that the article contained one or more of the following phrases: youth/juvenile violence, youth/juvenile offender, epidemic of violence, crime wave, town meetings/marches/protests/press conferences/church sermons on crime/violence, correctional facilities for youth, criminal/juvenile system and youth, gangs, gang prevention, random violence, reports on patterns/distributions/trends/rates of crime/violence, fear of crime/violence, and funds/resources/personnel allocated to crime/violence prevention programs.

36. We focus on youth and violent crime because this topic, more than any other, fueled local media coverage of the summer's violence.

37. The data for the 1994 summer are incomplete because the Aurora monthly report does include aggravated assault figures for August of that year. Combining Denver's complete figures with the partial information supplied by Aurora, we inferred that nonlethal, violent offenses were roughly 5% to 10% lower in the 1994 summer compared to the 1993 summer.

38. Our qualitative assessment of the media's coverage of the Summer of Violence analyzed articles published in both the *Denver Post* and the *Rocky Mountain News.* The *Denver Post* has the largest circulation in the state, whereas the *Rocky Mountain News* boasts the second-largest circulation in Colorado. Both papers are based in Denver.

39. *Denver Post* (1993, July 24), pp. A1, A2, A4; *Denver Post* (1993, July 28), p. A16; *Denver Post* (1993, July 24), pp. A1, A15; *Denver Post* (1993, July 31), p. A18.

40. *Denver Post* (1993, July 28), pp. A1, A4; *Denver Post* (1993, July 28), pp. A1, A11.

41. *Denver Post* (1993, July 29), pp. A1, A4; *Denver Post* (1993, July 29), pp. A1, A10.

42. Christie, N. (1986). The ideal victim. In E. A. Fattah (Ed.), *From crime policy to victim policy: Reorienting the justice system* (pp. 17-30). New York: St. Martin's; Luckenbill, D. (1977). Criminal homicide as a situation transaction. *Social Problems, 25,* 176-186.

43. Christie (1986), in *From crime policy to victim policy.*

44. We conducted interviews with 23 reporters, columnists, and editors involved in writing about youth crime for the *Denver Post* and the *Rocky Mountain News* during the 1993 summer. (We also conducted interviews with three local television reporters, a local talk-radio show host, and a reporter employed by *Westword,* an alternative Denver newspaper.) To protect the confidentiality we promised to those who spoke with us, we characterize all respondents generically as either journalists or reporters. The interviews were designed to elicit the meanings journalists were inviting their readers to accept, and reporters' comments and insights proved invaluable to our qualitative assessment of news themes.

45. Zelizer, V. A. (1985). *Pricing the priceless child.* New York: Basic Books.

46. *Denver Post* (1993, July 30), p. A16.

47. *Denver Post* (1993, July 31), p. A5.

48. *Denver Post* (1993, July 30), p. A15.

49. *Denver Post* (1993, July 31), p. A5.

50. *Denver Post* (1993, July 31), p. A5.

51. Best, J. (1990). *Threatened children: Rhetoric and concern about child-victims* (pp. 28-29). Chicago: University of Chicago Press.

52. *Denver Post* (1993, December 19), pp. A4, A45. The author of this story based his account on a computer search of Denver police records, which revealed that juveniles "attacked" 210 people during June, July, and August of 1993. From the story's context, it appears that this journalist defined juvenile violence broadly to include victims of homicide, forcible rape, aggravated assault, and nonaggravated assault. (The latter category is often omitted from social scientific discussions of serious youth violence.) This reporter was killed in a traffic accident a year before we began our research, and consequently, we could not ask for clarification about the data and sources used for this article.

53. Best (1990), *Threatened children,* pp. 28-29.

54. *Denver Post* (1993, May 5), p. A22.

55. *Denver Post* (1993, June 11), p. A1.

56. *Denver Post* (1993, June 10), p. A1.

57. *Denver Post* (1993, August 3), p. A1.

58. *Denver Post* (1993, June 11), p. A1.

59. *Denver Post* (1993, May 5), p. A1.

60. *Denver Post* (1993, August 8), p. A86.

61. *Denver Post* (1993, July 31), p. E1.

62. *Denver Post* (1993, August 12), p. A62.

63. *Denver Post* (1993, August 5), p. B9.

64. Durkheim, É. (1995). *The elementary forms of religious life* (pp. 118, 120). New York: Free Press. (Original work published 1912)

65. *Denver Post* (1993, July 13), p. B7.

66. Durkheim (1995), *The elementary forms of religious life,* p. 120.

67. Eliade, M. (1959). *The sacred and the profane: The nature of religion* (p. 48). New York: Harcourt, Brace & World.

68. *Denver Post* (1993, July 28), p. A13.

69. *Denver Post* (1993, June 15), p. A14; (1993, June 23), pp. A1, A11; (1993, July 1), pp. B1, B4.

70. *Denver Post* (1993, May 4), p. B6. Reprinted with permission.

71. *Denver Post* (1993, August 1), p. C4.

72. *Denver Post* (1993, August 8), p. D1.

73. *Denver Post* (1993, May 6), p. B1.

74. *Denver Post* (1993, June 11), A1, A4, A6; (1993, July 7), A5; (1993, July 13), A6; (1993, July 20), A12; (1993, July 23), A1, A14. *Denver Post* (1993, June 17), A21; (1993, June 23), A1; (1993, July 2), A1; (1993, July 3), B1; (1993, July 30), A12; (1993, July 31), A16; (1993, August 20), B1.

75. *Denver Post* (1993, August 10), p. A12; (1993, Sep. 7), p. A33. *Denver Post* (1993, July 13), p. B3; (1993, July 30), p. A1; (1993, August 15), pp. A1, A4; (1993, September 7), p. A12.

76. *Denver Post* (1993, June 11), A26; (1993, July 29), A20; *Denver Post* (1993, July 29), A9; (1993, August 1), C4; (1993, August 4), A1, A4, A6.

77. *Denver Post* (1993, July 17), pp. A1, A5; (1993, July 22), p. A16; (1993, July 25), pp. A1, A6, A26. *Denver Post* (1993, June 15), A1, A4; (1993, June 17), pp. A1, A27; (1993, August 2), p. A1.

78. *Denver Post* (1993, July 7), p. A5.

79. Acland, C. R. (1995). *Youth, murder, spectacle: The cultural politics of "youth in crisis"* (p. 4). Boulder, CO: Westview.

80. Gitlin, T. (1980). *The whole world is watching.* Berkeley: University of California Press.

81. *Denver Post* (1993, August 4), p. A32.

82. Colomy, P., & Kretzmann, M. (1995). Projects and institution building: Judge Ben. B. Lindsey and the juvenile court movement. *Social Problems, 42,* 1191-1215.

83. *Denver Post* (1993, July 12), p. A8.

84. *Denver Post* (1993, September 5), p. A93.

85. *Denver Post* (1993, September 1), pp. F1, F4.

86. *Denver Post* (1993, September 9), p. B7.

87. Durkheim, É. (1973). In Robert N. Bellah (Ed.), *Emile Durkheim: On morality and society* (p. 46). Chicago: University of Chicago Press. (Original work published 1898)

88. Durkheim (1995), *The elementary forms of religious life,* pp. 412-414.

89. Christie (1986), in *From crime policy to victim policy,* p. 25.

90. Christie (1986), in *From crime policy to victim policy,* p. 25.

91. Christie (1986), in *From crime policy to victim policy,* pp. 26, 28.

92. Christie (1986), in *From crime policy to victim policy,* p. 26.

93. Anderson, E. (1990). *Streetwise: Race, class, and change in an urban community.* Chicago: University of Chicago Press; Sampson, R. J., & Laub, J. H. (1993). Structural variations in juvenile court processing: Inequality, the underclass, and social control. *Law and Society, 27,* 285-311.

94. Sasson, T. (1995). *Crime talk: How citizens construct a social problem.* New York: Aldine de Gruyter.

95. *Denver Post* (1993, August 4), p. A32.

96. *Denver Post* (1993, August 4), p. A32.

97. Colorado Special Session on Youth Violence. Remarks delivered to House Judiciary Committee (September 9, 1993).

98. Colorado Special Session on Youth Violence. Remarks delivered to Colorado House and Senate (September 7, 1993).

99. Colorado Special Session on Youth Violence. Remarks delivered to Senate Appropriations Committee (September 8, 1993).

100. Colorado Special Session on Youth Violence. Remarks delivered to House Judiciary Committee (September 9, 1993).

101. Gusfield, J. R. (1981). *The culture of public problems: Drinking-driving and the symbolic order* (pp. 13-16). Chicago: University of Chicago Press.

102. Gusfield, J. R. (1981). *The culture of public problems,* p. 14.

103. Stallings, R. A. (1990). Media discourse and the social construction of risk. *Social Problems, 21,* 90.

104. Blumer, H. (1971). Social problems as collective behavior. *Social Problems, 18,* 304.

105. *Denver Post* (1993, June 23), p. B4.

106. *Denver Post* (1993, June 24), pp. A1, A4.

107. *Denver Post* (1993, September 5), pp. A20, A22.

108. *Denver Post* (1993, July 31), p. A16.

109. *Denver Post* (1993, July 20), p. A12.

110. *Denver Post* (1993, June 17), p. A21.

111. *Denver Post* (1993, July 13), p. A6.

112. *Denver Post* (1993, July 30), p. A12.

113. *Denver Post* (1993, July 3), p. B1.

114. *Denver Post* (1993, August 20), p. B1.

115. *Denver Post* (1993, July 23), pp. A1, A4. *Denver Post* (1993, July 23), p. A1.

116. *Denver Post* (1993, September 10), p. A11.

117. Colorado Special Session on Youth Violence. Remarks delivered to Joint Session (September 7, 1993).

118. Colorado Special Session on Youth Violence. Remarks delivered to Senate Judiciary Committee (September 7, 1993).

119. Colorado Special Session on Youth Violence. Remarks delivered to Senate Judiciary Committee (September 7, 1993).

120. Colorado Special Session on Youth Violence. Remarks delivered to House Appropriations Committee (September 10, 1993).

121. Lorch, R. S. (1983). *Colorado government* (p. 198). Boulder: Colorado Associated University Press.

122. *Denver Post* (1993, June 23), p. A1.

123. *Denver Post* (1993, July 23), p. A1.

124. *Denver Post* (1993, July 1), pp. B1, B4.

125. Colorado Special Session on Youth Violence. Remarks delivered to Joint Session (September 7, 1993).

126. Colorado Special Session on Youth Violence. Remarks delivered to Joint Session (September 7, 1993).

127. Colorado Special Session on Youth Violence. Remarks delivered to Joint Session (September 7, 1993).

128. Merton, R. K. (1936). The unanticipated consequences of social action. *American Sociological Review, 1,* 894-904; (1968). *Social theory and social structure* (pp. 73-138). New York: Free Press.

129. Report of the [Colorado] State Auditor. (1999). *Performance audit of department of corrections: Youthful offender system* (p. 52). Denver: Legislative Services.

130. *Westword* (1999, December 2-8), pp. 1, 24, 25, 27, 28, 30, 32.

Discussion Questions

1. This chapter argues that news organizations, like other institutions, are guided by a distinctive institutional logic. The media's institutional logic is structured around newsworthiness. How does the logic of newsworthiness affect the

coverage of crime in your town or city? Do some crimes seem to receive substantially more coverage than other crimes? Why? How does the status of crime victims affect that coverage? How might the size of a city and the overall volume of crime influence news coverage? Finally, what distinctive logics inform the functioning of other institutions—for example, science, religion, family, and government?

2. Many contemporary legislators and policy makers blamed a new breed of vicious teens for the surge in youth violence that occurred between the mid-1980s and mid-1990s. But the rates of youth violence have declined dramatically since 1995. What has happened to this supposedly new breed of offender? Did this new breed of offender ever really exist, or was it primarily a construction of the media and policy makers, a construction subsequently endorsed by the public?

3. Supporters of current "get tough" policies maintain that trying teens in adult (criminal) courts and sending those who are convicted to adult prisons (or to very punitive juvenile institutions) will deter both these offenders and other young people from committing crimes in the future. Do you agree with this argument? Why or why not? If you wanted to test this argument empirically, what type(s) of data would you gather?

CHAPTER 6

Why Do African Americans Pay More for New Cars?

A Structural Explanation

Christopher Prendergast

Christopher Prendergast received his BA from Brooklyn College (CUNY) in 1970 and then worked for the New York City Housing Authority for 2 years before pursuing an MA (1974) and a PhD (1979) from Southern Illinois University, Carbondale, where he concentrated on phenomenological sociology, Weber's methodology, Parsons, Lévi-Strauss, and the philosophy of science. For the past decade, he has centered his research on the concept of social structure in classical and contemporary social theory. He is Professor of Sociology at Illinois Wesleyan University in Bloomington. He served as president of the Midwest Sociological Society in 2003 and 2004.

This chapter develops a structural explanation to account for a disquieting and, on closer inspection, puzzling social fact—that African Americans in the Chicago metropolitan area pay more for new cars of comparable size and quality than do whites. Not a few dollars more, but hundreds of dollars more.

I explain what a structural explanation is later. For this chapter to succeed in its pedagogical purpose, however, readers should pause here and ask themselves, how is that possible? Most of you have some experience with the retail car business. What factors and circumstances could possibly account for this price disparity?

To spare you from heading off in the wrong direction altogether, I should inform you that the price differences were established by controlled experiment. Whites and blacks, matched for everything except race and gender, bargained for the same (or comparable) cars following the same bargaining script, and still the African Americans paid more—lots more.

While you are puzzling out the why and the how, I discuss structural explanations in sociology and introduce a few of the concepts I use in this chapter.

Structural Explanation in Sociology

A *structural explanation* is a type of causal explanation that is specifically designed to account for patterns of human actions and choices. These patterns are usually formulated as statistical frequencies and correlations, but any observed regularity or sequence of human behavior and belief can be subject to a structural explanation. A structural explanation takes the observed pattern or outcome as the fact to be explained. It then accounts for the pattern by identifying the social process or processes that produce it. The process usually amounts to a sequence of social interaction that leads each party to make an interdependent choice from a shrinking, often familiar, and even institutionalized menu of options. The process or processes that ultimately account for the pattern operate within a system of social relationships, practices, and beliefs called, appropriately, a *social system.* The process is just the way these relationships, practices, and beliefs operate dynamically to structure the choices and actions of individuals. The first step in a structural explanation is to describe the social system(s) whose processes generate the pattern, and the second is to forge a plausible link between the processes and the pattern.

That may sound simple enough, but in practice both steps are fraught with challenges because social systems crisscross and overlay each other in complex ways. That complexity has to be disentangled by abstraction into a series of interrelated models of structure and process aligned in a causal sequence. In the following explanation, several systems of relationships, practices, and beliefs are aligned into two causal streams that merge in the automobile showroom. One stream flows into the buyer and the other into the seller. The buyer-seller relationship is the social system closest to the decision to pay X amount for a new car. But it may not be the most important link in the causal sequence. In the following explanation, we will need to back up several levels of social structure to get a sense of the overlapping social systems involved. On the seller's side, we need to consider the dealership as a social system, the network of dealerships in the metropolitan area, the relationship between dealers and manufacturers, and, ultimately, the dynamics of the international automobile industry as a whole. On the buyer's side, we need to differentiate buyers by social network, community, and class position. Buyer and seller greet one another as bearers and emblems of structural position.

Bear in mind that the price disparity is an aggregate figure, an average cost difference per car. Because some African American buyers will get better deals than most whites, the explanation needs to identify the conditions and processes that produce that outcome as well as its opposite outcome. Some of these conditions and processes are bound up with individual performance, others with various kinds of empowerments (called social and cultural capital), and others with organizational characteristics and sales practices.

A model—or, rather, a collection of models—that tries to cover all the conditions and processes responsible for the price disparity would be too complex to present here, even if I had made a complete inventory of them. In fact, there are gaps even in crucial places. To forestall criticism, I admit that the explanation presented here amounts to a series of plausible guesses.

Because a structural explanation is a form of explanation, rather than a theory in its own right, it necessarily relies on a number of component theories to accomplish its task. The component theories employed here are represented by the following concepts: social capital, cultural capital, status characteristics, typification, power/dependency, and power-balancing operations.

The most important of these concepts, *power/dependency,* is taken from Richard Emerson's (1962) famous essay, "Power-Dependence Relations." Emerson's conception of power is entirely relational: One party's power in a relationship is equal to the other party's dependence on the rewards or resources derived from the relationship. It is significant that dependency is a two-sided concept. A's dependence on B increases proportionally to A's motivational investment in the goals or resources controlled by B, where *resources* refers to anything of value to A (e.g., a new car). Conversely, A's dependence on B decreases to the extent that A finds alternative suppliers of the resource controlled by B (i.e., another car dealer). When relationships are power imbalanced, the party with the greater power is tempted to seek a higher level of reward from the other, whereas the more dependent party is inclined to reduce dependency by seeking other exchange partners, by forming a coalition with others in their dependent condition, or by adjusting their desires and preferences. Emerson calls these strategic responses to dependency *power-balancing operations.* Being first cousin to the law of supply and demand, the concept of dependency provides a powerful conceptual bridge between structural conditions and bargaining processes.

For the concept of *cultural capital,* which refers to the quality and quantity of information that actors can deploy in social interaction, I draw on contemporary French sociologist Pierre Bourdieu (1984, 1985). For the concept of *social capital,* which refers to the pool of favors and obligations in one's social network, I draw on James Coleman (1988, 1990). The term *status characteristics* refers to the attributes commonly associated with statuses such as age, physical attractiveness, class, race, and gender. For my understanding of how status characteristics affect social interaction, I am indebted to Knottnerus (1994, 1997), Ridgeway (1991), Ridgeway and Berger (1988), and Wagner and Berger (1993).

The term *typification* is from Alfred Schutz (1962). It characterizes the degrees of knowledge that people have in different domains of experience. Some things we know in fine detail, others by name only. Both the salesperson and the customer can banter about the wonders of the "computer-controlled ignition system," but neither could explain how it works to an engineer. Having typifications of impressive depth and variety, and the linguistic competence to use them, is what cultural capital is all about. All status characteristics are known through typification.

Underlying the whole explanation is a theory of action derived from Carl Menger (1963) via Max Weber (1947) and developed further by March and Simon (1958), Kahneman and Tversky (Kahneman, Slovic, & Tversky, 1982), and White (1992). For the conception of social structure, I draw on social network analysis (Burt 1982, 1992; Knoke & Guilarte, 1994; Willer, 1999). For the concept of structural explanation, I rely on Boudon (1987), Coleman (1987), and Little (1991). Finally, in emphasizing typifications and cultural capital, I try to avoid the pitfalls of structural determinism and reductionism identified by Rubinstein (1986, 2000).

All that theory for one little explanation? You bet, and that is just the short list. But let's get back on task. While I have been assembling the concepts that are essential for my explanation, how is yours coming along?

Some Background Information

So why do African Americans in the Chicago metropolitan area pay hundreds of dollars more for new cars? It must have something to do with race. But what?

Like most facts, this one comes to us preinterpreted. So our first task is to question the interpretation that envelops it. We then marshal some background knowledge and try to work up a sociological explanation of the sort that I am promoting in this chapter. Because much of the information that you need for an alternative explanation is widely known, you should be able to keep a step or two ahead of the argument. But for those of you who are unfamiliar with the Chicago metropolitan area, let me share two essential bits of information.

First, the Chicago metropolitan area is highly segregated. According to the U.S. Bureau of the Census (1993, pp. 106-107), Chicago was 45% white and 39% black in 1990, whereas its suburbs were 87% white and 6.7% black. But that is just the tip of the iceberg. Most of the black population in Chicago is concentrated in two areas south and west of downtown. The city is so segregated that 91% of the black population would have to move for everyone to live in an integrated neighborhood (Massey & Denton, 1993, p. 72). Segregation extends into the suburbs as well: The majority of black suburbanites live in segregated towns and neighborhoods just across the city line (Massey & Denton, 1993, pp. 67-74). Two of these suburbs, near the abandoned East Chicago steel mills, are among the 15 poorest suburbs in the entire country (McCarron, 1989, p. 7). The term *hypersegregation* was coined to describe the extreme isolation and concentration of African Americans in metropolitan areas such as Chicago (Massey & Denton, 1993, p. 74).

Segregation may concentrate African Americans geographically, but that does not mean the population is highly integrated. On the contrary, African American social networks are shorter in length, range less widely across the social spectrum, and have fewer links to brokers of jobs, opportunities, and information (Fernández-Kelly, 1995; Patterson, 1998). College graduates who reside in segregated neighborhoods inhabit social networks as contact poor and isolated as those of people who never attended college (Patterson, 1998, p. 153).

Second, the median income of African Americans living in the city was just $20,282 in 1995 compared to $39,520 for the median family in suburban Cook

County and $60,686 for the median family in prosperous Du Page County (U.S. Department of Housing and Urban Development/U.S. Bureau of the Census, 1997, p. 23). As a result of both of these conditions, geographical concentration in areas served by public transportation and lower median income, fewer African Americans own cars. Slightly more than 60% of black households in Chicago owned an automobile in 1995 (U.S. Department of Housing and Urban Development/U.S. Bureau of the Census, 1997, p. 17). That is a major improvement over the late 1960s, when fewer than 30% owned an automobile. But it is no match for the collar counties, where two- and three-car families are commonplace.

Interesting. But what do these facts have to do with African Americans paying more for new cars?

Car Price Mystery

Some years ago, economist and law professor Ian Ayres sent a number of "testers" to auto dealerships in the Chicago area. Testers are employees in an experiment designed to detect discrimination against minorities, usually in housing and hiring. In this case, the Ayres team was responding to reports that African Americans paid more for new cars than did whites.

As is customary in this type of study, pairs of testers were matched for age, physical attractiveness, speech, dress, and socioeconomic status (all presented themselves as young professionals). In this case, all of the pairs included a white male; the other member of the pair was a white female, a black male, or a black female. Each member of a tester pair went separately to 90 different dealerships in the metropolitan area. Although they did not actually purchase cars, they bargained for the best price they could get and left with an offer in hand. All followed the same negotiating script, which they rehearsed for 2 days to minimize differences in personality and bargaining style. The script called for them to quickly select a car in the predetermined price range, ask how much the seller wanted for it, counteroffer at the wholesale price, then split the difference on subsequent counteroffers. Counteroffering at the wholesale price was supposed to suggest that the tester had done a little homework. That may have worked for the white male testers. But after 180 deals in 90 showrooms, the African American testers wound up agreeing to markups two and three times higher than their white counterparts. The results of this study are shown in column 1 of Table 6.1.

Because only 6 testers were involved in the study, the reliability of the findings could be challenged. So Ayres replicated the study using 38 testers who struck 404 deals at 225 dealerships (column 2 of Table 6.1). This time, testers were allowed to look at nine types of vehicles, and the script allowed salespersons to talk them up to a bigger car (which is why the markups were higher in the second study). Table 6.1 shows the differences between the average invoice price (roughly the cost of the car to the dealer) and the final bid price by status of tester in the two studies.

Rather amazing—and disturbing—isn't it? At the time the studies were undertaken, the income of the median black family in the city was nearly $20,000 less

Table 6.1   Car Price Markups by Status of Buyer

	1991 Study	1995 Study
White male	+$362	+$564
White female	+$504	+$656
Black male	+$783	+$1,665
Black female	+$1,237	+$975

SOURCES: Ayres (1991), Ayres and Siegelman (1995).

than that of the median family in suburban Cook County and $40,000 less than that of the median family in Du Page County. Yet car dealers seemingly gave white families a break in price while taking black families to the cleaners. It looks like a prima facie case of discrimination. Bias against African Americans must run pretty deep in the retail car business. Like exclusionary housing and hiring practices, price discrimination in car sales reinforces segregation and denies African Americans equal treatment and respect.

But there is something odd about this case, isn't there? Auto dealers are in the business of selling cars, not enforcing the color line. Salespeople rely on commissions for their livelihood. Both want to move product off the lot. Discriminatory pricing seems like a risky and self-penalizing way to express racial animosity. Even if one could avoid a lawsuit, what sense does it make to risk alienating a customer base as large as 40% of the population of Chicago?

Besides, just how does racial bias account for discriminatory pricing? Do dealers instruct salespeople to bargain in bad faith? Are they trying to enforce segregation by punishing those who cross the color line with higher prices? Do salespeople, acting on their own, just enjoy gouging their black customers? Is it company policy, maverick salespeople, or some deeply ingrained disposition on the part of whites to get the best of blacks when they have the chance?

Perhaps, auto sales are like housing sales. Where white homeowners are united in their desire to exclude blacks, realtors who break the ban face retaliation. If the analogy holds, suburban auto dealers try to keep black customers off the lot to ease the discomfort of white buyers, whom they placate further by giving them better deals. If so, the tactic of discriminatory pricing seems as ineffective as it is risky. Black customers take as long as anyone else to strike a deal. As far as race-sensitive whites who come on the premises during the negotiations are concerned, the dealership is integrated, whether the deal is struck or not and regardless of the markup. Besides, realtors who discriminate do not just bargain harder with African American buyers. They steer them into black-majority neighborhoods. Car dealers cannot do that without losing the sale.

Chicago suburbs are among the most highly segregated in the country. But the higher markups were not concentrated in the suburbs. They were just as high at dealerships located in and near majority black neighborhoods and at dealerships owned by blacks (Ayres, 1991, p. 847; Ayres & Siegelman, 1995, p. 315).

If protecting the color line is not the motive behind the higher prices, perhaps the explanation lies in the prejudice of individual salespeople. Everyone in this society has been exposed to racial stereotypes. Perhaps some white salespeople have passed these stereotypes back and forth within their social networks for so long that they cannot distinguish one African American from another anymore. All black customers are the same to them. They all fall for the same sales pitch. They are all equally gullible and uninformed and loose with their money. The testers' knowledge of what the dealer paid for the car, their professional middle-class status, and their business-like manner of negotiating are all screened out. The biased salespeople just keep interacting with a stereotype. They hardly budge on the price, while the testers keep splitting the difference. Bias wins, and the black testers leave with higher final offers than white testers.

That is a plausible theory with much good social psychology behind it. Many studies of prejudice document an out-group homogeneity effect, an expectation effect, and an assimilation effect (Fiske, 1993; Hilton & von Hippel, 1996). Taken together, these effects mean that prejudiced people operate with stereotypes that resist disconfirmation. But these studies also suggest that these effects diminish through social interaction, that people use more accurate subtypes rather than global stereotypes in practical affairs, and that subtypes eventually displace stereotypes when these practical needs persist (Brewer, 1988). Outcome dependency (relying on a minority for an outcome such as making a sale) also undermines stereotypes (Riley & Fiske, 1991). So does competition (Matheson, Holmes, & Kristiansen, 1991). Finally, being accountable to third parties—such as car manufacturers or the local Civil Rights Commission—also prompts people to attend to individual differences (Fiske, 1993, p. 174). All this suggests that car salespeople, biased or not, are occupationally predisposed to make finer, more accurate distinctions than the prejudice explanation requires.

But there is an even stronger reason to doubt this line of explanation: African American testers buying cars from African American salespeople suffered the same markups. The same was true for female buyers and female sellers (Ayres, 1991, p. 847; Ayres & Siegelman, 1995, p. 316). You read that correctly. The race and gender of the salesperson, like the location of the dealership, had no statistically significant effect on the markups.

If higher markups do not kick in at the suburban boundary, and if black and female salespersons extract the same markups as whites, correlation between race, gender, and car price remains a mystery. Bias and discrimination are a plausible first hypothesis. But try as we might, we cannot figure out the *causal process,* the step-by-step progression from bias to higher car prices. Before we start formulating an alternative explanation, however, we might ask whether the Ayres team got its facts straight in the first place.

Despite all their precautions, could the testers inadvertently have provoked these results? After all, they were employed to test for discrimination. In a kind of self-fulfilling prophecy, could black and female testers have caved in early in the price negotiations, whereas white male testers held out longer? Perhaps this occurred in the first study, but it did not in the second. The testers in the second study thought they were studying negotiating tactics and did not know that they were being paired with testers of a different race and gender (Ayres & Siegelman, 1995, p. 307).

The fact is that the Ayres study confirms what has been known since the early 1960s: Poor and minority residents living in segregated areas pay more for everything from furniture and appliances to rent, insurance, and loans (Caplovitz, 1967; see also Alwitt & Donley, 1996). Therefore, rather than pick apart the methodology, let us accept the price differentials as substantially correct and try to explain them differently.[1]

Bargaining Power, Capital, and Dependency

Let us begin by reviewing Table 6.1. Notice that among whites, the markup on new cars sold to women is also higher than it is for males—a full 40% higher in the first study. Why is that? When I ask my students this question, they usually point out that since they were kids, men and women have looked at cars differently. Notable exceptions aside, men are generally more interested and knowledgeable about cars and car dealing than women of the same age. Women pay more, my students suggest, because they know less about car models and features, the frauds and bluffs of bargaining, and car culture generally, which has largely remained a male preserve. This handicap, however, can be offset by coming from a two-car family or being coached by more knowledgeable family members or friends. Could something like this affect African American car buyers?

Here is where the fact that only 30% of black households in Chicago owned a car in the late 1960s, whereas 60% did 20 years later, comes in. Many African Americans going into the dealerships in the years before the Ayres study were first-time car buyers with all the informational deficits that implies. With fewer people in their social networks owning cars, the coaching factor was also minimized.

Do you know that you should research the invoice price of the car you are interested in before going in for a test drive? I did not when I bought my first car as a 23-year-old New Yorker. I paid the full sticker price plus a few options, without getting even the floor mats thrown in. According to the Consumer Federation of America (1990, p. 9), approximately one third of white Americans are as naive about sticker prices as I was. Given their ownership rates, it is not surprising that three-fifths of African Americans are as well.

Being carless not only hurts African Americans in the information department. It also limits their ability to drive to the big suburban dealerships with the large inventories, low overhead, and high-volume sales to get a lower bid. Instead, they are stuck with a few dealerships close to home. These dealers soon come to know their customers and get used to pretending that the sticker price is an impartial measure of market value. That is what the testers confronted when they stepped into the showrooms: salespeople and managers accustomed to bargaining down from the sticker price, and not very steeply, either.

Let's call the practical knowledge of car buyers their cultural capital and the number of potential coaches and advisers in their networks their social capital. Let's call the condition of having fewer alternative sources of information, advice, and bids dependency. Capital and dependency are inversely related: Bargaining power increases with social and cultural capital and decreases with dependency. For reasons of residential segregation, median economic standing, network structure, and carlessness, many African American buyers enter the showrooms relatively low in bargaining power. That is just a hard fact, a statistical frequency. But it is a fact associated with race.

In the alternative explanation we are developing here, race is just a rude proxy for bargaining power. The causally relevant conditions on the buyer's side are all the things that affect bargaining power: information about invoice prices, comparable cars, and bargaining tactics; the capacity to visit different dealerships to compare bids and prices; and the quality of social and cultural capital in one's social network—for example, the availability of a "purchase pal" (Furse, Punj, & Stewart, 1984) more knowledgeable than oneself. If these conditions were equal among white and black buyers, price differences in a controlled study such as this would be due to individual differences in personality and negotiating style, situational contingencies, and conditions affecting the dealer's bargaining power and dependency.

Because these conditions are not equal, race is a proxy for bargaining power. That puts all African Americans at a disadvantage, even young Buppies (black urban professionals) like our testers. For all the dealers know, these young, well-dressed African Americans are just upwardly mobile, first-generation car buyers, not the savvy negotiators they claim to be. Perhaps that is why the black testers were two and a half times more likely to be asked how they got to the dealership (Ayres, 1995, p. 139). When testers in the second study said that they did not own a car, the final bid was $127 higher. When they said that they had visited another dealership, it was $120 lower (Ayres, 1995, p. 139). Not owning a car means fewer opportunities for price comparison, less experience in price negotiation, and recent upward mobility (read: disposable income and status seeking).[2] The sellers were seeking clues to dependency and trying to fine-tune their buyer categories.

Sound like we are onto something? Then, let us take a quick look at a key social institution that we will return to soon—the sales commission. The higher the price, the higher the commission. That is well known. But what is not is this: A full 50% of dealer profit comes from just 10% of buyers (Ayres, 1991, p. 854)—those who pay the full sticker price, or close to it, as I did years ago. Given this profit profile, salespeople are on the lookout for the young, the naive, the enchanted, the free spending, and the stuck—whatever their race, class, gender, or favorite breakfast cereal may be.

Rather than trying to protect the color line or being unable to distinguish one African American from another, in all likelihood, the dealerships were only too glad to see the testers—or rather, the demographic stratum that they represented—walk in the door. Young, upwardly mobile African Americans just establishing themselves in dynamic new careers—when asked, the testers described themselves as "systems analysts" in the banking business and as residents of Streeterville, an upper-middle-class neighborhood in the city—they had profit opportunity written all over them.

Does that make sense? Statistically, the African American population in Chicago is relatively weak in bargaining power; race is associated with deficits in cultural and social capital and with greater dependency (i.e., less opportunity to get two or more dealerships into a bidding contest); and the testers represent a young, affluent stratum of the African American population that includes many inexperienced buyers, even if these particular customers seem to have done their homework. Tight-lipped, well-dressed white customers who split the difference between offers are readily typified as knowledgeable, self-reliant negotiators who could easily get a lower bid at another dealership. Socially and behaviorally similar black customers should be treated the same—in the abstract. But in the dealer's experience this combination of buyer attributes is rather rare. To them, the testers' age, race, gender, and socioeconomic status signal "inexperienced buyer with money." Perhaps that is why when they asked how much the dealer wanted for a car, 29% of the African American testers were told the full sticker price, as opposed to just 9% of white testers (Ayres, 1995, p. 141). In the end, the burden of proof was on them (on the burden of proof assumption, see Berger, Cohen, & Zelditch, 1966). The net result? Final bids $400 to $1,100 higher than white testers were offered for comparable new cars.

How does being African American or female fit into this explanation? To the extent that dealers associate these statuses with inadequate knowledge, less opportunity for price comparison, and lack of negotiating savvy, they matter a lot. If they also harbor typifications about the buyer's gullibility, spending habits, and cave-in point based on race and gender alone, they matter. But mostly, they count when the typical minority buyer actually is in a poor bargaining position. Residential segregation in areas of low economic opportunity, visible social mobility limited to members of two-income families and a small but growing upper-middle class, relative carlessness, and weak advice networks—these are the structural conditions that make dark skin a rough-and-tumble proxy for low bargaining power. Not an accurate measure, or a sufficient one. Certainly not a fair one. But a measure that hits the mark often enough to acquire presumptive validity.

The good news in this analysis, as opposed to the utter pessimism of the bias/discrimination account, is that a minority car buyer who is well informed, talks about offers tendered elsewhere, and is willing to walk out the door should prompt the salesperson to reflect on his or her own bargaining position: the other missed opportunities this week, the growing inventory problem, the lost commission, and the manager's chagrin. Projecting upper-middle-class standing and following a good bargaining script, as the testers did, is not enough. Given the structural handicaps of the African American population in the city as a whole, to get equal treatment one has to prove—through the social performance of bargaining—that one is no mere *arriviste* but someone with sufficient financial, social, and cultural capital to play the game well.

The alternative explanation we are developing here moves bias and discrimination to the periphery of the argument, but it does not deny their reality. Car dealers and salespeople may well hold overgeneralized, disparaging beliefs about African Americans. Such beliefs are easily grafted onto unequal outcomes and used to excuse the practices that generate them (Ridgeway & Berger, 1988). But the alternative we devised can also explain why black and female salespeople seek the same markups; why women pay more; and why blacks with equal financial, social, and cultural capital bargain nearly as effectively as whites with similar resources. I say "nearly" because, statistically, a large portion of the African American community is in a poor bargaining position, and dealers hit the full-sticker jackpot too often to alter their bargaining approach. As a result, even savvy African American buyers are going to pay slightly more on average than comparable whites, whose racial status signals a better bargaining position before they utter a single word.

The Contexts of Dealer Dependency

My purpose in introducing the car price mystery is not just to tickle your sociological imagination but also to illustrate the principles of structural explanation in sociology. I did that so far by showing how background structural conditions, such as residential segregation, carlessness, and recent social mobility, increase buyer dependency; reduce the cultural and social capital of black social networks; and allow sellers to use external status characteristics, such as age, class, race, and gender, as indicators of bargaining power. Yet, aside from seller typifications, the axis of explanation mainly ran down the buyer's side of the relationship. For a proper structural explanation, we need to do at least two additional things: look at the dependencies on the seller's side of the relationship and contextualize the buyer-seller relationship by looking at the retail car business more globally. A good structural explanation always strives to chart all the lines of social causation that collapse on the immediate context of action, in this case, the bargaining situation.

Let us resume, then, where we left off—with the discovery that in the Chicago area, 50% of dealer profit comes from just 10% of buyers. As you recall, we used that statistic to explain why certain social statuses provoke so many full sticker-price offers. But that statistic can be read the other way, too. In the good old days of the 1950s, when the Big Three automakers had a swell little oligopoly going, dealers did not rely on 10% of sales for their livelihood. They expected, and got, markups in the 20% to 25% range, even more on hot new models (Yates, 1983, p. 220). There was some dickering over the price but not the wide disparities that we see today.

Flipped around, that statistic signifies a continental shift in dependency. Empowered by higher cultural and social capital and assisted by national organizations such as the Consumer Federation of America, which broadcasts coaching tips to its members, and credit unions, which provide wholesale car prices to their members for the asking, increasingly more families are bargaining dealers down to markups of just $300 to $500 per vehicle. During the mid-1990s, for example, members of the Chicago Automobile Association could order a new car through a dealer consortium for just 5% above the invoice price. One consequence of this new landscape of dealer dependency is the somewhat desperate attempt to exploit whatever buyer dependencies are left to dealers, such as the naïveté of first-time car buyers. We saw how that affects African Americans in Chicago, almost two fifths of whom are still carless. But that is obviously a rearguard action. What happened to the retail car business since the glory days of 25% markups?

Competition happened, that's what. In 1950, the United States produced 80% of the world's automobiles; by 1980, the U.S. share fell to 30% (Yates, 1983, p. 15). In the spring of 1999, the world's top 40 car makers had enough industrial capacity to produce 23 million more cars a year than consumers could buy. With overcapacity like that, a price war would decimate the industry. To forestall that outcome, car makers are acquiring each other at an unprecedented rate. The mergers of Daimler-Chrysler, Ford-Volvo, and Nissan-Renault in 1998 and 1999 mark the beginning of a new merger wave that could end with just six or eight global firms dominating the industry ("The Car Industry," 1999, p. 24).

These trends first hit American shores in the 1970s, when European and Japanese imports began to crowd the domestic market. Smaller, cheaper, sleeker, more fuel-efficient, better engineered, and better assembled foreign imports forced the domestic car industry into a crisis of reengineering, marketing, and downsizing that lasted two decades, cost more than 400,000 jobs, and—in conjunction with similar developments in the steel industry—turned the ring of manufacturing cities around the Great Lakes into the Rust Belt.[3]

How did the crisis in manufacturing affect the retail car business? It left dealers holding the bag, for one thing. As Detroit mass-produced one overpriced dud after another, dealers found themselves with unsold inventory, unhappy customers, and declining product loyalty. Each new model and engineering makeover also meant additional employee training, new service equipment, and more advertising—costs borne by the dealer and passed on to customers in annoying new fees and charges. Getting an edge on the competition often meant moving the dealership to a bigger and better location, keeping more inventory on hand, and borrowing at high interest rates to finance the upgrades. By the early 1990s, the cost of marketing a new car had risen to $1,500 per vehicle (Wysner, 1994, p. 95). With ever-rising prices, approximately 800 models to choose from, and a wide range of quality on the market, savvy consumers began to shop around and to seek the aid of guidebooks and consumer organizations.

Caught between manufacturers and consumers, both of whom wanted lower prices, dealers had little choice but to deal. As markups slipped, dealer profits slipped with them, from 9% in 1985 to 6.5% a decade later, a difference of approximately $300 per car (Darin, 1996). In 1985, new car sales accounted for 78.5% of dealer profit. Ten years later, they accounted for only 6.3% of dealer profit, whereas used car sales and the parts and service business accounted for 47.8% and 45.9% of dealer profits, respectively (Naughton, 1996, p. 72). Many dealers did not make it. More than 1,000 closed their doors during the recession years of 1990 and 1991 alone ("Rabbit Is Poor," 1994, p. 68). Caught in the profit squeeze, many dealers either sold their franchise or used it to acquire trade-ins for their used car operations, where a quick turnaround could still garner a 25% markup, just like the old days.

The Social Structure of Dealer Dependency

Funny thing, context. Just flipping a statistic around or looking at a particular relationship from a more encompassing standpoint can dramatically alter your understanding of how things fit together. What have we learned from this contextualization of the buyer-seller relationship? Just this: The Ayres studies were undertaken at a particular point in time—in the midst of a recession that would close 1,000 dealerships, one of a series of recessions within a longer cycle of price deflation, industrial restructuring, dealership consolidation, and market segmentation. Dealership dependence was at a peak, but so was the need to exploit buyer dependence for all it was worth. Despite the price differences shown in Table 6.1, in all likelihood, the markups for African Americans and women were lower at the time of the Ayres studies than at any time in American history.

Perhaps this thought occurred to you as well: Just as bargaining power varies among categories of consumer, so it must vary among categories of dealer. Insofar as the buyer-seller relationship (like any relationship) exhibits this property of power-dependence, various things can shift the balance of power one way or the other. We saw how buyers can overcome dependency: by finding a purchase pal more knowledgeable than themselves, by obtaining multiple bids, and by joining the Consumer Federation or a credit union. Dealers can lessen their dependence on consumers and manufacturers, too, by adopting the right power-balancing strategies. To the extent that they succeed, dealers can ride the trends, even prosper by them. To the extent that they fail, they suffocate under the combined weight of indebtedness, price competition, and consumer dissatisfaction.

The question for us is, to what extent do the markups in Table 6.1 reflect the array of dealer strategies for overcoming dependence? In the main, the answer should be clear: Given their higher buyer dependence, African Americans should do better with dealerships that were unable to devise successful power-balancing strategies. Now, we do not have the data to test this hypothesis, but we can at least lay out the logic behind it. Because my purpose is to illustrate the principles of structural explanation, that will be good enough, although hardly ideal.

What we might call "the social structure of dealer dependency" is a heuristic model of five types of dealership, differentiated by sales volume, organization of the sales staff, and degree of dependence. Each type of dealership adopted different power-balancing strategies for overcoming dependence, which vary in their effectiveness. I summarize the model in Table 6.2. In the last column, I estimate how buyer and seller dependencies intersect. That is, I guess what the markups by race and gender would be under the five conditions of dealer dependence using the data in Ayres's second study as a guideline.

The first type of dealership is the traditional franchise, which comes in two varieties. The first is a low-volume, family-run operation with a small entrepreneurial sales staff whose income is derived from commissions (sometimes supplemented by a small salary). The traditional entrepreneurial salesperson is, in effect, an independent contractor hired by the dealer to resell merchandise for a cut of the profit (typically 25% of the markup). Highly vulnerable to price competition in recent years, the low-volume traditional franchise exploits buyer dependency where it finds it, but its own dependency is such that it must concede on price in the face of buyer resistance.

The second type of dealership is the traditional franchise as well, except it has a higher sales volume and its own niche of loyal, well-heeled customers. It survives on repeat business and customer service, making its customers feel special and elite—and disloyal and cheap for seeking bargains.

The third is the dual-franchise operation. Its response to the foreign competition was to hop on board. This strategy can produce headaches and higher costs; many

Table 6.2   Dealer Dependence by Type of Dealership

Sales Volume	Type of Dealership	Sales Force Organization	Power-Balancing Strategy	Dependence	Bargaining Strategy	Markups by Status of Buyer
Low	Traditional franchise	Entrepreneurial	None; withdrawal	High	Exploit dependence, cave-in	White male, $350 White female, $415 Black female, $620 Black male, $1,090
	Traditional franchise (niche)	Entrepreneurial	Status-giving	Low	"Fair price" for quality service	White male, $1,050 White female, $1,225 Black female, $1,815 Black male, $2,750
Medium	Dual-franchise (import)	Entrepreneurial or team	Network extension	Medium-high in weaker; low in stronger	Exploit, cave-in (weaker); "fair price" for quality car (stronger)	White male, $750 White female, $870 Black female, $1,290 Black male, $2,285 (average)
	High-volume (team)	Team concept	Coalition formation (internal)	Medium-high	Exploit dependence, hold the line, discount when necessary	White male, $500 White female, $585 Black female, $860 Black male, $1,490
High	Megadealer	Entrepreneurial in small shop; team in large shop	Coalition formation (external)	Medium (in 1990)	Strategy pegged to size of franchise; discount in high-volume shops	White male, $650 White female, $760 Black female, $1,020 Black male, $1,950

NOTE: Numerical values are hypothetical, reflecting the relative dependencies in column 5 (Dependence).

dual-franchise operations had to build separate showrooms for their domestic and import lines to keep salespeople from talking up the high-markup imports at the expense of the domestic franchise (Yates, 1983, p. 227). But it allows the owner to shift resources to the stronger franchise as market conditions dictate.

The fourth type of dealership uses a "sales team" approach to increase the volume of transactions while keeping labor costs down. In this type of shop, the first salesperson you meet handles the car selection process and steers you into the office, where the "closer" and the sales manager work the angles to maximize dealer profit on each aspect of the transaction (car price, trade-in, financing, and down payment) (for an insider account, see Parrish, 1992). The commission is then split between the salesperson and the closer (and sometimes the sales manager). In effect, the team concept allows a coalition of insiders to corral commission income at the expense of entry-level personnel. Dealer dependency remains fairly high and markups fairly low, but the higher sales volume carries the company.

The final type of dealership seeks to control price competition by gaining a retail monopoly in the franchise. With 10 to 20 showrooms in its fleet, the megadealership can achieve economies of scale in personnel, inventory, and financing, not to mention greater leverage over manufacturers and consumers. In the future, the megadealer may go head-to-head with corporate retailers selling all makes and models of cars on a fixed-price basis (for a discussion of this impending "revolution in retailing," see "Angst for the Angstroms," 1997, p. 56; Naughton, 1996). When this happens, the megadealer is likely to adopt similar sales and commission practices (Simison & Suris, 1997; Taylor, 1997). In the early 1990s, however, few high-volume dealers had anything approaching a retail monopoly. At that time, the nascent megadealership was indifferent to sales organization. It retained both entrepreneurial and sales team forms as it found them and relied on sales managers to limit and coordinate discounts.

So those were the kinds of dealership the testers approached with their common bargaining script during the recession of 1990 and 1991, matched for everything except race and gender. Some dealers were teetering on the edge of bankruptcy, others were cushioned by their import franchise or loyal customer base, whereas others were learning to live with lower profit margins by reorganizing their sales staffs or acquiring the competition. Now, we can pull both sides of the explanation together. Where they meet is in the bargaining process. There, in the real-time, face-to-face situation of social interaction, buyer and seller dependencies confront each other, and seller typifications of buyers are put to the test.

From Both Sides Now: The Bargaining Process

The testers' bargaining script allows us to develop a simplified model of the bargaining process. In the model, the 60- to 75-minute interaction is divided into three phases. Phase 1, devoted to information exchange and car selection, concludes with the seller's initial offer. Phase 2 begins with the tester's counteroffer at the invoice price and concludes with the seller's second offer. Phase 3 includes all subsequent rounds of price negotiation, concluding with the seller's final offer.

Given the testers' split-the-difference method of price negotiation, the crucial moments in the bargaining process are all controlled by the seller: the initial offer, the second offer, and the final offer. That is just what we want, of course, but we do need a way to represent or model the seller's decision-making process. The seller is a composite of up to 225 salespeople, so our model has to be highly generalized and fitted to our explanatory purpose. It can be made slightly more concrete by taking into account the five types of dealership and their associated bargaining strategies. To the extent that there is a good fit between the salesperson and the organization, we then have five sellers, or rather, five models of seller decision processes. Finally, we need to put some thoughts inside the sellers' heads as they interact with the testers. The thoughts are mostly tactical in nature, but they also involve typifications of car buyers, external status characteristics such as race and gender (provisional proxies for bargaining power), and the expectations and reactions of others, especially peers and supervisors.

This is the final step of our long explanatory journey, where it all comes together. Let us walk through it phase by phase.

Phase 1

Recall that the testers quickly select a car. In the second study (the one we are following here), they also allow the sellers to talk them into the deluxe model or a larger car. (Whichever one they pick, the other half of the tester pair picks as well.) During this phase, the salesperson gathers information about the tester's occupation, car knowledge, and ability to pay. The tester's speech, dress, and residential neighborhood also provide clues to socioeconomic status. What the salesperson, particularly the traditional entrepreneurial salesperson, is looking for is the "qualified buyer" (Parrish, 1992), a person with money who is ready to buy right away. A qualified buyer who has not shopped around much, is committed to a certain make and model of car, and knows or cares little about bargaining may be called a "prime profit opportunity." Young, first-time car buyers often fall into this category (Parrish, 1992). The testers do not ask for a test drive. Nor do they want time to think it over. After selecting the car they want, they ask, "How much do you want for it?"

Qualified buyers, right? If the women sounded insecure or smitten, they would be prime profit opportunities, for sure. They do not, so their shopping alone could be a sign of self-confidence. Given the widely known problems of black unemployment and blocked social mobility, the black male's age and socioeconomic status suggest recent and perhaps dramatic social mobility. He could really want this car. As for the white guy, he seems a little taciturn and businesslike. Probably a "retail shopper" (Furse et al., 1984), a guy who shops around for a good price.

But buyer typifications and typifications about age, race, class, and gender are not the only factors at work here. There is also the dealership's market position, its access to customers like the testers, its policy on discount pricing, and its sales targets for the week, not to mention the salesperson's stake in the matter, the sales commission. The greater the dealer dependence, the less it can afford to lose the sale. The niche and import dealers and some megadealer showrooms can afford to highball, but if the high-volume and low-volume shops try the same thing, they will have to back off quickly. Many African Americans coming into the dealerships are upwardly mobile, first-time car buyers. If anyone is to be highballed, it should be them.

Phase 2

A counteroffer at the wholesale price, a markup of zero. This is the crucial phase for the seller because buyer typifications have to be reassessed quickly. The salesperson's least favorite categories of buyer include "the negotiator" and "the retail shopper" (Furse et al., 1984). Both will walk away if they do not get a good bargain. The white guy now looks like a negotiator, and perhaps the white woman as well. The black woman moves up from profit opportunity to retail shopper, and the black male, too. How quickly the tables turn! How many low-markup sales did the sales manager approve this month? Not many to black males, that's for sure. Or to black females, for that matter. Then again, perhaps they have been coached. Or read that article in *Consumer Reports*. The white guy knows his way around, and the white woman is surely a feminist. How do these people stack up against our usual customers?

Phase 3

When the testers split the difference between their initial counteroffer and the seller's second offer, a minimum profit is assured at all dealerships. But although that has become all too customary at the low-volume and high-volume (team) dealerships, it does not cut the mustard at the niche, import, and megadealer showrooms. By this time, the salesperson is committed to an array of buyer and status typifications, most of them reinforced by the prevailing occupational culture, particularly in shops in which exploiting buyer dependency is considered playing by the rules in a dog-eat-dog world. So the bargaining continues for another round or two until a deal is struck or the seller refuses to discount any further.

The last column of Table 6.2 shows how the balance of dependencies works out theoretically. The dollar figures are hypothetical. They are the markups I imagine the testers would receive at that type of dealership. In the middle of the table, you will find the terms *withdrawal, status-giving, network extension,* and *coalition formation.* These terms refer to the four power-balancing operations in Richard Emerson's (1962) theory of power dependency. The correspondence between the dealers' organizational adaptations and Emerson's four responses to dependency is striking.

Loose Ends

That completes the task I set for this chapter. But because we invested so much time in this explanation, perhaps we should use what we learned to tidy up a few loose ends.

Do you recall Ayres's finding that the race and gender of the salesperson had no effect on the markups? That is what led us to reject the bias/discrimination account. Does that finding make better sense now? I think it should, given what we learned about the types of dealership. The marginalization of the low-volume dealership and the spread of the sales team concept dramatically affected the occupation of car selling. Today, car salespeople have less autonomy than ever before and less room to vary their bargaining style. Their bargaining behavior is shaped by the kind of dealership at which they work, particularly the way the sales force is organized. Three consequences of these occupational changes are relevant here.

One is lower income. Between 1974 and 1996, the inflation-adjusted income of car salespeople fell by 14% (Darin, 1996, p. 38). In commission-only shops today, the salesperson's salary averages just $24,000 to $28,000 a year, compared to the industrywide average of $35,000 (Henry, 1996, p. 54). Guess where the losses were concentrated. Right—in the smaller, traditional franchises and in entry-level positions in the high-volume dealerships. A second, related change is high employee turnover—50% in 1990 (Bohn, 1991, p. 1) and 61% during the economic recovery of 1993 to 1996 (Darin, 1996, p. 38).

A third trend follows directly from the previous two: the influx of female and African American salespeople. More than one fifth of the salespeople in Ayres's second study were nonwhite (Ayres, 1995, p. 135). As the new faces on the lot, women and blacks would bear the brunt of the occupational restructuring and diminished income, a pattern often associated with occupational desegregation by race and gender (Reskin & Roos, 1990, p. 80).

So why do the salesperson's race and gender have no effect on the markups? Female and African American salespeople hired by a megadealer follow the same script as anyone else. Those joining the sales team suffer split commissions until they deliver markups as high as the closer's. Those hired by traditional franchises either exploit buyer dependency or enjoy uncertain incomes of $24,000 to $28,000 a year or less. Those lucky enough to be hired by the low-dependency niche and import dealers find the testers' bargaining style—counteroffering at the invoice price—just as offensive as their white male colleagues. In short, the occupational position of the salesperson, the position of the dealership in the marketplace, and the give and take of the bargaining process determine the deals that salespeople offer to their customers.

Like their white counterparts, female and African American salespeople have little control over institutions and practices that predated their arrival—the franchise system, the sales commission, and the bargaining process—or the structural conditions affecting the industry in which they work—the distribution of social classes and populations across city and suburb, macroeconomic trends and conditions, or the social structure of dealer dependency. Nor do they control the social and cultural capital and dependency of their customers, black or white. Can we really expect them to risk their own income and job security in a counterinstitutional campaign to ensure that all customers pay the same price for the same car, regardless of their bargaining power or performance in the bargaining situation?

That would be a quixotic effort, given the institutions and practices of the industry. Yet, the franchise system and all its institutions and practices may be swept away by the impending "revolution in retailing" (Naughton, 1996). That would be an ironic development because the initiators of this transformation are interested not in social justice but in the more efficient accumulation of capital. Nevertheless, the passage of a social system in which some people are compelled to exploit the lower social and cultural capital and higher dependency of others for a share of the take will mark a small step toward a society in which all people are afforded equal concern and respect.

Conclusion

I introduced the car price mystery to illustrate the principles of structural explanation in sociology. The explanation, such as it was, was highly informal. Normally, one would define concepts and diagram the cause-and-effect relations with greater precision. It was also highly generalized. The car buyers and salespeople we talked about were mere stick figures (for flesh and blood, see Lawson, 1996). Moreover, without original data on seller typifications of African American car buyers pegged to social class, the discussion of race as a proxy for bargaining power remains hypothetical. Finally, we do not know the characteristics of the Chicago dealerships (traditional franchise, sales team, etc.) that sell the largest number of cars to African Americans. As a result, we cannot connect the two strands of the explanation as tightly as we need to do. That step, too, was hypothetical. Despite these shortcomings, I think our explanation makes better sense of the data than the bias/discrimination account or Ayres's (1995) own "willingness to pay" explanation.[4]

Let me close with a few encouraging remarks to student readers and a hint to their professors. C. Wright Mills (1958) once came within a hairbreadth of identifying structural explanation with the sociological imagination. Perhaps he overstated the case. But structural explanation satisfies an intellectual imperative deeply rooted in the discipline. In contrast to psychology and economics, which are (subspecialties aside) individualistic, law seeking, and ahistorical, sociology has been historical, holistic, and process seeking since Auguste Comte first chatted about social statics and social dynamics in 1839. Nowhere more than in the United States is this true, where figures such as Cooley (1909, 1918) and Mead (1934) ditched the language of statics and dynamics in favor of social organization and social process and developed a sociological social psychology that made each a reciprocal phase of the other. Since then, every generation of social theorists and researchers has reworked the structure/process formula in different ways, trying to find the best mix of composite theories or the synthesis that will bring the search to an end.

If structural explanation is so central to the sociological imagination, perhaps undergraduates should be encouraged to try one on for size. As the car price mystery shows, the form is easy to adopt. All you need, for starters, is some conception of the levels of social structure; a knack for identifying social systems and mapping them onto the levels scheme; and a sense of how social relationships, beliefs, and practices fit together dynamically to generate the facts you seek to explain. (The simplest levels scheme is the bilevel one of macro and micro [Coleman, 1987]. Slightly more realism can be gained by the addition of a mesolevel [Maines, 1982].

A six-level scheme has an intuitive appeal all its own [Prendergast & Knottnerus, 1994]. Systems theorists are particularly adept at levels construction [Bertrand, 1972; Pattee, 1973; Simon, 1981.])

Of course, you need other things, as well—a load of factual information, some composite theories for understanding the key processes, and a lot of time for research. Oh, and a good problem to work on, too. To accumulate factual material and find something interesting to explain, students may wish to return to aspects of the same research problem in different courses—for example, why priest resignations in the Catholic Church spiked after Vatican II (Seidler, 1979). To assemble the composite theories, students may need to approach the theory course differently. Perhaps, it is not just an exercise in intellectual history. Time is always scarce. But if two or three students work on the same explanation, using an effective division of labor. . . .

There is one other thing students can do to make the task of structural explanation more manageable: Develop simple models. Use Marx or Durkheim for the macrotheory and Mead, Emerson, or Dorothy Smith for the microtheory. Remember, you are trying to develop a chain of social causation. Pick the composite theories that get the job done. Which ones you select will depend in part on the social facts you want to explain. Cultural capital may not help you with priest resignations, although a theory of identity might. Just keep in mind Burt's (1992) dictum— "causation resides at the intersection of social relations" (p. 2)—if your theoretical musings wander far afield. Sociology allows enormous freedom in theory selection. Yet, the choice of composite theories is never arbitrary. If you think otherwise, read Burt's dictum again.

The real payoff in structural explanation, even with the gaps and hypotheticals, is the way it pulls things together. When you finally assemble all the parts, you really understand something. You see how a social system "works." And that is the point, isn't it?

Postscript

The explanation you just read was bounded in time, space, and scope by the car price data that law professor Ian Ayres collected in metropolitan Chicago in the early 1990s. Much has changed since then, far too much to review in a brief postscript. The changes would make worthy topics for collaborative student research, though. One team could examine the changes in African American communities, social networks, and social and cultural capital in order to estimate the degree of buyer dependency today. Another team could focus on the changes in the social structure of dealer dependency. With faculty help, both teams could develop better indicators of dependency than I employed. In this postscript, I limit myself to a simple empirical question: Do African Americans still pay more for new cars a decade after Ayres's studies, or has the racial disparity narrowed somewhat or even disappeared altogether?

The question continues to be researched, although no one replicated the paired-testers methodology of Ayres's studies. That methodology has many virtues, but it failed to see that sending Buppie testers into the showrooms would trigger a target-specific set of seller typifications, even if the sellers were themselves African American. But controlled comparison studies using actual sales data were conducted in the late 1990s. I won't hold you in suspense. African Americans still pay hundreds of dollars more for cars of the same size and sticker price, even after controlling for a variety of differences among buyers that reduce the disparity somewhat.

In a well-designed study using a random sample of 700,000 car sales in 1999, Scott Morton, Zettelmeyer, and Silva-Risso (2003) found that African American car buyers paid $1,700 over invoice price relative to nonminority Americans, a markup bonus of 30%. Controlling for income, education, region, type of car, and a host of other things, they reduced the initial price difference to approximately $500 on the average car. They also found a residual "price premium" for women of $100 but did not report differences between African American males and females. The price disparity persists.[5]

Scott Morton et al. (2003) did not stop with that finding. They also obtained sales data from the top company in Internet referrals. This company has contracts with 5,000 of the country's 22,000 dealerships. In exchange for a fee paid by the dealer, it obtains basic information from the buyer and then solicits a bid for the make and model of car that the buyer is interested in from the nearest dealerships in its network. Race can be inferred from name and address, but apparently little of that occurred because the price disparity virtually disappeared in online car shopping.

Makes your head spin, doesn't it? If nonminority Americans treat people of African ancestry differently just because they are black, name and address should be enough to trigger price discrimination. That does not happen because disparate treatment, to the extent that it exists, is situationally conditional. Here, the buyer-seller relationship has been altered by the introduction of a third party. The largely impersonal relations between the referral company and its affiliated dealerships insulate minority buyers from predatory pricing. These dealerships establish Internet sales departments that, by contractual agreement, operate separately from the rest of the showroom. The Internet salesperson, who is not supposed to handle walk-in traffic, is paid by sales volume, not a percentage of the markup (Scott Morton et al., 2003). The sales process has been standardized and reduced to procedures. Most of the contact between the customer and the Internet salesperson occurs by phone over content dictated by the paperwork that the referral company helps the customer to fill out, up to and including the financing. Ideally, the online buyer just shows up at the dealership to sign the papers and pick up the car. After the sale, the referral company surveys buyers to gauge their satisfaction with the process. Dealerships that try to restructure the deal when they get the buyer on the premises may be dropped from the network, although referral company dependency often precludes that outcome. (Dealer compliance is the weak link in the system.) Finally, the dealers who affiliate with the network are precisely those high-volume dealerships known to underprice the competition slightly (Zettelmeyer, Scott Morton, & Silva-Risso, 2001).

In short, the relative anonymity and routinization of the sales process insulate minority buyers. Sellers are denied the opportunity to deploy their well-honed buyer typifications that, when confirmed, lead to the extraction of increasingly more markup from the timid, the uninformed, and the credulous of all races and creeds. The key structural difference is the absence of bargaining. Online shopping is not color-blind, but it eliminates face-to-face negotiation over prices. It does not offer the same vehicle to all customers at the same price, as the revolution in retailing promised to do. But it standardizes the bids that a single dealership makes to a third party (the referral company), which has the effect of equalizing prices among demographic groups.

Online shopping is no panacea. Few sales are transacted online. Although more equalized, markups are higher than savvy bargainers can get on their own. Buying a car online saves consumers only approximately $450 on the average car (Scott Morton et al., 2003). But it benefits less savvy bargainers more (Zettlemeyer et al., 2001), a real advantage for many buyers, particularly first-timers. Alas, like other resources, Internet access is unequally distributed by class, race, and region. Whereas 62% of Asian Americans and 43% of nonminority whites use the Internet, only 39% of Hispanics and 27% of African Americans do so ("Minorities' Internet Usage," n.d.). The Internet may level the playing field for some, but the majority of African American buyers continue to fend off seller typifications in the showrooms.

They have a lot more fending off to do than we realized, too. It turns out that the price disparities we have been discussing—$564 to $1665 in Ayres's 1995 study and $350 to $500 under different control conditions in the Scott Morton, Zettelmeyer, and Silva-Risso's 2001 and 2003 studies—underestimate by half the extent of the disparity because none of them factored in finance charges.

Car makers finance 45% to 50% of car sales through their assurance operations. When you separate borrowers by race, and control for the usual sources of variation, the markups on African American borrowers are double those of whites— $970 per contract versus $462, a difference of $508, at one manufacturer's lending arm (Ayres, 2001). Part of the difference comes from poorer African Americans borrowing more money for longer periods of time. The rest comes from higher interest rates (after controlling for credit risk) and hidden charges. In the first controlled study that takes into account both sale price and finance charges, Ayres (2002) examined racial disparities in 1,000 "consummated sales" at a single dealership in Atlanta, Georgia. (Half of its customers were black and half were white.) He found that African American females paid markups $505 higher than white males on sale price and $589 higher in finance charges. Excess profits for African American males were higher, too—$405 more on the car and $471 more on the financing.

So African Americans continue to pay more for new cars. Economists have struggled for two decades to explain why. Perhaps sociologists, with our theoretical ears perked to issues of structure and process, should give it a try.

Notes

1. For methodological and ideological criticisms of the study, see Goldberg (1996) and Epstein (1992), as well as Ayres's (1994) reply to Epstein.

2. First-time car buyers, by definition, fit into the seller's category of "inexperienced shoppers." (For seller typifications of car buyers, see Furse et al., 1984.) In his exposé of the

retail car business, Parrish (1992) answers the question, "Why are first-time car buyers so vulnerable?" as follows: "Firstly, the young car buyer will do almost anything to get into a car. Secondly, he/she is very inexperienced at negotiating. And these people usually have no credit record" (pp. 235-236).

3. The auto makers were not entirely responsible for their own troubles. Like housing, steel, and agriculture, the auto industry took a beating in the drive to control inflation. Responding to complaints from bond holders and commercial banks that inflation was eroding the value of their long-term investments, the Federal Reserve System has restricted the supply of money and credit four times since 1969, generating four recessions and costing more than $800 billion in lost economic activity. During the worst of it, from 1979 to 1982, auto industry unemployment reached 23%, and overall industrial output fell 12%. After 3 years of 18% to 20% interest rates, personal income from interest (86% of which goes to the wealthiest 10% of Americans) grew by $148 billion (67%), the largest banks registered record profits, and the effective tax rate on the banking industry was reduced to 3.8% (Greider, 1987, pp. 401, 413, 456). This violent redistribution of wealth then fed the great stock market rally that began at the end of 1982. Because cars are bought on credit, automakers, dealers, and customers alike paid heavily for the restoration of bank capital.

4. Ayres (1995, pp. 131-135) also rejects what he calls an "animus" explanation of his data. In the end, he favors a willingness-to-pay account, although he also sees some animus in the treatment of black males and some reluctance on the part of black females to bargain tough with sellers (p. 141). My emphasis on carlessness and restricted search opportunities overlaps what Ayres calls a "cost-based" account. He rejects this account because there were no statistically significant differences between the markups in black-majority neighborhoods (representing low search costs) and those in white-majority neighborhoods (representing high search costs) (p. 136). What Ayres considers low search costs I consider a condition of buyer dependency. Originally, I expected dealerships serving African American customers regularly (even if black owned) to charge higher markups. When they did not, I put proportionally more emphasis on the sources of dealer dependency. If dealerships serving African Americans are mainly older, smaller franchises with low sales volume, dealer dependency may actually outweigh buyer dependency, particularly during a recessionary period such as 1990 and 1991. Indeed, as Ayres (p. 136) reports, dealers in black-majority neighborhoods did offer slightly lower prices to African American testers, although not low enough to be statistically significant at the .05 level. Why? Faced with customers of the tester's socioeconomic status and bargaining style, these low-volume dealers quickly abandoned full-sticker hopes and conceded more steeply in subsequent bargaining rounds, knowing that Buppie customers like the testers could and do shop outside the neighborhood. The same testers visiting less dependent dealerships would be treated as upwardly mobile, first-generation car buyers—that is, as prime profit opportunities. With 225 rather than 90 dealerships in the second study, the testers confronted more less dependent, suburban dealers just when the economy was beginning to pick up, resulting in higher markups for most categories of buyer.

5. The $500 price difference can be restated in percentage terms. So formulated, African Americans pay 1% more for the average new car. Some industry analysts are inclined to say "only 1% more" and to attribute the difference to African Americans' penchant for economizing on search costs. The price difference is statistically significant and reliable, and it amounts to a power-based extraction of millions of dollars a year from a positionally disadvantaged population. To use a less neutral term from the economist's lexicon, the auto dealers' exploitation of dependency amounts to "rent-seeking," an economic practice that has yet to find a persuasive apologist. In his most recent writings on price discrimination, Ayres (2001, 2002) discards his willingness-to-pay account (see Note 4) in favor of rent-seeking behavior he calls supracompetitive pricing.

References

Alwitt, L. F., & Donley, T. D. (1996). *The lower-income consumer: Adjusting the balance of exchange.* Thousand Oaks, CA: Sage.

Angst for the Angstroms. (1997, July 12). *The Economist,* pp. 56-57.

Ayres, I. (1991, February). Fair driving: Gender and race discrimination in retail car negotiations. *Harvard Law Review, 104*(4), 817-872.

Ayres, I. (1994). Alternative grounds: Epstein's discrimination analysis in other market settings. *San Diego Law Review, 31,* 67-87.

Ayres, I. (1995). Further evidence of discrimination in new car negotiations and estimates of its cause. *Michigan Law Review, 94,* 109-147.

Ayres, I. (2001). *Expert testimony of Ian Ayres.* Boston: National Consumer Law Center. Available at www.nclc.org

Ayres, I. (2002). *Pervasive prejudice? Unconventional evidence of race and gender discrimination.* Chicago: University of Chicago Press.

Ayres, I., & Siegelman, P. (1995). Race and gender discrimination in bargaining for a new car. *American Economic Review, 85*(3), 304-321.

Berger, J., Cohen, B. P., & Zelditch, M., Jr. (1966). Status characteristics and expectation states. In J. Berger, M. Zelditch, Jr., & B. Anderson (Eds.), *Sociological theories in progress* (pp. 29-46). Boston: Houghton Mifflin.

Bertrand, A. L. (1972). *Social organization: A general systems and role theory perspective.* Philadelphia: Davis.

Bohn, J. (1991, September 16). Half the sales staff is quitting. *Automotive News, 1,* 49.

Boudon, R. (1987). The individualistic tradition in sociology. In J. C. Alexander, B. Giesen, R. Münch, & N. J. Smelser (Eds.), *The micro-macro link* (pp. 45-70). Berkeley: University of California Press.

Bourdieu, P. (1984). *Distinction: A social critique of the judgement of taste* (R. Nice, Trans.). Cambridge, MA: Harvard University Press.

Bourdieu, P. (1985). The forms of capital. In J. G. Richardson (Ed.), *Handbook of theory and research for the sociology of education* (pp. 241-258). Westport, CT: Greenwood.

Brewer, M. B. (1988). A dual process model of impression formation. In T. K. Srull & R. S. Wyer (Eds.), *Advances in social cognition* (Vol. 1, pp. 1-36). Hillsdale, NJ: Lawrence Erlbaum.

Burt, R. S. (1982). *Toward a structural theory of action.* New York: Academic Press.

Burt, R. S. (1992). *Structural holes: The social structure of competition.* Cambridge, MA: Harvard University Press.

Caplovitz, D. (1967). *The poor pay more: Consumer practices of low-income families.* New York: Free Press.

The car industry: Barbarians at Bavarians' gates. (1999, February 13). *The Economist,* 23-25.

Coleman, J. S. (1987). Microfoundations and macrosocial behavior. In J. C. Alexander, B. Giesen, R. Münch, & N. J. Smelser (Eds.), *The micro-macro link* (pp. 153-173). Berkeley: University of California Press.

Coleman, J. S. (1988). Social capital in creation of human capital. *American Journal of Sociology, 94,* S95-S120.

Coleman, J. S. (1990). *The foundations of social theory.* Cambridge, MA: Harvard University Press.

Consumer Federation of America. (1990). *U.S. consumer knowledge: The results of nationwide test.* Washington, DC: Author.

Cooley, C. H. (1909). *Social organization: A study of the larger mind.* New York: Scribner's.

Cooley, C. H. (1918). *Social process.* New York: Scribner's.

Darin, A. T. (1996, November 11). Hiring, keeping sales people is nearly impossible. *Automotive News*, 38.

Emerson, R. M. (1962). Power-dependence relations. *American Sociological Review, 27,* 31-41.

Epstein, R. A. (1992). *Forbidden grounds: The case against employment discrimination laws.* Cambridge, MA: Harvard University Press.

Fernández-Kelly, M. P. (1995). Social and cultural capital in the urban ghetto: Implications for the economic sociology of immigration. In A. Portes (Ed.), *The economic sociology of immigration: Essays on networks, ethnicity, and entrepreneurship* (pp. 213-247). New York: Russell Sage.

Fiske, S. T. (1993). Social cognition and social deception. *Annual Review of Psychology, 44,* 155-194.

Furse, D. H., Punj, G. N., & Stewart, D. W. (1984). A typology of individual search strategies among purchasers of new automobiles. *Journal of Consumer Research, 10,* 417-431.

Goldberg, P. K. (1996). Dealer price discrimination in new car purchases: Evidence from the consumer expenditure survey. *Journal of Political Economy, 104,* 622-654.

Greider, W. (1987). *Secrets of the temple: How the Federal Reserve runs the country.* New York: Simon & Schuster.

Henry, J. (1996, May 27). Kicking the commission habit: Land Rover backs salary plan. *Automotive News, 3,* 54.

Hilton, J. L., & von Hippel, W. (1996). Stereotypes. *Annual Review of Psychology, 47,* 237-271.

Kahneman, D., Slovic, P., & Tversky, A. (1982). *Judgment under uncertainty: Heuristics and biases.* New York: Cambridge University Press.

Knoke, D., & Guilarte, M. (1994). Networks in organizational structures and strategies. In J. D. Knottnerus & C. Prendergast (Eds.), *Current perspectives in social theory: Supplement 1. Recent developments in the theory of social structure* (pp. 77-115). Greenwich, CT: JAI.

Knottnerus, J. D. (1994). Expectation states theory and the analysis of group processes and structures. In J. D. Knottnerus & C. Prendergast (Eds.), *Current perspectives in social theory: Supplement 1. Recent developments in the theory of social structure* (pp. 49-74). Greenwich, CT: JAI.

Knottnerus, J. D. (1997). Social structural analysis and status generalization: The contributions and potential of expectation states theory. In J. Szmatka, J. Skvoretz, & J. Berger (Eds.), *Status, network, and structure: Theory development in group processes* (pp. 119-136). Stanford, CA: Stanford University Press.

Lawson, H. M. (1996). Car saleswomen: Expanding the scope of salesmanship. *Current Research on Occupations and Professions, 9,* 53-71.

Little, D. (1991). *Varieties of social explanation: An introduction to the philosophy of social science.* Boulder, CO: Westview.

Maines, D. R. (1982). In search of mesostructure: Studies in the negotiated order. *Urban Life, 11,* 267-279.

March, J. G., & Simon, H. A. (1958). *Organizations.* New York: John Wiley.

Massey, D. S., & Denton, N. A. (1993). *American apartheid: Segregation and the making of the underclass.* Cambridge, MA: Harvard University Press.

Matheson, K., Holmes, J. G., & Kristiansen, C. M. (1991). Observational goals and the integration of trait perceptions and behavior: Behavioral prediction vs. impression formation. *Journal of Experimental Social Psychology, 27,* 138-160.

McCarron, J. (1989, June 5). Chicago has both poorest, richest suburbs. *Chicago Tribune,* pp. 1, 7.

Mead, G. H. (1934). *Mind, self, and society: From the standpoint of a social behaviorist.* Chicago: University of Chicago Press.

Menger, C. (1963). *Problems of economics and sociology* (F. J. Nock, Trans.). Urbana: University of Illinois Press.

Mills, C. W. (1958). *The sociological imagination.* New York: Oxford University Press.

Minorities' Internet usage. (n.d.). *Automotive Retailing Today.* Available at http://www.autoretailing.org/research

Naughton, K. (1996, February 19). Revolution in the show room. *Business Week,* 70-76.

Parrish, D. (1992). *The car buyer's art: How to beat the salesman at his own game.* Bellflower, CA: Book Express.

Pattee, H. H. (Ed.). (1973). *Hierarchy theory: The challenge of complex systems.* New York: Braziller.

Patterson, O. (1998). *Rituals of blood: Consequences of slavery in two centuries.* Washington, DC: Civitas/Counterpoint.

Prendergast, C., & Knottnerus, J. D. (1994). Recent developments in the theory of social structure: Introduction and overview. In J. D. Knottnerus & C. Prendergast (Eds.), *Current perspectives in social theory: Supplement 1. Recent development in the theory of social structure* (pp. 1-26). Greenwich, CT: JAI.

Rabbit is poor. (1994, February 26). *The Economist,* 68.

Reskin, B., & Roos, P. (1990). *Job queues, gender queues: Explaining women's inroads into male occupations.* Philadelphia: Temple University Press.

Ridgeway, C. L. (1991). The social construction of status value: Gender and other nominal characteristics. *Social Forces, 70,* 367-386.

Ridgeway, C. L., & Berger, J. (1988). The legitimation of power and prestige orders in task groups. In M. Webster, Jr., & M. Foschi (Eds.), *Status generalization: New theory and research* (pp. 207-231). Stanford, CA: Stanford University Press.

Riley, T., & Fiske, S. T. (1991). Interdependence and the social context of impression formation. *European Bulletin of Cognitive Psychology, 11,* 173-192.

Rubinstein, D. M. (1986). The concept of structure in sociology. In M. L. Wardell & S. P. Turner (Eds.), *Sociological theory in transition* (pp. 80-94). Boston: Allen & Unwin.

Rubinstein, D. M. (2000). *Culture, structure, and agency: Toward a truly multidimensional sociology.* Thousand Oaks, CA: Sage.

Schutz, A. (1962). *Collected papers I: The problem of social reality* (M. Natanson, Ed.). The Hague, Netherlands: Nijhoff.

Scott Morton, F., Zettelmeyer, F., & Silva-Risso, J. (2003). Consumer information and discrimination: Does the Internet affect the pricing of new cars to women and minorities? *Quantitative Marketing and Economics, 1,* 65-92.

Seidler, J. S. (1979). Priest resignations in a lazy monopoly. *American Sociological Review, 44,* 763-783.

Simison, R. L., & Suris, O. (1997, January 31). U.S. car buying practices are getting a big overhaul: Dealer consolidations, big chains indicate good news for customers. *Wall Street Journal* (Eastern ed.), p. B4.

Simon, H. A. (1981). The architecture of complexity. In H. A. Simon (Ed.), *The sciences of the artificial* (2nd ed., pp. 193-229). Cambridge, MA: MIT Press.

Taylor, A. (1997). Car wars: Wayne Huizenga vs. everybody. *Fortune, 135,* 92-94.

U.S. Bureau of the Census. (1993). *1990 census of the population, social and economic characteristics, urbanized areas.* Washington, DC: Government Printing Office.

U.S. Department of Housing and Urban Development/ Bureau of the Census. (1997). *American housing survey for the Chicago metropolitan area in 1995.* Washington, DC: Government Printing Office.

Wagner, D. G., & Berger, J. (1993). Status characteristics theory: The growth of a program. In J. Berger & M. Zelditch, Jr. (Eds.), *Theoretical research programs* (pp. 23-63). Stanford, CA: Stanford University Press.

Weber, M. (1947). *The theory of economic and social organization* (A. M. Henderson & T. Parsons, Trans.). New York: Free Press.

White, H. C. (1992). *Identity and control: A structural theory of social action.* Princeton, NJ: Princeton University Press.

Willer, D. (Ed.). (1999). *Network exchange theory.* Westport, CT: Praeger.

Wysner, J. W. (1994). *Every purse and purpose: General Motors and the automobile business.* Davisburg, MI: Wilderness Adventure Books.

Yates, B. (1983). *The decline and fall of the American automobile industry.* New York: Empire Books.

Zettelmeyer, F., Scott Morton, F., & Silva-Risso, J. (2001). *Cowboys or cowards: Why are Internet car prices lower?* (Working Paper No. 8667). Cambridge, MA: National Bureau of Economic Research. Available at http://faculty.haas.berkeley.edu/forian/

Discussion Questions

1. The author uses a number of concepts from a variety of theorists and theoretical research programs to explain why African Americans pay more for new cars than do European Americans. Chief among these concepts are social capital, cultural capital, status characteristics, typification, power dependence, and power-balancing operations. Define these terms in your own words. Briefly identify the theorists and theory groups that first employed these concepts in sociological explanation. Finally, suggest how some or all of them can be used to explain a curious social fact that interests you.

2. The author insists that a "proper structural explanation" of the car price mystery requires the sociologist to track the chains of social causation that operate on both sides of the buyer-seller relationship, right down to the face-to-face bargaining situation. First, trace the chain of social causation operating on the buyer's side of the relationship. Then, trace the chain of social causation operating on the seller's side. Be sure to keep buyer and seller dependencies at the forefront of your analysis.

3. In the postscript, the author discusses the differences experienced by African Americans buying a car in a face-to-face situation versus via the Internet. Apply a "proper structural explanation" to account for these differences.

CHAPTER 7

Critical Theory, Legitimation Crisis, and the Deindustrialization of Flint, Michigan

Steven P. Dandaneau

Steven P. Dandaneau *is Associate Professor of Sociology and Director of the Honors and Scholars Programs at the University of Dayton. He has taught social theory at the undergraduate level since receiving his doctorate in sociology from Brandeis University in 1992. His contribution to this volume is based on his book,* A Town Abandoned: Flint, Michigan, Confronts Deindustrialization *(1996), whereas his continuing interest in applied critical theory is exemplified in the book,* A Wrong Life: Studies in Lifeworld-Grounded Critical Theory *(1998), which he is coauthor of with Maude C. Falcone, and in his Pine Forge Press book,* Taking It Big: Developing a Sociological Consciousness in Postmodern Times *(2001).*

I n this chapter, I will apply the famous legitimation crisis theory of Jürgen Habermas (1929–), the world's leading contemporary exponent of critical theory, to the phenomena of deindustrialization in Flint, Michigan.[1] Growing from, but also fundamentally revising Marx's original theory of capitalist economic crisis, Habermas and other 20th-century critical theorists attempted to understand and explain the changing nature of capitalist society since Marx's time.[2] In agreement with Marx, critical theorists view capitalism as an irrational, contradictory, oppressive, albeit dynamic and productive, economic system. It is therefore understood as a leading cause of contemporary social problems, crisis, and domination, as well as a source of rapid social change and technological advancement. However, critical theorists have found it necessary to go beyond Marx's primary analytical focus on the internal dynamics of the capitalist economic system per se to include analyses of the political and cultural processes increasingly essential to the sustained and legitimate reproduction of 20th-century capitalist society.[3] Attention to the case of a medium-size midwestern American city's staggering loss of auto industry jobs allows us to better understand not only the complexities of contemporary capitalism but also the need for criticism and fundamental social change in our society. Indeed, Habermas's theory of legitimation crisis ultimately helps us see a variety of ways in which the continuation of capitalism as we know it causes unnecessary and unjustifiable social disruption and human suffering, damaging what Habermas dubs, in a poetic turn of phrase, the "grammar of forms of life."[4]

The student should know that Habermas's theoretical works are notoriously difficult, even for professional social theorists. Writing about Habermas has already caused me to use a host of difficult concepts, such as capitalism, legitimation, deindustrialization, and the notion of critical theory itself. Also, what might Habermas mean by the phrase "grammar of forms of life"? I would not blame the reader for thinking, "If this is the first paragraph, what lies in store?" Never fear, however; this chapter, like *Illuminating Social Life* as a whole, is premised on the idea that a good way to begin to understand abstract social theories is to witness their power in action with respect to a concrete case in point.

What Is Critical Theory (Doing in Flint)?

At first blush, the experience of the people of Flint, Michigan, is quite revealing and easy to appreciate.[5] This city of 142,300 (1990 census) is approximately 50 miles northwest of Detroit, Michigan, and is the historic hometown of both the General Motors (GM) Corporation (1908), America's largest and perhaps most recognized industrial firm, and the United Auto Workers (1937), America's largest industrial union. Flint is also the focus of Michael Moore's *Roger & Me* (1989), which depicts a decade's worth of the devastation and mayhem caused by massive unemployment in Flint.[6] Indeed, throughout its history, Flint's local experience has been an exaggeration of the main crisis tendencies of American capitalism such that close attention to its particulars brings into relief the structure and dynamics of this complex societal subsystem. One Flint resident noted,

> Flint would be to life what a cowboy movie is to life or [what] a football game is to life: It is uniquely and usefully simplified. So, we're anything but a microcosm. We are the essence of the issues with all the extraneous stuff stripped away.[7]

As Habermas's theory of legitimation crisis predicts, however, Flint also has a rich experience of displacing and transforming the effects of economic crisis into spheres of social life once largely free of direct integration into the capitalist system, such as family life and the educational system. Habermas's perspective not only draws our attention to this displacement tendency but also thereby allows us to view Flint as a community—with a history and a story to tell—rather than, through the imagery of economic science, as one abstract location of factories and jobs among others.

Before going beyond these prefatory remarks, it is also essential to reveal that Flint is my hometown as well. In reviewing what Habermas and others have to say about the "Flints" of the world, I am trying to make better sense of my own life's experiences as much as I am simply trying to understand and teach yet another social theory. Importantly, this reflexive approach[8] to theorizing is consistent with the spirit and purpose of critical theory because this term broadly applies to theories that set as their ultimate goal the emancipation of people from both historically specific situations that prevent them from realizing their human freedom and the kind of thinking that muddies their ability to fully understand the sources of their unfreedom.[9] If we call the former *domination* and the latter *ideology,* then we can say that critical theories are distinct from other types of contemporary social theory inasmuch as critical theories explicitly and purposely work from within conditions of domination and ideology to oppose domination and ideology.[10] In this sense, critical theories are partisan.[11] I write about critical theory and Flint primarily because my experience tells me that domination and ideology (bound together in a process of *deindustrialization*) are an important part of Flint's experience. Luckily, there is a rich theoretical tradition from which I can draw inspiration and orientation in my opposition to this state of affairs.

The two most important originators of critical theory are Karl Marx (1818-1883) and Sigmund Freud (1856-1939). Even though Marx thought of himself as a philosopher turned scientist, he could be understood to have created a new type of theory that was irreducible to either science or philosophy. Rather, as in the title of Habermas's famous treatise on the subject, Marx seemed to move "between philosophy and science" to "critique."[12] With the critical impulses of the Enlightenment tradition of Kant and Hegel, the French Revolution and its aftermath, and an emerging economic science serving as major influences, Marx developed a unique version of critique that meant self-conscious theoretical activity aiming to educate humanity about its actual and potential participation in history making.[13] How could humanity make its future? What prevented humanity from realizing, in Marx's youthful expression, "the meaning of its own struggle and its own desires"?[14] Whereas mainstream labor economics and "scientific management" theory view workers as mere labor commodities to be bought and sold like any market commodity and then fit like cogs into the machinery of industrial production, Marx's economics became, as in the subtitle of his greatest work, *Capital* (1867), a "critique of political economy."[15] In other words, Marx formulated his economics in opposition to the economic orthodoxy of early British and French political economy, which he regarded as benefiting the capitalist class by envisioning a social order in accordance with its interests. If this mainstream economic theory could be criticized and, thereby, in the minds of the majority working class, delegitimized, then such critique would affect the course of history by encouraging revolutionary social change. Paraphrasing his famous "Eleventh Thesis on Feuerbach" (1843), Marx discerned that philosophers had only interpreted the world, whereas in modern, scientific times, the point was to change it.[16]

Sigmund Freud thought of himself as a medical doctor treating psychological illness, but his new psychoanalytic method had similar revolutionary implications inasmuch as it aimed to dispel self-deception through a form of dialogical analysis.[17] His innovative "talking cure" treated humans as communicatively competent participants in their own illness and cure and is to be contrasted with other approaches, such as the use of drugs, lobotomies, shock therapies, and all manner of behaviorist conditioning, that treat humans as thing like phenomena to be manipulated. Freud's emancipatory theory and method sought to lessen the grip of irrational and unnecessary forms of repression that limited individual human self-development, much like Marx's critique of prevailing economic theory was meant to open space for theory and practice true to the experience of the working class and to the potentials of history making in his time. Also, much as Marx viewed the early industrial working class as a potentially self-directed (class-conscious) political force necessary to any sustainable and liberatory social revolution, Freud saw people as necessary participants in their own cure. Inspired by Marx and Freud, critical theorists oppose "bourgeois" economic and management theory and behaviorist psychology inasmuch as these theories lack reflexivity and thus fail to understand their own participation in a society ultimately based on the domination of humans by other humans.

Even though they are credited with forging a new type of emancipatory social theory, neither Marx nor Freud fully appreciated what he had achieved. Such a consistent self-understanding had to wait for Max Horkheimer's (1895-1973) seminal 1937 essay, "Traditional and Critical Theory."[18] Horkheimer was a German philosopher and social theorist and, beginning in 1931, director of the Institute for Social Research affiliated with the University of Frankfurt. Horkheimer coined the term *critical theory* to call attention to his goal to offer a self-conscious and generalized approach to social theory that would transcend its particular origins in Marx, Freud, and others. In part, too, Horkheimer found in the new terminology a politically useful euphemism for studies inspired by one so radical and controversial as Marx. Working from within the devastation that was Germany after the Great War (World War I) and anticipating the rise of such movements as Hitler's National Socialism, Horkheimer set out to update and synthesize the best that modern social theory could offer to put this critical social theory to work for his contemporaries, who in his view were in need of liberation from capitalist domination and the irrationalist ideology of an emergent German fascism.

The notion, then, of a "critical theory of society" is intimately associated with Horkheimer and his luminous "Frankfurt School" colleagues from this period.[19] Horkheimer's most prominent colleagues included Theodor W. Adorno (1903-1969), Herbert Marcuse (1898-1979), and Walter Benjamin (1892-1940). Each of these social theorists made scores of significant contributions to 20th-century philosophy and social theory. Each, like Jean-Paul Sartre, Albert Camus, and Michel Foucault, would be considered among the leading intellectual figures of the previous century. Even though this chapter treats only one important specific theory from today's preeminent living critical theorist, Jürgen Habermas, I encourage students to investigate the lives and work of Habermas's vitally important teachers and predecessors.[20]

Habermas and Legitimation Crisis

We may now consider the essentials of Habermas's theory of legitimation crisis and its applicability to the case of Flint. Although there are many discussions and explications of Habermas's theory, this study's empirical orientation seeks to direct attention to the concrete experience of Flint's citizens to illustrate the ongoing significance of Habermas's perspective. This discussion is, therefore, an attempt to demonstrate not only the continuing importance of Marx's original critique of capitalist society but also the need to extend and revise the Marxian analysis, as Habermas has done, to meet the challenges of today's "late capitalist" society.

Although Flint is today a notorious case of a depressed, Midwestern, Rust Belt community, this was not always the case. Indeed, it is possible to identify three distinct periods in Flint's 20th-century social and economic history, each of which corresponds to significant changes in the American capitalist-industrial system, and each of which is discussed by Habermas in his 1973 book *Legitimation Crisis.* By way of further introduction to Habermas via Flint and its telling contemporary experience, I briefly describe the periods of liberal, advanced, and late capitalism through their manifestation in 20th-century Flint.

Capitalism in Flint

The period of liberal or laissez-faire industrial capitalism occurred in Flint between the development of the horse-drawn carriage, and later, the automobile industry, and the Great Sit-Down Strike of 1936-1937. Carriage production mushroomed in late 19th-century Flint. By 1904, Flint was the world's leading center of horse-drawn carriage production, producing more than 150,000 carriages per year. In 1908, Henry Ford rolled out the first of his Model Ts in Detroit, while in Flint Billy Durant founded the GM Corporation. As a result of the rapid expansion of its local automobile industry, Flint quickly became an amazing boomtown, so much so that the city's population more than tripled between 1900 and 1930. As historian Ronald Edsforth documents, the automobile was the "primary driving force" behind America's 20th-century "second industrial revolution."[21] Flint was in the thick of these momentous developments, with the likes of Fisher Body, Chevrolet, Buick, AC Sparkplug, Cadillac, and DuPont fortifying the city's economic expansion.

This was still a time in American society when entrepreneurs like Durant had a relatively free hand in deciding where, when, and how to run their private businesses. Hence the notion of *laissez-faire,* which refers to the doctrine of government noninterference in the workings of the economic system.[22] Although it is true that the American economy by this time was characterized by very notable economic concentration (including the infamous "trusts" in steel, railroads, oil, and banking and the social struggles by immigrant workers, farmers, and other groups against these monopolies), in newly forming industries, such as Flint's fledgling automotive industry, independent inventor-entrepreneurs still played a vital role. Indeed, their ingenuity and inventiveness, their willingness to take risks, and their ultimate success at creating vast wealth are regularly celebrated by proponents of capitalism as proof of the system's robust social virtues.

In this period, capitalists such as Durant not only ruled over their own private property but also sought and obtained considerable power beyond their workplaces. This was certainly true in Flint. For example, in 1910, when a socialist, John H. Menton, was popularly elected as Flint's mayor, local business leaders rallied to defeat this challenge by electing in the following year one of their own—multimillionaire and GM board member Charles Stewart Mott. From 1911 to 1973, when Mott died as one of America's richest men, no other person exerted more influence in or over Flint. Mott's personal significance is suggestive of GM's structural dominance in Flint as the city's primary employer, just as GM's role in Flint is suggestive of big business's dominant place in American society as a whole. The era of liberal capitalism was a time of relatively little government interference with the workings of the private market economy, and a time when the social power of America's dominant capitalist class was effectively unquestioned.

The second period of 20th-century capitalist development began with the onset of capitalism's worst hour: the Great Depression. After the infamous stock market crash of 1929, the laissez-faire capitalist economy collapsed, causing widespread hardship in Flint and throughout America and the world. The private ownership of wealth and its use in the private pursuit of profit (capitalism) did not generate, as Adam Smith's theory of the "invisible hand" predicted, a new round of entrepreneurship, employment, and economic growth. Thus, the Great Depression was not only a pressing practical problem but also an ideological problem that threatened the economic theory that legitimized capitalism as a whole. The workings of the market "mechanism" had been touted by economists since Smith as a nature like system (*ordre naturel*) that, if left to correct its own imbalances, should have moved to a state of full-employment equilibrium. Much to the chagrin of economists, however, the market was unable to pull itself up by its own bootstraps, and, in Flint as elsewhere in America, the very real threat of social upheaval meant that something had to be done.

It is no surprise that Franklin Delano Roosevelt's activist New Deal program was enthusiastically welcomed by Flint's working class. Elected twice in the 1930s with the strong backing of Flint's industrial workers and other minorities, Roosevelt dramatically reversed the Hoover administration's traditional do-nothing policy toward the Great Depression in favor of an unprecedented surge in government involvement in economic affairs. In establishing his so-called alphabet soup of government job-creation and economic stimulus programs, and in supporting the rights of workers to unionize and claim power in the workplace as well as in the wider political arena (e.g., by supporting the National Labor Relations Act and castigating the nation's wealthy elite as an illegitimate "plutocracy"), Roosevelt forcefully challenged the exclusive power of the capitalist class to manage America's economic growth. In this era, there arose a new type of capitalist system significantly different from the liberal capitalism that collapsed into economic depression. Habermas calls this second phase of 20th-century capitalism *advanced capitalism.* It is also known as organized capitalism, monopoly capitalism, and, more popularly, "welfare state" capitalism.

Although the welfare state developed sooner and grew much larger in Europe, it could be said that America's period of advanced capitalism was born in Flint precisely when, during the Great Sit-Down Strike of 1936 and 1937, Michigan's New Deal governor placed National Guard troops *between* striking workers at Flint's GM facilities and the GM-controlled local police force that was attacking the "sit-down" strikers in an effort to rout them from their held positions in the factories.[23] The workers had struck the corporation primarily as a result of the physically intolerable working conditions but also because of the arbitrary and unjust use of managerial authority and the widespread insecurity and suffering that 6 years of economic depression had wrought—not, of course, on Mr. Mott and associates, but on the workers and their families, who owned little but their ability to labor. In a sense, then, the workers sat down in the factories to stand up for their rights as human beings and not factors of production. In total, 11 strikers were wounded by police gunfire during the 44 days of the strike action as thousands of fellow workers and strike sympathizers poured into Flint and filled the streets in a jarring conflict that garnered the attention of the nation and the world. As depicted in the Academy Award–nominated film *With Babies and Banners,* even members of the United Auto Workers' (UAW) Women's Emergency Brigade took the unusual and courageous step of placing themselves between the strikers and police, suggesting the depth of commitment and solidarity emerging from within Flint's working-class community.[24]

With the blessing of President Roosevelt and his secretary of labor, Frances Perkins, Michigan Governor Frank Murphy moved to protect the strikers and encouraged the negotiation of a settlement in which GM would for the first time recognize the UAW and thereby its workers' right to unionize. This development was part of a larger movement in American society to mitigate and in doing so salvage, if not laissez-faire capitalism, then at least capitalism in some form. While many capitalists at the time, such as Charles Stewart Mott, disliked Roosevelt's New Deal—and they *did* dislike it[25]—its ultimate effect was to bring a greater balance of the power between capital and labor and thus save American society from more extreme forms of political revolution, such as those that occurred at the time in Germany and earlier in Russia.

U.S.-advanced capitalism emerged from World War II virtually unscathed and, indeed, strengthened, by worldwide military conflict. In the mildly sardonic phrase of the sociologist C. Wright Mills, this was a time of an "American celebration."[26] Postwar America was a society that easily delivered the proverbial goods, creating material abundance for a growing and stabilizing middle class. The overt political upheavals associated with the "labor wars" of the 1930s were replaced by a postwar mass democracy that created political stability and ideological conformity. Aided by Cold War tensions abroad and McCarthyism at home, this "culture of abundance" encouraged, in Edsforth's phrase, the emergence of a "cultural consensus."

As a shining example of the celebration of postwar American prosperity, Flint enjoyed its *Leave It to Beaver* heyday. As Edsforth documents, one magazine in 1956 went as far as to dub Flint "The Happiest Town in Michigan."[27] In this new era of (as it turned out, temporary) consensus, the American automobile industry dominated the world's market for cars and trucks, providing an abundance of jobs and economic growth. The UAW, for its part, negotiated steadily increasing wages, benefits, and improved working conditions. This steady rise in income created the conditions for a parallel rise in consumption. It was not uncommon for Flint's working people to own a home, two or more cars, a boat, and perhaps a cabin "up north," where families might regularly vacation and for parents to ponder the likelihood of sending their children to the local college or one of the expanding state universities. Not only were individuals realizing what, at the time, constituted the "American Dream" but also whole communities were sprouting, as was Flint, all manner of museums, theaters, sports facilities, superhighways, libraries, and music halls. From 1945 to the late 1960s, the Big Business/Big Labor/Big Government advanced capitalist economy was good for GM and was absolutely great for Flint.

From the early 1970s onward, however, the stability of the advanced capitalist system has eroded, so much so that we may distinguish this period as the third phase of 20th-century capitalism. With the 1973 publication of *Legitimation Crisis* and its English translation 2 years later, Habermas helped to initiate discussion of late capitalism in terms of the "crisis tendencies of advanced capitalism." Because it is the burden of the remaining discussion to fully explain Habermas's theory of these "crisis tendencies," including in particular the potential in our time for "legitimation crisis," I conclude this background discussion of the changing shape of American capitalism by simply describing the emergence of late capitalism in Flint.

Once an expanding metropolis—a veritable boomtown—Flint is today closer to a ghost town.[28] According to one study, "at its peak in 1978, General Motors *directly* contributed 42.4 percent of the county's jobs and indirectly significant other auto-related jobs."[29] Auto industry jobs are crucial to the vitality of the area's economy because the typical pay and benefit level for these jobs far exceeds the national average. In fact, auto industry jobs are better paying than almost every other type of industrial job. For example, in 1987, automotive manufacturing occupations had annual average earnings of $39,500, which was in that year $13,800 more than the average manufacturing wage.[30] By 1996, GM employees averaged $69,000 a year.[31] In comparison to minimum-wage, service-sector employment, auto industry jobs are a gold mine. Since 1978, however, GM has cut its Flint workforce by more than 50,000 (from more than 80,000 in 1978 to roughly 30,000 in 1999).[32] This massive reduction of once-secure, high-wage jobs has resulted in "ripple effects" through the community, which register in Flint as a panoply of apparently disparate social problems.[33]

In *The Deindustrialization of America: Plant Closings, Community Abandonment, and the Dismantling of Basic Industry* (1982), economists Barry Bluestone and Bennett Harrison describe this general process as *deindustrialization*. They define deindustrialization as "the widespread, systemic disinvestment in the nation's basic productive capacity," which, they argue, can be traced to the way capital—in the forms of financial resources and of real plant and equipment—has been diverted from productive investment in our basic national industries into unproductive speculations, mergers and acquisitions, and foreign investment.[34]

For Bluestone and Harrison, deindustrialization has led to "shuttered factories, displaced workers, and a newly emerging group of ghost towns."[35] Sadly, Flint's experience is an exaggeration of these tendencies.

Although scratching only the surface of the human dimensions of widespread and sustained unemployment, a rehearsal of social statistics is one way to spark the imagination. According to a 1991 memorandum authored by staff at the Flint branch of Michigan's Department of Social Services, titled "State of Flint," Flint lost a quarter of its population in the 20-year period from 1970 to 1990. In 1990, Flint had more vacant businesses and boarded-up homes than at any time in its history as well as the 10th highest infant mortality rate in the nation. In this same year, Flint recorded an unemployment rate for black youth of nearly 60%. According to this source, public assistance caseloads in the Flint area increased by 79.6% during the period between 1973 and 1989, with the result that slightly more than 40% of Flint's total population was receiving some form of public assistance.[36]

Crime is also a problem. For example, in 1989, Genesee County ranked third from the top of the 333 largest U.S. metropolitan areas in the number of violent and property crimes committed.[37] In the 1980s, while Genesee County's overall youth unemployment rate grew to 25%, its homicide rate for youth rose 400%.[38] By 1990, Flint had the highest serious crime rates of any Michigan city, including Detroit.[39]

Additional indicators of Flint's depressed condition include statistics that document the following: Suicide rates for Genesee County's 15- to 19-year-olds increased 300% from 1982 to 1987; adolescent substance abuse increased by nearly 20% between 1988 and 1990; the number of domestic violence clients increased 10-fold in the period from 1984 to 1991; Genesee County's divorce rate was in this period 66% higher than the national average; reported cases of child abuse and neglect increased by more than 20% during the 1980s; and, finally, by the early 1990s, 58% of Flint's children were raised in single-parent households, which, as research suggests, are household types that suffer disproportionately from persistent poverty.[40] In 1987, *Money* magazine ranked Flint the least desirable American city in which to live.[41] By 1995, Flint's most depressed neighborhoods, populated disproportionately by Flint's majority African American population, had unemployment rates above 25% and concentrated rates of poverty ranging above 40%.[42]

Because Flint is singularly dependent on GM employment—an extreme case of the proverbial one-horse town—Flint's high rates of sustained, structural unemployment, as well as the social problems predictably related to this condition, are easily attributable to GM's local downsizing.[43] GM, however, is not legally or politically held responsible for Flint's economic ruination. GM was not, for example, charged with premeditated murder when Flint's crime and suicide rates shot up as an indirect, but predictable result of massive local unemployment. Even the thought of this probably seems strange. Nor did the federal, state, or local governments ask

GM to pay increased taxes to cover the soaring expenditures for social services caused by GM's widespread layoffs. On the contrary, governments at all levels are much more likely to grant tax breaks and provide other incentives in an effort to entice corporations to retain the reduced number of jobs remaining after a round of downsizing.

This was certainly the case in Flint, where GM received $400 million in local tax breaks during the 1980s, even as the company slashed its Flint-based employment.[44] The Flint City Council continues to approve GM tax-abatement requests, including eight abatement requests for a building constructed on top of the demolished GM factory recognized as the historic site of Flint's Great Sit-Down Strike. In the early 1990s, GM announced a new round of layoffs and local plant closings in Flint, and the local business class grew desperate.[45] By 1996, Flint-area business and political leaders predicted that local GM employment could drop to "between 26,000 and 15,000 by the end of the decade," which caused the head of the Flint-Genesee Economic Growth Alliance to speculate that Flint should consider following the lead of Amarillo, Texas, which taxes its citizens to pay prospective businesses a "bounty on jobs," as much as $10,000 up-front for every $12-per-hour job they promise to create.[46] It seemed as though the dominance of capitalism in Flint had in some sense come full circle: Instead of GM paying Flint's workers for their labor power, Flint's workers were, in effect, being asked to consider paying GM for the privilege of holding a job at a corporation that regularly earns annual profits in the billions.

A poignant moment in *Roger & Me* may serve to capture the deep social conflict engendered by capitalism. After years of trying, Michael Moore finally corners then–GM Chairman Roger Smith and asks him to come to Flint to witness the devastation caused by Smith's disinvestment decisions. Suggesting GM's legal and political unaccountability to the people of Flint, as well as, perhaps, the arrogance and sheer might of transnational capital in the increasingly freewheeling era of late capitalism, Smith tersely says to Moore, "I cannot come to Flint, I'm sorry," before he abruptly turns his back.

Habermas's Theory of Legitimation Crisis: Systems Crisis

Although Flint has experienced, as has been shown, something approaching Depression-like conditions during the past two decades, there has been no repeat of the kind of grassroots militancy and social upheaval that characterized Flint in the Great Depression. In Flint, there is no manifest development of a "proletarian" revolutionary consciousness; nothing like the class struggle predicted in the imagery of Marx's original theory of capitalist crisis; and no repeat of the Great Sit-Down Strike of 1936 and 1937.

Drawing from *Legitimation Crisis* as well as Habermas's two-volume magnum opus, *The Theory of Communicative Action* (1981), and other writings, we can make sense of this apparent departure from Marxian expectations by first taking into account the important changes in the capitalist system since Marx's time.[47] In contrast to Marx's original critique of liberal capitalism, Habermas directs our attention to advanced capitalism's integration of economic and political systems and, thus, to the displacement or shifting of the potential for economic crisis into a potential for political or government crisis, or what Habermas calls the tendency toward "rationality crisis." Unlike the situation in Marx's own time—before the Great Depression and the rise of the welfare state—today, governments take responsibility for smoothing out economic cycles and subsequent income disparities. Agreeing with Marx, Habermas sees these types of crises as endemic to the class-based structure of liberal capitalist society.[48] What of advanced capitalism, however? Thanks to the famous suggestion by economist John Maynard Keynes that government involvement in the capitalist economy could be a good and, from time to time, necessary thing, advanced capitalist governments had an economic theory that legitimized their attempts to manage economic growth (using fiscal and monetary policy, international trade policy, regulation of stock and bond markets, the expertise of the president's Council of Economic Advisors, etc.). This was especially the case in postwar Europe and in Japan, but it was also true to an important extent in the United States. Indeed, as we have seen, the postwar boom that made Flint "The Happiest Town in Michigan" also made it seem as though mass production and mass consumption, along with the government's Keynesian economics, had forever and peacefully solved the same contradictions of capitalism that, in *Capital,* Marx had suggested were resolvable only through wrenching class revolution.[49]

As a consequence of government intervention, Habermas observes that attempts to manage economic growth politicize that which had previously been seen as the nature-like, impersonal workings of the free market system. The results of Adam Smith's "invisible hand" became the all too visible outcomes of public policy decisions and labor-management collective bargaining. Constitutionally charged with promoting the general welfare, the post-New Deal federal government was called on to mitigate the short-term effects of unemployment and various other social problems and to create what today is often called the "social safety net." This implicit guarantee by the government to promote full employment and to protect individuals from the worst vicissitudes of the market is paid for by tax dollars and administered by government bureaucracies. Today, the expansion or contraction of this safety net is a matter of continual political debate.

In this regard, Habermas writes, "between capitalism and democracy there is an *indissoluble* tension; in them two opposed principles of societal integration compete for primacy."[50] As economic crises grow and multiply (as in Flint since the advent of GM's downsizing), the democratic governments of late capitalist society are therefore expected to provide more and more relief and protection from the harm engendered by economic crisis. Recall that 40% of Flint's citizens receive some form of public assistance. Governments, however, can provide and administer more services (e.g., increased unemployment benefits, medical care, educational benefits, and welfare services) only by increasing tax revenues or by borrowing to match the expenses caused by a rise in the number of "clients" of various government bureaucracies (such as the patients in veterans hospitals, senior citizens requiring government health care assistance, prisoners in America's jails, and the recipients of food stamps). Economic problems are in this way translated into political problems to be solved through the administration of welfare state bureaucracies.

It is also a problem because not only do average citizens generally dislike increased taxation, which diminishes the money they have to spend on themselves, but also increased taxation on business diminishes profits and in so doing discourages capitalist investment. Because capitalists invest, after all, to reap maximum private profits, capitalists might reasonably ask themselves, "Why invest (and create jobs and new products and services) if the government is just going to take a large share of my profits to pay for other people's problems" (e.g., the problems experienced by the people of Flint)? or "Why invest in GM stock, and thereby increase GM's ability to expand and improve its business, if the corporation's profits are just going to be redirected through government taxation and spending policies back to the people of Flint instead of into my personal bank account as stock dividends?" Even more plausibly, what is to prevent an investor from looking to make money in other countries, particularly those with more favorable "business climates" (i.e., countries with lower taxes, less government regulation to protect workers' rights and the environment, and a less powerful workforce, which is therefore less able to bargain or demand wage and benefit increases and less able to elect political leaders who will tax business and the wealthy to provide social services)? In any case, it stands to reason that the U.S. economy would suffer a loss of investment, which could lead to a vicious circle of decline: Less domestic investment or investment "offshore" means more domestic unemployment; more unemployment means more social problems; increasing social problems mean more pressure on government to increase social services to ameliorate the problems; but increased taxes could mean less investment, and so on.

There is also the possibility that this contradiction could cause political unrest, such as "tax revolts," in which voters reject local school millage increases, human service levies, property taxes, and candidates at all levels of government who would dare advocate increased taxation. In America, it is just this contradiction that produced the much-debated problem of the national debt. Although Reagan-era tax cuts were in themselves politically popular, they were not balanced by reductions in government spending, which, because so many depend on forms of government spending, tends to be politically unpopular. The resulting indebtedness of the government, which requires that an increasing proportion of the yearly budget go to paying interest on the debt, hinders the political system's ability to address social problems. For Habermas, this "crisis of the welfare state" is caused by the displacement of the contradictions in the capitalist system into the realm of politics, where they emerge in a different form. In Habermas's view, the contradictions of liberal capitalism (identified more or less correctly by Marx as rooted in the class structure of capitalist society[51]) are in advanced capitalism transformed into the persistent contradictions of the welfare state.

Therefore, why is it that GM is able to reduce its Flint-based employment by 50,000 jobs without sparking "class struggle"? Deindustrialization is a relatively smooth process, in part because the government is expected to ameliorate hardship, absorb the social costs, and diffuse the frustration and anger caused by GM's private business decision. It is expected, furthermore, that politicians will not explicitly discuss the class basis of capitalism or bring into question the legitimacy of the capitalist system as a whole. Instead, mainstream political leaders are expected to present this conflict in a technical or administrative light—for example, as a debate over "balancing the budget," which calls attention to the conflict between tax increases and the pressures on government spending and not between social classes as such. This kind of discourse tends to leave citizens demanding a contradiction: both more government-provided benefits and fewer taxes. This explains, in part, why political leaders as divergent as Ronald Reagan and Jesse Jackson could, in the 1980s, simultaneously be very popular in Flint because each spoke to a different dimension of Flint's experienced crisis.

Although the preceding discussion broadly captures what Habermas calls the rationality crisis of governments at the national and state levels, it is also instructive to closely examine the details of Flint's response to its GM-based deindustrialization. Even though Flint had for decades been overwhelmingly dependent on GM employment, Flint's government and community leaders showed surprising inventiveness and industry of their own in devising a plan to replace the permanently lost GM jobs. Acting in accordance with their implicit responsibility to promote the general welfare, and with more than $200 million in investment capital (including $80 million in backing from the Flint-headquartered Charles Stewart Mott Foundation, one of the country's largest charitable foundations), Flint's leaders set about to independently reinvent the city's image and economy.

Beginning in the late 1970s and gaining steam behind Reagan-era optimism and deficit spending, Flint's leaders hoped to take Flint from what it was—a decaying, Rust Belt, industrial city heavily dependent on its remaining and still substantial GM base—to, as one commentator put it, the "tourist and convention mecca of the Midwest."[52] The centerpiece of this would-be phoenix-like rebirth was "AutoWorld," an indoor theme park designed to attract more than 1 million visitors per year to Flint. Tax dollars also funded the construction of a new hotel in downtown Flint. With several additional developments, including a James Rouse-designed "festival marketplace," Flint readied itself to emerge as a major 1980s family vacation destination.

Of course, as *Roger & Me* depicts with such great effect, this government-inspired and -administered convention and tourism plan was a tremendous flop. The only conventions Flint could attract were on the order of statewide meetings of Scrabble players, and AutoWorld, the $80 million theme park, closed within 6 months of its opening due to lack of visitors. Apparently, the attraction of riding the world's largest indoor Ferris wheel and the sheen of Flint's new slogan—"Flint: Our Spark Will Surprise You!"—could not offset people's commonsense understanding of the bitter-hard realities of a Rust Belt auto town. In addition, Flint's downtown hotel eventually went bankrupt (although it has since reopened under new management), whereas its festival marketplace was transferred to the University of Michigan at Flint for a token sum. Michael Moore pointed out in his *Roger & Me* narration,

Expecting a million people to come to Flint was a little like expecting a million people to go to New Jersey to "ChemicalWorld," or to Valdez, Alaska, to "ExxonWorld." Some people just don't like to celebrate human tragedy while on vacation.[53]

Flint's community leaders' failed attempt at economic development easily exemplifies Habermas's notion of rationality crisis. With a grant from the C. S. Mott Foundation, tax dollars, and additional borrowing, the city tried to replace what it lost when GM removed so many jobs from the community. Instead of a viable alternative to capitalist development, however, Flint succeeded only in bringing the political nature of economic development into the open and placing in question the competence of government planners. Some years later, in a moment of frustration, Mark S. Davis, the head of Flint's new post-AutoWorld private business-led economic development coalition, exclaimed, "I mean, for God's sake, this is the town that built AutoWorld!"[54] Even for Davis—no radical social theorist— AutoWorld was symbolic of the inability of technically oriented government administrators to fundamentally solve the contradictions of capitalism. It is no wonder, then, that AutoWorld was eventually demolished, for it stood as a constant reminder that the old solutions to America's social problems have been eclipsed by the new realities of late capitalism.

Habermas's Theory of Legitimation Crisis: The Lifeworld

To this point, I have not addressed the especially unique aspect of Habermas's theory. Habermas in particular argues that a further displacement of the potential for crisis can and does occur, this time not as an exchange between the integrated economic and political systems (as previously described) but rather as an exchange from these machinelike societal subsystems to our community and personal lives or to what Habermas calls the *sociocultural system* or *lifeworld*. For Habermas, the truly unsettling crises of late capitalism are likely to occur along the "seams" between our contradiction-ridden social systems and the traditional, taken-for-granted cultural patterns (norms, values, and beliefs) that anchor our sense of reality, our personal identity, and guide and regulate our motivation as social actors.[55] In this way, Habermas moves the analysis of late capitalism in a distinctly sociological direction.[56] Drawing on the classic sociological theories of Durkheim, Mead, Parsons, and others, Habermas refocuses critical theory toward the tenuous and vulnerable processes of the symbolically mediated dialectic between self and society and the shared moral fabric that undergirds the abstract functioning of formal social systems. In *Legitimation Crisis,* Habermas names both the legitimation and motivation crisis tendencies associated with this part of his argument as types of identity crisis. This part of Habermas's theory has more in common with Durkheim's theory of anomie than it does, for example, with Marx's concern for the laws of capital accumulation and the falling rate of profit because what is at stake in Habermas's attention to the lifeworld is the nonrational underbelly of functionally differentiated social systems that provides societies their coherence and collective identity.[57]

Before applying this aspect of Habermas's theory to the case of Flint, it is necessary to point out that Habermas's theoretical approach is unique (and made even more complex!) because Habermas also identifies a type of top-down response to the crisis tendencies undermining late capitalism from below.[58] In effect, Habermas asks the following: If the New Deal welfare state (Big Government), increased unionization (Big Labor), and America's postwar global hegemony, among other factors, temporarily resolved the crisis of America's laissez-faire capitalism by creating a new type of advanced capitalism, then what might contemporaries do in response to the crises of advanced capitalism that continue despite government attempts to ameliorate them? Habermas's answer to this question allows us to make sense of the latest elite-driven responses to Flint's woes. Flint has not sat idly by after the Auto-World debacle and watched while its fortunes decline. Instead, there has arisen a new set of strategies designed to extend the tentacles of economic and political elites deep into the social and cultural fabric so as to vitiate the destabilizing effects of the crises of advanced capitalism.

Habermas uses the phrase "colonization of the lifeworld" to describe the tendency of corporations and government entities to work together in a desperate attempt to stabilize and reproduce late capitalism by attempting to manage and control more and more of everyday life.[59] The question then becomes, how much of everyday life can be successfully integrated into the operation of these social systems before new social and cultural pathologies are engendered as a result? Can people come to think of themselves, their families, and their community as mere cogs in turbulent bureaucratic corporations and mass political and economic systems and, at the same time, continue in good faith to wholeheartedly participate in such a society? Can people function, asks Habermas, when their "everyday consciousness is robbed of its power to synthesize; [when] it becomes fragmented"?[60]

Habermas does not think so. He sees a fundamental contradiction between the abstract calculus of instrumental rationality, which guides both the profit-maximizing firm and bureaucratic government, and the textured communicative rationality of everyday life, which guides us in our "action oriented to reaching understanding" and, in this way, secures and reproduces the integration of social life.[61] In other words, for Habermas, it is not possible to replace traditional values and beliefs with an artificial culture constructed only to further some corporation's profit-maximization strategy or some government's legitimacy. People cannot live as members of the "MTV" or "Pepsi Generation," at least not without serious and dysfunctional consequences. What Habermas calls the *internal colonization* of the lifeworld is, therefore, a contradictory process because it threatens to create forms of social *dis*integration, such as individual psychopathologies and collective anomie, even though its purpose is to stabilize and reproduce a coherent and integrated social order.[62]

This is where Habermas's theories of legitimation and motivation crisis become germane. We may think of these as crisis tendencies "from below" inasmuch as both refer to people's withdrawal of their connection to the society's institutionalized social systems.[63] In particular, Habermas understands the potential for people to lose confidence in a mass political system that is democratic in name but that in myriad ways discourages genuine participation and denies average citizens a meaningful political voice. Everyone knows, for example, that a "televised town meeting" is not a real town meeting but is instead a format designed for little more than the appearance of participatory democracy for a mass viewing audience. Moreover, because the political system regularly fails to solve the fundamental problems caused by a contradictory capitalist system (in part because the true nature of the problems cannot be openly identified and debated), citizens become disaffected, apathetic, and resigned, even if they are not consciously aware of the source of their disaffection and its relation to the prohibition against class-based political debate. Also, because the political and economic systems have become so tightly integrated, when both fail, and when the "colonization" tendencies identified by Habermas are, as a result, intensified, then torn and frayed is the very fabric of traditional values and beliefs that once motivated people to give over their lives to participation in the risky and difficult workings of the marketplace. For Habermas, this set of motivational resources includes a variety of specific dimensions, such as "civil" and "familial-vocational privatism," or the tendencies toward political nonparticipation in favor of attention to leisure, consumption, and status competition through careerism.[64]

For Habermas, there are no easy functional replacements for these traditional guiding values and norms, and it remains an open question whether the social systems can reproduce themselves without recourse to a pre-reflective, always implicit and shared culture. Habermas calls the withdrawal of mass political loyalty *legitimation crisis* and the withdrawal of motivation, especially the motivation toward achievement and participation in the occupational system, *motivation crisis*.[65] A combined realization of these closely related crisis tendencies would portend a radical transformation of society.

The development in 1989 of the Genesee Economic Area Revitalization, Incorporated (GEAR), a new umbrella public-private economic development partnership for the Flint area, illustrates Flint's colonizing response to the possibility of legitimation and motivation crises. Facing more GM downsizing (economic crisis) and stung by the AutoWorld debacle (rationality crisis), Flint's reeling elites implicitly sought (or so I argue) to ward off legitimation and motivation crises by adopting the attitude that any future economic development would have to be strategically—that is, self-consciously and systematically—tied to a human resource strategy and an education strategy.[66] In other words, GEAR's economic development mission involved what its executive director, Mark S. Davis, colorfully described as "defining" and "improving the product." Davis explained,

> The economic reality of GM shutting down jobs during the last couple of decades has created a political environment that has many effects on the social economy, the social fabric.
>
> But everybody in the past has been focused on the god-damned public sector. . . . For a long time, the way things got decided in our community was people waited for GM, the UAW, and the Mott Foundation to tell them what to do.

What's happening now, though, is there are massive structural changes in the economy taking place. So, as a community, we're recognizing, in a way, the ascendancy of the private sector in economic development in a way that has never been understood before.

My message here is economic development cannot succeed unless we improve the product. A community is a product. The product is the summation of what we are. What we have to offer to a business, to an employer, to an investor, is the summation of what we are. That is our product.[67]

Davis's notion that "a community is a product," or that a community's market or economic value to business is the "summation" of what a community is, jibes with Habermas's claim that the lifeworld (Davis's "social economy, the social fabric") is increasingly the focus of capitalism's efforts to stabilize itself.

If we follow the logic of this position, then everything that reproduces and characterizes human society becomes a potential object of cultural manipulation. GEAR's colonizing framework even defines Flint's evident social problems primarily in terms of their negative effect on the ability of "the product" to retain or attract outside business. For example, GEAR's 1991 strategic economic development plan states the following with regard to Flint's poverty: "Persistent poverty breeds understandable social resentment and conflict, dividing communities and prohibiting effective common action—*conditions that discourage enterprise and outside investment* [italics added].[68] The following is also from this same document:

Finally, but perhaps most importantly, there is the central issue of the human resource challenges in the Flint/Genesee County community that must be met if our economic future is to be bright.

Unless our people are provided with the material and spiritual resources needed to build a healthy, safe, and prosperous community—one in which people are permitted to dream and make choices about their futures—the prospect for more jobs is nothing but a hollow promise.

Poverty, inadequate health care, poor nutrition, racial discrimination, dysfunctional families, substandard housing, unsafe neighborhoods, drug and alcohol dependence and human despair: All are powerful enemies of economic development.

Therefore, we are of a strong and unanimous voice in recommending to the GEAR Board that the achievement of our vision for Flint/Genesee County's future requires that a human resources strategy be integrated with the economic development strategy we propose today.[69]

GEAR's Mark Davis puts this logic more simply and directly, and perhaps more honestly:

We better have a better educated workforce, we better have babies that come to school healthy, because no amount of slick marketing on my part is going to succeed in attracting a company from the outside unless we have a product that's competitive.[70]

In other words, GEAR recognized that its "product" is initially produced by individuals, families, neighborhoods. As an economic planning organization, however, GEAR had little or no direct control over these spheres of life. GEAR may have had influence in the economic and political systems, but its influence in Flint's social-cultural system was scant. Hence, GEAR proposed that a "human resources strategy be integrated with [its] economic development strategy," presumably to better integrate human and economic development. In this way, GEAR treats people's lives as variables in a strategic plan. GEAR's social engineers are not so much worried about poverty or young children's health in and of themselves—as though people were of intrinsic value, their suffering itself a matter of concern, and as though the people of Flint were subjects with whom one would speak and argue in the hope of reaching mutual understanding and perhaps even agreement and consensus. Rather, GEAR weighs people and their life's experience in an instrumental, cost-benefit calculus, adequate, at best, to the workings of social systems. A member of GEAR stated, "It doesn't make sense to try to drag in all this baggage, all these disenfranchised people."[71]

What if, however, in a different situation, it did "make sense" to drag in the baggage of disenfranchised people? What if it made good economic sense to employ workers in Mexico for $50 per week? Having eschewed an understanding of Flint as a community in favor of treating it as a product, GEAR took the strategic position that it could not in a cost-effective fashion sell Flint to prospective businesses unless Flint's people were competitively engineered at all stages of their socialization. It was decided, in other words, that Flint would "improve its product" and not ready it for a fire sale. Flint would set its sights high in hopes of attracting a handsome price. This would require strategic attention to the educational experience of Flint's citizens.

One might suppose that your study of the book in your hands is meant in some way to contribute to something as lofty as your full development as an intellectually empowered human being. Not surprisingly, perhaps, GEAR adopted a different way of looking at education. Because an important part of GEAR's early 1990s economic development strategy was to make Flint a "world center for applying information technology to manufacturing," GEAR recognized that this required Flint to also become home to a "world-class workforce."[72] The GEAR plan states the following:

> Every local economy must have a competitive advantage if it wishes to prosper in a global economy. In addition to the unique concentration of technically skilled workers that Flint/Genesee County proposes *to create* [italics added], the area has decided to develop a competitive advantage as a place where people know more about using information technologies and new organizational techniques in factory settings *than anywhere else in the world* [italics added].[73]

Because Flint's public educational system has the typical problems of school systems in most depressed urban areas, and because there are no major universities in Flint, one might reasonably ask how GEAR planned to "create" this base of "technically skilled workers." The answer is given in the strategic plan as follows:

The challenge of improving our work skills is great, because it will require that *every adult and youth* [italics added]—men and women already in the work-force as well as young people still in school—acquire the learning skills, social skills and job skills to earn a middle-class living and retain and attract good jobs to Flint/Genesee County. To meet this goal, *each person must better their individual skills, and have a positive attitude about work, family and education* [italics added].[74]

From GEAR's perspective, then, the educational system in Flint should not so much concern the students' enlightenment and personal growth, but instead focus its institutional power on developing job skills and even "positive attitudes" suffi-cient to "retain and attract good jobs" to the area. In this way, the value of "liberal education" (a conversation about ideas?) is erased in favor of the integration of educational institutions as a means to the larger economic end of an improved product. Indeed, the surprising emphasis given to "a positive attitude about work, family and education" is indicative of GEAR's attention to Flint's sociocultural system. In this regard, GEAR's plan for the reform of Flint's educational system is exactly akin to its human resources strategy; it's all about improving the product.

From Habermas's perspective, it is, however, doubtful whether GEAR's colo-nization strategy could be successful. Although this type of top-down manipulation of everyday life may not engender a response such as the class struggle that spilled into the streets of Depression-era Flint, neither is it likely that such a cynical pro-gram as GEAR's—which, for example, conceives of a baby's health in terms of its cost-benefit to prospective profit-maximizing business—will come to smoothly recast Flint's lifeworld in the form of a production process. As Habermas observes, culture is "peculiarly resistant" to such bureaucratic control.[75] It is simply too easy for people to see through such schemes to the cynicism concerning human life that lies at the heart of capitalism and any administrative attempts to contain the crises generated therein. Inasmuch as people, in solidarity with one another as human beings of intrinsic worth, do in fact resist the intrusion of such instrumental or "strategic" rationality into their lives, they withdraw their legitimation and their motivation from the integrated political and economic system that lives on little else.[76] In Habermas's view, and taking a more proactive stance, the protection and free development of the distinct form of human solidarity characteristic of the life-world necessitates the struggle against the colonizing tendencies of late capitalist society.[77]

Conclusion

It seems appropriate to conclude this application of Jürgen Habermas's critical theory of legitimation crisis by posing the following questions: (a) Will the pre-dicted withdrawal of legitimation and motivation create conditions for fundamen-tal social change? or (b) will the colonization of the lifeworld disrupt the symbolic reproduction through which social integration is maintained? If Habermas's theory is correct, it is as difficult to answer these questions as it is to ascertain the point at which an individual's or community's self-understanding as an administered and commodified product becomes unbearable, or to know why or even how these new conditions lead to self-debilitating or self-transformative responses or even to a radical political revolution—or to something in between, novel, or unprecedented.

What is clear, however, and what is appropriate to reveal, is that as a participant in the life of my hometown—which is to me, therefore, no mere product—I have a special interest in not further exposing Flint's lifeworld to any more top-down scrutiny than it has already received. In other words, as a reflexive critical theorist, I pursue sociology mindful of how sociological knowledge can itself contribute to the "colonization of the lifeworld."

Therefore, I choose to underscore but a single point. This discussion suggests that Flint's leaders are themselves at least tacitly aware of the crisis tendencies identified by Habermas as flaring up along the seams between system and lifeworld. Just as Habermas's analysis would lead us to predict "the repoliticization of the public sphere"[78] as the most probable crisis tendency to emerge out of a full-blown collapse of late capitalism, Mark Davis's following answer to my query concerning the origin of the GEAR board of directors' authority to manipulate Flint's "social fabric" suggests a parallel concern:

> To be honest, I've never looked, it wasn't important, and it's not important. It's only important to academics. In the real world, what is important is what are they doing, OK? And if we're going to get into legitimacy, and all these other sorts of stuff, I'm going to [pause]. I don't play that game because it's bullshit![79]

At this point, Davis threatened to short-circuit our pursuit of "mutual understanding" by ending my interview. Although Davis's wariness about questions of legitimacy does not, of course, verify the validity of Habermas's legitimation crisis theory, his concern suggests at least the salience of Habermas's line of questioning. As Habermas at one point dryly notes, in the absence of a rational, democratic response to the crisis tendencies of late capitalism, we should realize that "the scope of tolerance for merely instrumental attitudes, indifference or cynicism, is expanded."[80]

Notes

1. This chapter is based on my work, *A town abandoned: Flint, Michigan confronts deindustrialization.* (1996). Albany: State University of New York Press. The main sources of Habermas's legitimation crisis theory are the following: Habermas, J. (1975). *Legitimation crisis* (T. McCarthy, Trans.). Boston: Beacon Press. (Original work published 1973); Habermas, J. (1979). Legitimation problems in the modern state. In T. McCarthy (Trans.), *Communication and the evolution of society* (pp. 178-205). Boston: Beacon Press. (Original work published 1976); Habermas, J. (1982). A reply to my critics. In J. B. Thompson & D. Held (Eds.), *Habermas: Critical debates* (pp. 219-283). Cambridge, MA: MIT Press; Habermas, J. (1984). *The theory of communicative action: Volume I: Reason and the rationalization of society* (T. McCarthy, Trans.). Boston: Beacon Press. (Original work published 1981); Habermas, J. (1987). *The theory of communicative action: Volume II: Lifeworld and*

system: A critique of functionalist reason (T. McCarthy, Trans.). Boston: Beacon Press. (Original work published 1981)

2. In addition to the original works of Karl Marx, the beginning student might profitably consult the following: Tucker, R. C. (Ed.). (1972). *The Marx-Engels reader.* New York: Norton. A selection of prominent 20th-century analyses of Marxian crisis theory would include the following: Sweezy, P. M. (1942). *The theory of capitalist development.* New York: Monthly Review Press; Sweezy, P. M., & Baran, P. A. (1966). *Monopoly capital.* New York: Monthly Review Press; O'Conner, J. (1973). *The fiscal crisis of the state.* New York: St. Martin's; Offe, C. (1984). In J. Keane (Ed.), *Contradictions of the welfare state.* Cambridge, MA: MIT Press; Harvey, D. (1989). *The condition of postmodernity.* Cambridge, UK: Basil Blackwell.

3. For an excellent introduction to the distinctive Frankfurt School perspective on 20th-century capitalism, see the following: Held, D. (1980). *Introduction to critical theory: Horkheimer to Habermas* (pp. 40-76). Berkeley: University of California Press.

4. Habermas (1981/1987), *The theory of communicative action: Volume II,* p. 392.

5. In addition to *A town abandoned* (Dandaneau, 1996), key sources for the analysis of Flint's social and economic history include the following: Edsforth, E. (1987). *Class conflict and cultural consensus: The making of a mass consumer society in Flint, Michigan.* New Brunswick, NJ: Rutgers University Press; Lord, G. F., & Price, A. C. (1992, May). Growth ideology in a period of decline: Deindustrialization and restructuring, Flint style. *Social Problems, 39*(2), 155-169. The following are also informative because both books are grounded in Flint's experience: Hamper, B. (1991). *Rivethead: Tales from the assembly line.* New York: Warner; Kearns, J. (1990). *Life after the line.* Detroit, MI: Wayne State University Press.

6. Moore, M. (Producer & Director). (1989). *Roger & me* [Film]. Dog Eat Dog Production, released by Warner Brothers. For an extensive analysis of this film, see Dandaneau (1996), *A town abandoned,* pp. 107-157. For related sociological statements by Moore, see the following: Moore, M. (1989). GM and Flint, Michigan. In D. S. Eitzen & M. B. Zinn (Eds.), *The reshaping of America: Social consequences of the changing economy* (pp. 329-333). Englewood Cliffs, NJ: Prentice Hall; Moore, M. (1996). *Downsize this! Random threats from an unarmed American.* New York: Crown.

7. Dort, D. C. (1991). In *A town abandoned: Flint, Michigan confronts deindustrialization* (p. xix). Albany: State University of New York Press.

8. "Important to Habermas's work is the claim that critical theory is reflexive" [p. 190; Held, D. (1978, February). Extended review. *Sociological Review, 26,* 183-193]. In other words, critical theory must account for itself; it must understand its own position in the world and the history that it criticizes.

9. On the general notion of critical theory, see Geuss, R. (1981). *The idea of a critical theory: Habermas and the Frankfurt School.* Cambridge, UK: Cambridge University Press. Geuss writes, "A critical theory . . . is a reflective theory which gives agents a kind of knowledge inherently productive of enlightenment and emancipation" (p. 2). Similar works include the following: Kortian, G. (1980). *Metacritique: The philosophical argument of Jürgen Habermas.* Cambridge, UK: Cambridge University Press; Wellmer, A. (1971). *Critical theory of society* (J. Cumming, Trans.). New York: Continuum. (Original work published 1969); Bernstein, R. J. (1976). *The restructuring of social and political theory.* Philadelphia: University of Pennsylvania Press.

10. The notion of "ideology" is notoriously vague. See Geuss (1981), *The idea of a critical theory;* also see Thompson, J. B. (1990). *Ideology and modern culture.* Stanford, CA: Stanford University Press. I have chosen to stress the "immanent" nature of most critical theoretical activities, famously stated by Adorno, for example, as the need to "break out of

the objective context of delusion *from within* [italics added]" [p. 406; Adorno, T. W. (1973). *Negative* dialectics (E. B. Ashton, Trans.). New York: Continuum. (Original work published 1966)].

11. In this regard, note Nancy Fraser's concise discussion of the meaning of critical theory. She writes, "To my mind, no one has yet improved on Marx's 1843 definition of Critical Theory as 'the self-clarification of the struggles and wishes of the age.' What is so appealing about this definition is its straightforwardly political character. It makes no claim to any special epistemological status but, rather, supposes that with respect to justification there is no philosophically interesting difference between a critical theory of society and an uncritical one. But there is, according to this definition, an important political difference. A critical social theory frames its research programme and its conceptual framework with an eye to the aims and activities of those oppositional social movements with which it has a partisan though not uncritical identification. The questions it asks and the models it designs are informed by that identification and interest. Thus, for example, if struggles contesting the subordination of women figured among the most significant of a given age, then a critical social theory for that time would aim, among other things, to shed light on the character and bases of such subordination. It would employ categories and explanatory models that revealed rather than occluded relations of male dominance and female subordination. And it would demystify as ideological rival approaches that obfuscated or rationalized those relations. In this situation, then, one of the standards for assessing a critical theory once it had been subjected to all the usual tests of empirical adequacy, would be: how well does it theorize the situation and prospects of the feminist movement? To what extent does it serve the self-clarification of the struggles and wishes of contemporary women?" [p. 31; Fraser, N. (1987). What's critical about critical theory? The case of Habermas and gender. In S. Benhabib & D. Cornel (Eds.), *Feminism as critique* (pp. 31-56). Minneapolis: University of Minnesota Press].

12. See Habermas, J. (1973). *Theory and practice.* Boston: Beacon.

13. This interpretation of the influences on Marx follows the classic triad introduced by V. I. Lenin, who wrote that "the Marxist doctrine . . . is the legitimate successor to the best that man produced in the nineteenth century, as represented by German philosophy, English political economy [i.e., economics] and French socialism" [p. 20; Lenin, V. I. (1977). The three sources and three component parts of Marxism. In *Lenin: Selected works* (pp. 20-24). Moscow: Progress Publishers].

14. Marx, K. (1972). For a ruthless criticism of everything existing [a.k.a. Letter to Arnold Ruge, 1843]. In R. C. Tucker (Ed.), *The Marx-Engels reader* (2nd ed., pp. 12-15). New York: Norton.

15. Consider the description of labor found in one recent labor economics textbook: "There is a rumor that one recent Secretary of Labor attempted to abolish the term 'labor market' from departmental publications. He believed it demeaned workers to regard labor as being bought and sold like so much grain, oil, or steel. *True, labor is somewhat unique* [!] [italics added]. Labor services can only be rented; workers themselves cannot be bought and sold" [p. 2; Ehrenberg, R. G., & Smith, R. S. (1991). *Modern labor economics* (4th ed.). New York: HarperCollins]. Marxian theorists believe that humans and their ability to work is more than "somewhat unique." For the classic Marxian critique of Frederick Winslow Taylor's "scientific management" and an exemplary use of Marx's alienation theory, see Braverman, H. (1974). *Labor and monopoly capital: The degradation of work in the twentieth century.* New York: Monthly Review Press. For a comprehensive analysis of the "Taylor Paradigm," see Bushnell, P. T. (1994). *The transformation of the American manufacturing paradigm.* New York: Garland.

16. See Marx (1972), in *The Marx-Engels reader*, pp. 107-109. Thesis XI reads: "The philosophers have only *interpreted* the world, in various ways; the point, however, is to *change* it." For a noted discussion of Marx's modern historicity (or the reflexive use of historical self-understanding in the project of historical change itself), see Berman, M. (1982). *All that is solid melts into air*. New York: Simon & Schuster.

17. The parallels between Marx and Freud as originators of critical theory are discussed in Geuss (1981), *The idea of a critical theory* and Held (1980), *Introduction to critical theory*. A sampling of the various competing discussions of Freud among Frankfurt School critical theorists includes the following: Marcuse, H. (1955). *Eros and civilization: A philosophical inquiry into Freud*. Boston: Beacon Press; Fromm, E. (1962). *Beyond the chains of illusion: My encounter with Marx and Freud*. New York: Simon & Schuster; and Habermas's sympathetic treatment of Freud in Habermas, J. (1971). *Knowledge and human interests* (J. Shapiro, Trans.). Boston: Beacon Press. (Original work published 1968) (see especially Chapters 10-12).

18. Horkheimer, M. (1972). *Critical theory: Selected essays* (M. J. O'Connell et al., Trans.). New York: Herder & Herder. Additional collections of Horkheimer's work from this period include the following: Horkheimer, M. (1978). *Dawn and decline: Notes 1926-1931, 1950-1969* (M. Shaw, Trans.). New York: Seabury Press. (Original work published 1974); (1993). *Between philosophy and social science: Selected early writings* (G. F. Hunter, M. S. Kramer, & J. Torpey, Trans.). Cambridge, MA: MIT Press. Also see Horkheimer's magnum opus, with Theodor W. Adorno (1972), *Dialectic of enlightenment* (J. Cumming, Trans.). New York: Herder & Herder. (Original work published 1944)

19. In addition to previously cited sources, see the following: Jay, M. (1973). *The dialectical imagination: A history of the Frankfurt School and the Institute of Social Research, 1923-1950*. Boston: Little, Brown; Wiggershaus, R. (1994). *The Frankfurt School: Its history, theories, and political significance* (M. Robertson, Trans.). Cambridge, MA: MIT Press. (Original work published 1986)

20. Still the single best collective introduction to the work of Adorno, Horkheimer, Marcuse, and Benjamin is the following: Held (1980), *Introduction to critical theory*. For Habermas's own reflections on his predecessors, see Habermas, J. (1987). *The philosophical discourses on modernity* (F. Lawrence, Trans.). Cambridge, MA: MIT Press. (Original work published 1985); Habermas, J. (1985). *Philosophical-political profiles* (F. G. Lawrence, Trans.). Cambridge, MA: MIT Press. (Original work published 1981); Habermas, J. (1985). Psychic thermidor and the rebirth of rebellious subjectivity. In R. J. Bernstein (Ed.), *Habermas and modernity* (pp. 67-77). Cambridge, MA: MIT Press.

21. For population and other data, see Edsforth (1987), *Class conflict and cultural consensus*, p. 13.

22. See Gordon, H. S. (1986). Laissez-faire. In D. L. Sills (Ed.), *International encyclopedia of the social sciences* (Vol. 8, pp. 546-549). New York: Macmillian/Free Press.

23. On Flint's Great Sit-Down Strike, see Kraus, H. (1985). *The many and the few* (2nd ed., with an introduction by N. O. Leighton, W. J. Meyer, & N. Pendrell). Urbana: University of Illinois Press. (Original work published 1947); Fine, S. (1969). *Sit-down: The General Motors strike of 1936-1937*. Ann Arbor: The University of Michigan Press; Reuther, V. (1976). *The brothers Reuther and the story of the UAW*. Boston: Houghton Mifflin; Edsforth (1987), *Class conflict and cultural consensus*.

24. Bohlen, A., & Goldfarb, L. (Producers) & Gray, L. (Director). (1978). *With babies and banners: The story of the women's emergency brigade*. Women's Labor History Film Project.

25. In a 1970 interview with Studs Terkel, Mott derided Franklin Delano Roosevelt as "the great destroyer." Concerning the Great Sit-Down Strike, Mott stated, "[Frank Murphy] was the governor during the sit-down strikes, and he didn't do his job. He didn't enforce the

law. He kept his hands off. He didn't protect our property. They should have said [to the strikers], 'Stop that thing. Move on, or we'll shoot.' And if they didn't, they should have been shot" [p. 135; Terkel, S. (1970). *Hard times: An oral history of the Great Depression.* New York: Pantheon].

26. Mills, C. W. (1979). On knowledge and power. In I. L. Horowitz (Ed.), *Power, politics, & people* (pp. 599-613). Oxford, UK: Oxford University Press. (Original work published 1963)

27. See Edsforth (1987), *Class conflict and cultural consensus,* p. 218: Edsforth writes, "In articles like *U.S. News & World Report's* 'Labor Peace: It's Wonderful' (July 1950), *Look's* 'All American City' (February 1954), and *Coronet's* 'Happiest Town in Michigan'(June 1956), the national news media used Flint as an example of how the country had transcended the bitter, divisive class conflicts of the 1930s and early 1940s to enter a new era of consumer-oriented normalcy. Such publicity further legitimized the 'civilized relationship' between GM and the UAW, and it furthered the alienation of Flint's auto workers from their own union."

28. Flint is described as a ghost town in Zwerdling, D. (1982, July). And then there's the Disneyland solution. *The Progressive,* pp. 34-35. Zwerdling writes, "To see what 25 percent unemployment does to a community, take a stroll down Saginaw Street to the middle of town. It used to be a lovely place, lined with old brick buildings, with the kind of turn-of-the-century masonry you don't see much of any more. Saginaw, the main street, is paved with bricks, and the sidewalks are shaded by awnings. But there is almost nobody and nothing here. Virtually every second store is boarded up with plywood. Some businesses have fled to suburban malls, the rest of them have simply folded. Flint is a 1982 ghost town" (p. 34).

29. Data for the follow section are drawn mainly from research documents produced by and for Flint area organizations. For the most part, these are not sources readily available for public access and review. In this case, I label the source "document" and describe its organizational sponsor. The first case in point is: *The Genesis Project* report (document) (p. 4), prepared for the Genesee Area Economic Revitalization, Inc., by Price Waterhouse, Inc.

30. Grimes, D. (1990). *Diversification trends in Genesee County* (p. 2) (document), sponsored by the Project for Urban and Regional Affairs (PURA), University of Michigan at Flint.

31. Reported in Not being hurt, strikers say. (1996, March 12). *Dayton Daily News,* p. A1.

32. See Ananich, J. D., Leighton, N. O., & Weber, C. T. (1989, May). *Economic impact of GM plant closings in Flint, Michigan* (document), sponsored by PURA at the University of Michigan at Flint; Grimes (1990), *Diversification trends.* Indeed, near-term projections for Flint-area GM employment are as low as 22,000. See Buss, D. D. (1999, June). GM's Company town. *Automotive News,* pp. 26-28; (1999, July), City's Boom Replaced by Hollow Thud. *Automotive News,* pp. 34-35. Also, see Agrassia, P. I. (1998, June 30), A Long Road to Good Labor Relations at GM. *Wall Street Journal,* p. A18.

33. For a discussion of the "ripple effects" of plant closings, see Perrucci, C. C., Perrucci, R., Targ, D. B., & Targ, H. R. (1988). *Plant closings: International contexts and social costs.* Hawthorne, NY: Aldine.

34. Bluestone, B., & Harrison, B. (1982). *The deindustrialization of America: Plant closings, community abandonment, and the dismantling of basic industry.* New York: Basic Books. On deindustrialization and critical theory, see Agger, B. (1985). The dialectic of deindustrialization: An essay on advanced capitalism. In J. Forester (Ed.), *Critical theory of public life* (pp. 3-21). Cambridge, MA: MIT Press.

35. Bluestone & Harrison (1982), *The deindustrialization of America.*

36. *State of Flint* (document), a 1991 memorandum, State of Michigan Department of Social Services, Flint branch.

37. *The Genesis Project* report, p. 8.

38. From *The quality of life for children and their families in Genesee County* (document) (1991, June), sponsored by Priority '90s; see especially pp. 29-34.

39. Flint leads state in 1990 per-capita crime rate—FBI. (1991, August 11). *The Flint Journal*, pp. A1, A10; FBI figures still place Flint among most violent cities. (1992, April 26). *The Flint Journal*, pp. A1, A14.

40. *The quality of life for children and their families in Genesee County* (pp. 28-30, 12-13, 20, and "Summary: Changing social and economic conditions"). Also see Poverty spreads in Michigan. (1991, September 27). *The Flint Journal*, p. A3. A classic scholarly statement on the causes and effects of concentrated poverty is provided in the following: Wilson, W. J. (1987). *The truly disadvantaged*. Chicago: University of Chicago Press. This analysis has been carried forward in Wilson, W. J. (1996). *When work disappears: The world of the new urban poor*. New York: Knopf.

41. For an interesting reflection on this event, see Moore, M. (1996, July). Flint & me: Michael Moore returns to our first last-place city. *Money*, pp. 86-87.

42. *Synopsis of Flint area Enterprise Community Program* (document) (1995, March 6), provided by the City of Flint Department of Community & Economic Development.

43. Flint's dependency on GM employment is suggested by the fact that GM's local Flint payroll in 1988 exceeded $2 billion. See *Facts on Flint* (document) (1990, September 28), Office of the Mayor, City of Flint, Michigan.

44. See Lord & Price (1992, May), *Social Problems, 39*(2), 155-169.

45. See A city where hope runs on empty. (1992, February 26). *New York Times*, p. A8; Flint, Willow Run take hit. (1994, February). *The Flint Journal*, pp. A1-A2; Hurting: The GM fallout; Thousands still reel from impact of closings. (1992, February 25). *The Flint Journal*, pp. A1, A10; GM slashes—Michigan bleeds. (1992, February 25). *Lansing State Journal*, p. A1; Dupont leaving Flint, affecting 250 workers. (1992, January 14). *The Flint Journal*, pp. A1-A2.

46. See Flint preparing 'bold' package to keep GM jobs. (1996, June 21). *The Flint Journal*, pp. A1, A9. This estimate has, unfortunately, proven to be accurate since Flint-area GM employment is expected to dip below 26,000 in the next few years.

47. In addition to major sources cited elsewhere, I have also consulted the following: Miller, J. (1975, Fall). A review of Jürgen Habermas, "legitimation crisis." *Telos, 25*, 210-220; Shapiro, J. J. (1976, Spring). Reply to Miller's review of Habermas's "legitimation crisis." *Telos, 27*, 170-176; Held, D., & Simon, L. (1976, Winter). Toward understanding Habermas. *New German Critique, 7*, 136-145; Schroyer, T. (1975, Spring). The re-politicization of the relations of production: An interpretation of Jürgen Habermas's analytic theory of late capitalist development. *New German Critique, 5*, 107-128; Laska, P. (1974, Fall). Note on Habermas and the labor theory of value. *New German Critique, 3*, 154-162; Keane, J. (1975, Winter). On belaboring the theory of economic crisis: A reply to Laska. *New German Critique, 4*, 125-130; Camilleri, J. (1981, Summer). The advanced capitalist state and the contemporary world crisis. *Science and Society, 45*(2), 130-158; Roderick, R. (1986). *Habermas and the foundations of critical theory*. New York: St. Martin's; Alway, J. (1995). *Critical theory and political possibilities*. Westport, CT: Greenwood; Aune, J. A. (1994). *Rhetoric and Marxism*. Boulder, CO: Westview; White, S. K. (Ed.). (1995). *The Cambridge companion to Habermas*. Cambridge, UK: Cambridge University Press.

48. On this point, as well as for the explication of Habermas's "legitimation crisis" in its entirety, see McCarthy, T. (1978). *The critical theory of Jürgen Habermas*. Cambridge, MA: MIT Press (see especially Chapter 5). McCarthy writes, "Whatever its merits as an analysis of liberal capitalism—and Habermas holds them to be considerable—Marx's critique of political economy can no longer be applied to organized capitalism. There are a number of reasons for this, the primary among them being the changed relationship between the state

and the economy; the latter no longer has the degree of autonomy that justified the exclusivity of Marx's focus" (p. 363).

49. Marx did, however, hold for the possibility of a peaceful movement to socialism. See "The possibility of nonviolent revolution (1872)" in *The Marx-Engels reader* (1972), pp. 522-524: Marx states, "Institutions, mores, and traditions of various countries must be taken into consideration, and we do not deny that there are countries—such as America [and] England . . . where the workers can attain their goal by peaceful means" (p. 523).

50. Habermas (1981/1987), *The theory of communicative action: Volume II*, p. 345.

51. For example, in *Legitimation crisis*, Habermas (1973/1975) writes, "In the final analysis, [the] *class structure* is the source of the legitimation deficit" (p. 73).

52. Zwerdling (1982, July), *The Progressive*, p. 35.

53. Transcription by the author.

54. See Dandaneau (1996), *A town abandoned*, p. 228.

55. See Habermas (1981/1987), *The theory of communicative action: Volume II*, p. 395, in which Habermas writes, "The new conflicts arise along the seams between system and lifeworld."

56. See Habermas (1981/1987), *The theory of communicative action: Volume II*, pp. 332-403.

57. See Habermas (1973/1975), *Legitimation crisis*, p. 45.

58. Habermas also discusses the "new social movements" that might arise in response to the predicted tendency toward a colonization of the lifeworld. In *A town abandoned*, Dandaneau (1996) treats *Roger & Me*, the UAW-New Directions Movement (a dissident faction seeking to return the union to its radical roots in the Great Sit-Down Strike), and Flint's Center for New Work (1984-1988; organized by two university philosophy professors to teach Flint's unemployed and underemployed how to make the best use of nonworking time in the pursuit of "new," more meaningful forms of work) as examples of bottom-up local responses to Flint's economic and rationality crises.

59. See, for example, Habermas (1981/1987), *The theory of communicative action: Volume II*, p. 355.

60. Habermas (1981/1987), *The theory of communicative action: Volume II*, p. 345.

61. See Habermas's important discussion of "universal pragmatics" in *Communication and the evolution of society* (1976/1979, pp. 1-68), which is further elaborated and updated in Habermas (1981/1984), *The theory of communicative action: Volume I*, and Habermas (1981/1987), *The theory of communicative action: Volume II*.

62. A succinct statement of this position is found in "Reply to my critics" in *Habermas: Critical debates* (1982), in which Habermas discusses the primary importance of "the loss of meaning, anomie, and personality disorders" that result from the "colonisation of the lifeworld" (pp. 280-281).

63. Habermas (1982), in *Habermas: Critical debates*.

64. See Habermas (1973/1975), *Legitimation crisis*, pp. 75-92.

65. Note Habermas's 1982 (*Habermas: Critical debates*) clarification of his original argument in *Legitimation crisis*: "It is necessary to make a clear distinction that still escaped me in *Legitimation crisis*: A distinction between the deficits that inflexible structures of the lifeworld can give rise to in maintaining the economic and political systems on the one hand, and manifestations of deficiencies in the reproduction of the life-world itself on the other. Empirically the two are connected in a feedback process; but it makes sense to separate analytically the *withdrawal of motivation* affecting the occupational system and the *withdrawal of legitimation* affecting the system of domination, on the one side, from the *colonization of the life-world* that is manifested primarily in phenomena of loss of meaning, anomie, and personality disorders, on the other side. In 1973 I used the misleading catchphrase 'motivation crisis' for deformations of the life-world which make themselves felt in modern

societies as the destruction of traditional forms of life, as attacks on the communicative infrastructure of life-worlds, as the rigidity of a one-sidedly rationalised everyday practice, and which come to expression in the consequences of impoverished cultural traditions and disturbed socialisation processes. Now I would rather conceive of motivation crisis as a parallel case to legitimation crisis; and I would want to distinguish from both of these the pathological manifestations of a colonialised life-world" (pp. 280-281).

66. This discussion is drawn from Dandaneau (1996), *A town abandoned,* especially Chapter 7.

67. See Dandaneau (1996), *A town abandoned,* pp. 208-209, 212.

68. See Dandaneau (1996), *A town abandoned,* pp. 208-209, 212.

69. See Dandaneau (1996), *A town abandoned,* p. 212.

70. See Dandaneau (1996), *A town abandoned,* p. 212.

71. See Dandaneau (1996), *A town abandoned,* p. 213.

72. See Dandaneau (1996), *A town abandoned,* p. 206.

73. See Dandaneau (1996), *A town abandoned,* p. 207.

74. See Dandaneau (1996), *A town abandoned,* p. 211.

75. See McCarthy (1978), *The critical theory of Jürgen Habermas,* for a discussion of this point. McCarthy quotes Habermas: "There is no administrative production of meaning. The commercial production and administrative planning of symbols exhausts the normative force of counterfactual validity claims. The procurement of legitimation is self-defeating as soon as the mode of procurement is seen through" (p. 370). See especially Habermas (1976/1979), in *Communication and the evolution of society,* pp. 178-204.

76. See Habermas (1982), in *Habermas: Critical debates,* in which, in a concise statement, Habermas identifies the unacknowledged intrusion of strategic interaction into the realm of communicative interaction as the source for what he famously dubs "systematically distorted communication" (p. 264).

77. Habermas writes in support of "counterinstitutions" that are "intended to dedifferentiate some parts of the formally organized domains of action, remove them from the clutches of the steering media, and return these 'liberated areas' to the action-coordinating mechanism of reaching understanding" (Habermas [1981/1987], *The theory of communicative action: Volume II,* p. 396). He identifies a "new politics" in which "the issue is not primarily one of compensations that the welfare state can provide, but of defending and restoring endangered ways of life" (p. 392); "In terms of social statistics, the 'old politics' is more strongly supported by employers, workers, and middle-class tradesman, whereas the new politics finds stronger support in the new middle classes, among the younger generation, and in groups with more formal education" (p. 392); "The following catchphrases serve at the moment to identify the various currents in the Federal Republic of Germany [the former West Germany]; the antinuclear and environmental movements; the peace movement (including the theme of north-south conflict); single-issue and local movements; the alternative movement (which encompasses the urban 'scene,' with its squatters and alternative projects, as well as the rural communes); the minorities (the elderly, gays, handicapped, and so forth); the psychoscene, with support groups and youth sects; religious fundamentalism; the tax-protest movement, school protest by parents' associations, resistance to 'modernist' reforms; and, finally, the women's movement. Of international significance are the autonomy movements struggling for regional, linguistic, cultural, and also religious independence" (p. 393). Also see Habermas, J. (1990). *Moral consciousness and communicative action* (C. Lenhardt & S. Weber Nicholsen, Trans.). Cambridge, MA: MIT Press. (Original work published 1983)

78. This is Thomas McCarthy's formulation of "legitimation crisis." See McCarthy (1978), *The critical theory of Jürgen Habermas,* p. 385.

79. Dandaneau (1996), *A town abandoned,* p. 199.

80. Habermas (1982), in *Habermas: Critical debates,* p. 281. On June 20, 1996, Flint's mayor joined spokespeople for GM, the C. S. Mott Foundation, and the UAW to announce the formation of the "Billy Durant Automotive Commission," whose cynical raison d'être is well captured by one of its most intelligent members's terse summary of Flint's current situation: "The facts are simple. Most of our plants are obsolete. They are 40 years old with 30-year-old equipment, processes and systems. We are not competing effectively. The challenge is to persuade our major customer [who buys the product!], the GM corporation, that this community and its workers will partner up with the company to become absolutely best in class in everything we do. *We have no other option.*" Or so argues William Donohue, President of the Genesee Area Focus Council, as quoted in Billy Durant Automotive Commission formed to deal with GM losses in Genesee County (1996, June 27). *Headlight* (UAW Local 599), p. 1.

Discussion Questions

1. What makes critical theory a distinctive type of social theory? In what ways does Jürgen Habermas's theory of the legitimation crisis exemplify the essential features of critical theory?

2. Think about your own community. How similar or how different is it from Flint? Can you apply the four crisis tendencies of late capitalism discussed in the chapter to phenomena present in your community?

3. Habermas originally published his book on the legitimation crisis more than two decades ago. Obviously, much has changed in the world since that time. Do you think that there are features of Habermas's theory that need to be reformulated in light of those changes? Defend your position.

CHAPTER 8

The Socially Constructed Body

Insights From Feminist Theory[1]

Judith Lorber and Patricia Yancey Martin

Judith Lorber *is Professor Emerita of Sociology and Women's Studies at Brooklyn College and The Graduate School, City University of New York. She is author of* Gender Inequality: Feminist Theories and Politics *(1998; 2nd ed., 2001; 3rd ed., 2004),* Gender and the Social Construction of Illness *(1997; 2nd ed., 2002; with Lisa Jean Moore),* Paradoxes of Gender *(1994) (Italian translation,* L'Inventione dei sessi *[1995]; German translation,* Gender-Paradoxien *[1999]), and* Women Physicians: Careers, Status and Power *(1984), as well as numerous articles on gender, women as health care workers and patients, and social aspects of the new procreative technologies. She is coeditor of* Revisioning Gender *(1999, with Myra Marx Ferree & Beth B. Hess) and* The Social Construction of Gender *(1991, with Susan A. Farrell). She is currently working on a new book,* Breaking the Bowls: Degendering and Feminist Change, *and an anthology,* Handbook of Gender Studies and Women Studies *(with Mary Evans and Kathy Davis).*

Patricia Yancey Martin *teaches gender in relation to organizations, violence, and the women's movement. She uses feminist principles to question the invisible aspects of social life relative to gender and sexuality (and also race, social class, and age). She is Daisy Parker Flory Professor of Sociology at Florida State University, where she studies the social constructions of masculinities and femininities at work. She edited a collection of essays titled* Feminist Organizations: Harvest of the New Women's Movement *(with Myra Marx Ferree) and has a forthcoming book on "rape work" by police, hospitals, prosecutors, and rape crisis centers that explores how jobs and organizations* *influence rape workers to treat victims unresponsively. Recent publications focus on aesthetics and bodies in residential organizations for the elderly; the literal "practicing" of gender at work; and biases among lawyers and judges relative to rape, domestic violence, divorce/family disputes, and care of the family/household.*

> Body-reflexive practices . . . are not internal to the individual. They involve social relations and symbolism; they may well involve large-scale institutions. Particular versions of masculinity [and femininity] are constituted in their circuits as meaningful bodies and embodied meanings. Through body-reflexive practices, more than individual lives are formed: A social world is formed.[2]

In an undergraduate course on the sociology of gender, one of us invited some young bodybuilders to speak to the class. Two of the speakers were a married couple who did "customized" coaching of people who wanted to change their bodies in various ways. The husband coached young fat or skinny boys whose parents wanted them to be thinner or heavier. The wife coached women who wanted to be "more defined," meaning they wanted muscles that show when their bodies are at rest. The third person was a 20-year-old man who was tall and muscular.

All the speakers had been given a set of questions in advance to think about when addressing the class. The 20-year-old man had written his comments out and, when his turn to speak came, he held the paper out in front of him, with both hands, looked down at it instead of at the students in class, and in a voice choked with emotion, said,

> When I was 12 years old, my dad walked out on my mother and brother and me. I knew from that day I was now the "man of the house." So I had to do something. I started working out. I tried to get big so I could fill his shoes. I've never stopped working out. I have a kid today and I know I have to be there for her, be strong, be a man.

The class of 230 students sat in silence, touched by this unexpected confession. The young man had, as a boy, decided that having muscles and being "big" made him into the man of the house, which he was required to be because of his father's departure. To be a man, he felt he had to "get big."

The equation of big size, strong muscles, and "true masculinity" is a pervasive theme in U.S. culture. It is so ingrained that popular athletes have been secretly using body-building steroids, and up to 1 million adolescent athletes do too, to attain the same muscular bulk. Young people using steroids can suffer premature stunting of bone growth and height loss, and there have been reports of depression leading to suicide. The long-term effects can be infertility, liver damage, high blood pressure, and other physiological problems. But the desire to look "masculine" and be able to perform well as an athlete outweighs regard for physical health.[3]

The young man's story illustrates a major point of this chapter: Members of a society construct their bodies in ways that comply with accepted views of masculinity and femininity. That is, they try to shape and use their bodies to conform to their culture's or racial ethnic group's expectations of how a woman's body, a man's body, a girl's body, or a boy's body should look. This point does not deny the distinctiveness of material bodies, with their different physical shapes, sizes, strengths, and weaknesses. It does emphasize, however, that members of a society, not genes or biology, determine the proper shape and usage of women's, men's, boys', and girls' bodies.

The search for better looking bodies fuels the popularity of cosmetic surgery, growth hormones, anabolic steroids, body building, and fitness regimens for men and women. For example, men are the targeted market of plastic surgeons for gynecomastia or enlarged breasts. One ad said that "as many as one of three males are affected by this embarrassing problem" and that breast-reduction surgery can remove the "undesirable contour . . . restoring the normal male breast shape." For women, the "normal female breast shape" is large, but not too large, firm and lifted, so they get targeted with ads for "breast augmentation" and "breast reduction/lift" as well as reshaping faces, noses, lips, tummies, and buttocks.[4] The ads for body and facial surgery encourage men and women to judge their appearance against images that are culturally admired but that many, if not most, people find difficult to meet.

It is not surprising that 6.9 million Americans had cosmetic surgery in 2002, an increase of 228% from 1997. Of these, 88% were women or girls, and 12% were men or boys. Among the top five surgical procedures for women and men were liposuction, eyelid surgery, and nose reshaping. The other top procedures for women were breast augmentation and breast reduction; for men, they were hair transplantation and ear reshaping. Regarding age and racial ethnic group, 44% were between 34 and 50 years old, with 3% 18 or younger; 81% of the surgeries were performed on whites and 19% on racial or ethnic minorities.[5]

Given its high cost, cosmetic surgery appears primarily to be a method used mostly by affluent white women in their quest for the "perfect" shape, size, or look. But the popularity of expensive exercise clubs and home exercise equipment indicates that men and women of all racial ethnic groups are preoccupied with the search for the "perfect body." This preoccupation is not just for good looks but also for success.

How Bodies Matter: Appearance and Success

We may say that intelligence and competence count for much more than physical appearance, but only a few presidents of the United States have been shorter than 6 feet tall, and research on corporations has shown that approximately 10% of a man's earnings can be accounted for by his height.[6]

When one of the authors was doing interviews in the headquarters of a large, multinational corporation, she noticed that the men she was interviewing were very tall. As one interview with a man who was more than 6½ feet tall was about to begin, she asked, as a joke, "Are all the men at [the company] tall?" He smiled and said, "Well, a lot of us are," and he proceeded to explain that he has a bias toward tall people—men and women. He stated, "The last two women I've hired have been over 6 feet tall." He described his department's "winning" volleyball team and its "need [for] tall people to win." His comments may indeed reflect a preference for tall volleyball players by his department, but they may also reflect society's general preference for tall men. He may see tall men as superior, given society's valorization of height in men. Then, his concern to avoid "gender bias" leads him to favor tall women as well.

When it comes to filling positions of authority, the male sports hero, astronaut, and combat soldier—symbols of the "right stuff"—are often the first choices. Their physical strength, coolness under fire, motivation to succeed, and combination of self-promotion and team support are thought to make them the exemplars of leadership. Their exemplary characteristics are displayed, we believe, on their faces and bodies.

A very large oil portrait, 50 feet wide by 30 feet high, of World War I British military officers on display in the National Portrait Gallery in London shows approximately 50 men in their military uniform finery. With the exception of 2 somewhat short and rotund men, all are tall and thin in physique. Furthermore, all have square jaws, strong chins, similar hair styles (short cropped and no beards), and conventional "good" looks. The idea may seem fantastical that military officers are chosen on the basis of height, weight, race, or "jaw shape," given ideological claims in Western societies that ability, knowledge, and a track record of competence form the basis for such decisions. Recent research, however, shows that the shape of a man's jaw—for example, whether he has a receding or perpendicular chin—is a determinative factor in being chosen for high-ranking military office.[7] "Weak-faced" men are rarely advanced to the highest ranks.

West Point's curriculum is devised to produce military leaders, and physical competence is used as a significant measure of leadership ability. When women were accepted as cadets, it became clear that the tests of physical competence, such as the ability to scale an 8-foot wall rapidly, had been constructed for male physiques—pulling oneself up and over and using upper-body strength. Rather than devise tests of physical competence for women, West Point provided boosters that mostly women used but that lost them test points (in the case of the wall, West Point added a platform). Finally, the women figured out how to use their bodies successfully. Janice Yoder describes this situation as follows:

> I was observing this obstacle one day, when a woman approached the wall in the old prescribed way, got her fingertips grip, and did an unusual thing: She walked her dangling legs up the wall until she was in a position where both her hands and feet were atop the wall. She then simply pulled up her sagging bottom and went over. She solved the problem by capitalizing on one of women's physical assets: lower-body strength.[8]

Thus, if West Point is going to measure leadership capability by physical strength, women's pelvises will do just as well as men's shoulders.

The Social Construction of Gendered Bodies

The feminist view of bodies is that they are socially constructed in material and cultural worlds, which means they are physical and symbolic at one and the same time. To say that bodies are socially constructed is not to deny their material reality or universality. Bodies are born, and bodies die. Female breasts are able to produce milk for nursing infants, whereas male breasts cannot. Female mammals gestate and give birth; male mammals do not. Male bodies usually have less fat and more muscle than female bodies. But when we ask which women's and men's bodies are beautiful, or what are the physical capacities of human men and women in physical labor and sports, we are asking questions about social practices and judgments that vary by culture and ethnicity, time and place, and are different for the rich and the poor.

Social practices exaggerate and minimize differences and similarities among people, creating, through physical labor, exercise, sports, and surgery, the various masculine and feminine bodies social groups admire. Cultural views about the body are more than aesthetic; they are also moral judgments. When a person's body contradicts social conventions regarding weight, height, and shape, that person may be viewed as lacking in self-control and self-respect. Conversely, people whose bodies comply with valued conventions are admired, praised, and held up to others as ideals to be emulated. In short, by judging, rewarding, and punishing people of different body sizes, shapes, weights, and musculature, members of a social group persuade and coerce each other to construct socially acceptable—and similar-looking—bodies.

Gender is one of the most significant factors in the transformation, via social construction dynamics, of physical bodies into social bodies. In Western culture, dieting, breast enhancement, and face-lifts are ways that women have changed their appearance to fit ideals of feminine beauty, whereas men lift weights, get hair transplants, and undergo cosmetic surgery to mold their bodies and faces to a masculine ideal. These practices may lead to illnesses, such as eating disorders, infections, and systemic damage from leaking silicone implants, but by themselves they are not considered abnormal because they are responses to culturally idealized views of how women's and men's bodies should look.[9]

Because our bodies are socially constructed in deeply gendered societies, they will of necessity be gendered because a gender-neutral or androgynous or "unisex" body is an anathema in a world in which people must know quickly and precisely where to place others they encounter for the first time or in brief, face-to-face interactions. How you look to the other person (masculine or feminine) is tied to who you are (woman or man). Your social identity is a gendered identity, and all your identity papers and bureaucratic records document your gender over and over again. Who you are is therefore gendered. We will never know how much of this gendering is biology and how much is social construction unless we have a degendered society, one that does not produce or exaggerate differences through markedly different treatment and expectations of boys and girls.

Thus, although you may think the natural physiology and anatomy of female and male bodies dictate the ways women's and men's bodies look and are used, feminist theory argues that the "ideal types" of bodies that all are encouraged to emulate are the product of society's gender ideology, practices, and stratification system. Western societies expect men to be aggressive initiators of action and protectors of women and children; therefore, their bodies should be muscular and physically strong. Women are expected to be nurturant and emotionally giving, willing to subordinate their own desires to please men and their own interests to take care of children. Therefore, women's bodies should be yielding and sexually appealing to men when they are young and plumply maternal when they are older.

Of course, many perfectly acceptable variations of women's and men's bodies exist, including well-muscled women bodybuilders and graceful men ballet dancers. The underlying norms seep through, however. Men ballet dancers, such as Nijinsky, Nureyev, and Baryshnikov, awed audiences with their phenomenal leaps and turns, the specialty of men dancers. Competitive women bodybuilders downplay their size, use makeup, wear their hair long and blond, and emphasize femininity in posing by using "dance, grace, and creativity." Otherwise they do not win competitions or are called "butch" or "lesbian" and treated as an oddity or embarrassment to the other contestants, women and men alike.[10]

Gendered Bodies and Social Power

Feminist theory has increased awareness of the social construction of "gendered bodies" by making visible cultural and social dynamics that generally are invisible to members of a society. Feminists have called into question many accepted "truths" about gender and bodies and have challenged the evidence on which dubious claims are based. In addition, feminism has a political agenda that seeks to improve the status and treatment of women and girls by valuing women's bodies as much as men's bodies.[11]

According to feminist theory, claims about gender, which include bodies, fit into the social arrangements and cultural beliefs that constitute gender as a social institution.[12] As a social institution, gender produces two categories of people, "men" and "women," with different characteristics, skills, personalities, and body types. These gendered attributes, which we call "manliness" or "masculinity" and "womanliness" or "femininity," are designed to fit people into adult social roles, such as "mother," "father," "nurse," or "construction worker."

The institution of gender has many facets, from the societal patterns that put men into most of the positions of power in government and corporations to intimate relationships in which men have more power over women than women have over men. There are racial, ethnic, and class differences among women and among men, but gender similarities still exist. These similarities are socially produced, but their pervasiveness makes it seem as if they are biologically linked. Thus, women's learned emotional sensitiveness will be considered as evidence that they are naturally maternal, and men's learned coolness and objectivity will be considered as evidence that they are naturally logical and scientific. Yet recent events have shown that men do cry, and women can be heroes, warriors, and terrorists.[13]

Another common pattern is that men's characteristics are, for the most part, considered superior to women's, thus justifying men's social dominance. Cockburn notes that men's supposed greater strength rationalizes the gendered division of labor, even when it is machinery that does the actual physical labor:

Two qualities are combined in men's work: physical competence and technical competence. The men bind these two together and appropriate both qualities for masculinity. Each affords a little power. Not much, just a modicum of power that is enough to enable men to lever more pay, less supervision, and more freedom out of management.[14]

Cockburn further notes that men's "greater strength" is socially constructed, and it builds into gender stratification at work and in society in general:

Females are born a little smaller than males. This difference is exaggerated by upbringing, so that women grow into adults who are less physically strong and competent than they could be. They are then excluded from a range of manual occupations and, by extension, from the control of technology. The effect spills over into everyday life: Ultimately women have become dependent on men to change the wheel of a car, reglaze a broken window, or replace a smashed roof slate. Worse, women are physically harassed and violated by men: Women are first rendered relatively weak; the weakness is transformed to vulnerability; and vulnerability opens the way to intimidation and exploitation. It is difficult to exaggerate the scale and longevity of the oppression that has resulted.[15]

Feminists argue that domination requires difference; thus, claims that women and men are different become fodder for the development and perpetuation of a gender hierarchy or a dominance system favoring men over women.

On Telling Men From Women

Imagery, ideology, and practice are the social processes by which supposedly natural bodies are socially constructed. One of the most crucial aspects of the social construction of gendered bodies is that women and men should be easy to tell apart. You may say that anyone can tell a female from a male. Physical differences between male and female bodies certainly exist—a roomful of naked people or a walk on the beach would tell us at least that. Paradoxically, however, when dressed in unisex clothing, their differences are not as obvious as you may think.

When four women students were admitted to the formerly all-male military academy, The Citadel, they were warned that they would have to have "nob" haircuts (shaved heads). Soon thereafter, however, they were told that they would have only very short haircuts—in a "feminine" style. Unhappy with this distinction, three of the four women cadets shaved each other's heads and were disciplined for it.[16] Although the commander insisted it was so that the women would not be humiliated, a picture of a woman Citadel cadet with her regulation hat showed how difficult it would be to tell the boys from the girls—unless they had a visible gender marker such as longer hair.

In most situations involving bodies, women and men are physically marked and physically separated, and overlaps between female and male bodies are ignored.

Separating women from men is not such a simple matter. In the past, chromosomal testing was thought to be an infallible sex detector. But an anomaly common enough to be found in several feminine-looking women at every major international sports competition is the existence of XY chromosomes that have not produced male anatomy or physiology because of other genetic input. Even with evidence of overlapping physiology and physical capabilities, sports authorities continue to uphold the principle of separate competitions for women and men.[17] Part of the reason is that men's sports have higher prestige, more extensive media coverage, and greater economic rewards.

Feminists have studied areas in which bodies are crucial and found that the social construction of masculine and feminine characteristics represents men as superior. Ideas about bodies and physical capacities produce social practices that result in gendered bodies. These ideas and practices, and their bodily outcomes, do not just produce visible differences between women and men; they also reproduce a hierarchy, or gender stratification system, in which men's bodies are viewed as superior to women's bodies.

Sports is a prime cultural arena for the social construction of men's and women's bodies. In sports, men's bodies have an extremely high value, paying off in prestige and income. Women's sports do not pay off as well, even though the bodies of women athletes have physical capabilities most ordinary men and women could not emulate. Another area in which gender norms affect bodies is health and illness. Here, men are more disadvantaged. Young men put themselves at risk for accidents, homicides, and drug and alcohol abuse, which reduce their life span. Young women with eating disorders also put themselves at risk, but the death rates are not as high. Regarding risk of HIV/AIDS, young women are becoming even more vulnerable than young men. Both women and men are disadvantaged by physical disability, but gender norms affect them in somewhat different ways. In the following sections, we detail the gendered aspects of sports, risk behavior, weight and eating problems, and able-bodiedness.

Gender and Sports

Sports competitions are almost always gendered, and different kinds of sports construct different kinds of women's and men's bodies. In the process, they also construct masculinity and femininity and men's superior status.[18]

Talent for sports seems to come early, but it is carefully encouraged in the United States—and it is carefully gendered. Many gendered body characteristics we think of as inborn are the result of social practices. The phenomena of boys' boisterousness and girls' physical awkwardness in Western societies are examples. When little boys run around noisily, we say, "Boys will be boys," meaning that their physical assertiveness has to be in the Y chromosome because it is manifest so early and so commonly in boys. Boys the world over, however, are not boldly physical—just those who are encouraged to use their bodies freely, cover space, take risks, and play outdoors at all kinds of games and sports. Conversely, what do we mean when we say, "She throws like a girl"? We usually mean that she throws like a female child, a carrier of XX chromosomes. After all, she is only 4 or 5 years old, so how could she have learned to be so awkward? In fact, as Young notes, she throws like a person who has already been taught to restrict her movements, to protect her body, and to use her body in ways that are approved of as feminine:

> Not only is there a typical style of throwing like a girl, but there is a more or less typical style of running like a girl, climbing like a girl, swinging like a girl, hitting like a girl. They have in common first that the whole body is not put into fluid and directed motion, but rather . . . the motion is concentrated in one body part; and . . . tends not to reach, extend, lean, stretch, and follow through in the direction of her intention.[19]

The girl who experiences her body in such a limited way at an early age is a product of her culture and time. As she learns to restrict her moves, she simultaneously closes opportunities to develop the fluid, whole-bodied, unconstrained moves that are associated with outstanding achievement in sports. As social practices change, and girls are encouraged to use their bodies the way boys do, they become formidable sports competitors.

On June 23, 1996, the *New York Times* devoted its Sunday magazine to the forthcoming Olympics. What was startling was that the athletes featured in the special issue were all women. These women athletes, who were from all over the world, were champions in basketball, running, jumping, swimming, diving, sculling, kayaking, judo, gymnastics, heptathlon, shot put, mountain biking, and softball. They competed in Atlanta in 95 women-only sports as well as in 11 mixed teams sports, including badminton doubles, yachting, and equestrian. There were 3,800 women competitors in Atlanta, two fifths of the total number of competitors. The featured final event, followed by the closing ceremony on television, was women's basketball.

One hundred years ago, the first modern Olympics was all-male—female bodies were supposedly not made for serious athletics. Have female bodies changed in 100 years? Yes, they have. Women did not run in marathons until approximately 20 years ago. In 20 years of marathon competition, women have reduced their finish times by more than 1.5 hours. They are expected to run as fast as men in the 26-mile marathon in the near future, and they might catch up with men's running times in races of other lengths within the next 50 years because they are increasing their speeds more rapidly than are men.[20]

What has particularly changed women's bodies are the norms and expectations of their capabilities. For example, before Fanny Blankers-Koen, two-time mother, won four gold medals in sprinting in the 1948 Olympics, it was thought that childbirth ruined the female athlete's body. In 1952, June Irwin won a bronze medal in diving while she was 3.5 months pregnant.[21] The rules governing women's competitions, however, have not always recognized their strength. In the Grand Slam tennis contests, men must win three of five games, whereas women must win two of three. In response to Martina Navratilova's call for the same rules for women as men (and the same prize money), Bud Collins stated in a letter to the *New York Times* that approximately 100 years ago, women played three-out-of-five matches (and in much more clothing). Their ability to match men's endurance "alarmed" the U.S. Tennis Association officials (all of whom were men), and they downgraded women's abilities by reducing the number of games they had to play to win a match.[22]

An important part of the changed view of women athletes is that they are no longer seen as masculinized oddballs.[23] Muscles on women are now sexy. Holly Brubach, in "The Athletic Esthetic," the "style" piece in the special issue of the *New York Times,* stated the following:

> Muscles bestow on a woman a grace in motion that is absent from fashion photographs and other images in which the impact resides in a carefully orchestrated, static pose. Muscles also impart a sense of self-possession, a quality that is unfailingly attractive.[24]

This new image of women was visually evident in the photos of the special issue. All but 2 of the 28 photos showed the women in action or in power poses, with muscles bulging and arms akimbo. In contrast, in 1 of the 2 feminized photos, a Belorussian gymnast was shown lolling on her bed in a black satin jumpsuit, like an odalisque in a painting. In the other, which was from 1926, a woman tennis player looked like a ballet dancer doing a leap, with skirt flying.

Television broadcasts of the Olympics, news and magazine photos, product endorsements, and other popular media depictions make new images of women's bodies routine and everyday. No one would think of organizing an all-male Olympics anymore.[25] Not only would it be unthinkable but also it would be unprofitable. Olympic women athletes are good business; they attract audiences, men as well as women, and they sell products. But the prestige and financial rewards of sports for women are far less than for men, even though women—just like men—sustain many injuries, play through pain, and undergo orthopedic surgery and other such procedures. For women, pain and injuries are the price of high-level competition. For men, they are marks of manhood. If men sports stars fail to ignore injuries and pain and refuse to use their bodies aggressively on the field, their masculinity is impugned by coaches and fellow players.[26]

Sports is a path to upward mobility for poor and working-class boys, even though few become successful professional athletes. Those who break into professional teams have only a few years to make it, and they cannot afford to be sidelined by injuries. Alcoholism, drug abuse, obesity, and heart disease also take their toll. The life expectancy of professional football players in the United States is approximately 15 years less than that of other men.[27] Their payoff, and that of all the successful athletes in men's sports, is very high income and fame. Successful women athletes do not get the same amount of income, media coverage, or prestige.

Messner, Duncan, and Jensen found that in 1989 in the United States, men's sports received 92% of the television coverage and women's sports 5%, with the remaining 3% mixed or gender neutral. In 1990, in four of the top-selling newspapers in the United States, stories on men's sports outnumbered those on women's sports 23 to 1. There is also an implicit hierarchy in naming, with women athletes most likely to be called by first names, followed by African American men athletes; only white men athletes were routinely referred to by their last names.[28] Similarly, women's collegiate sports teams are named or marked in ways that symbolically feminize and trivialize them—for example, the men's team is called Tigers, whereas the women's team is called Kittens or Lady Tigers, with all the gendered meanings of the term *lady*.[29]

Given the association of sports with masculinity in the United States, many women athletes manage their contradictory status through a postgame ritual of dressing and fixing their hair. One study of women college basketball players found that although they "did athlete" on the court—"pushing, shoving, fouling, hard running, fast breaks, defense, obscenities, and sweat"—they "did woman" off the court, using the locker room as their staging area:

> While it typically took 15 minutes to prepare for the game, it took approximately 15 minutes after the game to shower and remove the sweat of an athlete, and it took another 30 minutes to dress, apply makeup, and style hair. It did not seem to matter whether the players were going out into the public or getting on a van for a long ride home. Average dressing time and rituals did not change.[30]

Another way these status dilemmas are managed is by redefining the activity or its result as feminine or womanly. Thus, women bodybuilders claim that "flex appeal is sex appeal."[31]

The ideological subtext in Western culture is that physical strength, as demonstrated in sports, the military, and bodybuilding, is men's prerogative and justifies men's physical and sexual domination of women.[32] Women's physical capabilities challenge these assumptions. As MacKinnon says,

> It's threatening to one's takeability, one's rapeability, one's femininity, to be strong and physically self-possessed. To be able to resist rape, not to communicate rapeability with one's body, to hold one's body for uses and meanings other than that can transform what *being a woman means*.[33]

Resistance to that transformation was evident in the policies of American women physical education professionals throughout most of the 20th century. They minimized exertion, maximized a feminine appearance and manner, and left organized sports competition to men for a long time.[34]

Today, when girls and women are professional and amateur players in all kinds of sports, women and men are not allowed to compete against each other, so actual comparisons of men's and women's and boys' and girls' physical prowess are rarely made. One student noted that he and the other boys were glad that they did not have to play against the best athlete in their elementary school—a girl. Sex segregation of sports by school officials kept her from playing with the boys and probably from showing them up. Another young man, who had played Little League baseball with girls, believed that most girls were "no good"—even though three or four girls were very good. The girls who played well were ignored by the boys. He said,

About this time I participated in Little League baseball. This was a boy-dominated organization where a team was "unlucky" to have a girl teammate. Approximately 1 out of every 12 kids in Little League at that time were girls. I remember them quite well. Most were really not that good at baseball. They would usually play at the end of the game and bat last in the lineup. Then there were the three or four girls who stuck out in the league. They competed with the best of us. They could outhit just about any boy and played aggressively. Although they were good, they were also outcasts. Everyone considered them "tomboys" because they would dive for a fly ball or slide headfirst into home plate. Their teammates loved them on the field but once the game was over, so was the friendship. Girls just didn't fit into the norms of Little League. I have always wondered what it was like for those girls to play a boy-dominated sport.

The girls' willingness and ability to "play like boys" were valued and celebrated on the field, but the same boys who praised them on the field viewed these girls as "freaks" off the field.

If gender ideology about girls' and boys' bodies says girls are not athletically skilled, at least in sports defined as appropriate for boys, girls who do well in these sports are viewed as deviant. If teachers and principals forbid gender-mixed teams in schools, and if boys will not recognize girls' abilities when they play on teams outside of school, there is little opportunity to challenge the stereotypes of girls' versus boys' physical prowess.[35]

The belief that only men are "true athletes" plays out in media representation of women's and men's sports and in unequal distribution of financial rewards and prizes. Media images of modern men athletes glorify their strength and power, even their violence. Media images of modern women athletes tend to focus on their feminine beauty and grace (so they are not really athletes) or on their thin, small, wiry androgynous bodies (so they are not really women). As Lorber notes, "believing is seeing."[36] If members of society are told repeatedly that women's bodily limitations prevent them from doing sports as well as men, they come to believe it, and the belief is reinforced by the media. The result is that even women's championship teams falter and fail.[37]

Risk Behavior

The masculine code of demonstrable physical strength valorized in men's sports is part of the body imagery of men in general. Men in the working class prove their masculinity by being tough, making fun of danger or hardship on the job, and lording it over women and weaker men.[38] For the middle-class man, power over resources and people seems to be the primary route of proving oneself a man. To get that power, a man may have to push himself so hard on the job that he ends up with a heart attack.

Because of multiple risk factors, young African American men living in disadvantaged environments are the most likely to die before they reach adulthood. In 1998, in the United States, the leading cause of death for all individuals in the 5- to 44-year-old age range was accidents, largely motor vehicle. However, the leading cause of death for young African American men aged 15 to 24 in 1998 was homicide.[39] Because of the 1990s trend of early death rates due to homicides, suicides, and accidents, young African American men have been called an endangered species.[40]

Young men's "taste for risk" has been attributed to sociobiological factors, but more plausible explanations are the seductiveness of danger, displays of masculinity, and, for African American men, despair about restricted opportunities and the future. If a man cannot honorably walk away from a fight, he may end up a homicide statistic. One research study analyzed 80 cases in which men who were strangers killed each other and found that the homicide frequently occurred in encounters in which one insulted the other and the dares escalated.[41]

Unsafe sex practices and shared needles in illegal drug use put both women and men at risk for AIDS. In the United States, the estimate of people with HIV/AIDS as of 2000 was 920,000, 25% of whom are women. African American women represent only 13% of the U.S. female population, but they accounted for 63% of new AIDS cases among women in 1999. Women and men with HIV in the United States cluster in different exposure categories. In 1998, of 10,398 women with HIV, 61% had been exposed through heterosexual contact and 36% through injection drug use. Of 33,289 men with HIV, 53% were exposed by having sex with men and 27% through drug use.[42]

There is a possible "second wave" of infection among young homosexual men who believe that AIDS is now treatable, so they are less vigilant about safer sex practices. A similar denial of vulnerability may be occurring among young women as well. According to data from 25 states, the rate of HIV infection from heterosexual sex among teenage girls increased by approximately 117% between 1994 and 1998, and there was a 90% increase due to injection drug use.[43] Transmission of HIV/AIDS is embedded in relationships, and whether heterosexual or homosexual, the closer the relationship, the less likely the partners are to practice safer sex.[44]

Health-threatening behaviors, such as smoking, drinking, illegal drug use, and unsafe sex, are also influenced by social norms expressed in peer group pressures on young men and women of all racial ethnic groups. Women and men who drink heavily are likely to hurt themselves physically and others emotionally and to do poorly in school. College men drink more often and more heavily than college women and are much more likely to get into fights, hurt others, drive while drunk, and cause damage to property.[45]

Young women tend to adopt a somewhat healthier lifestyle than young men on such measures as using seat belts, getting adequate amounts of sleep and exercise, eating a healthy diet, taking care of their teeth, and managing stress. Young middle-class women, however, are vulnerable to eating disorders, such as anorexia nervosa and bulimia, especially in the college years.[46] Often, these eating disorders are direct reflections of gender norms.

Weight and Eating Disorders

If a young woman's boyfriend says of a photo of her in a majorette uniform, in which she had thought she looked both pretty and important, "You look like a whale," she may stop eating to control her weight and thus, in time, develop a medically recognized eating disorder, as well as depression and low self-esteem.

Many students are surprised at how body norms change. The average weight of Miss America contestants has declined by more than 20 pounds since the 1970s. The average adult in the United States, however, weighs 10 pounds more than he or she weighed a decade ago. Therefore, if women are fatter, but Miss Americas are thinner, there is going to be much dissatisfaction with bodies. When Rubens painted naked women in the 17th century, fleshy women with large stomachs, butts, and breasts had ideal bodies. Many current cultures want the most marriageable women to be full-breasted and full-hipped; their weight shows that they are fertile and healthy, and that their families are prosperous. In other times, thinness in women showed religiosity. Sometimes, it is men who starve themselves for beauty; other times, it is women.[47]

Anorexia (self-starvation) and bulimia (binge eating and induced vomiting) are extreme ways to lose weight to meet Western cultural standards of beauty and to maintain control over one's body. Eating disorders are extremely difficult to reverse and can lead to hospitalizations and even death. Otherwise well-protected against health risks, young white middle-class college women who are dissatisfied with their body image are vulnerable to eating disorders.[48] A study of teenagers found that more than 50% of girls in a national sample were trying to alter their weight by dieting, exercising, or using more extreme measures (pills, vomiting, etc.), a pattern that was most pronounced among girls who made good grades, were more involved in school activities, and had more friends.[49] These findings suggest that the pressure to have a "conforming" body begins early in life, at least for girls.

The significance of society's views of compulsory heterosexuality and femininity is highlighted by research comparing heterosexual women, who are subject to pressure from the media and the significant men in their lives to stay thin to be sexually attractive, and lesbians, whose views of beauty are not influenced by men's opinions. Lesbians are heavier than comparable heterosexual women, more satisfied with their bodies, and less likely to have eating disorders.[50] Men also have an idealized body image, which may encourage anorexia and bulimia, especially among those with sexual conflicts or who identify as homosexual.[51]

Women and men college athletes are prone to anorexia and bulimia when they have to diet to stay in a weight class.[52] A study of 695 athletes in 15 college sports found that 1.6% of the men and 4.2% of the women met the American Psychiatric Association's criteria for anorexia, and 14.2% of the men and 39.2% of the women met the criteria for bulimia.[53] The reasons for strict weight control are not standards of beauty but the pressures of competition, to meet weight category requirements, to increase speed and height, and to be able to be lifted and carried easily in performances. Eating disorders here are an occupational risk taken not only by young athletes but also by dancers, models, jockeys, and fitness instructors, as well as professional gymnasts, figure skaters, runners, swimmers, and wrestlers.

The norms about weight or thinness as markers of beauty and strength are part of a larger issue in the social construction of gendered bodies: What is a "good body"? What is an "able body"?

What Is an Able Body?

Able-bodiedness is a relative concept, dependent on the physical environment and social supports. When the physical environment is adapted to a range of needs, and technological devices that enhance hearing, speech, sight, and dexterity are available on a widespread basis, people with all kinds of bodies and physical capabilities can work, travel, and socialize. John Hockenberry, a paraplegic due to an automobile accident, has gone around the world as a reporter in his wheelchair, openly flaunting his physical state and constructing an image of masculine strength.[54]

Women, too, can enhance their self-image by overcoming adversity. Nancy Mairs says she prefers to consider herself a cripple rather than disabled or handicapped:

> People—crippled or not—wince at the word "cripple," as they do not at "handicapped" or "disabled." Perhaps I want them to wince. I want them to see me as a tough customer, one to whom the fates/gods/viruses have not been kind, but who can face the brutal truth of her existence squarely. As a cripple, I swagger.[55]

Unlike Hockenberry, who wants to present a strong, masculine image, Mairs's presentation of self is "tough"—a stance for women or men who want to confront the world on their own terms.

The conventional norms of femininity lock women with disabilities into a paradoxical situation: As women, it is alright for them to be helpless and dependent, but because they are disabled, they are unlikely to have a man to take care of them. Feminists have argued that norms of independence and economic self-support provide a better model for all women, and that giving women with disabilities the means to accomplish these goals would go a long way to enhancing their self-esteem and quality of life.[56]

For men with disabilities, the change has to come in challenges to conventional masculinity. Examining the problem of masculinity and physical disability in the lives of 10 men, one study discovered three strategies: reliance on conventional norms and expectations of manhood, reformulation of these norms, and creation of new norms.[57] The men who relied on the predominant ideals of masculinity believed they had to demonstrate physical strength, athleticism, sexual prowess, and independence. Their self-image was tied to heroics and risk taking, but they often felt inadequate and incomplete because they could not do what they wanted or go where they wanted. The men who reformulated these norms defined their ways of coping with their physical limitations as demonstrations of strength and independence. For example, two quadriplegics who needed round-the-clock personal care assistants did not believe they were dependent on others but, rather, had hired helpers whom they directed and controlled. The men who rejected the standard version of masculinity put more emphasis on relationships than on individual accomplishments.

To erase the status dilemmas of women and men with physical disabilities, conventional norms about bodies, functions, and beauty need to be reexamined. A woman without arms or legs claimed the statue of Venus de Milo as her model of beauty.[58] At the opening ceremony of the 1996 Olympics in Atlanta, the torch was lit by Muhammad Ali, the famous heavyweight champion and 1960 gold medalist. Weakened by Parkinson's disease, his left arm shook, his face was immobilized, and he could hardly walk. Why was he chosen to represent the spirit of athleticism when he seemed its very contradiction? As a man who was overcoming the limits of his body, he was celebrated once more as a hero.[59]

Able-bodiedness is an impermanent state because illness, traumas, pregnancy, and old age render all of us disabled sooner or later. At the 1996 Academy Awards ceremony in Hollywood, the appearance on stage of two men, one young and one old, dramatized the body's fragility. Kirk Douglas, receiving a lifetime career award, was clearly counteracting the effects of a stroke in his walk and his thank-you speech. Later, the curtain went up on Christopher Reeve, paralyzed from the effects of a fall from a horse. He was completely propped up and spoke with the aid of a breathing tube. When the mostly young audience members, gorgeous in body and face, rose to applaud these men, each must have had a sinking feeling in the pits of their stomachs and a whisper on their lips asking whatever higher being they believed in to spare them these fates, at least for a long while.

Degendering Social Bodies

Feminists do not deny that bodily differences between women and men exist; rather, they claim that many, if not most, of the uses of these differences are ideological. They oppose the use of bodily differences to benefit men and exclude or oppress women.

Changing the social construction of gendered bodies is difficult because our identities are tied up with how our bodies look and act or perform. Self-identity as a women or man and self-esteem are translated into bodily markers. Sometimes, self-pride is exaggerated—we talk of strutting, swaggering, preening, and flaunting it. The playing field is not level for women and men, however: "For men, as for women, the world formed by the body-reflexive practices of gender is a domain of politics—the struggle of interests in a context of inequality. Gender politics is an embodied-social politics."[60]

Men have the advantage because all men's bodies are stereotyped as bigger, stronger, and physically more capable than any woman's body. Realistically, we know that a well-trained woman, a tall and muscular woman, a woman who has learned the arts of self-defense, a woman soldier, or a woman astronaut is a match for most men. If women and men of the same size and training are matched, men may not necessarily be physically superior because women have greater endurance, balance, and flexibility. The type of competition makes a difference; most sports are made for men—that is, they are organized around men's bodily capacities.

Although feminists have different views regarding how much and in what ways men's and women's bodies differ, all object to claims that bodily differences between the sexes confirm men's superiority. Feminists who believe that women's and men's bodies are different tend to view women as superior in some ways and men as superior in others. They challenge assertions that differences between women and men require them to occupy different social positions or have different opportunities in society. They view claims about bodily differences between women and men as social rather than biological in character, meaning that, like the clothing individuals "put on" to cover their bodies, cultural beliefs about bodies are put on—or imposed—by society onto the bodies of women and men, through gendered beliefs and practices, as part of the society's gender order.[61]

A second theme of feminist analysis of the body is dominance with regard to questions of power, gender hierarchy, privilege, and oppression. Who says men's or women's bodies are one way or another? How many women MTV producers and Hollywood film directors decide how bodies are depicted in videos and movies? Who benefits when the media depict women's bodies as sexy and fragile but strong enough to lift children, clean houses, and carry home the groceries (and work to pay for them, too)? Feminists assert that most of the naming, depicting, and promoting of the images of women are done by powerful, privileged men. Although only some men—white, economically privileged, powerful, middle-aged, and ostensibly heterosexual—create cultural images of women, all men benefit if the images influence most women to seek men's approval; cling to one man to receive protection from the rest; doubt their physical abilities because of their "feminine limitations"; or quit trying to get well-paying jobs in construction, mining, and truck driving.

A third aspect of feminist analysis of the body concerns subversion and relates to feminism's political agenda. Subversion refers to resistance to and undermining of cultural ideals and practices. Women may be depicted as less "talented" sports figures than men; Dot Richardson, U.S. Olympic softball star and physician, and Lisa Leslie, U.S. Olympic basketball star, however, ignore the depiction. They are "girls" who "play like boys," developing their bodies and skills to the maximum. Some women refuse to shave their legs or wear makeup, much less submit to liposuction or breast implant surgery. Some men refuse to worry about balding, height, and body shape and support women who compete in athletic events and apply for combat roles in the military. People who dress as "punks" resist mainstream society's views about tattooing and body piercing.[62] Resisting cultural pressures to adorn, shape, and judge bodies according to conventional standards, especially in relation to gender, is a subversive act.

Conclusion

What is beautiful, admired, rejected, or unattractive about women's and men's bodies? What is normal? What are the body's capacities?

Feminists raise these questions in an attempt to unveil the social processes that produce and maintain the invisible gender-related assumptions and beliefs that undergird so many claims about women's and men's bodies. The most important process is the maintenance of power differences. When we ask, "Who says? Who decides? Who benefits? Who is harmed?" we are asking who has the power.

Currently, men's greater power in society allows them to represent women's bodies in ways that are often untrue and harmful to girls and women. In questioning power in gender relations, feminist theory also asks questions about race and ethnicity, social class, sexual orientation, age, and able-bodiedness, in addition to gender. When the "woman question" exposes women's exclusion or representation as inferior, awareness of the situation raises questions about who else is excluded. By questioning accepted norms and challenging the prerogatives of the powerful to set standards, feminists make room for differences—in bodies and in behavior. Affirmation of differences and resistance to stereotyping foster the rejection of restrictive gender images, standards, and practices, increasing the odds that all can realize their full potential.

Notes

1. Some of the material in this chapter was adapted from Lorber J. (2001). *Gender inequality: Feminist theories and politics*. Los Angeles: Roxbury; Lorber, J., & Moore, L. J. (2002). *Gender and the social construction of illness*. Walnut Creek, CA: AltaMira; Lorber, J. (1994). *Paradoxes of gender*. New Haven, CT: Yale University Press.

2. Connell, R. W. (1995). *Masculinities* (p. 64). Berkeley: University of California Press.

3. Klein, A. M. (1993). *Little big men: Bodybuilding subculture and gender construction*. Albany: State University of New York Press. For a detailed account of drug use in sports and predications of genetic manipulation of bodies to produce superathletes, see Sokolove, M. (2004, January 18). The lab animal: In pursuit of doped excellence. *New York Times Magazine*, pp. 28-33, 54, 58. For accounts of steroid use, see Longman, J. (2003, November 13). Drugs in sports creating games of illusion. *New York Times*, pp. D1-D2; Longman, J. (2003, November 26). An athlete's dangerous experiment. *New York Times*, pp. D1, D4; Longman, J. (2003, December 5). Inquiry on steroid use gets Bonds testimony. *New York Times*, pp. D1, D3.

4. The ad for men appeared in *New York Times Magazine*. (1997, January 5), p. 56. For comments on breast surgery for women, see Goodman, E. (2003, November 2). Beauty and the breast. *Boston Globe*, p. G11; Kolata, G. (2003, October 19). A sexual subtext to the debate over breast implants. *New York Times*, p. 4.

5. The top five nonsurgical procedures were botox and collagen injections, skin abrasion and chemical peel, and laser hair removal. Statistics provided by the American Society for Aesthetic Plastic Surgery Web page (2002).

6. Collins, M. A., & Zebrowitz, L. A. (1995). The contributions of appearance to occupational outcomes in civilian and military settings. *Journal of Applied Social Psychology, 25*, 129-163; Hensley, W. E., & Cooper, R. (1987). Height and occupational success: A review and a critique. *Psychological Reports, 60*, 843-849.

7. Mueller, U., & Mazur, A. (1996). Facial dominance of West Point cadets as a predictor of later military rank. *Social Forces, 74*, 823-850.

8. Yoder, J. D. (1989). Women at West Point: Lessons for token women in male-dominated occupations. In J. Freeman (Ed.), *Women: A feminist perspective* (4th ed., p. 530). Mountain View, CA: Mayfield.

9. Bordo, S. R. (1993). *Unbearable weight: Feminism, Western culture, and the body*. Berkeley: University of California Press; Davis, K. (1995). *Reshaping the female body: The dilemma of cosmetic surgery*. New York: Routledge; Gullette, M. M. (1993). All together now:

The new sexual politics of midlife bodies. *Michigan Quarterly Review, 32,* 669-695; Hesse-Biber, S. (1996). *Am I thin enough yet? The cult of thinness and the commercialization of identity.* New York: Oxford University Press.

10. Mansfield, A., & McGinn, B. (1993). Pumping irony: The muscular and the feminine. In S. Scott & D. Morgan (Eds.), *Body matters: Essays on the sociology of the body* (pp. 143-167). London: Falmer.

11. Butler, J. (1993). *Bodies that matter: On the discursive limits of "sex."* New York: Routledge; Jacobus, M., Fox Keller, E., & Shuttleworth, S. (Eds.). (1990). *Body/politics: Women and the discourses of science.* New York: Routledge; Price, J., & Shildrick, M. (Eds.). (1999). *Feminist theory and the body.* New York: Routledge; Weitz, R. (Ed.). (1998). *The politics of women's bodies: Sexuality, appearance and behavior.* New York: Oxford University Press.

12. Lorber (1994). *Paradoxes of gender.*

13. Lorber, J. (2002). Heroes, warriors, and burqas: A feminist sociologist's reflections on September 11. *Sociological Forum, 17,* 377-396.

14. Cockburn, C. (1985). *Machinery of dominance: Women, men and technical know-how* (p. 100). London: Pluto Press.

15. Cockburn, C. (1983). *Brothers: Male dominance and technological change* (p. 204). London: Pluto Press.

16. Allen, M. (1996, November 9). Women at The Citadel get shorter hair, and in trouble. *New York Times,* Section 1, p. 9.

17. Grady, D. (1992, June). Sex test of champions: Olympic officials struggle to define what should be obvious: Just who is a female athlete. *Discover, 13,* 78-82; Purcell, K. (1996). In a league of their own: Mental leveling and the creation of social comparability in sport. *Sociological Forum, 11,* 435-456.

18. Hargreaves, J. A. (1994). *Sporting females: Critical issues in the history and sociology of women's sports.* New York: Routledge; Messner, M. A. (2002). *Taking the field: Women, men, and sports.* Minneapolis: University of Minnesota Press; Messner, M. A. (1992). *Power at play: Sports and the problem of masculinity.* Boston: Beacon; Messner, M. A., & Sabo, D. F. (1994). *Sex, violence, and power in sports: Rethinking masculinity.* Freedom, CA: Crossing.

19. Young, I. M. (1990). *Throwing like a girl and other essays in feminist philosophy and social theory* (p. 146). Bloomington: Indiana University Press.

20. Fausto-Sterling, A. (1985). *Myths of gender: Biological theories about women and men* (pp. 213-218). New York: Basic Books.

21. Wallechinsky, D. (1996, June 23). Vaults, leaps and dashes. *New York Times Magazine,* pp. 46-47.

22. Collins, B. (1996, September 2). Navratilova against history: Love-15 [Letter to the Editor]. *New York Times,* Section 1, p. 27.

23. Cahn, S. K. (1993). From the "muscle moll" to the "butch" ballplayer: Mannishness, lesbianism, and homophobia in U.S. women's sport. *Feminist Studies, 19,* 343-368.

24. Brubach, H. (1996, June 23). The athletic esthetic. *New York Times Magazine,* p. 51.

25. In ancient Greece, women ran races in their own Olympics, as depicted on the vase in the Vatican. Their athletic events were in honor of Hera for women spectators. See Pomeroy, S. B. (1975). *Goddesses, whores, wives, and slaves: Women in classical antiquity* (p. 137). New York: Schocken.

26. Messner, M. A. (1992). *Power at play,* pp. 61-84.

27. Messner, M. A. (1992). *Power at play,* p. 71.

28. Messner, M. A., Duncan, M. C., & Jensen, K. (1993). Separating the men from the girls: The gendered language of televised sports. *Gender & Society, 7,* 121-137.

29. Eitzen, S. D., & Zinn, M. B. (1989). The de-athleticization of women: The naming and gender marking of collegiate sport teams. *Sociology of Sport Journal, 6,* 362-370.

30. Watson, T. (1987). Women athletes and athletic women: The dilemmas and contradictions of managing incongruent identities. *Sociological Inquiry, 57,* 441, 443.

31. Duff, R. W., & Hong, L. K. (1984). Self-images of women bodybuilders. *Sociology of Sport Journal, 2,* 378.

32. Hargreaves, J. A. (1986). Where's the virtue? Where's the grace? A discussion of the social production of gender relations in and through sport. *Theory, Culture, and Society, 3,* 109-121; Izraeli, D. (1997). Gendering military service in the Israeli Defense Forces. *Israel Social Science Research, 12;* Messner, M. A. (2002). *Taking the field;* Theberge, N. (1987). Sport and women's empowerment. *Women's Studies International Forum, 10,* 387-393.

33. MacKinnon, C. A. (1987). *Feminism unmodified* (p. 122). Cambridge, MA: Harvard University Press.

34. Mangan, J. A., & Park, R. J. (1987). *From fair sex to feminism: Sport and the socialization of women in the industrial and post-industrial eras.* London: Cass.

35. Fine, G. A. (1987). *With the boys: Little League baseball and preadolescent culture.* Chicago: Chicago University Press.

36. Lorber, J. (1993). Believing is seeing: Biology as ideology. *Gender & Society, 7,* 568-581.

37. Longman, J. (2003, September 16). Women's soccer league folds on World's Cup eve. *New York Times,* pp. A1, D6; Vecsey, G. (2003, November 16). Great sport had bad bottom line. *New York Times,* pp. D1, D6.

38. Connell, R. W. (1995). *Masculinities.*

39. *National vital health statistics reports.* (2000). Centers for Disease Control and Prevention Web site.

40. Gibbs, J. T. (Ed.). (1988). *Young, black and male in America: An endangered species.* Dover, MA: Auburn House; Staples, R. (1995). Health among Afro-American males. In D. Sabo & D. F. Gordon (Eds.), *Men's health and illness: Gender, power and the body* (pp. 121-138). Newbury Park, CA: Sage.

41. Polk, K. (1994). Masculinity, honor, and confrontational homicide. In T. Newburn & E. Stanko (Eds.), *Just boys doing business: Men, masculinities, and crime.* New York: Routledge. Also see Wilson, M., & Daly, M. (1985). Competitiveness, risk taking, and violence: The young male syndrome. *Ethology and Sociobiology, 6,* 59-73; Staples, R. (1995). In *Men's health and illness.*

42. *Women and HIV/AIDS, fact sheet.* (2001). Kaiser Family Foundation Web site.

43. Lee, L. M., & Fleming, P. L. (2001). Trends in human immunodeficiency virus diagnoses among women in the United States, 1994-1998. *Journal of the American Medical Women's Association, 56,* 94-99.

44. Browne, J., & Minichiello, V. (1996). Condoms: Dilemmas of caring and autonomy in heterosexual safe sex practices. *Venereology: Interdisciplinary International Journal of Sexual Health 9,* 24-33; Lear, D. (1995). Sexual communication in the age of AIDS: The construction of risk and trust among young adults. *Social Science and Medicine, 41,* 1311-1323.

45. Johnson, V. (1988). Adolescent alcohol and marijuana use: A longitudinal assessment of a social learning perspective. *American Journal of Drug and Alcohol Abuse, 14,* 419-439; Perkins, H. W. (1992). Gender patterns in consequences of collegiate alcohol abuse: A 10-year study of trends in an undergraduate population. *Journal of Studies on Alcohol, 53,* 458-462; Van Roosmalen, E. H., & McDaniel, S. A. (1992). Adolescent smoking intentions: Gender differences in peer context. *Adolescence, 27,* 87-105.

46. Oleckno, W. A., & Blacconiere, M. J. (1990). Wellness of college students and differences by gender, race, and class standing. *College Student Journal, 24,* 421-429; Hesse-Biber, S. J. (1989). Eating patterns and disorders in a college population: Are college women's eating problems a new phenomenon? *Sex Roles, 20,* 71-89.

47. Miller, M. N., & Pumariega, A. J. (2001). Culture and eating disorders: A historical and cross-cultural review. *Psychiatry, 64,* 93-110.

48. Ben-Tovim, D. I., Walker, K., Gilchrist, P., et al. (2001, April 21). Outcome in patients with eating disorders: A 5-year study. *Lancet, 357,* 1254-1257; Bordo, S. R. (1993). *Unbearable weight: Feminism, Western culture, and the body;* Brumberg, J. J. (1988). *Fasting girls: The emergence of anorexia nervosa as a modern disease.* Cambridge, MA: Harvard University Press; Cooley, E., & Toray, T. (2001). Body image and personality predictors of eating disorder symptoms during the college years. *International Journal of Eating Disorders, 30,* 28-36; Gremillion, H. (2002). In fitness and in health: Crafting bodies in the treatment of anorexia nervosa. *Signs, 27,* 381-414; Hesse-Biber, S. (1996). *Am I thin enough yet?*

49. Boyd, E. (2002). *Eating practices, body image, and social relationships in girls.* Unpublished master's thesis, Florida State University, Tallahassee.

50. Herzog, D. B., Newman, K. L., Yeh, C. J., & Warshaw, M. (1992). Body image satisfaction in homosexual and heterosexual women. *International Journal of Eating Disorders, 11,* 391-396.

51. Herzog, D. B., Bradburn, I., & Newman, K. (1990). Sexuality in males with eating disorders. In A. E. Andersen (Ed.), *Males with eating disorders* (pp. 40-53). New York: Brunner/Mazel; Herzog, D. B., Norman, D. K., Gordon, C., & Pepose, M. (1984). Sexual conflict and eating disorders in 27 males. *American Journal of Psychiatry, 141,* 989-990; Kearney-Cooke, A., & Steichen-Asch, P. (1990). Men, body image, and eating disorders. In A. E. Andersen (Ed.), *Males with eating disorders* (pp. 54-74). New York: Brunner/Mazel.

52. Black, D. R. (Ed.). (1991). *Eating disorders among athletes.* Reston, VA: American Alliance for Health, Physical Education, Recreation and Dance.

53. Burckes-Miller, M. E., & Black, D. R. (1991). College athletes and eating disorders: A theoretical context. In D. R. Black (Ed.), *Eating disorders among athletes* (pp. 11-26). Reston, VA: American Alliance for Health, Physical Education, Recreation and Dance.

54. Hockenberry, J. (1995). *Moving violations: War zones, wheelchairs, and declarations of independence.* New York: Hyperion.

55. Mairs, N. (1986). *Plaintext* (p. 9). Tucson: University of Arizona Press.

56. Asch, A., & Fine, M. (1988). Introduction: Beyond pedestals. In M. Fine & A. Asch (Eds.), *Women with disabilities: Essays in psychology, culture, and politics* (pp. 1-37). Philadelphia: Temple University Press.

57. Gerschick, T. J., & Miller, A. S. (1994). Gender identities at the crossroads of masculinity and physical disability. *Masculinities, 2,* 34-55.

58. Frank, G. (1988). On embodiment: A case study of congenital limb deficiency in American culture. In M. Fine and A. Asch (Eds.), *Women with disabilities* (pp. 41-71); Wendell, S. (1996). *The rejected body: Feminist philosophical reflections on disability.* New York: Routledge.

59. Vecsey, G. (1996, July 21). Choosing Ali elevated these games. *New York Times,* Sports section, p. 1.

60. Connell, R. W. (1995). *Masculinities,* p. 66.

61. Davis, K. (1997). Embodying theory: Beyond modernist and postmodernist readings of the body. In K. Davis (Ed.), *Embodied practices.* London: Sage.

62. Thomson, R. G. (Ed.). (1996). *Freakery: Cultural spectacles of the extraordinary body.* New York: New York University Press.

Discussion Questions

1. What does your culture or racial or ethnic group think is the ideal body for a man and a woman? Address such features as the ideal weight, height, musculature, and so on. What attributes about the person are those ideal body norms supposed to show others?

2. List all the businesses and professions you can think of that profit from the social construction of idealized bodies in the United States.

3. How do men in feminized sports, such as figure skating, physically demonstrate masculinity? How do women in male-identified sports, such as basketball, physically demonstrate femininity?

CHAPTER 9

Wild Thoughts

An Interactionist Analysis of Ideology, Emotion, and Nature

Gary Alan Fine and Kent L. Sandstrom

Gary Alan Fine is Professor of Sociology at Northwestern University. He specializes in social psychology, sociology of culture, and sociological theory. Part of this chapter is based on his ethnographic research published in his book, Morel Tales: The Culture of Mushrooming *(University of Illinois Press, 2003). He has written other studies of Little League baseball, Dungeons and Dragons, restaurant kitchens, high school debate, and the market for self-taught art.*

Kent L. Sandstrom is Professor of Sociology at the University of Northern Iowa. He believes that sociological theory should be linked to social action, and he is actively involved in organizations that promote peace and human rights. He teaches courses in social psychology, medical sociology, and peace studies. He is coauthor of Symbols, Selves, and Social Reality: A Symbolic Interactionist Approach to Social Psychology *(Roxbury, 2003). He is Executive Officer of the Midwest Sociological Society. He is currently working on a book titled* Social Structure and Human Interaction: A Sociological Approach to Social Psychology.

In this chapter, we use *symbolic interactionist* theory to examine how people define and experience the reality of "nature." In doing so, we highlight how people's understandings and experiences of nature are not natural; instead, they are profoundly shaped by culture, ideology, and social organization. We also demonstrate how the concept of ideology, often confined to macrosociological theory, can be incorporated into microsociological research and analysis. We use basic interactionist concepts, such as emotion, identity, interaction, impression management, frame, and network, to reveal how ideologies (particularly ideologies about nature) are generated and enacted. In the process, we illustrate how the reality of nature is constructed and mediated through the template of culture.

Sociology, Ideology, and Symbolic Interactionism

Sociologists have frequently emphasized how ideologies alleviate social strains or advance the political and economic interests of groups or classes.[1] They have also asserted that ideologies are conditioned by larger social structures, such as modes of production, political apparatuses, or forms of bureaucratic rationality.[2] Most sociologists view ideology as a set of ideas shaped by more fundamental social forces.

Recently a growing number of social analysts have challenged this orthodox view. Some highlight the independence of ideology as a cultural system, whereas others stress that ideology and social structure have a dialectical, or mutual, relationship with one another.[3] Even Marxist theorists, who accentuate the material and economic bases of social life, have placed increased emphasis on the independent effects of ideology.[4] In general, both mainstream and Marxist sociologists now assign greater weight to ideological factors in structuring social reality. Yet while paying more attention to ideology and its effects, most sociologists overlook the question of how ideology shapes and gets shaped by specific social interactions.[5]

Symbolic interactionist analysis can fill this gap in social theory, particularly because it highlights how collective meaning is constructed and how it is embedded in social interaction. Whereas cultural and neo-Marxist theories illustrate how ideological beliefs and symbols are not reducible to social structural factors, an interactionist approach provides distinctive insights by exploring how ideology is linked to action and meaning and, correspondingly, how it helps people communicate concerns, announce their identities, build networks of solidarity, and cope with their lived realities.

Before considering how ideology is connected to meaning and action, we need to define this concept, especially because it has been described as "the most elusive concept in social theory."[6] Drawing on interactionist (and related social psychological) insights, we contend that ideology has two core components. First, it consists of beliefs that are connected to attitudes.[7] Attitudes, as routinely defined by social psychologists, have cognitive, affective, and behavioral dimensions; they provide a way of looking at objects or realities, a guide for evaluating them emotionally, and a disposition for action. Attitudes are moral statements that link depictions of the world (images of what "is") to judgments of those depictions (feelings about what "ought to be"). Attitudes have truth claims, evaluative emotions, and behavioral tendencies associated with them. Ideology, in turn, consists of bundles of interconnected attitudes that form a pattern of beliefs.

A second key component of ideology is that these bundles of attitudes provide an interpretation of the social or political order. Interactionists emphasize that people are driven by problematic events, ranging from terrorist bombings to broken romances, to make sense of the world and to determine how to respond to it. Ideologies become relevant in these processes because they provide individuals and groups with diagnoses of what is and is not problematic in the social and political world. They also offer guidelines for how individuals and groups should address or resolve those things that they define as problematic.

Based on the previous contentions, we suggest that an *ideology* consists of a set of interconnected beliefs and their associated attitudes, shared and used by members of a group or population, that relate to problematic aspects of social or political issues.[8] These beliefs have an explicit evaluative and implicit behavioral component. We recognize that this definition, like most, has a measure of ambiguity, but it clearly highlights (a) the linkages among beliefs and among beliefs and attitudes, indicating that ideology is part of an interpretive system; and (b) the relevance of ideological beliefs in guiding people's views of and actions in the sociopolitical realm. Another important feature of this definition is that it locates ideology squarely in a group or population. In addition, it challenges, or at least sidesteps, the arguments of some theorists that ideological beliefs are necessarily grounded in false consciousness or faulty thinking.

In our analyses of ideology, we are guided by the following three premises articulated by Herbert Blumer, the founder of symbolic interactionism[9]:

1. People act toward things based on the meanings that they have for them.

2. These meanings are derived from their interaction with other people.

3. These meanings are managed and transformed through the processes of interpretation and self-reflection that individuals use to make sense of and handle the things they encounter.

In his first premise, Blumer suggests that if we want to understand human behavior, we must know how people define those things—objects, events, individuals, and structures—they encounter in their environment. These things do not have an inherent or unvarying meaning. Rather, their meanings differ based on how we define and respond to them. For instance, the thing we call a "tree" will have a different meaning depending on whether we identify it as something to chop, climb, decorate, prune, or turn into lumber. If you cut down a tree, chop it into smaller pieces, and burn it in a fireplace, it becomes "fuel." On the other hand, if you take it into your house, put it in a stand, and trim it with lights and ornaments, it becomes a "decoration" marking the arrival of Christmas. A tree has different meanings depending on how we define and respond to it. In the same way, a person will mean different things to us and call out different responses depending on whether we define him or her as a teacher, lover, terrorist, parent, or friend. The crucial factor, then, is how we name, or give meaning to, the things we encounter because that will shape our actions toward them.

Blumer's second premise indicates where these meanings come from—social interaction. We are not born knowing the meaning of things. Nor do we learn these meanings simply through individual experiences. Instead, we learn what things mean through our interactions with others. For example, in the United States we learn what a "football" means through taking part in a team game that consists of quarterbacks, running backs, receivers, linemen, defenders, punts, passes, handoffs, touchdowns, and field goals. As we play this game with others, including friends, parents, and coaches, we quickly discover that a football is something you are supposed to throw if you are a "quarterback," catch if you are a "wide receiver," kick if you are a "punter," and intercept if you are a "defensive back." Before we find out these things, a football does not have a self-evident meaning. We learn that it is something to throw, catch, kick, or intercept through observing how others act with respect to it.

In his third premise, Blumer makes the crucial point that the meanings of the things we encounter change through our understandings or interpretations. While acknowledging that the meaning of a thing is formed through social interaction, Blumer stresses that we should not see an individual's use of that meaning as automatic. Instead, the use of meanings by a person occurs through interpretation and self-reflection. As Blumer argued, interpretation should not be viewed as merely an unthinking application of previously established social meanings. Instead, it should be regarded as a process in which meanings are used and revised as tools for guiding and shaping our actions.[10]

In essence, then, while acknowledging that social definitions guide action, Blumer stresses that the interpretive process involves more than a reflex-like application of these definitions. When we find ourselves in a situation, we must decide which of the many things present in that situation are relevant. We must determine which objects or actions we need to give meaning and which we can neglect or ignore. Moreover, we must figure out which of the many meanings that can be attributed to a thing are the appropriate ones in this context. For example, if you are walking through the woods and you see a deer standing behind a clump of trees approximately 100 yards away, you have to determine what meanings to give to it. Let's imagine that the deer glances in your direction nervously and looks like it is prepared to bound away. If you are a hunter looking for a deer to shoot, you would assess its meaning in this situation by asking the following: Has the deer detected my presence? Can I take a clear shot at it in this thicket of woods before it runs away? And if I shoot it, will I be able to drag it out of the woods on my own? If you answer yes to these questions, you would give the deer the meaning of "prey." In contrast, if you see the deer while you are on a "nature walk," you might assess its meaning by asking the following: How could anyone shoot such a docile and beautiful creature? Is it going to run away in fear or will it stand there for awhile so I can admire it? And will I have time to get my camera out so that I can take a nice photograph of it? In the process, you would define and respond to it as a "natural wonder."

As this example illustrates, the same object can have very different meanings, and as we decide how to respond appropriately in a given situation, we have to determine which of these meanings best applies. Unfortunately, we sometimes find ourselves in situations in which no established meanings pertain. As a result, we must be flexible enough to learn or construct new meanings. We have this flexibility because we develop the capacities of "mind" and "self" through our social interactions. That is, through interacting with others we develop the ability to see and respond to ourselves as objects. This gives us the capacity to think or to interact with ourselves. When we think, we shape the meaning of objects in our world, accepting them, rejecting them, or changing them in accord with how we define and act toward them. We respond to these objects in terms of a dynamic and creative process of interpretation—a process based on socially shared symbols or language. This process allows us to generate new or different meanings and to adjust our actions accordingly.

Guided by Blumer's three premises of symbolic interaction, we focus this chapter on how people construct and enact ideology, particularly as they define "nature" and "the environment." We highlight (a) the connections among ideology, folk images, naturework, and moral order; (b) the emotional context and underpinnings of ideology; (c) the dramaturgical techniques and framing conventions used in the public presentation of ideology; and (d) the connection of ideology to small groups and the activation of networks and social movements.

In elaborating these themes, we draw from research about environmental ideologies. We also rely on readings of nature tracts and draw on the ethnographic observations of mushroom collectors conducted by Gary Alan Fine.[11] In studying mushroom collectors, he sought to learn about the relationship between human behavior and the natural environment. In particular, he was interested in how people who spend time "in nature" conceive of the relationship between nature and culture and how they put this orientation into practice. Through referring to the data he collected, we give empirical grounding to our generalizations about how people do ideology.

Ideology, Images, and Moral Order

Throughout the academic community and in public discourse, discussions of the meaning of nature and the relationship between human beings and the natural world abound. These discussions have been triggered not only by the serious problems emerging in the natural environment but also by the rapid growth in the size and number of environmental organizations. Not surprisingly, many academics and environmentalists agree that human beings are treating nature poorly. They disagree, however, about who or what is to blame for this situation. Some argue that the key villain is the corporation, whereas others point to larger social or economic forces, such as capitalism, patriarchy, or anthropocentrism. Typically, these approaches distinguish between humans and nature. Although they see humans as animals, they do not permit them the same freedom of action as "real" animals. Humans are blamed for their behavioral choices in a way that bears, beavers, and mosquitoes are not. Regardless of who or what they blame, most academics and environmentalists argue that humans should tread less harshly on nature, showing greater consideration for animals and plants and leaving them in peace as much as possible.

Although there is much to be said for environmental approaches that fret about the degradation of the natural world, these approaches typically focus little attention on the specific images and symbols through which people understand their environment as a meaningful other. They also neglect or downplay the processes through which people's interpretations of nature are transformed into a set of action claims.

Drawing on interactionist insights, we point out that people's understandings of nature are not "natural." Instead, these understandings, like all human understandings, are shaped by language and its implicit images, which are rooted in culture. We are not suggesting that the objects we associate with nature, including the things we call trees, birds, lakes, and mushrooms, exist only as a product of human language and culture. They are quite real. Rather, we are proposing that nature as a concept derives from human cognition and cultural activity; that is, the meaning of nature derives from the names and classification schemes created by human beings. Labels such as "nature," the "wild," and "the environment" as categories of objects are socially constructed, linked to ideologies of nature. These ideologies of nature are grounded in "folk ideas" and pools of cultural images through which individuals establish models for experiencing the wild, for describing that experience, and for analyzing the existence and severity of natural problems.

As Alan Dundes has observed, folk ideas are traditional notions that a group of people have about the nature of humanity, the nature of the world, and the nature of human life in the world.[12] These notions operate like master images, informing and guiding the interpretations of individuals and groups as they interact with the world around them. Folk ideas provide people with a collective "description of the nature of reality"[13] and, thus, frame their definitions of situations and events. For instance, the "notion of unlimited good" is a central folk idea in American ideology. Americans apply the idea of unlimited good as a rule of thumb in addressing may problems. For example, until the past couple of decades many Americans believed that they could use natural resources without limitation; they imagined there was a "bounty of nature." This theme was evident in Fine's research with mushroom collectors: Most collectors opposed government limits on picking mushrooms because they claimed that there would always be a new crop. The collectors objected to areas being cut off from mushrooming because of fear of overpicking, arguing that there was not good evidence that such restrictions were necessary.[14] Mushrooms were regarded as a renewable resource, and collectors mobilized this image in a way that legitimated their self-interest.

Most crucially, people experience the world, including the world of nature, in terms of *concepts*—regularized ways of thinking about real or imagined objects or events. These concepts enable them to picture things, to describe or represent these things to themselves and one another, and to grasp their meaning. People use concepts because they are "cognitive misers," and they want to find relatively simple ways to deal with all the stimuli they experience. By sorting these stimuli into related and manageable units and giving them names, such as "roommate," "professor," "exam," "flower," "weed," or "lake," they simplify the world—they chunk and cluster its elements into meaningful symbols and thus see it in terms of images, metaphors, and simple slogans.[15] Ideology depends on this chunking and clustering process. It is a filter that activates and organizes selected contents of our consciousness. In particular, it activates certain attitudes and emotions "and permits these to be communicated via reflexive, articulate, and shared ideas."[16]

Modern ideologies are uniquely reliant on printed discourse in their dissemination to a larger public. Yet the subtlety and detailed content that characterize written texts are lost on many, if not most, of those who embrace and share the ideologies. Individuals are predisposed to accept ideology without thinking because the labels or categories are accepted as natural or inevitable.[17]

With respect to the environment, Americans draw on a variety of contrasting images and concepts, such as Mother Nature, the land ethic, earth as a lifeboat, the vulnerability of nature, stewardship, interdependence, wise use, sustainability, renewable resources, abundance, and unlimited good. These images become linked to larger, competing (but sometimes overlapping) ideologies of what relationship humans have or should have to their natural surroundings. Those people who embrace an "anthropocentric" (or human-centered) ideology regarding nature are often guided by images such as abundance, unlimited good, and the renewability of natural resources. They see nature as subordinate to humans and as something for them to use for their own purposes. In contrast, those who embrace a "protectionist" ideology are likely to be influenced by images such as Mother Nature and the vulnerability of the natural world. They give nature primacy over people. They also see the natural environment as a relatively fragile preserve that needs to be separated from and protected against the "civilized" world. In accord with this view, some protectionists stress the "civil rights" of plants and animals. For example, Dave Foreman of Earth First! asserts,

The other beings—four-legged, winged, six-legged, rooted, flowering, etc.—have just as much right to [exist] as we do, they are their own justification for being, they have an inherent value, value completely apart from whatever worth they have for . . . humans.

You protect a river because it's a river. For its own sake. Because it has a right to exist for itself. The grizzly bear in Yellowstone Park has as much right to her life as any one of us has to our life.[18]

When embracing these types of ideological beliefs, people transform natural objects into symbols and, thus, into cultural meanings. They also make sense of and express their relationship to the natural world, engaging in the process of *nature-work*. Through this process, people act on ideological beliefs that specify the relationship between culture and nature, and they evaluate the moral character of that relationship. They correspondingly construct rhetorics of nature—rhetorics that define it in terms of dramatic images and moral metaphors.

Ideology, Metaphor, and Moral Order

Ideology is closely connected to rhetoric. Dramatic and persuasive images are, as in a good speech, central to ideological commitment.[19] The images that guide people's reactions are those that have emotional resonance. These images are a lens through which individuals see the world rather than ideas that must be applied cognitively and rationally.

Although the "form" of ideology may seem logical on the surface, it is imbued with metaphor. As Raynor contends, the linguistic form of ideology

> is picturesque and flamboyant; in particular, it abounds with metaphor. . . . Metaphor is an important brush in the ideologist's paintbox, filling in the picture with a broad sweep, creating connections with the range of associations which a well-turned metaphor has at its disposal.[20]

Metaphor, then, is a handy tool for the ideologist in presenting pictures of "how things are" and of "how they ought to be"—pictures that resonate with people's experiences and offer them an appealing sense of how they can and should live. Through metaphors, the ideologist mobilizes evocative images that encourage people to experience and feel the moral, or what ought to be.

Although metaphor is an important component of ideology, we must be careful not to overemphasize its significance. As several analysts have observed, people's interpretations of their world are inevitably and necessarily grounded in metaphorical understandings.[21] Metaphor is not a distinctive feature of ideology—it is built into the structure of all human thought and communication. Nevertheless, ideologies are characterized by the abundance of metaphorical usage, not only in the conscious figures of speech that ideologists use but also in their choices of images when they are "just communicating."[22]

By focusing on the significance of metaphor in activating images of what ought to be, we emphasize the central position of ideology within social order, which is inevitably a moral order.[23] Typically, the moral statements characterizing an ideology are most effectively employed by containing them within an example, emphasizing their topical relevance. Examples work better than abstractions for framing and mobilizing attitudes. When leaders of social movements wish to mobilize or strengthen the support of a public, they rely on instances that crystallize widely held moral beliefs, focusing on an action that can be effective locally. This strategy is conveyed in the popular slogan that advises members of environmental and human rights movements to "think globally and act locally." By focusing on a recognized local or personal danger, activists hope that individual troubles and sentiments, such as "not in my backyard," will be generalized to systemic problems and outlooks. For instance, mushroom collectors were motivated to express opposition to housing developments that impinged on their collecting sites, and they generalized this personal loss to global statements about stopping human "progress" that harmed nature, but they did so with their concern focused on what was happening to local mushroom ecology.

Advocates of the environmental movement consciously try to align people's actions with a symbolic moral order by transforming personal passion into movement support. Consider the mobilization of public concern over acid rain. For scientists and policymakers, acid rain may be a technical concern, but for the public (and mushroomers as a case in point) the controversy is moral and personal. The impact of "acid rain" begins with the term. The decision of environmentalists to use the label acid rain was consequential.[24] Reactions to this label were conditioned by the image of drops of acid pelting down—the powerfully paradoxical link of "acid" and "rain." This image was further dramatized by linking it to images of "dead lakes."[25]

The technical details of the acid rain debate were unclear to most mushroomers, but the belief that it could affect them was not. The issue became relevant in their discussions of what acid rain could do and already had done to mushroom fruitings and in their political conversations. After one poor year of chanterelle fruitings, collectors speculated that a connection existed between their personal situation and this environmental issue. By inferring this connection, they activated an environmental ideology grounded in dramatic images and folk ideas: the belief that nature should be autonomous from human action, but that it is threatened by these actions.

These images, of course, are not inevitable or unchangeable. Although images are often taken for granted, they may eventually become problematic. In many cases, they are challenged or undermined by the occurrence of a dramatic event that gets manipulated by a *moral entrepreneur,* an individual or group that crusades to translate its concerns into laws and to have violators of these laws defined as "deviants" who need constraint or punishment.[26] The "construction of social problems" approach, grounded in symbolic interactionist theory, emphasizes how moral entrepreneurs take dramatic and concrete events and shape them for their own ends—for example, the kidnapping of young Elizabeth Smart as a means of focusing on the problems of "abducted children" or the shooting of schoolchildren at Columbine as a way to focus on the problems of media violence or the easy accessibility of guns.[27] The new "image" becomes a topic for which some response is needed, crystallizing a set of personal difficulties that had been ignored or downplayed. With respect to the environment, the effects of the massive Exxon oil spill on the Alaskan wilderness provided a dramatic symbolic circumstance that demanded a response. The emergence of such an event, and the mobilization of related dramatic images, sparks a questioning of the existing moral order, provoking action by an aroused public.

In summary, three components are necessary for an ideology to direct people's thoughts and actions. First, the context must be dramatically labeled to link it to widely held moral concerns or "ought beliefs." Second, a set of images must connect to these moral beliefs. Third, the problem, whether acid rain, global warming, or deforestation, must be made personally relevant. Although ideology is a set of moral concerns that become activated when perceived as relevant, it must be enacted, or put into practice, to have an impact. We offer an approach that is distinctively different from traditional macrosociological perspectives. We link ideology to the processes of labeling, claims making, and symbolic interaction that characterize the construction of social problems, highlighting how moral entrepreneurs search for and manipulate dramatic events to make their ideology appealing to a public that often is uninspired by abstract arguments.

Ideology and Emotion

Ideology and emotion are joined at the hip, working in tandem and directing each other. For several decades, sociologists, especially feminists and symbolic interactionists, have focused on how ideology shapes and constrains emotion, particularly through feeling rules and gender expectations.[28] Unfortunately, sociologists have not devoted much attention to the other side of the equation; that is, they have not examined how emotion informs and shapes ideology.

Ideology reveals the transformation of feelings, known through images and metaphors, into beliefs about political order and the social system. People understand and embrace ideology through emotional experiences that help them make sense of the world. Through ideology, people's emotional reactions are generalized beyond specific situations or contexts. In saying this, we do not deny that ideology has a logical or analytical component; instead, we emphasize that emotions are at its heart. We also stress that emotional responses cannot be separated from cognitive ones. The emotions that people experience sensitize them to beliefs and attitudes. These beliefs and attitudes are then linked to cognitive choices, producing an integrated worldview. Stated simply, images of the morally proper structure of society influence which solutions feel "right." These images operate "in our gut" as emotional tools and suggest that the conclusions we draw about morality and social order are based in our felt experiences. Thus, environmentalists such as mushroomers may feel emotionally upset, even angry, when they discover that a favorite collecting site has been cleared for new housing. This anger may lead to an increased commitment to fight to preserve open land.

Environmental ideology derives as much from the emotional responses of individuals as from logical analysis, and it represents the interconnections of the two. As David Wilson observes,

> Nature is present to naturalists the way God is to saints or the past is to humanists—not simply as a matter of fact but as an insistent and live reality. . . . Part of the delight [of nature is] the joy of things, things not as poor shadows of some ideal reality but solidly affecting and significant in themselves.[29]

A key point, made by nature writers from Thoreau to Dillard, is that our experience of nature is profoundly emotional. Our feelings, or emotional responses, help translate nature into mental categories, ideological beliefs, and policy initiatives. Feelings of love, inspiration, or exhilaration make protecting the natural environment necessary; just as feelings of fear or anxiety in nature lead to efforts to "tame" that danger.

Nature, then, is an emotionally laden and culturally potent concept that has effects separate from logical or analytical reflection. Although people's views of nature are affected by their socialization, their attitudes toward nature are grounded not only in learning but also in feeling.[30] The experience of "being in nature" is a deep, authentic reality and is not simply derived from social guidelines or instructions about how one should feel in the natural world. Naturalists commonly claim that being in the woods is like being in church, but this does not mean they use this metaphor because of empirical similarities between the two realities; rather, it is because these realities can be meaningfully compared in their experienced qualities, especially in terms of the feelings (serenity, inspiration, and connection to the divine) they evoke.

If being in the woods, including recalling being in the woods, produces a strong emotional response, then beliefs, attitudes, and policy considerations that facilitate this response are likely. Powerfully felt emotions shape ideology and social policy. In the United States, many people consider it desirable to be "in touch with nature"— they learn that contact with nature is an unqualified good. For city and suburban dwellers, contact with nature refers to a special occasion, such as a vacation or planned outing. These times are culturally and ideologically marked as being "in nature," and when they are satisfying, nature is valued as authentic. Many mush-roomers, like naturalists generally, fondly recall childhood occasions in which they went hiking or camping with their parents or other significant adults. They also recall how these experiences influenced their lives and sense of self. Their current attitudes toward nature are, in turn, informed by these pleasant memories of childhood, pro-viding an illustration of how emotional experiences shape ideological beliefs.

Ideology, Dramaturgy, and Action Frames

Interactionists emphasize that ideologies are not merely held by individuals or groups but also are presented by individuals and groups to others and, conse-quently, serve as a form of dramaturgy. As Erving Goffman noted, dramaturgy is behavior through which we communicate information about ourselves to others, thereby managing their impressions of us.[31] People selectively express and act on ideological beliefs when their presentation contributes to smooth interaction, enhances their self-image, or justifies their claims to resources or power. Individuals or groups can discretely hide, alter, or slant ideological beliefs when this seems appropriate or advantageous, and they often do so when speaking about contro-versial social issues.

But what do we mean by the "presentation of an ideology"? Given that ideology can be a broad and vague bundle of attitudes and beliefs, the dramaturgical pre-sentation of an ideology involves reference to specific strands of that bundle. The locations of people's behavior, such as bars, church services, political rallies, or wilderness hikes, condition how they talk and act and how others define this talk and activity. The underlying question individuals ask as they act and interact is, "What is going on here?" That is, how is this situation defined?[32] Their answers to these questions have a significant impact on their behavior. For instance, when visiting a national park, such as Yellowstone, people act and talk very differently depending on whether they define the park as a setting for leisure and entertain-ment or as a place where they can have a genuine experience of the wild. When defining situations, people often draw on ideology, with its implicit bundles of beliefs and attitudes. These beliefs and attitudes get mobilized as they are enacted in inter-action with others.

In highlighting the relational nature of ideology, our approach differs from traditional theoretical approaches that emphasize the existence of a definitive set of beliefs separate from the situation in which it is announced. Although we acknowledge that beliefs can exist outside of particular situations, we contend that the most important issue is when and how they become announced and displayed in collective action. As William Gamson and colleagues have noted, collective action often depends on the existence of "an injustice frame" or the belief that the unimpeded operation of the current authority system would result in an injustice, at least in regard to a particular issue or event.[33] Drawing on Goffman's insights, Gamson and associates refer to how experiences are structured by socially established meanings, and they focus on those events that "key" or inform the understandings of social movement participants, thereby providing a new framework for interpreting reality.[34] For a social movement to be effective, it must facilitate a process of *frame alignment*.[35] In other words, leaders must link their ideology with the attitudes of potential recruits, the public, leaders of the established order, or other movement groups. Frame alignment occurs as people construct frameworks of meaning that draw on the ideas and beliefs of the movement so that collective action makes sense on a personal level. As David Snow and Rob Benford have observed, members of social movements are continually searching for interpretive frameworks, or collective action frames that enable them to understand problematic events and inspire them to respond to these events. Some frames legitimate violent protest (the frame of oppression), whereas others (the frame of moral justice) diminish the probability of violence.[36] Through drawing on and manipulating such frames, movement leaders set a guiding tone for group understandings and actions, such as when environmentalists point to some violation of nature as a means of mobilizing protest.

In stressing these points, interactionist scholars recognize that ideological beliefs are not sufficient cause for group action; rather, people must define their experiences in a way that suggests it is legitimate for them to implement their beliefs through collective action. To the degree that people believe that something can be done about a problem and that they have the right and resources to do it, they are likely to translate their ideology into collective action.[37] To the degree that a community supports the nature, form, and timing of such action, collective power is enhanced and ideology becomes socially cemented.

Beyond these collective assumptions, perhaps what is most central to the embracement and presentation of ideologies are identity labels, including labels such as feminist, peace activist, Republican, or pro-life advocate. When presenting an ideology, a person engages in identity work, announcing that he or she is a certain kind of person, such as a "nature lover." At the same time, he or she provides a means for others to label and place him or her as a social actor. With regard to contemporary ideologies about nature, the dramaturgical displays and self-presentations of individuals are often linked to the belief that they are "environmentalists"—a label so vague that almost every citizen or corporation can claim rights to it. More than 80% of the mushroomers interviewed described themselves in this way, but the meaning of this label varied considerably, referring to different levels and types of political action and a broad range of political beliefs. A master status such as "environmentalist" encompasses a wide variety of views and covers individuals who vigorously disagree. By embracing the ambiguous label of environmentalist, mushroomers can gain the social benefits of this identity while denying its undesirable implications. The degree to which they act on or alter the meanings attached to this label depends in part on who they interact with regularly and how these others define environmentalism.

In their daily lives, people continually make adjustments between their beliefs and their understandings of the demands of the larger culture and a given situation. They sometimes deliberately hide feelings or identities, or in extreme cases deny their beliefs, to maintain relationships, avoid negative labeling, and sustain desired action. This type of interactional and ideological adjustment occurs in the course of many relationships. Mushroomers each have ideas about how human beings (and communities) should treat nature—for example, they believe that people should not throw garbage on the ground, trample on flowering plants, build subdivisions on wetlands, or burn fossil fuels. These specific rules are the outcroppings of an underlying, if vague, ideology. Mushroomers must decide whether, when, and how violations of their ideological standards should be brought to the attention of others. In making these decisions, they must grapple with questions such as the following: "When does an annoyance become a legitimate cause for action?" and "How important is it to preserve a relationship by ignoring what a person believes?" A trade-off exists between asserting an ideological belief and preserving their relationship with the individual who challenges it. The mushroomer with a prospective complaint must gauge the likely reaction of the person who is the target of the complaint, and he or she may consider how to communicate concerns in a way that coincides with the beliefs of the target and his or her level of understanding. Thus, when directing a complaint toward novices, a veteran mushroomer will give them more latitude, as well as more advice, than those who should "know better."

The dynamics involved in the dramaturgical presentation of ideology can also be illustrated on a more collective level. Groups with a complaint based on their moral codes and ideological expectations have tactical problems. They are likely to encounter powerful others who benefit from maintaining the status quo and thus resist proposed changes. Members of an oppositional group must determine the most effective tactics for presenting their complaints and framing their demands, and they must consider the responses they might receive from potentially supportive and hostile elements of the larger society. They must also confront the power of prevailing ideological outlooks. People generally accept these outlooks as a ready made part of their lives or simply as "how the world works." It is difficult for them to question dominant ideas because this requires them to relearn how they view themselves and their environment. These ideas are also held in place by those in power, and they restrict or deny access to oppositional views.[38] For instance, environmentalist groups may find that their complaints are not seen as sufficiently privileged for them to enter into a dialogue with developers, industry spokespersons, or political officials. In these circumstances, the groups must be highly cohesive to opt for confrontation, unless they can mobilize powerful social actors such as the mass media to generate that cohesion. In the absence of such support, the strategy of confrontation threatens the possibility of any dialogue with authorities and potentially undercuts group solidarity. In general, when striving for enhanced power or legitimacy, oppositional groups strive to strike a balance that appeals to and includes as large a community as possible while achieving tactically possible ends. The more extreme the demands of the group, the more difficult they are to achieve because of the threats posed to solidarity and the costs that result from loss of solidarity.

These tensions are evident within the environmental movement in debates between radicals ("deep ecologists") and those who work within the system. Environmentalism cuts broadly across the political spectrum, and environmental interest groups must decide which audience they wish to persuade and through which types of media and strategies. In fact, these groups may have different audiences, and they may or may not share similar outlooks on particular issues (e.g., the need to change pollution laws or to limit access to wilderness areas). At times, they may even find themselves on opposite sides of political debates. Among mushroomers, these debates provoke hostility between those who wish to pick edible mushrooms for profit and those who object to the "massive desecration" of the forests and, not incidentally, to the competition for these scarce resources. Anger and bitterness linger as mushroom clubs debate whether commercial pickers should be licensed and controlled by government. Ultimately, such debates can disrupt and tear apart the organizational structure of these clubs, especially if overarching agreement is lost. Yet these debates are important, and even necessary, because they allow groups to mark ideological boundaries and validate specific claims to authority and resources.

Group Identity, Networks, and Ideology

Ideology is both personal and shared. It is simultaneously a property of the individual, enacted in interaction, and also a property of the group or community. In its cognitive and emotional dimensions, we see the importance of the individual; in its enactment, we see the role of community, class, or social network.

It is fruitful to regard the small group, a tightly bounded social network, as a cornerstone of culture.[39] A national culture or subculture is, at bottom, a loose network of groups. Ideology, in turn, is grounded in an interactional network, such as a small group, and through the interconnections among small groups it radiates throughout a larger social network. In making this point, we do not suggest that ideologies, or other beliefs or cultural elements, are created in each of the small groups within which they get expressed. Rather, we propose that the small group is often the place where ideologies get enacted and where general values take on specific contents while also becoming invested with communal meanings.

This perspective on ideology has several notable merits. First, it emphasizes that ideology is developed and maintained in small groups and diffused through social networks and institutionalized channels of communication, including the mass media.[40] Second, it highlights that ideology must be enacted.[41] Groups are frequently the staging area for ideology. They serve as an organizing arena for several key processes involved in ideological work: identification, boundary maintenance, rituals, emotion management, and the mobilization of resources.

Identification and Boundary Maintenance

Ideology depends on identity and on identification. As Manning writes,

A political ideology is intended, via action, to establish the identity of a body of persons who are thereafter to be understood to be related to one another in a particular way. The relationship is only one among many that each of the potential members of this group may, at a given time, have with a number of other persons, but it is the only relationship which ought, according to the ideology, to embrace them all.[42]

Most small groups, as Robert Freed Bales observed, "develop a subculture that is protective for their members, and is allergic, in some respects to the culture as a whole. . . . [The members] draw a boundary around themselves and resist intrusion."[43] Groups do more than retreat into themselves, however; they also attempt to influence those outside of the group through recruitment or calls for change. Ideology is crucial in this regard, providing a mechanism that facilitates and controls communication with outsiders. That is, ideology offers a means by which a group member can try to affect or recruit outsiders. This is evident in the political activism of committed environmentalists. Even mushroomers, who are sometimes less politically aware than other naturalists, plaster bumper stickers on their cars ("I Brake for Fungi") or wear T-shirts ("Save the Forests") that convey environmental concerns and invite others to share these concerns.

In addition to facilitating communication with others, ideology establishes the boundaries of acceptable belief and inoculates the member from being influenced by the beliefs of nonmembers. An ideology thereby "constructs a boundary with a special one-way permeability,"[44] allowing members to reach outside the group to influence outsiders while simultaneously restricting the penetration of outside beliefs into the group.

Rituals

An ideology is, above all, a tool through which a group cements members to itself, legitimating calls for commitment, identification, and practical assistance. Words are generally less effective than deeds in building group loyalty and solidarity. As a result, groups typically connect members to themselves and to each other through ritual actions.[45] Ideology can become ritualized through the "meaning" of a secret handshake or blood brotherhood. Rituals display the central features of an ideology in symbolic and behavioral form: They provide the basis of common concerns and attitudes. For example, the ritualistic structure of meetings of the Minnesota Mycological Society in which the president stands before the club displaying, naming, and describing the mushrooms that members have brought in demonstrates in concrete form the bounty of nature, the desirability of species diversity, and the joys of mushroom picking and consumption. This group ritual enacts and dramatizes certain ideological beliefs held by these naturalists. It also links the organization of the meeting to these beliefs.

Emotion Management

As reflected in rituals, groups "hook" members and bond them to their ideological beliefs through emotions and emotion management. People often join groups because of the "emotional promise" they offer, either to remedy negative feelings, such as anger, confusion, or loneliness, or to allow for the enactment of positive ones, such as connection, pleasure, or acceptance.[46] Indeed, individuals initially may feel skeptical about joining a group, but its emotional promise, particularly the promise that membership can make them feel better and perhaps also make the world better, draws them in and persuades them to consider the group's ideological message.

After they become involved in a group, especially an activist or environmental group, members must learn and enact "identity codes" or ways of expressing that they are a specific kind of person.[47] These codes are ideological prescriptions for not only how they should act but also how they should feel and how they should express those feelings. For example, the Minnesota Mycological Society defined a good mycologist (or mushroomer) as someone who upheld the belief and practice that the natural world was to be treasured. By implication, good mycologists should be environmentally sensitive by picking fungi carefully and should take care not to damage other plants or flowers. They should demonstrate in their activities in nature—even while picking specimens—that they care about the wild.

In addition to learning identity codes and their implicit feeling rules, members of a group, such as a mycological society, build and sustain a collective identity, or a shared sense of "we-ness," through their articulation of shared emotions. As Michelle Wolkomir observed, group members do this "through the expression of two kinds of shared emotions: those that solidify resistance to opposing groups and those that support group ideologies and desired identity."[48] We can see this dichotomy among mushroomers in their resistance and objections to being seen by outsiders as weird or as living dangerously and in their often proclaimed beliefs of the value of being in the wild to collect what might otherwise be expensive and gourmet food.

Resource Mobilization

Beyond their grounding in community, rituals, and emotion work, ideologies are connected to a resource base, which shapes and constrains the speech, actions, and recruitment of supporters. Sociologists understand social movements in light of the central role of resources. Yet, in their efforts to go beyond traditional resource mobilization approaches to social movements, interactionists contend that analysis of resources should focus not only on the use value of resources but also on the centrality of symbols and symbolic goods as resources. Zurcher and Snow propose that "ideology is probably the best example of a resource that functions in a symbolic fashion and that is importantly related to a movement's mobilization efforts and organizational viability."[49] They suggest that ideological phrases, slogans, and patterns of rhetoric are vital resources that symbolize the nature and causes of discontent for movement actors and energize and justify their actions. Zurcher and Snow also point out that the concept of resources should be extended to incorporate symbols and symbolism, and the concept of mobilization should include symbolization, the process by which physical and social objects acquire meaning.[50] For mushroomers and other leisure groups, T-shirts, tote bags, bumper stickers (e.g., "I Break for Mushrooms"), and organizational handouts are important means of symbolization and mobilization.[51]

The presentation and enactment of ideologies involve the mobilization of those symbolic, emotional, and material resources necessary to create collective action frames. A key resource is the recognition that others feel similarly about an issue or event, or they can be made to feel that way—the realization of potent images and beliefs. Although necessary, recognition of the existence of a like-minded community is not sufficient for the enactment of ideology. This recognition must be coupled with a communications network that allows for the dissemination of beliefs and the coordination of action; a leadership or authority system that guides, controls, and routinizes action; and material resources that enable the expression of appropriate actions. Membership cards, newsletters, club elections, and objects such as mushroom guides serve these purposes. Thus, four conditions—public support, communications, authority, and material resources—are necessary for the effective expression of ideology.

The specific resources required for the enactment of an ideology depend on whether it is *challenging* (calling for systemic change) or *identificatory* (presenting a position that opposes or does not require change). Challenging enactments of ideology typically demand tighter organization and more powerful resources because of the socially consequential nature of the demands and the prospective hostile responses of those whose privileges are being attacked.

Each "ideological community" is based on a network of social relations, and each network has access to a set of resources. Holding an ideology does not mean that one must be a member of a social movement, but it does suggest that those who share particular images and metaphors belong to a group or collectivity that can be activated in certain circumstances. This process is dramatically evident in the case of environmental ideology and the environmental movement.

Environmentalism existed prior to the development of the latest wave of environmental movements in the 1970s.[52] The key to energizing the movement in the early 1970s was moral entrepreneurs finding symbolic images and personal threats that galvanized people, built on their values, and triggered the organization of groups with local angles that could direct action.[53] Because the environmental movement was particularly successful in appealing to wealthy and middle-class individuals who saw their lives and satisfaction threatened, it tapped into resources that enhanced its ideological impact.[54] Different groups appealed to segments of the environmentally aware public, and when coalitions were built and occasions for action defined, the movement became politically powerful. Access to resources combined with persuasive cultural images made environmentalism a crucial public concern. Environmental ideology has become increasingly central to public policy, in part because of the resources that environmental organizations can bring to bear on public debate. Ultimately, ideology is facilitated by social networks and their resources to have an impact. Ideologies provide "the cognitive map articulating the problem, focusing blame, and justifying action. However, social networks channel the diffusion of these ideas for action."[55]

Conclusions: Ideology in Action

Throughout this chapter, we have tried to examine ideology in a creative way. In doing so, we have drawn on insights from symbolic interactionist theory. Guided by interactionist insights, we have illustrated how people define and respond to nature in terms of ideological beliefs, which are linked to broader cultural images and definitions. In the process, we have revealed that (a) ideologies are based on a set of dramatic metaphors and images to which people respond based on their shared experience and expectations; (b) ideologies are not purely cognitive but depend crucially on emotional responses, expressions, and experiences; (c) the enactment of ideologies is fundamentally dramaturgical and relational—ideologies are presented at such times and in such ways as to enhance the public image (and justify the claims, feelings, or resources) of its presenters and supporters; and (d) ideologies are linked to groups and to the relationships between groups, which in turn depend on a set of resources to put ideologies into practice effectively. In making these arguments, we have illustrated how ideologies are symbolic, emotional, behavioral, and relational.

In focusing on these themes, we have avoided an overly abstract view of ideology, divorced from individual actors, that is frequently found in social scientific literature. We agree with anthropologist Clifford Geertz's (1973) claim that ideology is a "muddy river," and we have highlighted some useful concepts that can help social theorists filter and clarify it. Using symbolic interactionist theory, we have emphasized how ideologies can be linked to identity, emotion, dramaturgy, small groups, and social interaction, thereby portraying the value of this concept for microsociological analysis and, ultimately, for sociological understanding.

Notes

1. Parsons, T. (1951). *The social system*. New York: Free Press; Johnson, H. (1968). Ideology and the social system. *International Encyclopedia of the Social Sciences, 7*, 76-85; Marx, K., & Engels, F. (1976). The German ideology. In *Karl Marx-Frederick Engels Collected Works* (Vol. 5). New York: International (original work published 1846); Mannheim, K. (1936). *Ideology and utopia*. New York: Harcourt.

2. Ritzer, G. (2003). *The McDonaldization of society* (3rd ed.). Thousand Oaks, CA: Pine Forge Press; Williams, H. (1988). *Concepts of ideology*. New York: St. Martin's; Wuthnow, R. (1985). State structures and ideological outcomes. *American Sociological Review, 50*, 799-821; Althusser, L. (1971). *Lenin and philosophy*. London: New Left Books.

3. Sewell, W. H. (1985). Ideologies and social revolutions: Reflections on the French case. *Journal of Modern History, 57*(1), 57-85; Wuthnow, R. (1987). *Meaning and moral order*. Berkeley: University of California Press; Wuthnow, R. (1985). *American Sociological Review*.

4. Geertz, C. (1973). *The interpretation of culture.* New York: Basic Books; Hall, S. (1986). The problem of ideology: Marxism without guarantees. *Journal of Communication Inquiry, 10,* 28-44; Therborn, G. (1982). *The ideology of power and the power of ideology.* London: New Left Books.

5. Although ideology is not a central concept in Goffman's theory, his writings are closely connected to ideological themes. For instance, it is clear that ideological components (e.g., the desire to get by and to fit in) are heavily implicated in his Asylums and Stigma.

6. McLellan, D. (1986). *Ideology* (p. 1). Minneapolis: University of Minnesota Press.

7. Brown, L. (1973). *Ideology.* Harmondsworth, UK: Penguin.

8. Fine, G. A., & Sandstrom, K. (1993). Ideology in action: A pragmatic approach to a contested concept. *Sociological Theory, 11*(1), 21-38.

9. Blumer, H. (1969). *Symbolic interactionism: Perspective and method* (p. 2). Englewood Cliffs, NJ: Prentice Hall.

10. Blumer, H. (1969). *Symbolic interactionism,* p. 6.

11. For 3 years, Fine attended meetings of a local mycological society (with a membership of approximately 200) and spent dozens of hours in fields and forests with amateur mycologists searching for edible, beautiful, or intriguing mushrooms. In conjunction with this ethnographic observation, he conducted in-depth, audiotaped interviews with two dozen of these amateur mushroomers.

12. Dundes, A. (1972). Folk ideas as units of world view. *Journal of American Folklore, 84,* 95.

13. Dundes, A. (1972). *Journal of American Folklore 84,* 102.

14. Some bitter debates did occur over whether "commercial" enterprises should be regulated, particularly if these firms exported mushrooms. In this case, the discussion of "overpick" became tied to discourse about ecological nationalism and unemployment rates in the logging industry.

15. Thomas Gieryn proposes that scientists are similar to laypeople in this regard—that is, they are also guided by predominant cultural images, metaphors, and folk ideas in doing their research and in constructing or maintaining the boundaries of "science." See Gieryn, T. (1983). Boundary-work and the demarcation of science from non-science: Strains and interests in professional ideologies of scientists. *American Sociological Review, 48,* 781-795.

16. Gouldner, A. (1976). *The dialectic of ideology and technology* (p. 82). New York: Seabury.

17. Berger, P., & Luckmann, T. (1966). *The social construction of reality.* Garden City, NY: Doubleday.

18. As quoted in Nash, R. F. (1989). *The rights of nature* (p. 4). Madison: University of Wisconsin Press.

19. Billig, M. (1987). *Arguing and thinking.* Cambridge, UK: Cambridge University Press.

20. Raynor, J. D. (1980). The uses of ideological language. In D. J. Manning (Ed.), *The form of ideology* (pp. 104, 107). London: Allen & Unwin.

21. Dundes, A. (1972). *Journal of American Folklore;* Brown, R. H. (1977). *A poetic for sociology.* Chicago: University of Chicago Press; Gusfield, J. (1976). The literary rhetoric of science: Comedy and pathos in drinking driver research. *American Sociological Review, 41,* 16-33; Lakoff, G., & Johnson, M. (1980). *Metaphors we live by.* Chicago: University of Chicago Press; McCloskey, D. (1990). *If you're so smart: The narrative of economic expertise.* Chicago: University of Chicago Press; Nisbet, R. (1976). *Sociology as an art form.* New York: Oxford University Press.

22. Gieryn suggests that ideologies may have stylistic variations (regarding their use of hyperbole, irony, sarcasm, etc.) and stresses the need for analysts to "specify the social conditions in which ideologies might be expected to take one or another stylistic form." His point is well taken, although the specific tropes that make ideological metaphors

distinctive are not our concern here. See Gieryn, T. (1983). *American Sociological Review, 48,* 777-778.

23. Wuthnow. R. (1987). *Meaning and moral order.*

24. Imagine how public reaction would have differed if the term had been "acidic rain" or even "slightly acidic rain."

25. Garrett Hardin suggests that the existence of a label may also provoke a counter-movement, which now perceives that it has something to defend. See Hardin, G. (1974). Foreword. In C. D. Stone (Ed.), *Should trees have standing?* (p. x). Los Altos, CA: Kaufmann.

26. Becker, H. S. (1963). *Outsiders: Studies in the sociology of deviance* (pp. 147ff.). New York: Free Press; see also Sandstrom, K., Martin, D., & Fine, G. A. (2003). *Symbols, selves, and social reality* (p. 155). Los Angeles: Roxbury.

27. See, for example, Best, J. (1987). Rhetoric in claims-making: Constructing the missing children problem. *Social Problems, 34,* 101-121; Best, J. (1990). *Threatened children.* Chicago: University of Chicago Press.

28. Hochschild, A. (1983). *The managed heart.* Berkeley: University of California Press; Clark, C. (1987). Sympathy biography and sympathy margin. *American Journal of Sociology, 93,* 290-321; Kleinman, S. (1996). *Opposing ambitions: Gender and identity in an alternative organization.* Chicago: University of Chicago Press; Martin, D. (2000). Organizational approaches to shame: Management, announcement, and contestation. *Sociological Quarterly, 41,* 125-150; Pierce, J. (1995). *Gender trials: Emotional lives in contemporary law firms.* Berkeley: University of California Press.

29. Wilson, D. S. (1978). *In the presence of nature* (pp. 1, 11). Amherst: University of Massachusetts Press.

30. This "feeling" is not localized to a single cultural system as a wide array of cross-cultural evidence suggests. A powerful bond exists between people and their world, a bond that transcends individual cultural systems, even though its expression is dependent on them. Because human society depends for its survival and satisfaction on the natural environment, an attempt to connect oneself to this reality is faced by all (or most) human systems.

31. Goffman, E. (1974). *Frame analysis* (p. 11). Cambridge, MA: Harvard University Press.

32. Wuthnow. R. (1987). *Meaning and moral order,* p. 147.

33. Gamson, W. A., Fireman, B., & Rytina, S. (1982). *Encounters with unjust authority.* Homewood, IL: Dorsey.

34. Goffman, E. (1974). *Frame analysis,* p. 44.

35. Snow, D., Burke Rochford, E., Worden, S., & Benford, R. (1986). Frame alignment processes, micro-mobilization, and movement participation. *American Journal of Sociology, 51,* 464-481.

36. Snow, D., & Benford, R. (1998). Ideology, frame resonance, and participant mobilization. *International Social Movement Research, 1,* 197-217.

37. McAdam, D. (1982). *Political process and the development of black insurgency, 1930-1970.* Chicago: University of Chicago Press; Piven, F., & Cloward, R. (1979). *Poor people's movements.* New York: Vintage.

38. Schwalbe, M. (2001). *The sociologically examined life* (2nd ed., p. 16). Mountain View, CA: Mayfield.

39. Fine, G. A. (1979). Small groups and culture creation: Idioculture of Little League baseball teams. *American Sociological Review, 44*(5), 733-745.

40. We are not claiming that ideologies can only be transmitted within the framework of the small group, denying the pervasive power of the mass media. Rather, our claim is that ideologies, like culture, can be understood as arising out of group interaction.

41. Mullins, W. (1972). On the concept of ideology in political science. *American Political Science Review, 66,* 509.

42. Manning, D. (1976). *Liberalism* (pp. 154-155). New York: St. Martin's.

43. Bales, R. (1970). *Personality and interpersonal behavior* (pp. 153-154). New York: Holt, Rinehart & Winston.

44. Gouldner, A. (1976). *The dialectic of ideology and technology,* p. 81.

45. Collins, R. (1981). On the micro-foundations of macro-sociology. *American Journal of Sociology, 86,* 984-1014; Turner, J. (1988). *A theory of social interaction.* Stanford, CA: Stanford University Press.

46. In the following discussion, we draw heavily on Michelle Wolkomir's cogent insights regarding the links between emotion, identity work, group commitment, and ideological enactment. See Wolkomir, M. (2001). Emotion work, commitment, and the authentication of the self: The case of gay and ex-gay Christian support groups. *Journal of Contemporary Ethnography, 30,* 305-334.

47. Schwalbe, M. L., & Mason-Schrock, D. (1996). Identity work as a group process. In B. Markovsky, M. Lovaglia, & R. Simon (Eds.), *Advances in group processes* (pp. 113-147). Greenwich, CT: JAI.

48. Wolkomir, M. (2001). *Journal of Contemporary Ethnography, 30,* 322.

49. Zurcher, L., & Snow, D. (1981). Collective behavior: Social movements. In R. Turner & M. Rosenberg (Eds.), *Social psychology* (pp. 447-482). New York: Basic Books.

50. Zurcher, L., & Snow, D. (1981). In *Social psychology,* p. 471.

51. For a more extensive discussion of resource mobilization among mushroomers, see Fine, G. A. (1998). *Morel tales: The culture of mushrooming* (pp. 164-204). Cambridge, MA: Harvard University Press.

52. Fox, S. (1981). *The American conservation movement: John Muir and his legacy.* Madison: University of Wisconsin Press; O'Brien, J. (1983). Environmentalism as a mass movement: Historical notes. *Radical America, 17,* 7-27.

53. See Ennis, J., & Scheuer, R. (1987). Mobilizing weak support for social movements: The role of grievance, efficacy and cost. *Social Forces, 66,* 390-409; Klandermans, B. (1984). Mobilization and participation: Social psychological expansions of resource mobilization theory. *American Sociological Review, 49,* 583-600.

54. According to Paul Mohai, this belief is a function of environmental activists being largely upper-middle class, whereas environmental supporters transcend class lines. This argument is not, of course, inconsistent with ours, which suggests that the resources have been successfully acquired from upper-middle-class activists and supporters. See Mohai, P. (1985). Public concern and elite involvement in environmental-conservation issues. *Social Science Quarterly, 66,* 820-838.

55. Zurcher, L., & Snow, D. (1981). In *Social psychology,* p. 458.

Discussion Questions

1. How does the authors' view of ideology differ from more traditional sociological views? What do the authors see as the key components of ideology? Do you agree or disagree with their argument that ideology is grounded in dramatic images and moral metaphors? How do they support this argument through their discussion of environmental ideologies? What are some of the limitations of their analysis? For instance, how might you critique it from a Marxist or Weberian point of view?

2. The authors claim that human understandings of nature are not "natural." What do they mean by this? Do you agree or disagree with their claim? What is your view of "nature" and people's relationship to it? Do you think that nature should have rights of any kind, such as the right to be preserved? What do you see as the important aspects of nature? What ideological beliefs and cultural images guide you as you make these judgments?

3. Imagine you want to start a movement on your campus to raise concern about an environmental issue, such as global warming or the privatization of our natural parks. How would this chapter be useful to you? For instance, what images or metaphors would you draw on to appeal to your fellow students? How would you try to align your beliefs and "action frame" with theirs? If you successfully formed an environmental group, what role would ideology play in shaping the emotions, identities, and interactions of group members? How would it serve as a boundary with "one-way permeability"?

CHAPTER 10

Goffman's Dramaturgical Sociology

Personal Sales and Service in a Commodified World

Peter Kivisto and Dan Pittman

Peter Kivisto *is the Richard Swanson Professor of Social Thought and Chair of Sociology at Augustana College, where he has taught continuously since obtaining his PhD in sociology from the New School for Social Research in New York City. It was in the unique environment of the New School that he came to appreciate the importance of social theory for making sense of the social issues that are important to him. His major interests revolve around exploring the implications of racial and ethnic groups living in a society that is both capitalist and democratic. His dissertation research, for example, involved a historical excursion into the world created by Finnish American political radicals, which appeared as his first book,* Immigrant Socialists in the United States *(1984). He coauthored, with Ronald Glassman and William H. Swatos, Jr., For* Democracy *(1993) and published* Multiculturalism in a Global Society *(2002). He has recently published a second edition of his brief theory text for Pine Forge titled Key* Ideas in Sociology *(2004). With Thomas Faist, he is currently working on a book on the future of citizenship.*

Dan Pittman *is a Phi Beta Kappa graduate of Augustana College, where he majored in sociology and philosophy. He grew up in an academic environment in Iowa City. He completed law school at New York University, where he served as a staff editor for the* Annual Survey of American Law. *He is a member of the New York bar, employed by the New York City law firm of Carter, Ledyard, and Milburn. At the moment, he is also* *pursuing a master's degree in taxation at NYU. As an avocation, he remains engaged in a project concerned with the cultural roots of the blues, in which he examines the movement of the blues out of its rural origins in the Mississippi Delta to northern cities.*

The original inspiration for dramaturgical sociology, the subject of this chapter, derives from the greatest playwright in the English language: William Shakespeare. It was Shakespeare who adorned London's famous Globe Theater with the Latin motto, *Totus Mundus Agit Histrionem* (All the World Is a Theater) and who wrote the following lines for Jacques in *As You Like It:* "All the world's a stage, and all the men and women merely players."

For Erving Goffman (1922-1982), arguably the most original American theorist of the second half of the 20th century, the metaphor of life as theater is rich in meaning. He sees all human interaction as, in some ways, very much like a grand play. He is not, however, as concerned with sweeping generalizations about the human condition as he is with the particulars of daily life—the microlevel interactions between individuals that, when taken together, constitute the human experience. At this microlevel, he argues, the world is much more like a stage than we commonly realize.

For Goffman, the subject matter of dramaturgical sociology is the creation, maintenance, and destruction of common understandings of reality by people working individually and collectively to present a shared and unified image of that reality. The brilliant insight that makes Goffman's book *The Presentation of Self in Everyday Life* (1959) so significant is that this process, which he believes lies concealed deep within every interaction, is familiar to all of us in the form of the theater. In a play, actors try to convey to an audience a particular impression of the world around them. Through the use of scripted dialogue, gestures, props, costumes, and so on, actors create a new reality for the audience to consider.

It is Goffman's claim that if we understand how a contemporary American actor can convey an impression of an angst-ridden Danish prince during a presentation of *Hamlet,* we can also understand how an insurance agent tries to act like a professional operating with a combination of expert knowledge and goodwill. If we can understand how a small stage can be used to represent all of Rome and Egypt in *Antony and Cleopatra,* we can also understand how a Disney store creates a sense of adventure and wonder in any local mall. Also, if we can understand the process by which two paid actors convince us that they are madly in love in *Romeo and Juliet,* we can understand how flight attendants manage and use their emotions for commercial gain. In this chapter, we will attempt to explain aspects of Goffman's metaphor by taking insurance agents, employees of the Walt Disney corporation, flight attendants, and car salespeople as examples of how people create alternate realities. Beyond the metaphor of social life as dramatic ritual, Goffman sensed the potential for alienation brought about because of the problems of authentically embracing a role rather than feeling a certain ambivalence or distance from it. This alienation is also critical to Goffman's analysis.

Before directly reviewing Goffman's dramaturgical analysis of social interaction, we must briefly consider his rather unique conception of selfhood because it is crucial to his method of analysis. Goffman does not believe in a "self" in the traditional sense; he does not think that we can discuss people's selves abstracted from their social situations. He writes,

> This self itself does not derive from its possessor, but from the whole scene of his action . . . this self is a product of a scene that comes off, and not a cause of it. The self, then, as a performed character, is not an organic thing that has specific location . . . [the individual and his body] merely provide the peg on which something of collaborative manufacture will be hung for a time. And the means for producing and maintaining selves do not reside inside the peg.[1]

Goffman is arguing here that the self is not an entity that is in some sense antecedent to its enactment but rather that it arises in the very process of performance. What is crucial is a recognition that, for Goffman, talking about the individual as some sort of autonomous agent is incorrect; rather, the individual should be thought of always in relationship to a social whole. Thus, the fundamental unit of social analysis, for Goffman, is not the individual but rather what he refers to as the "team." He writes, "a teammate is someone whose dramaturgical cooperation one is dependent upon in fostering a given definition of the situation."[2] Teams, then, are responsible for the creation of perceptions of reality in social settings. The crux of his dramaturgical social theory is that the analysis of how teams cooperate to foster particular impressions of reality reveals a complex system of interactions that, in many ways, is like the presentation of a play.

Goffman assumes that his theory could be applied to all social activities, but it is especially visible in certain commercial settings. This will be illustrated in the four examples we have chosen to employ. The first is Arlie Hochschild's *The Managed Heart* (1983), in which she looks at the world of airline flight attendants. She describes the types of social interaction found among flight attendants, contending that the entire flight crew must form a coherent, unified team intent on conveying to passengers a sense of competence and friendliness. If any attendant started behaving rudely or, worse, incompetently, the entire project would fail. Similarly, employees in the Disney store, the focus of Kelly Kraft's ethnographic study, must all foster a sense of adventure and wonder for customers; if one employee looks sullen and bored, the atmosphere will be lost, and the team's attempt to convey a particular understanding of reality will be deemed a failure. The final examples we use come from Guy Oakes's study of insurance salespeople and Stephen Miller's car salesmen, who, as we shall see, must expend considerable energy to establish a particular impression of who they are and what they can do for a customer if they are to be successful.

How do people convince other people—specifically consumers—to adopt a particular understanding of various social scenes? Goffman says that this is accomplished by using the tools of the theater. It takes collaborative effort to stage a convincing performance, complete with roles, scripts, costumes, and a stage. Only when all these are employed to create a coherent picture of reality can a team be successful.

Roles

A crucial part of Goffman's dramaturgical metaphor is the role. Generally, the role is the particular image that a single actor wants to convey. It is the essence, the contrived sense of self, that the individual wants to project to the world. Just as an actor may adopt the role of a troubled Danish prince or a blues-loving ex-con, individuals in social settings must adopt the traits necessary to the understanding of reality they want to project. For instance, Guy Oakes argues that to effectively sell insurance, one must adopt the role of the dedicated and knowledgeable professional.

Of course, most people in white-collar careers must put on a display of professionalism. In many ways, however, Oakes suggests, the insurance agent has a more difficult task than other professionals. For various reasons, there is a widespread public perception that insurance agents are sleazy and underhanded. As one of the insurance agents Oakes interviewed stated, "You really get shit on in this business."[3]

The more insurance agents in general are believed to be sleazy, the harder particular insurance agents must work to avoid demonstrating these qualities. Being perceived as a "professional" is an ideal way to provide agents with the credibility they so desperately need to close sales. The aspiring agent must figure out precisely what is required to successfully convey a professional role, which, Oakes states in the following passage, involves an emphasis on expertise and advice rather than a single-minded emphasis on selling a product:

> Like . . . other professionals, the agent claims to be an expert in the solution of certain problems in which the public has a substantial interest. The agent places this expertise at the disposal of a client, who receives confidential advice. . . . This is why training manuals describe the agent as a "financial doctor." The buyer/seller conception of salesmanship is relegated to the pioneer days of personal selling. It is replaced by the professional/client relationship, in which the function of the agent is to assist clients in solving their problems by applying specialized skills and offering expert advice.[4]

Insurance agents must understand not only that they are to present themselves as experts who want to help but also that they have enough knowledge of the life insurance industry to actually be of assistance. Most insurance agencies provide comprehensive training to prospective agents. This training process serves a dual purpose. First, of course, is to make sure that agents have all the information they will eventually need. It is difficult to look like a credible professional if one does not understand what one is selling. Second, although the training process itself has value to the industry, if there is a public perception that agents need special education, agents will instantly get a certain credibility—they will look like professionals—when they obtain some kind of educational credential. Goffman explains this as follows:

> Labor unions, universities, trade associations, and other licensing bodies require practitioners to absorb a mystical range and period of training . . . in part to foster the impression that the licensed practitioner is someone who has been reconstituted by his learning experience and is now set apart from other men.[5]

Airline flight attendants must adopt a role that imposes rather different demands and expectations from that of insurance agents. Flight attendants have more direct contact with the public than anyone else in an airline and therefore have many responsibilities associated with the comfort and safety of passengers. Ultimately, when customers remember a particular flight, they will almost certainly remember the flight attendants more than any other airline employee. Flight attendants represent the public face of the entire company. The most basic role of the flight attendant is to be pleasant and reassuring. This is emphasized in airline advertisements:

> Through the 1950s and 1960s the flight attendant became a main subject of airline advertising, the spearhead of market expansion. The image they chose, among many possible ones, was that of a beautiful and smartly dressed Southern white woman, the supposed epitome of gracious manners and warm personal service.[6]

The stewardess[7] is supposed to represent all the things passengers would like to see in servants—they are graceful, elegant, friendly, and, above all, constantly smiling. This is such a crucial component of the flight attendant's job that it is emphasized even before the interview. Hochschild noted,

> Applicants are urged to read a preinterview pamphlet before coming in. In the 1979-1980 *Airline Guide to Stewardess and Steward Careers,* there is a section called "The Interview." Under the subheading "Appearance," the manual suggests that facial expressions should be "sincere" and "unaffected." One should have a "modest but friendly smile" and be "generally alert, attentive, not overly aggressive, but not reticent either." Under "Mannerisms," subheading "Friendliness," it is suggested that a successful candidate must be "outgoing but not effusive," "enthusiastic with calm and poise," and "vivacious but not effervescent."[8]

In addition to these components of the role, individual airlines add other requirements. There are relatively few qualitative differences between airlines, but to the extent that airlines want to individuate themselves, to stand out in a crowded market, their flight attendants must be in some way unique. Thus, during the time of her study, Hochschild found that, "United Airlines, the consensus has it, is 'the girl-next-door,' the neighborhood babysitter grown up. Pan Am is upper class, sophisticated, and slightly reserved in its graciousness. PSA is brassy, fun-loving, and sexy."[9]

Some companies have tried to further individuate themselves by making their flight attendants adopt semisexualized roles in an attempt to appeal to certain segments of the market. Hochschild noted the following:

> The omnipresent smile [in airline advertisements] suggests, first of all, that the flight attendant is friendly, helpful, and open to requests. But when words are added, the smile can be sexualized, as in "We really move our tails for you to

make your every wish come true" (Continental) or "Fly me, you'll like it" (National). Such innuendoes lend strength to the conventional fantasy that in the air, anything can happen. . . . The sexualized ad burdens the flight attendant with another task, beyond being unfailingly helpful and open to requests: She must respond to the sexual fantasies of passengers. She must try to feel and act as if flirting and propositioning are "a sign of my attractiveness and your sexiness," and she must work to suppress her feelings that such behavior is intrusive or demeaning.[10]

The role of the flight attendant is very tightly circumscribed. At a minimum, the flight attendant must project an impression of friendliness and pleasantness; usually more requirements are added to the role to fit the desires of the particular airline. Of course, flight attendants have other requirements as well. They must know where safety equipment is located, they must make sure that passengers are complying with safety regulations, and they must be able to efficiently and calmly instruct passengers about what to do in case of various types of emergencies. Airlines do not want to play up these features, however, because to mention them would be to raise questions about the airline's safety.

No matter how well an actor understands his or her role, he or she must be capable of conveying it to an audience. In Goffman's sociology, the common or shared understanding of reality *is* reality. A "friendly" flight attendant who seems surly will not please management; a wealthy insurance agent who dresses shabbily probably will not sell many policies. An actor who cannot manipulate the common understanding successfully will be a failure. Goffman's sociology, then, is the study of how people get other people to see things in a certain way. They do this, he claims, by using a variety of theatrical tools.

Scripts

Perhaps the most important means of getting an audience to understand a role is a script; certainly theater as we know it relies on them. Goffman claims that scripts are vital to interpersonal interaction as well. Of course, most interpersonal communication is relatively improvisational—we make it up as we go along. In everyday life, however, some elements of conversation are pretty well scripted. If a person asks a casual acquaintance how he or she is doing, he or she is likely to reply with a simple "Fine, yourself?" rather than a sincere, well-thought-out description of what he or she is really thinking or feeling at the moment. This is a fragment of conversation that we are so used to employing that it feels automatic. Thus, scripts can allow us a great deal of convenience; they constitute a taken-for-granted quality in which, rather than creating our lines out of whole cloth, we borrow from a stock of well-worn scripts.

Commercial settings often make use of increasingly formalized scripts, which can provide distinct advantages to all parties. Often, retail store managers write scripts that are passed down to the people who must actually go about making sales. One extreme example of this is provided by the Disney company, which, as Kraft discovered in her research, gives staffers (or "Cast Members," in their words) a set of rigidly prescribed scripts:

> These scripts offer verbatim responses Disney Store executives would like to hear used by Cast Members. . . . Frequently, a Cast Member becomes dependent on the scripts and mindlessly repeats the same message to every guest he or she encounters. The greeting traditionally offered at the front of the store is an example of how closely the scripts are followed. When a Cast Member was trained in 1991, he or she received a handout [which included the statement] "When you are greeting, the exact script is 'Hi! Welcome to the Disney Store!' There are to be no variations of this script used . . . ever."[11]

In this case, a script is used to control and limit employee autonomy. The management has a particular role that it wants employees to adopt: friendly, cheerful, and helpful, but somewhat aloof, like a cartoon character. Disney corporate officials have concluded that the best way to ensure that employees actually adopt this role is to force it on them. It should also be noted that the scripts sometimes have advantages for the clerks. Kraft noted that cast members frequently become reliant on the scripts, using them as convenient crutches. Similarly, many telephone solicitors use obviously scripted messages when they call people; reading scripts is a simple process that requires little training or thought and thus makes the solicitor's job much easier.

Script use in direct sales is in no way limited to controlling employees or providing a convenience in place of more sophisticated kinds of training. Frequently, scripts are used to control customers to compel them to buy a given product. Car sellers need to have a very comprehensive understanding of their customers, and to gain it they often employ an almost ritualized conversation. For instance, Stephen Miller learned the following in his study of this much maligned occupation:

> The salesman employs the demonstration ride to establish a situation in which the customer will communicate to the salesman what he values in an automobile and why, information which can be used to stress the merits of the automobile being considered and influence a decision.[12]

One salesman explained this technique, claiming, "I ask him how he likes the way it handles, how about the power and a lot of other things. . . . By the time we finish the ride, I have a good idea of what he wants in a car."[13]

By using a strictly patterned conversational format, the agent can gain insights into what will make the customer buy a car. To the extent that these conversations follow a predictable form, they are scripted, even though the particulars of the discussion will change from one customer to the next.

Furthermore, there is a sense in which the entire sales transaction follows a loose script. Miller divides the process of selling a car into three stages, the second and third arising as a logical result of the previous stage. First comes the "contact," when a salesperson first interacts with someone who may or may not be interested in buying a car. If the potential customer shows any interest, the transaction moves into the second stage, the "pitch," in which the agent attempts to size up precisely what the customer wants and how much he or she will pay for it. Finally, if the customer does not walk out during the pitch, the transaction proceeds to the final stage, the "close," in which the agent tries to get the customer to agree with the agent's understanding of this particular social reality—that is, tries to convince the customer to pay a certain amount for a particular car.

In a sense, these distinct stages of the transaction look like different scenes in a play; each has it own rules, each follows from the developments of the preceding scenes, and the action (if the agent is successful) rises to a cathartic agreement and ultimate resolution in the final act. In a sense, then, sales transactions seem scripted at the level of both individual lines and the broad outlines of the play. In both cases, the script is used to control the customer, to get him or her to see reality the same way the car seller sees it.

In a play, the script is often the most important aspect of one's role—ultimately we are more likely to remember Hamlet's soliloquies than the stage directions or what kind of jewelry he wore. In social interaction, this is not always the case. First, scripted interaction in real life is rarely mutual; the seller is following a script that the buyer is generally unaware of and therefore may not follow. Also, as noted previously, scripted interaction is rarely formal; although the car seller has a general notion of what kinds of things need to be said and when, how to phrase individual lines is usually improvisational so that the script is more of a general outline than a specific blueprint. Because the script is not quite as important in social interaction as it is in theater, we can expect many other tools of the actor to play a slightly larger part in conveying a person's role in a social interaction than those same tools do in a play. An individual selling a car cannot control with precision what the customer will say, so he or she must focus attention more on those things that can be controlled.

Costumes

One element that most actors have complete control over is their costume. This is fortunate, because what a person is wearing is probably the quickest way to form an impression of them and their social status. Before a word is uttered in a play, we can size up characters on stage; the one wearing tattered rags is probably much poorer than the one wearing a fine suit, and so on. In precisely the same way, an individual's wardrobe is vital to presenting to the audience his or her particular role in the drama being played out at the moment.

For instance, as noted previously, insurance sellers have a tremendous incentive to look like professionals. This suggests several aspects about their wardrobe. First, of course, because professionals are supposed to be relatively well-off financially (especially, one would hope, professionals in financial services), agents would be wise to adopt the dress and habits of the financially secure. This might partially explain why companies frequently give prizes such as gold watches and vacations to exotic locales to agents who are especially productive[14]—flashy watches and nice tans are luxuries that come with relative wealth. Although insurance agents generally do not make enough money to qualify as rich, it is helpful if their costumes suggest that they do qualify.

Second, there is more to the costume of the agent than just a suggestion of wealth. One of the selling points of most insurance policies is that they are relatively secure investments; agents urge potential customers to take a fiscally conservative approach to investing. Obviously, it is easier to take someone dressed in a sober business suit seriously on this point than, for example, someone wearing leather pants and an outrageous jacket.

Not all costumes are intended to say the same things, however. Roles that do not involve notions of professionalism may require different types of clothing. At the Disney Store, for example, employees must conform to a very strict dress code, which includes white shoes, pink shirts, and blue cardigans with an "M" on the lower left-hand side. Men must wear gray polyester pants; women must wear gray polyester skirts.[15] Obviously, these costumes are not designed to suggest that the cast members are part of the educated professional class; rather, they tie into a notion of nostalgia that Disney is trying to establish and exploit.

Stages and Sets

The other major tool the actor can employ to control audience reaction is the stage and its setting. If, as the curtain rises, the audience sees what looks like the inside of a mansion, they will assume certain things about what the play will be about— things they would not assume if the curtain rose on a jungle scene. The physical environment of a play, then, can provide a context for the action that is to follow, locating it at a particular point in space and time in the audience's mind. Similarly, the use of the physical environment can establish a context for social interaction; if used skillfully, it can help one team convince the other to adopt the preferred understanding of reality.

Perhaps the most obvious aspect of using stages is the introduction of scenery. Of course, some sellers have very little control over the scenery at their place of work; the door-to-door salesperson, for instance, must work with whatever scenery he or she finds in a particular home. Sometimes, however, sellers have a great deal of control over their environments and use it effectively. The Disney Corporation has spent tremendous amounts of time and money designing the scenery in its retail stores to foster an impression of a fantasy world of some sort, right down to selecting the soundtracks that best evoke this conjured reality. Kraft noted that

> The music playing in the background is a mixture of classic and new Disney tunes. The songs are designed to remind one of a special childhood memory or a much loved movie. . . . The music is intended to capture the imagination and transport the shopper further into the depths of the Magic Kingdom. It is easy to become captivated by the shelves stuffed with familiar characters. Before too long, the shopper has become completely enveloped by the package. The Disney Store is intended to offer more than the average retail shopping experience. It attempts to bring a piece of the Magic Kingdom to all who "visit."[16]

With this manipulation of the physical surroundings, Disney tries to make the process of shopping less like a banal consumer experience and more like some kind of mild adventure, or at least a nostalgia trip. Manipulation of scenery is part of a conscious effort to replace the mundane with the fantastic—that is, to change people's perceptions of reality.

Another use of stages that is common in many social interactions is the division between front and back stages. The front stage is what confronts the audience: It is what they see. The back stage, by contrast, is a place where all the support activities necessary for maintaining the performance on the main stage will go on. In theater, the back stage is where actors who are not involved in the scene going on at the moment mill about, where props that will be used at other times are stored, and where the counterbalances, lights, and so on that make the scenery convincing to the audience are hidden. Goffman points out that the crucial element that allows the back stage to be useful for these purposes is that "the back region will be the place where the performer can reliably expect that no member of the audience will intrude."[17] Thus, most back regions are clearly divided from the public fronts so that only team members have access. Manifestations of region-specific behavior abound in everyday life. Goffman claims that putting locks on bathroom stall doors exhibits a certain region behavior because presumably while one is in the stall the public front cannot be maintained.[18] Houses are divided along these front stage/back stage lines as well; guests are frequently confined to living and dining rooms and rarely invited to see bedrooms or bathrooms. Similarly, many houses have front doors that are used primarily for more formal situations; family members often use back or side doors for day-to-day admission.

Offstage regions have two major purposes, both related to the maintenance of the proper front on stage. They must serve as a storing ground for physical items that cannot be on stage, and they must also provide employees a place to recoup, a place where they take care of their emotional needs. The physical requirements of back stage may not be particularly surprising. Most retail shops, for instance, try not to clutter the stage with too much stuff but want to have enough of certain popular items to ensure that they will not run out. A storeroom, then, is crucial. Shoe stores offer perhaps the best example of this; most of them leave one pair of each style of shoe on display, but because they need several pairs of each size of shoe in each style to satisfy customers, they have a need for a well-organized back stage, where piles of shoe boxes can sit without being observed. Back regions are also helpful for storing things not sold by the business but that are vital to the maintenance of the proper atmosphere on stage. Retail stores are almost uniformly clean; this means that vacuum cleaners, mops, glass cleaners, and so on must be kept where they can be accessed regularly, but because cleanliness usually mandates a lack of visible cleaning supplies, the equipment must be hidden from public scrutiny.

The physical requirements of back regions in commerce are frequently rather mundane, as these examples show. Back stages often have a more interesting purpose as well; they often provide for the emotional needs of employees so that they can continue to give the proper performance on stage. One crucial element is the informality afforded by the back stage. During a performance, people have to be constantly vigilant to ensure that they do not betray their roles; they must stay in character, follow whatever script they are using, and so on. Such rigidity can be exhausting, and the ability to go to a place where the audience will not see or hear anything provides a safety valve for employees. Thus, backstage areas provide employees with an opportunity to take a break. Indeed, this is frequently the chief function of one backstage region, the break room, where employees can sit down, have some coffee, and relax for a few minutes before continuing the show at hand.

Backstage areas are also useful in that they allow team members to discuss with each other what could be changed about the performance if, for example, one member of the team is failing or if the customer is behaving oddly. In retail stores, then, one would expect most discussions that are not directly parts of the performance to only occur backstage, and almost all parts of the early training process in almost all vocations occur away from the public arena.

The degree to which region behavior is engraved in the consumer's consciousness can be highlighted by an example that shows how this very awareness of the difference between front and back stages is exploited by some businesses to further the impression they want to foster. Car buyers, according to Miller, are not often given access to information such as the actual cost to a dealership of a car or the average selling price of the car, so they have to negotiate, to a certain extent, blindly. This allows the dealerships to get the best possible deal for themselves while leaving the customer, who presumably has haggled a few thousand dollars off the sticker price by the end of the negotiation, feeling satisfied. One technique many dealers employ to guarantee this satisfaction is "changing sides," in which salespeople seem to come to the conclusion that the customer is getting the better end of the deal but that, because they like the customer, they will act as advocates for the customer and get the deal approved by the hostile sales manager. This is where the use of space comes into the picture. At this point in the negotiations, the seller will go into the sales office. This is an office inside the dealership where the sales manager approves contracts. The customers see the seller walk into the office but cannot hear what goes on inside it. Presumably, then, the office is a backstage area. The seller and the sales manager, however, are fully aware that the customer is waiting, outside, paying close attention to the office. They frequently use this knowledge to dupe the customer. Miller quotes one sales manager, describing what goes on in the office as follows: "He [the salesman] comes to me and says, 'Here you are' . . . I OK the deal . . . he ain't going to come to me with a bad one . . . he waits, sits down, smokes a cigarette, then goes back to the customer."[19]

Although the process need only take a few moments, it is prolonged so that the customer will get nervous. Presumably, the customer will think the only reason this could take so long is that the deal is being debated hotly. As time passes, the customer will get increasingly nervous and increasingly confident that he or she has indeed driven a hard bargain—perhaps too hard. This is confirmed when

the salesman, on his return to the customer, says he encountered difficulty in having the deal accepted ("you sure got me in a lot of trouble") but that he managed to convince the sales manager ("I got him to accept your deal"). By further implication, the salesman manages to communicate to the buyer that he is a unique and shrewd negotiator ("I'm glad I don't get many like you").[20]

The office, in this case, serves as a tool for fostering the impression of reality that the dealership hopes to convey to the customer, although only because it is thought of as a backstage region even by the customer. This is especially the case in dealerships in which the sales office has windows through which the customer can peek; one would expect to see wild gesticulations and some red faces, although in all probability the manager and seller would be discussing where to go to lunch because the performers know that aurally they are back stage while visually they are on stage.

In this case, the car dealership is participating in a complex interaction; it is a version of what Goffman called a play within a play, used to make audience members think they are seeing a behind-the-scenes interaction that is, of course, on stage:

> In brief, a glimpse behind the scenes can be a device for inducing the belief that you are seeing the backstage of something. Obviously, once you've got the staging area and the backstage you've got the whole thing and can feel secure in your frame anchorage. And the moment you feel secure, of course, is the moment you can be diddled.[21]

The sense of security the customer gets in seeing the supposedly offstage rituals of the salesman and sales manager allows the final stage of the sales process to be completed successfully and amicably, although a good deal of manipulation and misinformation is engaged in before this conclusion can be reached.

Impression Management and Sincerity

Stages and region behavior provide important tools for the manipulation of public perceptions of reality. Combined with scripts, props, and costumes, they allow teams a great deal of control over the impression of reality they convey to audiences. Goffman's analysis is concerned with more than the process of manipulation, however; he is also concerned with the effects of manipulation on the actor. At the most basic level, all the methods described previously, and indeed the very idea of projecting a particular impression of reality, can lead to a certain insincerity. Goffman is very interested in how this insincerity comes about, what actors do to counteract it, and what happens if they are unsuccessful in the attempt to deal with insincerity. The theater example we have been following becomes less relevant at this point; obviously, actors in a play know that the impression of reality they want to project is not "real"; they know they are not Danish princes or poor Londoners. Rather, Goffman is interested in the problems caused by living life like a play—on how that affects a person's psychological state and behavior.

As Goffman claims in the following, whenever actors adopt a role, they must take a position on their belief in the role—they must decide whether they feel that the impression of reality they will project is "true":

> At one extreme, one finds that the performer can be fully taken in by his own act; he can be sincerely convinced that the impression of reality which he stages is the real reality. . . . At the other extreme, we find that the performer may not

be taken in at all by his own routine. This possibility is understandable, since no one is in quite as good an observational position to see through the act as the person who puts it on. . . . When the individual has no belief in his own act and no ultimate concern with the beliefs of his audience, we may call him cynical, reserving the term "sincere" for individuals who believe in the impression fostered by their own performances.[22]

It is important to note that although individuals can be anywhere in between these two extremes of belief in their own performance, they must be somewhere— that is, every performer must, consciously or not, have some level of acceptance of the part he or she is playing.

Obviously, in most cases, it will be much easier to present a convincing performance if one is relatively sincere about one's performance, and consequently, many teams will go to great lengths to convince individual performers of the reality of their presentation. The insurance industry goes to great lengths to prevent agents from becoming cynical because buyers find it difficult to trust agents who are not committed to their product and because agents are very likely to "burn out" quickly if they do not believe in what they are doing.[23] Agencies are well aware of this and go to great lengths to convince their vendors to believe in the product they are selling. To foster genuine belief in the value of life insurance, they promote what Oakes calls "the philosophy of financial security."[24] This philosophy claims that, macroeconomic trends and luck notwithstanding, each individual is directly responsible for his or her economic lot in life. Furthermore, the purpose of life is, according to this philosophy, to provide financial security for one's self and loved ones. Because each individual is capable of attaining this goal, it is simple to measure people's goodness by their net worth and, more generally, their ability to provide for their family.

Once the insurance agent begins to believe this simple but compelling picture of his or her role, the agent can often be convinced that the role he or she is about to assume is not one of huckster trying to profit off other people's misfortunes but instead approaches that of hero because, as Oakes explains,

Life insurance agents constitute the priesthood of the religion of life insurance, the ministers and guardians of financial security planning. Because life insurance sales is legitimated as a high calling based on ethical imperatives, conscientious agents do not wait for financial exigencies in the lives of prospects to bring in business. For the prospect whose health and security are at stake, tomorrow may be too late. Because of their obligation to safeguard the financial future of prospects, agents are able to take pride in the fact that they are sales personnel. Agents justify their work by conceiving it not as a commercial transaction, but as an exercise of moral responsibility.[25]

In Goffman's language, the industry has an interest in fostering sincerity on the part of their agents. Insurance, for them, must not be merely another commodity but must be something whose value they deeply believe in. Otherwise, the industry suggests, agents will find it impossible to succeed at selling policies because, as the

Prudential company's training manual claims, "if you are insincere, your prospect will sense it."[26]

At the other end of the spectrum of belief, according to Miller, are some car salespeople. Rather than trying to convince themselves that they are doing unappreciative customers a tremendous favor, they tend to realize that they are exploiting buyers but construct a worldview that uses skill in haggling as the basis for determining worth. As Miller explains,

> A majority of automobile salesmen admit that their customers regard them as "con men," who attempt to "put one over" on the buyer. In informal conversations regarding what makes a "good salesman," salesmen describe their role in much the same way: for example, "Anybody can sell something they [the customers] want but the real bit is to make them think they need exactly what you got to sell, only more of it." The consensus appears to be that the "good" salesman is highly proficient at manipulating the situation and customer in such fashion as to produce a favorable deal for the salesman. The object of the sales transaction, as an experienced older salesman expressed it, is to "make them think they are getting something instead of losing anything." . . . Their behavior appears organized around the premise that monetary and social success are the results of opportunistic dealing.[27]

This highly cynical view treats the impression of reality the salesperson wants to project as a sham; furthermore, everyone but the customer knows that it is a sham.

Depending on how cynical people are, it may be possible for them to operate on a day-to-day basis with this assessment of their role. Most people, however, are uncomfortable with the view that they are actively exploiting suckers; they want to think of themselves as decent people. Car salespeople frequently justify their cynicism by claiming that the customers are just as bad or worse; they project the negative aspects of their own roles onto customers. Thus, as Miller writes, the salesperson sees customers as

> opportunistic, "out to make or save a buck any way they can." By selectively perceiving and, if necessary, by misinterpreting the behavior of the customer to fit his own pattern of expectations, the salesman is able to rationalize the exploitative and manipulative aspects of his role, making his work acceptable to himself and tolerable to others.[28]

Why is it necessary for the salesperson to go to such lengths to justify his or her behavior? The profit motive in deceiving and manipulating customers is quite clear, so it might seem obvious that sellers should do anything possible within the law to rip customers off and not worry about it. The near-universal desire not to do so suggests that people are not comfortable with a tremendous amount of cynicism about their roles. They would prefer not to have to establish and maintain what Goffman calls "role distance,"[29] which means that they dissociate themselves from, rather than wholeheartedly embrace, the role.

The role of salesperson is critical to the sales process. The individual selling the car, however, has more roles than just salesperson to maintain at any given time.

A particular performer, for instance, may want to project the images of "parent," "nice guy or nice person," "music lover," and "good friend" all at once. All these roles, however, are at least to a certain extent counteracted by a willingness to glee-fully exploit uninformed customers; the individual probably does not want to think of himself or herself, and certainly does not want to be thought of by others, as a greedy, underhanded jerk. Thus, conflicting roles in an individual's life may cause distinct problems because the demands of one role may be incompatible with the demands of other roles.

There are various ways to attempt to reconcile these roles. The salespeople described previously did it by claiming that they were simply protecting themselves from greedy, exploitative customers; the customers are the bad guys, and the seller unfortunately has to respond in kind to survive. This does not make the seller a "bad guy" or "bad person" because, in normal circumstances, the seller would never resort to manipulating people the way he or she does to sell cars. Other methods of coping that Goffman suggests include joking or including other parts of contra-dictory roles in the situation at hand; the seller may try to prove that he or she is a good friend by acting unnecessarily friendly toward the client, or the seller may take an ironic stance toward one of his or her roles; this is not easy to pull off in car sales, but it could occur if, for instance, a salesperson made subtle jokes about the company's promotional literature, fellow employees, or even the act of selling.

These attempts to reconcile roles all involve, to a certain extent, emotion man-agement. As noted previously, flight attendants have a somewhat unique job—one that focuses considerable attention on managing their emotions. The most impor-tant tool of the flight attendants, they are frequently told in training, is a ready smile.[30] Particular airlines emphasize that flight attendants should enjoy being flirted with or should go out of their way to be friendly to rude, drunk, or unrea-sonable passengers. In cases of role conflict, however, flight attendants cannot, like many workers, resort to the expression of emotions common to other roles to resolve the tension because their employers specifically stake out the emotional space of the attendant as a vital part of the attendant's role. As Hochschild observes,

> Some workers conclude that only one self (usually the nonwork self) is the "real" self. Others, and they are in the majority, will decide that each self is meaningful and real in its own different way and time. . . . Such workers are generally more adept at acting, and the idea of a separation between the two selves is not only acceptable but welcome to them. They speak more matter-of-factly about their emotional labor in clearly defined and sometimes mechanis-tic ways: "I get in gear, I get revved up, I get plugged in." They talk of their feelings not as spontaneous, natural occurrences but as objects they have learned to govern and control.[31]

In either case, flight attendants must recognize that their roles are fundamentally incompatible and must draw a clear division between them.

As soon as attendants realize that they are operating with contradictory goals, they will be in trouble; they will have increasing difficulty in appreciating their jobs and their passengers. Airlines, not surprisingly, do everything possible to put off this realization because the simplest way to convince passengers that the emotions of their attendants are sincere is for the emotions to actually be sincere. Thus, airlines spend a great deal of time in training suggesting ways that flight attendants may merge the seemingly contradictory emotional roles they are forced to deal with. Early in the education process, and frequently thereafter, flight attendants are trained in methods designed to actively manipulate their emotional states to avoid conflict. Delta hopes that, if flight attendants can somehow connect with passengers on some level, they will be able to put forth a show of genuine emotion. For this reason, Hochschild notes,

> The deepest appeal in the Delta training program was to the trainee's capacity to act as if the airplane cabin (where she works) were her home (where she doesn't work). Trainees were asked to think of a passenger as if he were a "personal guest in your living room."[32]

One graduate elaborated,

> You think how the new person resembles someone you know. *You see your sister's eyes in someone sitting at that seat.* That makes you want to put out for them. I like to think of the cabin as the living room of my own home. When someone drops in [at home], you may not know them, but you get something for them. You put that on a grand scale—thirty-six passengers per flight attendant—but *it's the same feeling.*[33]

This approach, if successful, could merge many of the roles that are likely to come into conflict for the flight attendant. The attendant's role demands a display of genuine affection, but for most people, genuine affection is reserved for friends and relatives. By inviting flight attendants to think of passengers as friends or relatives, it may be easier for them to reconcile their emotional needs with their employer's emotional demands.

Of course, most passengers are not relatives, friends, or even acquaintances; therefore, the attempt to see them as such is likely to break down fairly quickly, especially in the case of the troublesome passengers whom flight attendants are likely to be forced to deal with more often than they would like. Training programs anticipate this and attempt to build in safeguards to delay the moment when a flight attendant simply can no longer deal with the stresses of the job. One way is to think of irate, unruly, or otherwise troublesome fliers as children attempting to get attention; this not only helps the attendant connect with the customer, in an emotional way, but also allows flight attendants to rationalize their role distancing by claiming that it is caused only by particularly immature customers and not by a fundamental problem in the constitution of the role.

There is only so much value to this coping strategy, however; at some point, flight attendants will not be able to think of drunken businessmen as children. Training programs tend to stress one last check on role-distancing behavior, this one more social than those mentioned previously. Flight attendants tend to work in teams and generally form a strong sense of group unity while flying particular routes. Companies exploit this by training attendants to recognize morale problems among coworkers and to try to counteract them.[34] This does not really do much to address the problem at hand, however; although friends may be able to cheer each other up, they will not be able to reconcile the conflicting roles that got the flight attendant into trouble in the first place. At the end of the day, the cynical flight attendant still must wrestle with the options of seeing his or her role as "fake" or "real."

Whatever option employees adopt, they must, to a certain extent, be insincere. If employees decide that only their "natural" (i.e., off-job) role is real, each action mandated by their role as flight attendants will come off as "phony" because it does not reflect their nonwork, real self. If employees decides that it is impossible to adopt both roles at once, they will constantly be aware, as flight attendants, that they are in some significant sense not being "true to themselves." Insincerity thus becomes a fundamental component of their daily life. Because of the special emotional demands placed on flight attendants, the ways in which their role by definition forces them to feel some insincerity are quite apparent.

According to Stanford Lyman and Marvin Scott, "Goffman seems to see that a brooding and suspicious sense of inauthenticity is the basic condition of performative human existence."[35] Roles always have a great potential to come into conflict, in countless ways. A working mother, for instance, may feel that, by working long hours, she is not dedicating enough time to her children and simultaneously feel, while spending time with her children, that she is neglecting her work.

Conflicting Role Expectations

Minor conflicts arise in all kinds of work situations. One very common source of trouble is an inability to reconcile the demands of a sales job with perceived ideals of service. Kraft reports a discrepancy between messages handed down by management as follows:

> [Sales contests] imply that it is the quantity of the product that one sells that determines the quality of the clerk's work performance. The obvious message [is that] what is important becomes how much of any one thing is sold. . . . However, the company would, at other times, lead staff to believe that it is more concerned with the overall quality of service delivered. . . . They appear to contradict the sales contest message by claiming [Disney] is not exclusively "hard sell." In short, they expect and explicitly train the Cast Member to practice two contradictory styles.[36]

For clerks, if this problem exists, it arises only because management forces it. Insurance agents also find this problem inherent in the sales process. Insurance agents must convince others and must themselves believe that they are professionals dedicated to the financial well-being of their customers. What counts most to them and their employment future, however, is the ability to generate sales. Generally, professionals do not have to convince people that their services are valuable; doctors do not call people during dinner, convince them that they are ill, and try to schedule an appointment for surgery as soon as possible. Insurance agents, however, are forced to convince people of the need for coverage and then offer a range of alternatives to fulfill this newfound need. There is, therefore, an obvious and necessary friction for any insurance agent between two conflicting role expectations. To be professionals, they must worry about what their client needs and wants. To be salespeople, however, they must be most concerned with the bottom line.

Another type of conflict arises when it becomes impossible to reconcile demands for service and speed. Retailers, for instance, might be told to be personable to customers, to converse with them, and so on. They might be called to task if the actual application of these instructions leads to delay, however—that is, if in talking to a customer they seem to be neglecting other aspects of their job. A revealing example is again provided by flight attendants, who found in the 1970s that, due to an industry-wide speed-up, they were forced to give the same amount of emotional labor in significantly less time.[37] In the 1980s, this got even worse because airlines found that, to stay in business, they had to make fewer flight attendants attend to more customers in less time. Something had to give, as stated in the following:

> Before the speed-up, most workers sustained the cheerful good will that good service requires. They did so for the most part proudly. . . . After the speed-up, when asked to make personal human contact at an inhuman speed, they cut back on their emotion work and grew detached.[38]

Of course, the ideal of service is not abandoned by either management or the flight attendant. The role demands placed on the employee do not change but must for better or worse be negotiated by each individual flight attendant.

The demands of the market, whether for speed or raw sales, sometimes are simply incompatible with the roles it compels individuals to adopt. When role distancing occurs, it might seem logical for people to recognize the conflicting nature of their situation and attempt to reconcile their discrepant roles. It is often very difficult, however, for agents caught up in the action to understand that their problems are caused by fundamental inconsistencies in the roles they are expected to adopt; rather, they tend to blame themselves, assuming that the problem is not that roles or role expectations are incompatible but that they are somehow "not good enough" to live up to their assigned roles, because, as Lyman and Scott note,

> When people experience a suspension in their own belief in the naturalism or "authenticity" of the performance put on by themselves or others they approach a phenomenological understanding of the dramatic fundament of human existence. These suspensions, however . . . are not usually taken to be a clue to the phenomenology of human existence itself, but rather to be an exposure of the "fraudulence" and "bad faith" of certain [performers].[39]

"Real" Selves in a Commodified World

For insurance agents who cannot convince themselves of the authenticity of their own performances, instead of blaming the fundamental contradiction implicit in the roles they are asked to adopt, there is a tendency to blame themselves. Thus, they will think something similar to the following: "A *real* professional could manage to reconcile the demand to sell at all costs with the need to make service their utmost priority. I cannot. Therefore, I am flawed." Of course, if they want to keep eating, they must continue to pretend to be professionals, and every performance will highlight some way in which professionalism is antithetical to their identity.

Similarly, flight attendants caught up in the inauthenticity of their emotional displays will find themselves torn between a desire to continue the job and find some way to fake the emotions they "should" authentically experience, on the one hand, and a growing recognition that each painted-on smile is more strained and further suggests that they are not cut out for this job, on the other hand. Role distancing thus tends to get increasingly worse as time goes on and more and more inauthentic productions are delivered. Due to the very nature of role conflict, it is difficult to resolve distancing without fundamentally changing the definition of either the self or the situation that one wants to project. The alienated actor must either quit the job that is causing the role problems or somehow learn to deal with the conflict, either by becoming highly cynical or somehow changing the personal roles that are thought of as constituting the "real" self.

Of course, it is always much more pleasant to give up a work self than a real self; we should not expect people to abandon their perceptions of themselves. In a tight labor market, however, we also should not expect people to give up their jobs, especially because they have frequently received years of training and to switch careers would make them start at the bottom of the employment ladder again, which for someone approaching midlife can be financially disastrous. Cynicism, it seems, becomes a pretty reasonable option by default. Insurance agents might give up their ideals of service and professionalism and only pretend to offer these to the extent that they help the bottom line. Flight attendants might learn to effectively display friendliness, good cheer, and so on when feeling the absolute opposite. In both cases, the alienated professional will turn to a reliance on acting to reconcile his or her unpleasant circumstances.

Therefore, Goffman's dramaturgy comes full circle. Social reality is a performed event, highly dependent on the various components of theater. For particular individuals to effectively communicate the social reality most advantageous to them, they must adopt roles regarding their vocations. At a certain point, however, these work roles will almost inevitably collide with the nonwork roles individuals hold dear, their supposed real selves. When this happens, individuals have a wide variety of options, but ultimately none of them are likely to fully resolve the conflict; the best solution, in many cases, is to gloss over the conflict by acting—by using the tools of the stage. Goffman emphasizes that he is using theater as a metaphor and claims that ultimately, the world is not a stage, and it should not be difficult for readers to find major differences between the two.[40] Given the complexity and compelling character of his dramaturgical sociology, however, it can be hard for readers to share Goffman's asserted willingness to abandon the metaphor of the theater.

Notes

1. Goffman, E. (1959). *The presentation of self in everyday life* (pp. 252-253). Garden City, NY: Doubleday. Although this book will be central to our analysis, we also relied on the following: *Encounters.* (1961). Indianapolis, IN: Bobbs-Merrill; *Interaction ritual.* (1967). Garden City, NY: Doubleday; *Relations in public.* (1971). New York: Harper & Row. For thoughtful commentaries on Goffman's contribution to sociology, see the following: Fine, G. A. & Manning, P. (2000). Erving Goffman, in G. Ritzer (Ed.), *The Blackwell Companion to Contemporary Social Theorists* (pp. 456-85). Oxford: Blackwell; Lemert, C. (1997). Goffman, in *The Goffman Reader* (pp. ix-xiii). Oxford: Blackwell; Burns, T. (1992). *Erving Goffman.* London: Routledge; Drew, P., & Wotton, A. (Eds.). (1988). *Erving Goffman: Exploring the interaction order.* Boston: Northeastern University Press; Lyman, S. M. (1973). Civilization: Contents, discontents, and malcontents. *Contemporary Sociology, 2*, 360-366.

2. Goffman (1959), *The presentation of self in everyday life,* p. 83.

3. Oakes, G. (1990, Fall). The American life insurance salesman: A secular theodicy. *International Journal of Politics, Culture, and Society, 4*(1), 102.

4. Oakes (1990, Fall), *International Journal of Politics, Culture, and Society, 4*(1), 99.

5. Goffman (1959), *The presentation of self in everyday life,* p. 46.

6. Hochschild, A. (1983). *The managed heart* (pp. 92-93). Berkeley: University of California Press. Reprinted with permission of The Regents of California and University of California Press.

7. Hochschild tended to use "stewardess" and "flight attendant" interchangeably because, during the time of her study, most were women, and even today the vast majority of flight attendants are women. In airline advertisements, most images of flight attendants depict females. We generally prefer the more gender-neutral "flight attendant," although the subjects of Hochschild's study were overwhelmingly women.

8. Hochschild (1983), *The managed heart,* pp. 95-96.

9. Hochschild (1983), *The managed heart,* p. 97.

10. Hochschild (1983), *The managed heart,* pp. 93-94.

11. Kraft, K. (1994). *The rationalization of fantasy* (p. 8). Unpublished paper, Augustana College.

12. Miller, S. (1964). The social basis of sales behavior. *Social Problems, 12*(1), 19. Reprinted with permission.

13. Miller (1964), *Social Problems, 12*(1), 19.

14. Oakes (1990, Fall), *International Journal of Politics, Culture, and Society, 4*(1), 107.

15. Kraft (1994), *The rationalization of fantasy,* p. 6.

16. Kraft (1994), *The rationalization of fantasy,* pp. 1-2.

17. Goffman (1959), *The presentation of self in everyday life,* p. 113.

18. Goffman (1959), *The presentation of self in everyday life,* p. 121.

19. Miller (1964), *Social Problems, 12*(1), 20.

20. Miller (1964), *Social Problems, 12*(1), 20.

21. Goffman, E. (1974). *Frame analysis* (p. 475). New York: Harper & Row.

22. Goffman (1959), *The presentation of self in everyday life,* pp. 17-18.

23. At this point, Kraft's analysis of Disney stores becomes less relevant because sales jobs with Disney are conceived of not as careers but, for the most part, as short-term work. Certainly, all the features of alienation and role distancing discussed here would apply to someone who tried to model his or her professional role around that advocated by the Disney corporation.

24. Oakes (1990, Fall), *International Journal of Politics, Culture, and Society, 4*(1), 104.

25. Oakes (1990, Fall), *International Journal of Politics, Culture, and Society, 4*(1), 106.

26. W. Walsh as cited in Oakes, G. (1989, Winter). Sales as a vocation: The moral ethos of personal sales. *International Journal of Politics, Culture, and Society, 3*(2), 247.

27. Miller (1964), *Social Problems, 12*(1), 22.

28. Miller (1964), *Social Problems, 12*(1), 20.

29. Although Goffman hints at role distance briefly in *The presentation of self in everyday life* (1959), he offers a much more thorough exposition of the phenomenon in a later essay titled simply "Role Distance." For an analysis of this essay, see Burns (1992), *Erving Goffman.*

30. Hochschild (1983), *The managed heart,* p. 105.

31. Hochschild (1983), *The managed heart,* p. 133.

32. Hochschild (1983), *The managed heart,* p. 105.

33. Hochschild (1983), *The managed heart,* p. 105.

34. Hochschild (1983), *The managed heart,* p. 115.

35. Lyman, S., & Scott, M. (1974). *The drama of social reality* (p. 107). New York: Oxford University Press.

36. Kraft (1994), *The rationalization of fantasy,* pp. 10-11.

37. Hochschild (1983), *The managed heart,* p. 122.

38. Hochschild (1983), *The managed heart,* p. 126.

39. Lyman & Scott (1974), *The drama of social reality,* pp. 110-111.

40. Goffman (1959), *The presentation of self in everyday life,* p. 254.

Discussion Questions

1. Enter the same store in a local shopping mall on three or four different occasions and determine the operative sales script. Describe it. What does this corporate-written script say about the kinds of customers the store is catering to and the image of the store's products that is being conveyed?

2. When people interview for a job, they frequently define the process as amounting to an attempt to "sell themselves" to a would-be employer. Use your own experience to describe the techniques you have used in job interviews to accomplish the presentation of self that you think will make you as attractive an applicant as possible (think about both backstage and onstage aspects of your performance).

3. The idea that we are all actors playing various roles has been interpreted by some critics of Goffman to mean that we are all basically presenting ourselves out of a manipulative self-interest, and therefore we cannot speak about an authentic self beneath the surface. In other words, these critics think Goffman offers a cynical view of human nature. What do you think?

CHAPTER 11

The "New" Means of Consumption

A Postmodern Analysis

George Ritzer

George Ritzer has published a number of books in sociological theory, including Postmodern Social Theory *(1997) and a book on metatheory,* Metatheorizing in Sociology *(1991). He has written a number of essays on the theory of rationalization, and they provided the base for his best known work,* The McDonaldization of Society *(1993/1996/2000). He is also author of a work in applied social theory,* Expressing America: A Critique of the Increasingly Global Credit Card Society *(1995) as well as* Enchanting a Disenchanted World *(1999). He has recently completed editing the two-volume* Encyclopedia of Social Theory *(2004) and the 6th edition of* Sociological Theory *(2004). His work has been or is being translated into many languages, including Croatian, Czech, Danish, Farsi, German, Hungarian, Italian, Korean, Portuguese, Russian, and Spanish.*

In previous works, I have analyzed the rise of fast-food restaurants[1] and credit cards[2] largely from a modern point of view. For example, I have associated both with a characteristic rationality that most analysts see at the heart of modern society. Furthermore, I have used a modern epistemology to describe both fast-food restaurants and credit cards in terms of grand narratives: McDonaldization and Americanization. Although I think that these and related phenomena are usefully analyzed from a modern point of view, this chapter is devoted to demonstrating that other insights into these phenomena come to light when they are analyzed from a postmodern perspective.

The objective in this chapter is to apply at least some key aspects of postmodern social theory not only to fast-food restaurants and credit cards but also to a broader set of phenomena that can be combined under the heading of what I (and others) call the "means of consumption."[3] Specifically, I have in mind a number of relatively new means of consumption that are largely products of American society.[4] Two of these new means of consumption are the fast-food restaurant and the credit card. Related innovations in the means of consumption include shopping (including mega-) malls, superstores, cybermalls, theme parks, home shopping via television, infomercials, telemarketing, and even the somewhat older supermarkets.

This raises an immediate issue: How can these phenomena be discussed under the heading of postmodernism when two of them have already been discussed as modern phenomena? The answer is that, in this context, I am adopting not the chronological view that postmodernity supplants modernity but rather the view one can analyze any social phenomena from the point of view of both modern and postmodern theory.

In fact, it may be far more useful to regard modernism and postmodernism not as one epoch that follows another but as different "modes" of analysis.[5] In analyzing social phenomena alternately from a modern and then a postmodern perspective, one would be following the logic employed by Weinstein and Weinstein in their recent postmodern analysis of Simmel:

> To our minds "modernism" and "postmodernism" are not exclusive alternatives but discursive domains bordering each other. . . . We could be working the modernist side of the border (as we have in the past) if we didn't think that the postmodernist side contained more resources for mapping present culture.[6]

Having worked the modern side of the border in my previous work on fast-food restaurants and credit cards, in this chapter, I will be working the other side of the border to discuss them and, more generally, the new means of consumption. One is quite safe in doing so because the postmodernists themselves have tended to look at similar phenomena as representative of postmodernism.

It should be pointed out that I (and many others) tend to look at the new means of consumption in a very material (Marxian) sense, but most postmodernists (and poststructuralists) tend to focus far more on nonmaterial signs associated with such phenomena and their place in the nonmaterial code. These two approaches, however, are not mutually exclusive, and I will have many things to say about signs and the code in the context of a discussion of these means of consumption.

Postmodern Society as a Consumer Society

The place to begin a postmodern analysis of these means of consumption is with the view that *postmodern* society is a *consumer* society.[7] Indeed, one often sees the terms used synonymously. French social theorist Jean Baudrillard's early work was focused on consumer society[8] and, recently, Zygmunt Bauman has viewed postmodernity in these terms.[9] Capitalist society has undergone a shift in focus from production to consumption. In the early days of their economic system, capitalists focused almost exclusively on controlling production in general and production workers in particular. As factories have moved out of advanced capitalist nations, the focus in those nations has been moved toward controlling consumption in general, especially the thoughts and actions of consumers. Although producing more and cheaper goods remains important, attention is increasingly being devoted to getting people to consume more and a greater variety of things.

In the realm of consumption, the focus is usually on marketing and advertising. Although these are certainly important, what I focus on, as pointed out previously, are the new means of consumption as both social structures that constrain people and signs (and as producers, sponsors, and so on of signs). In doing so, I follow Baudrillard, who discussed such means of consumption in some of his early work.[10] He focused on the distinctively French drugstore as such a (then) new means, but closer to my foci he also discussed the shopping mall in these terms.

The new means of consumption are just that—means to allow people to consume. The concept is obviously derived from Marx's focus on the means of production: tools, raw materials, machines, factories, and so on. Just as such means are necessary to and facilitate production, means of consumption perform the same roles in the sphere of consumption. Furthermore, this helps us to see that there are important analogies between workers and consumers. In fact, as we will see, consumers now "work" in conjunction with these new means of consumption, and to the constant joy of capitalists (and their profit margins), they perform that work without compensation.

On the surface, means of consumption and their functions seem benign, even quite positive. Looked at more deeply, however, they are means to gently, and not so gently, lead consumers to consume in ways that are most advantageous to manufacturers and sellers. This means that at least some of the time, they act to the detriment of consumers. For example,

- Fast-food restaurants lead people to eat foods that are detrimental to their health because they are high in cholesterol, sugar, salt, and so on.
- Credit cards induce people to spend more that they should and beyond their available capital.
- Shopping malls entice people into buying things they often do not need.
- TV shopping networks and cybermalls permit people to shop 24 hours a day, 7 days a week, thereby increasing the likelihood that they will spend more than they should and buy things that they should not.
- Catalogs allow people to purchase products from anywhere in the world, and people may be induced into buying unneeded products.

The point is that these and other new means of consumption enable people to do things they could not do before, but they also encourage them to buy more than they need—to spend more than they should.

The fact is that capitalists need customers to consume in this way to keep the economy operating at a high and growing level. Thus, capitalism is a major force in the invention of these new means of consumption. Furthermore, capitalism needs to keep inventing them so that it can continue to be the kind of economic system we have known it to be. In fact, more attention seems to be devoted these days to inventing new means of consumption than to the more traditional course of creating new means of production. If postmodern society is consumer society, at least in part, then these new means of consumption are key elements of the postmodern world.

There is an enormous amount of money spent on advertising the glories of the growing importance of consumption in modern capitalism. Although we usually associate labor with production, Baudrillard has made it clear that consumption has become a kind of labor.[11] Thus, in a sense, we all perform labor in trekking to a half-dozen or more fast-food restaurants each week. Not only must we (usually) drive to them and back but also we must often wait in lines in or out of our cars. If we eat in the restaurant, we must literally perform a series of jobs (serve as waiters by carrying our own food and serve as buspersons by cleaning up after ourselves) that restaurants of old had to pay people to perform. If we go through the drive-through and take the food with us, we do the work of sanitation workers by disposing of the debris left over after our meal is completed. Similarly, we work during our treks to shopping malls, supermarkets, and even Las Vegas casinos. All this, and much more associated with the new means of consumption, is work, and capitalism must keep us at it to keep expanding and to prevent the consuming masses from thinking about anything remotely resembling revolution. In addition, capitalism wants to keep us at work because instead of paying workers, people are willing, even eager, to pay for the privilege of working as consumers. Most important, capitalism needs us to keep on spending at ever-increasing levels to be and remain capitalism. Without ever-increasing consumerism, capitalism as we have come to know it would collapse or at least be transformed dramatically. As a result, the focus of capitalism has shifted from exploiting workers to exploiting consumers.

The new means of consumption also led to the proliferation of goods and services. Bauman recognizes this and relates it to Simmel's "tragedy of culture."[12] The tragedy is that our capacities do not develop fast or far enough to allow us to deal with the enormous profusion of commodities. In addition to the expected goods and services, in the postmodern world, virtually every aspect of culture (art, music, and so on) is for sale. In other words, we come to be overwhelmed by objects of consumption, to say nothing of the increasingly wide array of means in existence to dispense these goods and services.

Given this contextualization of our discussion of the new means of consumption from a postmodern perspective, let us turn to a more general postmodern analysis of these phenomena. Because postmodernism is not a coherent theory—indeed, it generally denies the possibility of such a theory—in the following section, I present a pastiche of postmodern ideas and their applicability to an analysis of the new means of consumption. In the concluding section, I address a rather surprising topic, given the usual association of postmodern social theory with nihilism: ways of dealing with the new means of consumption.

A Postmodern Analysis

The new means of consumption are characterized, to a very high degree, by simulacra. For example, instead of "real" human interaction with servers in fast-food restaurants, with clerks in shopping malls and superstores, with telemarketers, and so on, we can think of these as simulated interactions. Employees follow scripts, and customers counter with canned responses, with the result that no authentic interaction ever takes place.[13] In fact, so many of our interactions in these settings (and out) are simulated, and we become so accustomed to them, that we lose a sense of genuine interaction. In the end, all we have are simulated interactions; there are no more real interactions. In fact, the entire distinction between the simulated and the real is lost; simulated interaction is the reality.

The same point applies to objects associated with the new means of consumption. Any given credit card is a simulation of all other cards of the same brand; there was no "original" card from which all others are copied; there is no real credit card. Furthermore, credit cards can be seen as simulations of simulations. That is, credit cards simulate currency, but each bill is a simulation, a copy, of every other bill and, again, there was no original bill from which all the others have been copied. Currencies, in turn, can be seen as simulations of material wealth, of the faith one has in the treasury, or of whatever one imagines to be the real basis of wealth. Thus, the credit card shows how we live in a world characterized by a never-ending spiral of simulation built on simulation.

Of perhaps greatest importance, in this regard, is the fact that credit cards are simulated goods and services being created in contemporary society and being sold through other new means of consumption—for example, shopping malls, theme parks, and catalogs. Thus, the credit card can be seen as a means to all the other means of consumption: a "meta-means." For example, to build on one of Fredric Jameson's examples,[14] we could charge a copy (a simulation) of Andy Warhol's (simulated) painting of Campbell soup cans, or we could even charge a copy (a simulation) of a second artist's reproduction (another simulation) of Andy Warhol's "original" (yet another simulation). We could even go so far as to charge a real can of Campbell's soup (which is, of course, a copy of perhaps billions of other such cans in label, design, physical structure, and contents) in our local supermarket (which is undoubtedly a simulation of many other such markets). Most generally, we can say that the credit card is a simulation that helps to enable all other simulations. Thus, as credit cards (and other forms of electronic funds transfer) increase in importance in the coming years, we will see a society dominated even more by simulations.

Simulations also characterize the fast-food industry—for example, the simulated playgrounds that grace the entrances to many fast-food restaurants. Then, there are the foods—the hamburgers, the pizza, the tacos—that, although they may be very good simulations of others of their genre, are poor copies of their ancestors, bearing only the faintest resemblance to the homemade hamburgers, pizzeria pizzas, and roadside-stand tacos that may still be found. In fact, such real food, if it ever existed, has largely disappeared under an avalanche of simulacra. Today, to most Americans under the age of 30 or 40, the McDonald's burger is the real burger or, more accurately, there are nothing but simulated hamburgers. One who wants to unmask these simulacra for what they are runs the risk of discovering that there are no real hamburgers—there is no "true" hamburger (or anything else, for that matter). Also, there are completely invented foods—for example, the millions, perhaps billions, of virtually identical (and simulated) Chicken McNuggets. The latter fits perfectly Baudrillard's idea of a simulacrum as an identical copy for which no original ever existed.[15] The original, the chicken, had the temerity to be created with bones, skin, gristle, and so on. Chickens themselves, however, given modern factory farming, are nothing more than simulations that bear little resemblance to the dwindling number of their "free-ranging" kin.

In addition, the structure and decor of the fast-food restaurants are also simulations. The Roy Rogers' chain is modeled, I suppose, after the movie cowboy's ranch house—a ranch house that never existed, except perhaps in the movies in which, of course, it was a simulation. The whole western atmosphere created by the chain, and its commercials, has much more to do with the movies (simulations) than it does with the real Old West (whatever that was). Another example that comes to mind is the Arthur Treacher chain of restaurants, which are modeled after an old English fish and chips shop (whatever that may be). For those of you too young to remember, Arthur Treacher was a British actor who was most associated with butler roles in the movies. This simulated British butler was the symbol of this chain of simulated fish and chips shops. A similar point could be made about the fictional Long John Silver (known best to the public, of course, from the movie [i.e. simulated] version of *Treasure Island* rather than the original book) chain of seafood restaurants as well as many other simulated purveyors of simulacra.

As simulated worlds selling simulated products, the new means of consumption in general, and the shopping mall in particular, have a hyperreal quality to them; they seem more real than real. A typical mall has a cold sterile quality; it is not quite of this world; it is not quite real, or rather it is a little bit more real than real shopping plazas in large cities as well as in small towns. The malls are outdone by the theme parks (although malls are coming to look more and more like theme parks) such as Disney World, in which Disney products are sold in a world that seems more real than reality. The products purveyed in glossy catalogs (e.g., the lingerie marketed in the Victoria's Secret catalog) and on the home shopping networks are made to appear far more real than they will be when they find their way into our homes and onto our backs. Obviously, even more hyperreal are the new cybermalls. Can we be far from "virtual shopping"?

Baudrillard describes America as a dry and emotionless desert,[16] and it is not surprising that fast-food restaurants, perhaps the quintessential American product, are similarly desertlike. Lacking in depth and emotion, every fast-food restaurant seems like every other. Ultimately, the entire terrain of fast-food restaurants seems like some vast desert in which it is difficult to differentiate one superficial landmark from another. Each fast-food restaurant seems like one more meaningless outpost in the desert. People are dashing from one outpost to another, but there is nothing meaningful about any of the outposts or the monotonous process of moving from one to another. People seem to be coming from nowhere and headed to nowhere. Also, America is rapidly exporting this mode of consumption to the rest of the world, which eagerly awaits it, or at least the seemingly desirable features of it. From Baudrillard's perspective, the rest of the world is rushing headlong in the direction of creating a similar consumer, and ultimately social, desert.

Although they are characterized by a certain flat, desertlike quality, there is, as Jameson points out, a peculiar kind of euphoria ("intensities") associated with these postmodern settings.[17] There is, for example, the sense as one arrives at the fast-food restaurant that one is in for excitement or at least some fun. Indeed, what fast-food restaurants really sell is not food but rather a (simulated) kind of fun. The clowns, the cartoon characters, the setting (e.g., a carnival, a ranch, or a pirate ship) all promise excitement, even if the food is of the most prosaic type one can imagine. What could be less exciting to most Americans than eating yet another fast-food hamburger, chicken wing, or pizza slice? We seem to be fooled (or to fool ourselves) continually by the peripherals, however, into believing that we are in for some excitement when we pass through the portals of the fast-food restaurant.

Of course, this excitement pales in comparison to the intensity of feeling on the part of the consumers who enter yet another shopping mall with credit card at the ready. Malls, like fast-food restaurants, promise, and seem to deliver, excitement, especially those such as the Mall of America in Minneapolis with its amusement park, which even includes a roller coaster. Just as fast-food restaurants are not really peddling food, malls are not really selling goods, or at least they are not selling themselves on the basis of the goods they have to offer, because those same goods can be purchased almost anywhere else. What they are peddling is their version of an enchanted environment in which to buy those goods. Lo and behold, in come the customers and what do they have at the ready? The magical credit card; the keys to the kingdom! What could be more exciting? Here we are in a magical world, and we have got the golden key that will unlock every door. Better yet, and even more magical, it appears as if it is all free! Merchants gladly take our plastic, we sign our names, and off we go with as many goods as we can carry (and as many as our credit limits will allow). Of course, we know that a downer (the credit card bill) awaits us down the road, but who cares? We are too excited to worry about such future consequences. Even if we "max" out on one card, some other bank will admire our profligacy and give us another card. We might even be able to take a cash advance on the new card to make a minimal payment on an overdue bill from the old card.

Related to the idea of intensities is the sense that Bauman[18] and others convey that postmodern systems are intent on offering "spectacles."[19] Examples include the garishness of fast-food restaurants and their amusement-park qualities, such as playgrounds for children, and modern malls that contain theme-oriented amusement parks. Thus, Disney World seems to be only marginally different from Mall of America.[20] Disney World has a few more attractions and a few less shops than Mall of America, but both have a healthy mix of each. Also, both are oriented to using the spectacle to attract as many buyers as possible. Cruise ships, casinos, hotels, and even supermarkets seek to present themselves as spectacles so that they can elicit an intensity that is otherwise made so difficult to experience by the unemotional and affectless character of most postmodern systems.

There is a fragmented and discontinuous character of life associated with the new means of consumption. Tacos today, burgers yesterday, and pizza tomorrow add up to fragmentation and discontinuity. Credit cards are perhaps the ultimate means to a fragmented and discontinuous life. Limited only by the number of cards in our possession and their collective limit, we can be anywhere we want and buy anything we wish. We can spend a little time here, and a bit more time there, and we can put it all on the card. The only continuity in this fragmented and discontinuous life is the constant spending and the fact that an inevitable reckoning will be appearing in our mailboxes. The package tour is another wonderful example of this as vacationers whirl through a series of fragmented sites often so quickly that they hardly know where they are, let alone the significance of what they are seeing.

Baudrillard describes much of this experience with the term *ecstasy*.[21] Each and every fast-food restaurant can be seen as but one of a series of empty forms that endlessly differentiate themselves from one another (even though they are all essentially alike). In the process, they are constantly reinventing the same products over and over again, with only slight variation from one to another. Fast-food restaurants and their products are *hypertelic*, increasing at astronomical rates without any reason (besides new or greater sources of profit) for their increase; there is an ecstasy associated with this pure movement. Involved in this is a kind of empty inflation. As a result, we find ourselves adrift in an ecstatic system in which fast-food restaurants (or shopping malls, supermarkets, or superstores) and their endlessly different, but surprisingly similar, products whirl about us. We are lost in a world of relentless, but meaningless, expansion. Thus, customers, fast-food restaurants, their products, and the resulting signs are all madly and meaninglessly spinning about in this hyperreal world. Fast-food restaurants (and the other new means of consumption) are contributing to a world in which there is too much meaning (we actually know the meaning of Chicken McNuggets and Egg McMuffins), much of it superfluous (do we really need to know the difference between a Whopper and a Big Mac?). We are left with a feeling of vertiginousness. Things in the world of fast food go round and round at a dizzying pace, but there is no essential meaning to the process.

It is worth noting that as significant and highly visible sponsors, the fast-food restaurants play a key role in the proliferation of signs by the media, perhaps the main source of sign overload in contemporary society. Through the media, the fast-food restaurants not only bombard us with all their own signs but also through their sponsorship, they help support a media system that produces a daily avalanche of signs. In so doing, the fast-food restaurants help contribute to the perception that everything is available for communication, signification, banalization, commercialization, and consumption.

Of course, all this is much truer of credit cards and the world of shopping they have helped spawn: communication, signification, banalization, commercialization, and consumption are all very apt terms to describe that world. As means to means, credit cards have not only increased enormously but also contributed to the hypertelic expansion of all the other means of consumption. Shopping malls, casinos, cruise ships, package tours, and the like have exploded because, at least in part, credit cards have permitted people to use them more quickly and easily and, more important (at least sociologically), they have permitted people to spend far beyond their cash on hand. An interesting case in point is the coming growth in cybermalls. At the moment, the use of cybermalls is still restrained by consumer concerns about the safety of using their credit card numbers to charge products over the Internet. The major credit card companies have been working on solutions and are assuring customers that such protection is in place. Once people feel safe in using their credit card numbers on the Internet, we can expect to see a hypertelic proliferation of such malls, the businesses that participate in them, the goods sold through them, and the consumers who buy through them.

There is a new type of technology associated with postmodern society and the new means of consumption. Instead of productive technologies such as the auto-mobile assembly line, there is the dominance of reproductive technologies, especially electronic media such as the television set and the computer. Rather than the exciting, explosive technology of the industrial revolution, there are flattening, implosive technologies such as television. The technologies of the postmodern era give birth to very different cultural products, and a very different way of life, than the explosive, expanding technologies of the modern era.

All the new means of consumption can be seen as *implosive* technologies. They are not technologies that better permit us to get what is already in existence and that entrepreneurs want us to purchase. In the vast array of fast-food restaurants, the range of different foods available to us implodes into an undifferentiated black hole of hard-to-differentiate salty-sweet foods. Subtlety of taste is not the strong suit of fast-food restaurants. Similarly, in the mad race to acquire as many goods as we can with our credit cards, the goods implode into a mass of largely undifferen-tiable stuff—stuff that we do not really want, do not need, and will likely replace as soon as our credit card limits will allow. Again, there is no explosive production of goods with credit cards but rather an implosive consumption of wares. Much the same can be said about virtually all, if not all, the new means of consumption.

Although they may be implosive technologies, they are undergoing explosive growth—that is, there is enormous expansion of fast-food restaurants, credit cards, and the other new means of consumption in postmodern society.

To some postmodern social theorists, especially Jameson, the multinational capitalistic system is a key element of the postmodern world.[22] In fact, it can be seen as lying at the base of the development and expansion of all the new means of con-sumption. Given a focus on the economy, it is clear that Jameson, unlike many other postmodernists, does not accord central importance to technologies but rather sees them as a means by which we can begin to grasp the postmodern capitalistic world.

Although the same could be said for all the new means of consumption, the fast-food restaurant and the credit card fit well into this aspect of Jameson's approach; they are central aspects of contemporary capitalist society. The credit card, for example, is an American innovation that has led people to buy more than they otherwise would. In fact, as we have pointed out previously, the credit card allows people to spend money they do not have. Much like the treasury, credit cards create money. Of course, Visa does not actually print currency, but it does imprint credit cards with varying limits. With these cards, people can spend all the currency in their possession printed by the treasury and then they can spend the additional "money" available in the collective credit limits of their cards. This additional money has been created by the credit card companies (not the treasury), and it allows capitalism to operate at a far higher level than it could if it was limited to extracting all the consumer's available cash.

Most of the other new means of consumption assist the capitalist system by devoting themselves to getting people to buy things they otherwise would not or to spend more than they intend. Take, for example, megastores such as Costco: The whole idea behind these stores is to get people to buy things they do not need and, more important, to buy things in far larger quantities than they ordinarily would, sometimes in larger quantities than they could ever use. Thus, multiples of a given item are packaged together so that instead of one, several must be purchased. Similarly, enormous containers, jars, bottles, and so on are used so that people buy far larger quantities of things. People go to outlets such as Costco to save money. Although the unit prices are ordinarily lower, people in fact often end up spending more money than they otherwise would.

Today, credit card firms (and fast-food restaurants) are concentrating on international expansion. This will mean greater profits for them. More important, it will allow more people around the world to do what Americans are doing—spend far beyond their available cash resources. Consuming more like Americans, they will inevitably consume more American goods as well as the goods of other capitalist nations. The result will be a more active capitalist system and greater profits to the capitalist firms.

International expansion is certainly not restricted to fast-food restaurants and credit cards. Shopping malls and supermarkets are finding greater international acceptance; television shopping networks are now found outside the confines of the United States; and of course the cybermalls, like the Internet of which they are part, are inherently international in scope—indeed, this is a great source of the attraction to sellers of a wide array of goods and services.

Of course, Jameson is an atypical postmodernist in viewing postmodernism as continuous with capitalism and therefore modernity. In contrast, for example, Baudrillard sees us as having moved from the industrial era, in which there is serial production of simulacra by the industrial system, to an era in which the code predominates and in which simulacra are reproduced by the code.[23] The era of the code brings with it a possibility of control that far exceeds that of the industrial-capitalist system. Furthermore, whereas the industrial-capitalist era is marked by production, the era of the code is one of reproduction.

The new means of consumption reproduce the same products over and over and, more generally, they serve to reproduce the code and the system. For example, although the fast-food restaurant exerts control through more modern industrial-capitalist mechanisms and contributes to capitalistic expansion, it is also a significant contributor to, and part of, the code, and it is through that code that it also manifests control. We can, following Baudrillard, think of the code as a "code of signification"[24]—that is, the code is a set of signs that exert control over people. In the postmodern world, objects and commodities are signs; in using or consuming them, we are using or consuming signs. Thus, in patronizing fast-food restaurants and consuming their products, we are making statements about ourselves. Of course, those statements are controlled and kept in a narrow range by the code. It is much like the referenda to which Baudrillard devotes so much attention.[25] In a referendum, our ostensibly free choices are defined for us in advance; our free choices are, in fact, tightly constrained. Similarly, our ostensibly free choice of food is constrained by the fact that fast-food restaurants are driving the alternatives out of business. More important, the differences that they appear to offer turn out to be, at best, superficial. Thus, following Baudrillard's notion of the referendum, when we "vote" on which fast food to eat on a given day, that choice can hardly be deemed a free one.

I use Wal-Mart to further illustrate this point. A discount department store focusing at least initially on small towns eschewed by other large retailers, Wal-Mart clearly qualifies as an example of one of the new means of consumption. Typically, when a Wal-Mart arrives in a small town, it drives out many of the competing "downtown" businesses. In a sense, it becomes virtually the only game in town. Thus, when people choose to shop at Wal-Mart, it is because, in many instances, it has helped create a situation in which there are few if any alternatives to it.

In addition to material constraints and characteristics, and of far greater importance to most postmodernists, is the fact that the new means of consumption are busy fabricating and manipulating signs, and it is those signs that are controlling our behavior. For example, fast-food restaurants clearly signify "fast." To the degree that the sign *fast* has become part of the code, we are led in the direction of doing many things, not just eating, quickly and efficiently, and conversely we are led away from slow, cumbersome processes in most, if not all, settings. Concretely, this means that we will be drawn to fast-food restaurants and away from traditional restaurants in which it might take an hour or two to dine.

Another sign associated with fast-food restaurants is "fun" (the bright colors, the clowns, the toys, and so on). Again, with fun food part of the contemporary code, we are going to gravitate toward the fast-food restaurants and away from the "old-fashioned" restaurants that offer only good food in staid surroundings. More generally, we are led to look for fun in most, if not all, other means of consumption. In Neil Postman's terms, we are intent on "amusing ourselves to death."[26] Thus, one of the cruise lines is the Carnival line: We are getting not just a cruise but also a carnival, and what could be more fun than that?

The code, and the fact that we all implicitly understand it, enables us to understand what people are saying about themselves when they utilize one of the new means of consumption. In eating in one fast-food chain rather than another, or in eating one type of food rather than another, we are saying, at least implicitly, that we are like some people and different from others. In other words, our eating habits constitute a text that is possible to read. "Reading McDonald's" might involve such aspects as understanding what some people are saying when they consume "value meals" and what others are saying by eschewing such meals. Those who are regulars at Taco Bell are telling us something about themselves and how they differ from those who are habitués of Burger King, Kentucky Fried Chicken, or Popeye's. For example, those who eschew McDonald's for higher-status McDonaldized chains such as Red Lobster are communicating a message, and that message is even stronger from those who avoid all fast-food restaurants and frequent restaurants in which meals are cooked from scratch with fine ingredients by culinary experts. Because it is all coded, there is no end to our ability to read the signs associated with people's eating habits.

There are also signs associated with different credit cards. Use of American Express, Diner's Club, and Carte Blanche communicates that one is of higher status than one who uses the more prosaic and widely used Visa and MasterCard. Using a gold or platinum card, rather than one of the basic cards (and colors), communicates the same message. There is also the significance of using cash rather than a credit card. A rich person using cash may be saying one thing, whereas a poor person who pays in cash is saying something quite different. Thus, one can read credit card use (or its absence) just as one can read fast-food preferences; indeed, utilization of all the new means of consumption is coded and therefore can be, and is, read.

From the perspective of signs and the code, eating, shopping, vacationing, and so on have little or nothing to do with "needs" as they are conceptualized conventionally. For example, we do not eat in fast-food restaurants because we need to eat there (as opposed, for example, to eating at home). More to the point, we do not eat Chicken McNuggets (as opposed to any other food) because we need them and only them. The desire to eat Chicken McNuggets has been manufactured, like all other needs, by the code (and the economic system). Indeed, the human race survived quite nicely for the eon before the Chicken McNugget was "invented." We do not eat what we need but rather what the code tells us we should eat; the code produces our needs (if they can still be called needs when they are manufactured externally). In general, we eat to express our similarities to and differences from other humans and not to satisfy our need for food and, more generally, to survive. When we eat a Big Mac, we may think that we are consuming a glorified hamburger, but in fact we are eating an object-sign. By eating that object-sign and not others, we are expressing much about our position within the system.

One tangential point worth mentioning briefly relates to the focus of postmodernists (and poststructuralists) on expressing differences in the signs we consume. Although there is certainly much truth in this, it is also the case that we use signs to express our commonalities with others. The consumption of signs associated with fast-food restaurants is clearly much more an expression of commonality than difference. There will always be signs of difference, but they are increasingly dwarfed by signs of commonality: McDonald's golden arches and, as an example from another realm, Nike's "swoosh" logo.

Returning to the thrust of the argument on signs, many of the same kinds of things said about fast-food restaurants can be said about the other means of consumption. When we whip out our credit card at the mall, we are saying, among other things, that we are "players" in the postmodern economy. A similar sign is communicated when we take a cruise or gamble in a Las Vegas casino (many cruise ships offer casinos). In these cases, we are demonstrating that we are not merely players but also "high rollers" (when, of course, most of us are not, and we will need to spend months or years paying off the trip or the gambling debt or both). There are also times, however, when we demonstrate that we are knowledgeable and cautious consumers. A trip to Costco might be designed (although not consciously) to demonstrate that fact, even though, as we have already seen, we often spend more money and buy more goods than we intended or should have bought. Making a purchase via a cybermall is a sign that we are among the most progressive of consumers utilizing the latest technological advances.

At one level, most of this section has been devoted to a discussion of the new means of consumption from the perspective of postmodern social theory. At another level, there is a great deal of, perhaps even a pervasive, critique of those means of consumption and of the postmodern world of which they are part. This raises several issues. For example, if, as they do, postmodernists see no hope of ever finding the "truth," how can they be critical of things such as these means of consumption? Following Jameson, we can respond that the inability to discover truth does not inhibit the critique of the falseness (e.g., simulacra) associated with them.

This begs the question, however, at least in part. Without a fundamental sense of what is true, and without such an Archimedean point, how do we determine what is, or is not, false? This is a serious, perhaps even a fatal, problem for postmodern social theory. It is especially true if we accept the postmodern argument that the real is disappearing, or has already disappeared, in a sea of simulacra. If all we have are simulations, what basis do we have to critique some rather than others?

Even if we are willing to concede the obviously highly dubious point that postmodernists might be able to critique that which is false, they cannot, following Bauman and others, come up with an alternative sense of truth.[27] Thus, we cannot await the emanation of a new grand narrative of what is true from the practitioners of postmodern social theory. As a result, we are doomed to perpetual ambivalence as well as to the need to find individual ways of coping with postmodern society. (This is linked to Foucault's idea that because power exists at the microlevel, resistance must also take place at the microlevel.[28]) Although ambivalence and such a lonely search for ways of coping may be problems, they are preferable, in Bauman's (and others') view, to the terrorism of the single grand truth. Thus, we are largely on our own in the postmodern social world in general and in our relationships with the new means of consumption in particular.

Dealing With the New Means of Consumption

Postmodern theorists identify a number of ways of responding to the problems associated with postmodernism, and many of them can be applied to the new means of consumption. Jean Baudrillard's work is particularly rich with such responses. It should be pointed out that in his view, it was far easier to respond to the modern capitalist system in which the proletariat had a clear adversary (the capitalist) than it is to cope with the postmodern code because there is no obvious antagonist associated with it. Furthermore, capitalist hegemony was largely restricted to the economy, whereas the code is and seems everywhere; it is omnipresent. Therefore, it is difficult to figure out ways of combating the code, and even if one is successful in one domain, problems are likely to persist in many other areas. Given these caveats, I examine some responses derived from postmodern theory and their application to the new means of consumption.

Like many other postmodernists, Baudrillard sees the contemporary world as plagued with disenchantment. In various ways, he seeks to reenchant the world, and reenchantment constitutes a way of dealing with the excesses of contemporary society. Thus, for example, one of the problems with exchanges between customers and employees in superstores (among other new means of consumption) is that they have lost their symbolic qualities. This is true not only for the economic exchange of money for commodities but also for the social exchanges between customers and employees in these settings, which have taken on a mechanical, non-human quality. In other words, a world of simulation (including simulated human relationships) has replaced symbolic exchanges between humans. This implies that one way of responding to this, and more generally to the disenchantment in settings such as the superstore, is by reestablishing symbolic exchange among and between workers and customers. Involved in such symbolic relationships is a continual cycle of giving and receiving rather than the self-limiting exchanges that characterize such settings. Furthermore, a wide range of things would need to be exchanged rather than the highly specific and very limited types of exchanges found in super-stores. That is, not just money and goods would be exchanged but also a range of things such as emotions, feelings, experiences, knowledge, insight, and so on. Work in such settings would involve unlimited giving and receiving rather than the limited exchange of money for services. To customers, employees in superstores are like the dead discussed by Baudrillard; they are physically separated from customers and prevented (by scripts, rules, counters, and so on) from engaging in symbolic exchange with them.[29] In engaging in symbolic exchange with employees, customers would be striking a blow against the powerful but fragile code that serves to keep both in their places.

Similarly, Baudrillard suggests that we respond to the system by offering it "gifts" to which it is constitutionally unable to reciprocate.[30] This is based on Baudrillard's belief that all systems are based on symbolic exchange and that those systems that defy such a system of exchange have a fatal flaw that will ultimately prove to be their downfall. In the contemporary world, systems are set up to give but not receive, or to engage in a highly circumscribed round of giving and receiving (e.g., products for money). The death of the system (which is its fate) is hastened if consumers offer it gifts it is incapable of returning. Thus, I suppose, in the case of the fast-food restaurant, we might take to overpaying for our food, performing unpaid and unex-pected services for those restaurants, or literally bring them gifts on anniversaries and openings. This would make their inability to engage in symbolic exchange even more glaring and hasten their downfall. Unless one buys into Baudrillard's argu-ment fully, however, it does seem to strain credulity to believe that such acts as overpaying for a Big Mac would jeopardize the current system.

The ability of such minor actions to make a difference, let alone bring down the system, is based on Baudrillard's belief that although this system appears to be omnipotent, it has in fact grown progressively unstable.[31] Thus, such mundane actions do, in fact, have the capacity, at least in Baudrillard's view, to topple the hegemony of fast-food restaurants, the system, and the code. Of course, these actions cannot occur only in fast-food restaurants, or even just in the new means of consumption, but rather must take place at every site at which the code is represented and re-created.

Paying extra for food at McDonald's is related to another of Baudrillard's concepts: reckless expenditure.[32] Squandering money on a series of useless expenditures is, in a sense, making gifts to the code and the system that they do not know what to make of and to which they are unable to respond. Baudrillard believes that this, like more specific gifts to entities such as the fast-food restaurant, will help set the system on a course to self-destruction.

Alternatively, Jameson's ideas on homeopathic remedies[33] can be applied to the issue of dealing with the new means of consumption. Instead of responding with things postmodern systems cannot produce or respond to (such as symbolic exchange), homeopathic remedies involve responding to postmodern systems in the same way that they deal with us—using the elements of that world to push it to its limits and beyond. In the case of fast-food restaurants, this might involve formally rational responses to the formally rational system. For example, customers might adhere strictly to all the rules, formal and informal, that govern the fast-food restaurant. Such adherence would be time-consuming and demanding of the system and its staff; it might well cause the system to slow to a crawl, thereby giving the lie to the label "fast food."

The world of fast-food restaurants and many other new means of consumption may be viewed, in Baudrillard's terms, as an obscene world in which seemingly everything is visible—indeed hypervisible.[34] Note, for example, the visibility of the food-preparation area in contrast to the traditional restaurant, in which the kitchen is almost always hidden from view, or the obvious and abundant trash receptacles rather than the way trash and its disposal are hidden from view in a traditional restaurant. To Baudrillard, the traditional restaurant is a "scene" in which some things are hidden and in which some mystery (e.g., just how the foods are prepared and how trash is disposed of) continues.[35] Fast-food restaurants are obscene because almost nothing is hidden; everything is visible. Baudrillard's solution to this problem is the return of some invisibility—some mystery; in other words, the return, to use another of his terms, of seduction. Instead of fast-food restaurants that bludgeon customers into submission, we need restaurants that retain the ability to seduce rather than overwhelm customers.

For example, the issue of the taste of the food: Fast food tends to overwhelm our taste buds with strong and obvious tastes, especially very sweet and highly salty ones. In contrast, of course, a gourmet restaurant (or a home-cooked meal) is oriented to seducing our taste buds. Even the decor of such restaurants is seductive in contrast to the bright, loud, and powerful colors and decorations of the typical fast-food restaurant. The logic of Baudrillard's argument leads us to see the creation and patronage of seductive restaurants as a way of coping with the contemporary world.

Seduction is related in Baudrillard's work to the fatality of the objects,[36] in this case the customers who frequent fast-food restaurants (or utilize the other means of consumption). Instead of being constrained by these restaurants, Baudrillard suggests that it is possible that the restaurants are being seduced by the customers (objects). For example, the seemingly ever-increasing parade of customers is seducing the fast-food chains into endless rounds of expansion and proliferation, a game that will ultimately prove fatal as fast-food restaurants eventually proliferate beyond their ability to survive. The same process, of course, affects all the other means of consumption. For example, millions and millions of people can be seen as seducing the credit card companies by accepting offer after offer for new credit cards and overture after overture to increase their spending limit once the old limit has been exceeded. The result is that the banks and credit card firms are extending untold billions of dollars in unsecured credit. This could eventually cause this vast "house of cards" (literally) to collapse when it becomes clear that there is no way that the masses will be able to repay much of this debt, or even the interest on it.

These are two examples of the masses' "fatal strategies." Baudrillard believes that such strategies will lead the world into an ever-spiraling downward trajectory that will end only in catastrophe for the system and the code.[37] The fatal strategies of the "evil genies," the masses, will lead not to revolution in the traditional, grand-narrative sense of the term but rather to a gradual devolution as the code, and the system on which it is built and that sustains it, gradually unravels.

With regard to looking for agents (the masses, as objects, cannot be seen as agents) to respond to the new means of consumption, one can, for example, point to those who have avoided their pervasive presence and influence. The problem is that in the United States, and increasingly in many other parts of the world, it is difficult to identify very many who have been able to avoid their effects. The young, those most likely in most conditions to form the base of a revolutionary movement, are the most profoundly affected by the influence of the new means of consumption. The working class, the traditional revolutionary subject, would be similarly affected and, in any case, would have no obvious material reason to be the vanguard of such a revolution. One can only hope that isolated pockets of people relatively immune to the influence of the new means of consumption (e.g., the Amish) can provide the base for a social movement whose objective is to at least limit their impact.

More promising is the postmodern idea that the revolution is not the grand product of a group of revolutionary agents, but such a revolution is possible, even necessary, here and now in the everyday practices of individuals. In postmodern terms, especially in the work of Derrida, everyone, all of the time, has the capacity to "write"—that is, to create innovative responses to the code and more specific oppressive structures.[38] For example, by demanding things of fast-food restaurants that they do not want to deliver (e.g., a rare hamburger or extra-brown French fries), people are engaging in a form of writing that can alter the nature of the fast-food restaurant and perhaps ultimately the code. Clearly, we are talking of millions of very specific behaviors repeated over and over again; we are talking about innumerable microlines of resistance.

A related set of actions would involve scrambling the signs associated with the code. Baudrillard sees graffiti artists as playing this role within the city,[39] but what form might it take in a setting such as the fast-food restaurant? Graffiti on the walls of the local McDonald's would certainly represent an assault on its fetish for cleanliness and, more generally, on it as a system. Another example might involve a deliberate misreading of the signs that dominate the fast-food restaurant. People might come in and sit down and wait for service rather than following the code and waiting in line to order their own food. Also, people might do the latter but then leave their food on the counter, indicating an expectation that the food will be delivered to them. These efforts to scramble the code at the fast-food restaurant might serve to destabilize what, as we have seen, Baudrillard regards as an already fragile system.

Ultimately, Baudrillard favors any kind of indeterminacy as a way of responding to the determinacy of the code with its reproduction and endless repetition. Death, not as a final event but as a model of indeterminacy, is Baudrillard's paradigm for responding to the system.[40] This, of course, does not mean that people should take to dying in droves at the counters of fast-food restaurants, but it does mean that any kind of indeterminacy would serve to disrupt the smooth operation of the system and the code. More specifically, Baudrillard recommends that we inject some risk—some small measure of death—into otherwise meticulously regulated systems such as fast-food restaurants. This suggests a range of actions anywhere from taking the chance and ordering a Big Mac without special sauce to actually eschewing fast-food restaurants and taking the plunge and preparing a meal from scratch at home.

Although most of the responses discussed in this section are nonrational or irrational, there are more rational responses to be found in postmodern social theory. One example is Jameson's suggestion that what we need are new cognitive maps.[41] Adrift in the hyperspace of postmodernity, we need new kinds of guides to help us find our way. On the one hand, this means that we need, and need to do, new kinds of social analyses and critiques of the world of the new means of consumption. On the other hand, we need maps that will help us find the increasingly scarce alternatives to those things.

A more rational task, mainly for scholars and intellectuals, would be to engage in Jameson's transcoding.[42] That is, a scholar can examine what one can say, think, and do in, for example, the fast-food restaurant and compare and contrast that to the possibilities in other systems. Such a contrast might serve to point out the problems in the fast-food restaurant as well as some alternatives to it.

Conclusion

The purpose of this chapter has been to explore fast-food restaurants, credit cards, and many other new means of consumption from the perspective of postmodern theory. This chapter is a supplement to previous interpretations by the author of fast-food restaurants and credit cards from a modern perspective. It is clear that the new means of consumption can be analyzed just as easily and effectively from a postmodern perspective as they can from a modern viewpoint. Furthermore, and more important, a postmodern perspective leads to a different set of insights into the new means of consumption than are derived from a modern viewpoint. They are not better, or poorer, insights than those derived from modern theory; they are simply a different set of insights. The analysis of the new means of consumption clearly indicates the utility of both modern and postmodern theory; indeed, it demonstrates the great strength of using both approaches simultaneously.

The new means of consumption are not modern or postmodern phenomena. They are social phenomena that can be usefully analyzed from both perspectives. There is not much utility in worrying about whether we have moved from a modern to a postmodern society. Indeed, such thinking is often counterproductive, leading to endless wrangling of whether we have undergone some kind of epochal change. The body of postmodern theory, however, especially the thinking of such people as Baudrillard, Lyotard, Jameson, and Bauman is, as is demonstrated in this essay, of great utility in thinking about contemporary social developments. Good theory is good theory, whether it carries a modern or postmodern label. We need to spend less time worrying about how we label theory and spend more time developing and using strong, useful theoretical perspectives.

Notes

1. Ritzer, G. (1996). *The McDonaldization of society* (rev. ed.). Thousand Oaks, CA: Pine Forge Press. (Original work published 1993)

2. Ritzer, G. (1995). *Expressing America: A critique of the increasingly global credit card society.* Thousand Oaks, CA: Pine Forge Press.

3. Baudrillard, J. (1988). Consumer society. In *Jean Baudrillard: Selected writings* (p. 54). Stanford, CA: Stanford University Press. (Original work published 1970)

4. Ritzer, G. (in press). *Consuming society.* Thousand Oaks, CA: Pine Forge Press.

5. Lyotard, J.-F. (1992). *The postmodern explained* (p. 24). Minneapolis: University of Minnesota Press. (Original work published 1988)

6. Weinstein, D., & Weinstein, M. A. (1993). *Postmodern(ized) Simmel.* London: Routledge.

7. Featherstone, M. (1991). *Consumer culture and postmodernism.* London: Sage.

8. Baudrillard (1988), in *Jean Baudrillard: Selected writings,* p. 54.

9. Bauman, Z. (1992). *Intimations of postmodernity.* London: Routledge.

10. Bauman (1992), *Intimations of postmodernity,* p. 54.

11. Bauman (1992), *Intimations of postmodernity,* p. 54.

12. Bauman (1992), *Intimations of postmodernity,* p. 54.

13. Schutz, A. (1967). *The phenomenology of the social world.* Evanston, IL: Northwestern University Press. (Original work published 1932)

14. Jameson, F. (1984). Postmodernism, or, the cultural logic of late capitalism. *New Left Review,* 59-92; (1991). *Postmodernism, or, the cultural logic of late capitalism.* London: Verso.

15. Baudrillard, J. (1983). *Simulations.* New York: Semiotext(e).

16. Baudrillard, J. (1989). *America.* London: Verso. (Original work published 1986)

17. Baudrillard (1986/1989), *America.*

18. Baudrillard (1986/1989), *America.*

19. Debord, G. (1977). *The society of the spectacle.* London: Rebel Press.

20. Fjellman, S. M. (1992). *Vinyl leaves: Walt Disney World and America.* Boulder, CO: Westview.

21. Baudrillard, J. (1990). *Fatal strategies.* New York: Semiotext(e). (Original work published 1983)

22. Jameson (1984), *New Left Review,* pp. 59-92; Jameson (1991), *Postmodernism, or, the cultural logic of late capitalism.*

23. Baudrillard, J. (1993). *Symbolic exchange and death.* London: Sage. (Original work published 1976)

24. Baudrillard (1990). *Fatal strategies,* p. 146.

25. Baudrillard (1990). *Fatal strategies,* p. 142.

26. Postman, N. (1985). *Amusing ourselves to death: Public discourse in the age of show business.* New York: Viking.

27. Bauman (1992), *Intimations of postmodernity,* pp. 187-204.

28. Foucault, M. (1979). *Discipline and punish: The birth of the prison.* New York: Vintage.

29. Baudrillard (1990). *Fatal strategies,* p. 68.

30. Baudrillard (1990). *Fatal strategies,* pp. 130-142.

31. Baudrillard (1990). *Fatal strategies,* p. 135.

32. Baudrillard (1990). *Fatal strategies,* p. 132.

33. Stephanson, A. (1989). Regarding postmodernism: A conversation with Fredric Jameson. In *Postmodernism: Jameson: Critique.* Washington, DC: Maisonneuve Press.

34. Gane, M. (Ed.). (1993). *Baudrillard live: Selected interviews.* London: Routledge.

35. Gane (1993), *Baudrillard live,* p. 62.

36. Gane (1993), *Baudrillard live,* p. 62.

37. Gane (1993), *Baudrillard live,* p. 70.

38. Derrida, J. (1978). *Writing and difference.* Chicago: University of Chicago Press.

39. Baudrillard, J. (1990). *Seduction.* London: Macmillan.

40. Baudrillard (1990). *Seduction,* p. 146.

41. Jameson, F. (1989). Afterword—Marxism and postmodernism. In D. Kellner (Ed.), *Postmodernism: Jameson: Critique* (pp. 369-387). Washington, DC: Maisonneuve Press.

42. Jameson (1989), in *Postmodernism: Jameson: Critique,* pp. 369-387; Best, S. (1989). Jameson, totality, and the poststructuralist critique. In D. Kellner (Ed.), *Postmodernism: Jameson: Critique* (pp. 333-368). Washington, DC: Maisonneuve Press.

Discussion Questions

1. Discuss Ritzer's analysis of the difference between productive and reproductive technologies. Use either television or the computer as an example, and indicate whether you agree or disagree with the distinction he makes.

2. Keep a diary for one day and identify and describe all the instances you encounter in which the social relations can be characterized as simulacra.

3. Although credit cards are a convenience (and sometimes a necessity), there is a negative side to them. On the basis of your own experience or that of someone you know well, do you think that Ritzer's criticisms of the credit card society are on target? Do you think the negatives outweigh the positives, or is the reverse the case? Defend your position.

CHAPTER 12

The Cinematic Society, the Interview, and the Postmodern Self

Norman K. Denzin

Norman K. Denzin is Professor of Sociology, Communications, and Humanities at the University of Illinois, Urbana-Champaign. He is the author of numerous books, includ-ing Children and Their Caretakers, Sociological Methods, The Research Act, Inter-pretive Interactionism, Images of Postmodern Society, The Recovering Alcoholic, The Alcoholic Self, The Cinematic Society, Reading Race, *and* Interpretive Ethno-graphy. *He has served as the editor of several sociological journals, including* The Socio-logical Quarterly, Studies in Symbolic Interactionism, *and* Qualitative Inquiry. *He has coedited several books with Yvonna Lincoln, including* Handbook of Qualitative Research *and* Collecting and Interpreting Qualitative Materials. *He is past president of the Midwest Sociological Society.*

Think about how much we learn about contemporary life by way of interviews. Larry King introduces us to presidents and power brokers. Barbara Walters plumbs the emotional depths of stars and celebrities. Oprah and Geraldo invite the ordinary, tortured, and bizarre to "spill their guts" to millions of home viewers (Holstein & Gubrium, 1995, p. 1).

We inhabit a secondhand world, one already mediated by cinema, television, and the other apparatuses of postmodern society. In this world, culture is driven increasingly less by the technological innovation of the written word and increasingly more by the interactive conventions of dramaturgy, performance, and the media. We have no direct access to this world; we only experience and study its representations. A reflexive sociology studies society as a dramaturgical production. The reflexive interview is a central component of this interpretive project.

In this chapter, I examine the nexus of the cinematic and the interview society. I show how the postmodern has become an interview society, how our very subjectivity "comes to us in the form of stories elicited through interviewing" (Holstein & Gubrium, 2000, p. 129; Atkinson & Silverman, 1997). The interview, whether conducted by social researchers, mass media reporters, television journalists, therapists, or counselors, is now a ubiquitous method of self construction (Holstein & Gubrium, 2000, p. 129). Of central concern herein is the ways that the self is constructed in postmodern times. As such, this is in part an exercise in social psychology from the perspective of a theorist who is grounded in the symbolic interactionist tradition but has also been open to various currents of postmodern social thought. Herein, I seek to blend the insights of both theoretical approaches in coming to understand some of the unique characteristics of self formation in contemporary society.

I discuss the concept of the active, dialogical interview, anchoring this complex formation in the postmodern, cinematic society (Denzin, 1995a, 1995b, 1997; Holstein & Gubrium, 1995, 2000; Jackson, 1998; Scheurich, 1995). The reflexive interview is simultaneously a site for conversation, a discursive method, and a communicative format that produces knowledge about the self and its place in the cinematic society—that society which knows itself through the reflective gaze of the cinematic apparatus. A cinematic sociology requires a concept of the reflexive interview.

A single two-sided question organizes my argument, namely "How does the postmodern, cinematic world mediate the ways in which we represent ourselves to ourselves?" and "What is the place of the interview-interviewer relationship in this production process?" My argument unfolds thusly. I begin by discussing the meaning of postmodernity and outlining the central features of the postmodern, cinematic, interview society. I then show how the interview and the interviewer as a voyeur are basic features of this society. I thicken this argument by demonstrating how popular media representations shape and define situated cultural identities. I show how these representations become anchor points for the postmodern self. In other words, I seek to indicate that they occupy a central place in the background of our cultural consciousness. They mediate structures of meaning in the cinematic-interview society. A circular model of interpretation is thus created. Interviews, interviewers, and storytellers are defined in terms of these dominant cultural images and understandings. Thus does the cinematic society structure the interview society and vice versa. I conclude with a series of epistemological observations on the significance of the relation between the cinematic society and the reflexive interview (Bourdieu, 1996; Burawoy, 1998; Heyl, 2000; Mishler, 1986).

What Is the Postmodern?

The term *postmodern* is an oxymoron with a short history. How can something be post, or after, the modern when the modern represents the present or recent moment (Hassan, 1985, p. 121)? What comes after the present but another present, or period in history, that is a continuation of the present (Updike, 1984)? It is an oxymoron because it comes at the end of a series of post-isms, most important poststructuralism, that amorphous theoretical formation that has theorized language, meaning, and textuality after the semiotic-structural movement inspired by theoretical influences from earlier in the 20th century, particularly those originating in the work of Ferdinand de Saussure and Claude Lévi-Strauss.

Users of the word *postmodern* are attempting to describe fields of political, cultural, aesthetic, scientific, and moral experiences that are distinctly different from those that were taken for granted in an earlier historical period, commonly called the modern or Enlightenment phase. It is not possible to give a precise date for the beginning of the postmodern period. Just as Virginia Woolf claimed that modernism began "in or about December, 1910" (Hassan, 1985, p. 122), however, there are those who have tried to identify a point at which the postmodern took root. Thus, Hassan (p. 122) argued that the postmodern began in approximately September, 1939, at the moment World War II and its attendant horrors commenced, whereas architectural critic Charles Jencks contends (somewhat tongue-in-cheek I suspect) that it began at 3:32 p.m. on July 15, 1972—the moment when St. Louis's Pruitt-Igoe public housing project was demolished by a series of controlled dynamite blasts (Kivisto, 2004, p. 123). Although other "precise" dates could be chosen, the point of these examples is that the dawn of the postmodern begins with a sense of disillusionment with the modernist project and its optimism about the capacity for social progress and harmony as well as for our capacity to know and to translate knowledge into power. Among other things, postmodern theorists are suspicious about the capacity to comprehend the totality of the world, a suspicion that takes the form of critiquing what are referred to as the "grand narratives" of modernity.

Postmodern social theory may be read as a response to this skepticism. Refusing the modernist agenda to theorize societies as totalities interpreted from within any of the familiar grand metanarratives advanced by the classic founders of sociology—including Marx on the dynamics of capitalism, Weber on the rationalization of the world, and Durkheim on the shift from mechanical to organic solidarity—postmodern social theory has the following characteristics. It seeks to produce theoretical-interpretive analyses that illuminate the social world through the close-up analyses of selected slices of social life that are treated as texts. It argues, following the symbolic interactionist tradition (Blumer, 1933), that society in the here and now, society at hand, is best understood as an interactional accomplishment that is shaped by preexisting and emergent political, economic, and moral structures of crystallized social experience. Postmodern theory operates with the assumption that the exercise of power involves the control and manipulation of knowledge and quickly translates into the control and application of knowledge structures. Furthermore, postmodern social theory orients itself to and focuses its gaze on the modern, computerized, mass media-saturated world in which information technologies define what is real.

What, then, is the postmodern? In my view, the postmodern consists of four elements. First, it describes a sequence of historical events from World War II to the present, including the Vietnam War, the deindustrialization of the advanced industrial nations, the triumph of neoliberalism and the concurrent failure of the political Left, the end of the Cold War with the collapse of communism and the dissolution of the Soviet Union, and what has become known in shorthand as 9/11 and its aftermath. Second, postmodern refers to the transnational forms of capitalism that have introduced what Fredric Jameson (1991) has referred to as the "cultural logic" of late capitalism. Third, it describes a movement in the visual arts, architecture, cinema, popular music, and cultural theory that goes against the grain of classic realist and modernist formations. Finally, it references a form of theorizing about the social that is postpositivist, interpretive, and critical.

Although some theorists of postmodernism focus particular attention on the penetration of consumerism into all facets of social life (see Chapter 11), I propose that postmodern society is first and foremost a cinematic, dramaturgical production. The postmodern terrain is defined in visual terms, which includes notions of the display, the icon, representations of the real seen through the camera's eye, captured on videotape, and given in the moving picture (Ulmer, 1989). In particular, I am convinced that film and television have transformed contemporary societies into visual or "cinematic" societies.

The Postmodern Cinematic Society

By 1930, the cinema had become an integral part of modern industrial societies. In America and other industrial nations, going to the movies became a weekly pastime for huge audiences. Not only did a majority of Americans attend the cinema regularly, but also American films were exported to Europe and elsewhere, as Hollywood stars became the personal idols of millions. Fan clubs were formed, and the movie theater marquee became a permanent part of virtually every American community. A new visual literacy was being produced. Americans (and others) were learning to look at and see things that they had not seen before. Although cinema clearly had a profound impact on rapidly industrializing and urbanizing societies, with notable exceptions—including the Chicago school's Robert Park, symbolic interactionist theory's founding voice Herbert Blumer, and some critical theorists associated with the Frankfurt school—sociology ignored the impact of the film industry.

Hollywood's cinematic apparatus ushered into American civil society a new scoptic regime that initially privileged the visual over the aural. This visual culture muted the voice of the other, producing a loss of aurality (the silent film). This loss of voice was quickly overturned, however, merging the panoptic with the panauditory. American cinema created a space for a certain kind of public, communal life. Inside the new movie palaces, Americans entered the public realm. But this was a self-contained realm, the public made private by the darkness of the theater, and here in these dark places a version of Bakhtin's (1968) carnival was enacted.

Thus was born within a few decades American cinema and its counterpart, the cinematic society. Fittingly defined in the early modern form by D. W. Griffith's racist film *The Birth of a Nation,* the movies entered American culture under a cloud of suspicion. Introduced as a new form of entertainment for the masses, an art form for some, a source of profit for a few, a challenge to Christian morality for others, a threat to the human eye to some, and an educational vehicle for others, this new apparatus fundamentally transformed American society.

Members of postmodern society know themselves through the reflected images and narratives of cinema and television. On this, Altheide (1995) observes that "culture is not only mediated through mass media . . . culture in both form and content is constituted and embodied by the mass media" (p. 59). The postmodern landscape is distinguished, as Gottschalk (2000) argues, by "its constant saturation by multiple electronic screens which simulate emotions, interactions, events, desires. . . . From TV screens to computer terminals, from surveillance cameras to cell phones, we increasingly experience everyday life, reality . . . via technologies of spectacle, simulation and 'telepresence.'" (p. 23).

Consider the following exchange between ESPN sports journalist Sal Paolantanio and Kurt Warner, quarterback of the St. Louis Rams and the most valuable player of the 2000 Super Bowl (*Sports Center*, 2000; see also Vecesy, 2000):

Sal:	There's a minute and 54 seconds left in the game. The Titans have just tied the score. Now look. Let me show you your 73-yard winning pass to Isaac Bruce. Kurt, what were you thinking when Isaac caught that pass?
Kurt (looks up at replay):	We'd called the same play earlier and Isaac was open. So we thought it would work. It was a go route. We thought we could get a big one right off the bat. I just thought it was meant to be, it was meant to work.
Sal:	This has been a terrific year for you. Five years ago you were sacking groceries in the IGA. Two years ago you were playing arena football in Cedar Rapids, Iowa. This is better than a Hollywood script. Tell me how you feel about what has happened to you this year?
Kurt:	I don't think of it as a Hollywood story. It's my life. I take it one day at a time.
Sal:	It has not been easy, has it?
Kurt:	I was getting to the point of thinking how much longer am I going to have before people say he is too old to give him an opportunity. It has been tough for us until this last year. Even when I was playing arena football we did all right, but a lot of tough decisions. . . . When I first started dating my wife, she was on food stamps, and I was in between jobs. That is why I ended up stocking shelves; I had to do something at nights so I could work out and keep my chances in football. A lot of things like that have helped keep things in perspective, even though we are not making a million dollars, we are very fortunate to be where we are at, in this position, and don't look beyond that, don't take anything for granted.
Sal:	Thanks Kurt. Is there anything else you want to say?

Kurt: I'm truly blessed. If I can be a source of hope to anybody, I'm happy to be a part of it. The good Lord has blessed me. I am on a mission. He has called me to do this. I can only share my testimony with others. Thank you Jesus.

Kurt's self-narrative is grafted into the replay of the winning touchdown pass. Indeed, this Super Bowl victory symbolizes the larger than life triumph that Warner has experienced during the course of the preceding 5 years. Sal elicits this self-story by asking Warner how he feels about his award-winning year, comparing it to a Hollywood script. Kurt complies by giving him a socially acceptable answer; indeed, Paolantanio's questions establish the right for Warner to give this extended account of his life and what it means (Holstein & Gubrium, 2000, p. 129). The viewer vicariously shares in this experience.[1]

The ingredients of the postmodern self are modeled in the media. The postmodern self has become a sign of itself, a double dramaturgical reflection anchored in media representations on one side and everyday life on the other. These cultural identities are filtered through the personal troubles and the emotional experiences from the individual's interactions with everyday life. These existential troubles connect back to the dominant cultural themes of the postmodern era. The electronic media and the new information technologies turn everyday life into a theatrical spectacle in which the dramas that surround the decisive performances of existential crises are enacted. This creates a new existential "videocy," a language of crisis coded in electronic, media terms.

The media structure these crises and their meanings. A 38-year-old male alcoholic is standing outside the door to where Alcoholics Anonymous (AA) meetings are held. He asks (Denzin, 1995b)

How do I get into one of those AA meetings? What do I say?. . . I seen them in the movies. That Michael Keaton in *Clean and Sober.* . . . He went to one of them. He just stood up and said he was an alcoholic. Do I have to do that? I ain't even sure I am one, but I drank a fifth of Black Jack last night and I started up again this mornin.' I'm scared. (p. 260)

This is a postmodern story waiting to be heard, already partially told through the figure of Michael Keaton, himself an actor, playing a fictional character (Daryl), who went to a fictional AA meeting in a Hollywood film that gave audiences the first extended view of life in a treatment center. Texts within texts, movies, everyday life, a man down and out on his luck, AA, a door into a building in which meetings are held, anxiety, and fear. The everyday existential world connects to the cinematic apparatus, and our drunk on the street hopes to begin a story that will have a happy ending, like Michael Keaton's. What this indicates is that alcoholism films are simultaneously visual records of and a part of everyday life.

The Birth of Cinematic Surveillance

The cinematic, surveillance society soon became a disciplinary structure filled with subjects (voyeurs) who obsessively looked and gazed at one another as they became, at the same time, obsessive listeners, eavesdroppers, persons whose voices and telephone lines could be tapped, voices that could be dubbed, and new versions of the spoken and seen self. A new social type was created—the voyeur, or Peeping Tom, who would, in various guises (ethnographer, social scientist, detective, psychoanalyst, crime reporter, investigative journalist, innocent bystander, or sexual pervert), elevate the concepts of looking and listening to new levels. In other words, the cinematic society is one in which the form and content of the motion picture industry spill out from the confines of the theater, pervading our everyday lives so that the boundaries between the world of the movies and the world of "real life" become increasingly blurred. Life mirrors art and vice versa.

With the advent of color and sound in the mid-1920s, there was a drive toward cinematic realism. This impulse to create a level of realism that mapped everyday life complimented the rise of naturalistic realism in the American novel and the emergence of hard-nosed journalistic reporting by the major American newspapers and radio (and later TV) stations (Denzin, 1997, pp. 21-22). During the same time period, an ethnographic, psychoanalytic, and life history approach was taking hold in the social sciences and society at large. Like journalists, sociologists and market and survey researchers were learning how to use the interview to gather and report on the facts of social life (Denzin, 1997, p. 129, 2000; Fontana & Frey, 1994, p. 362).

Robert E. Park, a founder of the Chicago school of ethnographic research (Vidich & Lyman, 1994, pp. 32-33), clarifies this relationship between journalism, social science, and the use of the interview (Park, 1950):

> After leaving college, I got a job as a reporter. . . . I wrote about all sorts of things. . . . My interest in the newspaper had grown out of the discovery that a reporter who had the facts was a more effective reformer than an editorial writer. . . . According to my earliest conception of a sociologist he was to be a kind of super-reporter. . . . He was to report a little more accurately, and in a little more detail. (pp. v, vii-ix)

Thus, although sociologists and journalists both used interviews, the duties and practices of the two occupational groups were separated. They go about their business organizing surveillance in their distinct ways.

The Interview Society

The interview society emerges historically as a consequence, in part, of the central place that newspapers, the cinema, and television came and continue to occupy in daily life. The media, human service personnel, market researchers, and social scientists "increasingly get their information via interviews" (Holstein & Gubrium, 1995, p. 1). The interview society has turned the confessional mode of discourse into a public form of entertainment (Atkinson & Silverman, 1997, pp. 309-315; Holstein & Gubrium, 2000, p. 129). The world of private troubles, the site of the authentic or real self, has become a public commodity.

The Interview Goes to Hollywood

It remained for Hollywood to authorize the interview as a primary method of gathering information about social issues, selves, and the meanings of personal experience. Soon Hollywood was telling stories about newspaper reporters (*The Front Page*, 1931), detectives and private eyes (*Maltese Falcon*, 1931, 1941), psychoanalysts and psychiatrists (*Spellbound*, 1945), spies and secret agents (*Saboteur*, 1942), and market researchers (*Desk Set*, 1957; *Sex and the Single Girl*, 1964) and offering spoofs about sociologists (*The Milagro Beanfield War*, 1988) and anthropologists (*Krippendorf's Tribe*, 1998).

Each of these film genres glamorized the interview as a form of interaction and as a strategy and technique for getting persons to talk about themselves and others (Holstein & Gubrium, 1995, p. 3). Journalists, detectives, and social scientists were presented as experts in the use of this conversational form. It was expected that they would use this form when interacting with members of society. Furthermore, it was expected that persons, if properly asked, would reveal their inner selves to such experts.

Thus, the key assumptions of the interview society were soon secured. The media and Hollywood cinema helped solidify the following cluster of beliefs: Only skilled interviewers and therapists (and sometimes the person) have access to the deep, authentic self of the person; sociologists, journalists, and psychoanalysts know how to ask questions that will produce disclosures, often discrediting, about the hidden self; and members of the interview society have certain experiences that are more authentic than others, and these experiences are keys to the hidden self. (These are the experiences that have left deep marks and scars on the person.) Adept interviewers can uncover these experiences and their meanings to the person. Nonetheless, persons also have access to their own experiences; this increases the value of first-person narratives, which are the site of personal meaning.

When probing for the inner self, or when seeking information from the person, interviewers are expected to use some method to record what is said in the interview. In the film *True Crime* (1999), Clint Eastwood plays Steve Everett, a burnt-out, alcoholic reporter who becomes convinced that Frank Beachum, a black man due to die within 24 hours in San Quentin, is innocent. Eastwood tracks down Mr. Porterhouse, the man whose testimony led to Frank's conviction. Everett and Porterhouse meet in a café and the following exchange unfolds:

Everett: Let me get this straight, you didn't really see the murder?

Porterhouse: I never said I did.

Everett: What did you see?

Porterhouse: I can't tell you how many times I've been over this. I went into Pokeums to use the phone. My car had overheated. Beachum jumped up from behind the counter. He was covered with blood and had a gun in his hand. He was bending over, stealing her necklace.

He got one good look at me and then he ran out the store. My concern was for the girl. So I immediately dialed 911. I figured why should I run after a killer, when the police should do their job.

Everett: And they sure did it, didn't they.

Porterhouse: Aren't you gonna take some notes, or somethin'? Or use a tape recorder? Usually when I'm talkin' to a reporter they wanta keep some sort of record of what I've been sayin'.

Everett: I have a photographic memory (points to head). I have a notebook right here (which he pulls out of his jacket pocket, holding a pen in his hand).

Eastwood refuses to write anything in his notebook, and Porterhouse challenges him, "I did some checking on you. You're the guy who led the crusade to get the rapist released. That lying what's his name? Had all your facts straight on that one too, didn't you."

Everett next interviews Frank in his prison cell. Frank's wife is with him (the reporter assigned to the case was killed in an auto accident):

Frank: I guess you wanta hear how it feels to be in here.

Everett: Yeah, it's a human interest piece.

Frank: I feel isolated. I feel fear, pain, fear of prison, fear of being separated from my loved ones. All those fears rolled up into one.

Everett takes his notebook out of his pocket.

Frank: I want to tell everyone that I believe in Jesus Christ, our Lord and Savior.

Everett scribbles the following in his notebook: BLV, JC.

Frank: I came into my faith late in life. Did a lot of bad things. . . . I believe that the crooked road remains straight, that's what the bible says.

Everett scribbles the following in his notebook: LORD, SAV, CARO, STRAIT.

Frank: Is there anymore that you want?

Everett: You don't know me. I'm just a guy out there with a screw loose. Frankly I don't give a rat's ass about Jesus Christ. I don't even care what's right or wrong. But my nose tells me something stinks, and I gotta have my faith in it, just like you have your faith in Jesus. . . . I know there's truth out there somewhere. . . . I believe you.

Wife: Where were you?

Everett: It wasn't my story.

Frank clearly expected Everett to ask him how he felt about being on death row. Frank expected to tell a reporter a deeply personal story about what this experience means to his inner, authentic self. Indeed, Everett's presence in the prison elicits such a story from Frank. Paraphrasing Holstein and Gubrium (2000, p. 129), the prison interview with a journalist is now a natural part of the death row identity landscape. But Everett, through his note taking, mocks this assumption. He has no desire to record the inner meaning of this experience for Frank. This is unlike Sal Paolantanio, who sought and got from Kurt Warner a self-validating, self-congratulatory story about hard work and success in American life.

The Interview Machine as an Epistemological Apparatus

The interview society uses the machinery of the interview to methodically produce situated versions of the self. This machinery works in a systematic and orderly fashion. It structures the talk that occurs in the interview situation. There is an orderly mechanism "for designating who will speak next" (Holstein & Gubrium, 2000, p. 125). Using the question-answer format, this mechanism regulates the flow of conversation. Talk occurs in question-answer pairs because the asking of a question requires an answer. Turn-taking structures this give-and-take. The rule of single speakership obtains, one person speaks at a time. In this sense, interviews are orderly, dramaturgical accomplishments. They draw on local understandings and are constrained by those understandings. They are narrative productions; they have beginnings, middles, and endings.

The methodology of asking questions is central to the operation of this machine. Different epistemologies and ideologies shape this methodological practice. Four epistemological formats can be identified: the objectively neutral format, the entertainment and investigative format, the collaborative or active interview format, and the reflexive, dialogical interview.[2]

For each format, the asking of a question is an incitement to speak, an invitation to tell a story; in this sense, the interview elicits narratives of the self (Holstein & Gubrium, 2000, p. 129). The place of the interviewer in this process varies dramatically. In the objectively neutral format, the interviewer, using structured or semi-structured interview schedules, attempts to gather information without influencing the story that is being told. Holstein and Gubrium correctly observe that the demands of ongoing interaction make the "'ideal' interview a practical impossibility, because the interview itself always remains accountable to the normative expectancies of competent conversation as well as to the demand for a good story to satisfy the needs of the researcher" (p. 131).

In the entertainment format, the interviewer often acts as a partisan, seeking to elicit a story that will sell as an entertainment commodity or be marketed as a new piece of information about a story that is in the process of being told. In the entertainment-investigative format, the interviewer asks leading, aggressive questions as well as friendly questions—questions that allow the subject to embellish on a previous story or to give more detail on the meanings of an important experience.

Paolantanio's interview with Warner employs the entertainment format. This is a friendly interview that shows both Warner and Paolantanio in a good light. Steve Everett's interview in *True Crime* with Mr. Porterhouse deploys the investigative version of this format. Everett is aggressive and hostile. He seeks to discredit Porterhouse as a witness.

In the collaborative-active format, interviewer and respondent tell a story together (Holstein & Gubrium, 1995, pp. 76-77). In this format, a conversation occurs. Indeed, the identities of interviewer and respondent will disappear. Each person becomes a storyteller, or they collaborate in telling a conjoint story. This is what occurs in the ESPN interview: Together, Sal and Kurt tell a story about the meaning of this victory for Kurt's life.

With the reflexive, interview format, two speakers enter into a dialogical relationship with one another. In this relationship, a tiny drama is played out. Each person becomes a party to the utterances of the other. Together, the two speakers create a small dialogical world of unique meaning and experience. In this interaction, each speaker struggles to understand the thought of the other, reading and paying attention to such matters as intonation, facial gestures, and word selection (Bakhtin, 1986, pp. 92-93).

Consider the following exchange taken from Wayne Wang's 1981 *Chan Is Missing.* Set in contemporary San Francisco, the film mocks popular culture representations of stereotypical Asian American identities. It also mocks social science and those scholars who point to language as an answer to cultural differences. The following Lily Tomlin–like monologue is central to this position. In the speaker's monologue, racial and ethnic identities are constructed. This construction is directly connected to the use of the objective interview format. The speaker is a female Asian American attorney. She is attempting to find Mr. Chan, who had an automobile accident just days before he disappeared. She is speaking to Jo, a middle-aged Chinese American cabdriver, and his young "Americanized" nephew, Steve. They are at Chester's Cafe. The young attorney is dressed in a black masculine-style suit with a white shirt and dark tie (Denzin, 1995a):

You see I'm doing a paper on the legal implications of cross-cultural misunderstandings [nods head]. Mr. Chan's case is a perfect example of what I want to expose. The policeman and Mr. Chan have completely different culturally related assumptions about what kind of communication [shot of Steve, then Jo] each one was using. The policeman, in an English speaking mode, asks a direct factual question—"Did you stop at the stop sign?" He expected a "yes or a no" answer. Mr. Chan, however, rather than giving him a yes or a no answer began to go into his past driving record—how good it was, the number of years he had been in the United States, all the people that he knew—trying to relate different events, objects, or situations to what was happening then to the action at hand. Now this is very typical. . . . The Chinese try to relate points, events, or objects that they feel are pertinent to the situation, which may not to anyone else seem directly relevant at the time. . . . This policeman became rather impatient, restated the question, "Did you or did you not stop at the stop sign?" in a rather hostile tone, which in turn flustered Mr. Chan, which caused him to hesitate answering the question, which further enraged the policeman so that he asked the question again, "You didn't stop at the stop sign, did you?" in a negative tone, to which Mr. Chan automatically answered "No." Now to any native speaker of English "No" would mean "No I didn't stop at the stop sign." However, to Mr. Chan "No I didn't stop at the stop sign" was not "No I didn't stop at the stop sign" [Jo shakes head, looks away]. It was "No, I didn't not stop at the stop sign." In other words, "Yes I did stop at the stop sign." Do you see what I'm saying? [camera pans room]. [Jo (voice-over):"Chan Hung wouldn't run away because of the car accident. I'm feeling something might have happened to him."] (p. 105)

Here our speaker, the young attorney, attempts to dialogically enter into and interpret the meanings that were circulating in Mr. Chan's interview with the policeman. In so doing, she criticizes the concept of cross-cultural communication, showing through her conversation that meanings are always dialogic and contextual.

The text from Wang's film is an example of how the reflexive, dialogic interviewer deconstructs the uses and abuses of the interview—uses that are associated with the objectively neutral, entertainment, and investigative formats. Wang's text suggests that interpretations based on the surface meanings of an utterance sequence are likely to be superficial. To paraphrase Dillard (1982, p. 46), serious students of society take pains to distinguish their work from such interpretive practices.

At another level, reflexively oriented scholars, such as Bakhtin, contend that there is no essential self or private or real self behind the public self. They argue that there are only different selves, different performances, different ways of being, for instance, a gendered or racialized person in a social situation. These performances are based on different interpretive practices. These practices give the self and the person a sense of grounding or narrative coherence (Gubrium & Holstein, 1998, p. 165). There is no inner or deep self that is accessed by the interview or narrative method. There are only different interpretive (and performative) versions of who the person is.

Steve Everett embodies one version of the reflexive interviewer. He has no interest in the inner self of the person he is interviewing, no interest in right or wrong. He only seeks the truth—the truth that says an injustice may have been done. Wang's Asian American attorney is another version of this interviewer; she understands that the self is a verbal and narrative construction.

The Interview and the Dramaturgical Society

The text from the Kurt Warner interview suggests that the metaphor of the dramaturgical society (Lyman, 1990, p. 221) or "life as theater" (Brissett & Edgley, 1990, p. 2; Goffman, 1959, pp. 254-255) is no longer a metaphor. It has become interactional reality. Life and art have become mirror images of one another. Reality, as it is visually experienced, is a staged, social production.

Raban (1981) provides an example of how life and television coincide. In a TV ad "beamed by the local station in Decorah, an Iowa farmer spoke stiffly to the camera in testimony to the bags of fertilizer that were heaped in front of him"

(p. 123). Here, the personal testimony of the farmer, a hands-on expert, authorizes the authenticity and value of the product. This message is carried live, staged in the frame of the TV commercial; a real farmer says this product works. The farmer's awkwardness comes, perhaps, from the fact that he must look at himself doing this endorsement, knowing that if he sees himself looking this way, others will as well.

The reflected, everyday self and its gendered presentations are attached to the cinematic/televisual self. Blumer (1933) provides an example from an earlier era. An interview respondent connects her gendered self to the Hollywood screen:

Female, 19-year-old white college freshman: When I discovered I should have this coquettish and coy look which all girls may have, I tried to do it in my room. And surprises! I could imitate Pola Negri's cool or fierce look. Vilma Banky's sweet and coquettish attitude. I learned the very way of taking my gentlemen friends to and from the door with that wistful smile, until it has become a part of me. (p. 34)

Real, everyday experiences are judged against their staged, cinematic, video counterpart. The fans of Hollywood stars dress like the stars, make love like the stars, and dream the dreams of the stars. Blumer (1933) provides an example.

Female, 24-year-old white college senior: During my high school period I particularly liked pictures in which the setting was a millionaire's estate or some such elaborate place. After seeing a picture of this type, I would imagine myself living such a life of ease as the society girl I had seen. My day-dreams would be concerned with lavish wardrobes, beautiful homes, servants, imported automobiles, yachts, and countless suitors. (p. 64)

With this dramaturgical turn, the technology of the media "disengages subjects from their own expressions. . . . Individuals become observers of their own acts. . . . Actions come to be negotiated in terms of a media aesthetic, both actor and spectator live a reality arbitrated by the assumptions of media technicians" (Eason, 1984, p. 430). Altheide and Snow (1991; see also Oudes, 1989, p. 46) provide an example from the Richard Nixon Presidency. In a December 1, 1969, memo to H. R. Haldeman, Nixon wrote:

We need a part- or full-time TV man on our staff for the purpose of seeing that my TV appearances are handled on a professional basis. When I think of the millions of dollars that go into one lousy 30-second television spot advertising deodorant, it seems to me unbelievable that we don't do a better job of seeing that presidential appearances on TV always have the very best professional advice. (p. 105)

Because of the same media aesthetic, Kurt Warner has learned how to talk that form of sports talk Ron Shelton mocks in *Bull Durham.* So too does Frank Beachum expect Steve Everett to record his moral story.

The main carriers of the popular in the postmodern society have become the very media that are defining the content and meaning of the popular; that is, popular culture is now a matter of cinema and the related media, including television, the press, and popular literature. A paradox is created because the everyday is now defined by the cinematic and the televisual. The two can no longer be separated. A press conference at the 1988 National Democratic Political Convention is reported thusly: "A dozen reporters stood outside CBS's area, and as was so often the case at the convention, one began interviewing another. A third commentated wryly on the interview: 'Reporter interviews reporter about press conference'" (Weiss, 1988, pp. 33-34; also quoted in Altheide & Snow, 1991, p. 93)—reporters reporting on reporters interviewing reporters.

Studying the Interview in Cinematic Society

The cinematic apparatuses of contemporary culture stand in a twofold relationship to critical inquiry. First, the cultural logics of the postvideo, cinematic culture define the lived experiences that a critical studies project takes as its subject matter. How these texts structure and give meaning to the everyday must be analyzed. At the same time, critical ethnographies of the video-cinematic text must be constructed, showing how these texts map and give narrative meaning to the crucial cultural identities that circulate in the postmodern society.

Consider race, the racial self, and Hollywood cinema. Lopez (1991) reminds us that "Hollywood does not represent ethnics and minorities; it creates them and provides an audience with an experience of them" (pp. 404-405). Consider Lopez's arguments in terms of the following scene from Spike Lee's highly controversial 1989 film, *Do the Right Thing*. Near the film's climax, as the heat rises on the street, Lee has members of each racial group in the neighborhood hurl vicious racial slurs at one another (Denzin, 1991):

Mookie (to Sal and his Italian sons, Vito and Pino):	Dago, wop, guinea, garlic breath, pizza slingin' spaghetti bender, Vic Damone, Perry Como, Pavarotti.
Pino (to Mookie and the blacks):	Gold chain wearin' fried chicken and biscuit eatin' monkey, ape, baboon, fast runnin', high jumpin', spear chuckin', basketball dunkin' ditso spade, take you fuckin' pizza and go back to Africa.
A Puerto Rican man (to the Korean grocer):	Little slanty eyed, me-no speakie American, own every fruit and vegetable stand in New York, bull shit, Reverend Sun Myung Moon, Summer '88 Olympic kick-ass boxer, sonofabitch.
White policeman (to Puerto Rican youth in the area):	You goya bean eatin' 15 in the car, 30 in the apartment, pointy red shoes wearin' Puerto Ricans, cocksuckers.

Korean grocer (directed to	I got good price for you, how am I doing?
then–New York Mayor Ed Koch):	Chocolate, egg cream drinking, bagel lox, Jew asshole.
Sweet Dick Willie	Korean motherfucker . . . you didn't do a god-
(to the Korean grocer, then to	damn thing except sit on your monkey ass here
his friends):	on this corner and do nothin. (pp. 129-130)

Lee wants his viewers to believe that his speakers are trapped within the walls and streets of a multiracial ghetto that is the Bedford-Stuyvesant area of New York City. Their voices reproduce current (and traditional) cultural, racial, and sexual stereotypes about blacks (spade and monkey), Koreans (slanty eyed), Puerto Ricans (pointy red shoes and cocksuckers), Jews (bagels and lox), and Italians (dago and wop). The effects of these "in-your-face insults" are exaggerated through wide-angled, close-up shots. The speaker's face literally fills the screen as the racial slurs are heard.[3]

Lee's film presents itself as a realist, ethnographic text. It asks the viewer to believe that it is giving an objectively factual, authentic, and realistic account of the lived experiences of race and ethnicity. The film performs race and ethnicity (Lee's Pino talking to Mookie) and does so in ways that support the belief that objective reality has been captured. The film "realistically" reinscribes familiar (and new) cultural stereotypes—for example, young gang members embodying hip-hop, rap culture. Lee's text functions like a documentary film.

Cinematic Society and the Documentary Interview

It is this documentary impulse and its reliance on the objectively neutral interview format that I now examine. I do so through an analysis of Trinh T. Minh-ha's 1989 film, *Surname Viet Given Name Nam*. This is a film about Vietnamese women whose names change and remain constant, depending on whether they marry a foreigner or a Vietnamese. In this film, Trinh (1992, p. 49) has Vietnamese women speak from five different subject positions representing lineage, gender status, age status, leadership position, and historical period. This creates a complex picture of Vietnamese culture (p. 144).

The film is multitextual, layered with pensive images of women in various situations. Historical moments overlap with age periods (childhood, youth, adulthood, and old age), ritual ceremonies (weddings, funerals, war, the market, and dance), and daily household work (cooking) while interviewees talk to off-screen interviewers. There are two voice-overs in English, and a third voice sings sayings, proverbs, and poetry in Vietnamese (with translations as texts on the screen). There are also interviews with Vietnamese subtitled in English and interviews in English synchronized with the on-screen image (Trinh, 1992, p. 49). The interviews are reenacted in Trinh's film by Vietnamese women, who are then interviewed at the end of the film and asked about their experiences of being performers in the film (p. 146).

The film allows the practice of doing reflexive interviews to enter into the construction of the text; thus, the true and the false, the real and the staged, intermingle. Indeed, the early sections of the film unfold like a traditional, realist documentary film (Trinh, 1992, p. 145). The viewer does not know these are actresses reenacting interviews. Nor does the viewer know that the interviews were conducted in the United States, not Vietnam. (This only becomes apparent near the end of the film.)

In using these interpretive strategies, Trinh creates the space for the critical appraisal of the politics of representation that structure the use of interviews in the documentary film. In undoing the objectively neutral interview as a method for gathering information about reality, Trinh (1992, p. 145) takes up the question of truth. Whose truth is she presenting—that given in the on-screen interview situation or that of the women-as-actresses who are interviewed at the end of the film?

Trinh begins by deconstructing the classic interview-based documentary film that enters the native's world and brings news from that world to the world of the Western observer. In its use of the traditional, nondialogical interview method, the documentary film, such as Spike Lee's *Do the Right Thing,* starts with the so-called real world and the subject's place in that world. It uses an aesthetic of objectivity and a technological apparatus that produces truthful statements (images) about the world. Trinh (1991, pp. 33-39) argues that the following elements are central to this apparatus:

- There is a relentless pursuit of naturalism, which requires a connection between the moving image and the spoken word.
- There is authenticity—the use of people who appear to be real and locating these people in "real" situations.
- The filmmaker interviewer is presented as an observer, not as a person who creates what is seen, heard, and read.
- Only events, unaffected by the recording eye, should be captured.
- The film interview captures objective reality.
- Truth can be dramatized.
- Actual facts should be presented in a credible way, with people telling them.
- The film interview text must convince spectators that they should have confidence in the truth of what they see.

These aesthetic strategies define the documentary interview style, allowing the filmmaker-as-interviewer to create a text that gives the viewer the illusion of having "unmediated access to reality" (Trinh, 1991, p. 40). Thus naturalized, the objective, documentary interview style has become part of the larger cinematic apparatus in American culture, including a pervasive presence in TV commercials and news (p. 40).

Trinh (1991, p. 41) brings a reflexive reading to these features of the documentary film, citing her own texts as examples of dialogic documentaries that are sensitive to the flow of fact and fiction, to meanings as political constructions. Such texts reflexively understand that reality is never neutral or objective—that it is always socially constructed. Filmmaking and documentary interviewing thus become methods of "framing" reality.

Self-reflexivity does not translate into personal style or a preoccupation with method. Rather, it centers on the reflexive interval that defines representation, "the place in which the play within the textual frame is a play on this very frame, hence on the borderlines of the textual and the extra-textual" (Trinh, 1991, p. 48). The film becomes a site for multiple experiences.

A responsible, reflexive, dialogical interview text embodies the following characteristics (Trinh, 1991, p. 188):

- It announces its own politics and evidences a political consciousness.
- It interrogates the realities it represents.
- It invokes the teller's story in the history that is told.
- It makes the audience responsible for interpretation.
- It resists the temptation to become an object of consumption.
- It resists all dichotomies (male/female, etc.).
- It foregrounds difference, not conflict.
- It uses multiple voices, emphasizing language as silence, the grain of the voice, tone, inflection, pauses, silences, and repetitions.
- Silence is presented as a form of resistance.

Trinh creates the space for a version of the cinematic apparatus and the interview machine that challenges mainstream film. She also challenges traditional ethnography and its use of objective and investigative interview formats.

Reflexive texts question the very notion of a stable, unbiased gaze. They focus on the pensive image, on silences, on representations that "unsettle the male apparatus of the gaze" (Trinh, 1991, p. 115). This look makes the interviewer's gaze visible. It destabilizes any sense of verisimilitude that can be brought to this visual world. In so doing, it also disrupts the spectator's gaze, itself a creation of the unnoticed camera—the camera that invokes the image of a perfect, natural world, a world with verisimilitude (p. 115). In using these interpretive strategies, Trinh creates the space for the viewer (and listener) to critically appraise the politics of representation that structure the documentary text.

Cultivating Reflexivity

Learning from Trinh, I want to cultivate a method of patient listening—a reflexive method of looking, hearing, and asking that is dialogical and respectful. This method will take account of my place as a coconstructor of meaning in this dialogic relationship. As an active listener (Bourdieu, 1996), I will treat dialogue as a process of discovery. I will attempt to function as an empowering collaborator. I will use the reflexive interview as a tool of intervention (Burawoy, 1998). I will use it as a method for uncovering structures of oppression in the life worlds of the persons I am interviewing. As a reflexive participant, I will critically promote the agendas of radical democratic practice.

In so doing, I hope to cultivate a method of hearing and writing that has some kinship with the kinds of issues Gloria Naylor (1998) discusses in the following passage:

Someone who didn't know how to ask wouldn't know how to listen. And he coulda listened to them the way you been listening to us right now. Think about it: ain't nobody really talking to you. . . . Really listen this time; the only voice is your own. But you done just heard about the legend of Saphira Wade. . . . You done heard it in the way we know it, sitting on our porches and shelling June peas . . . taking apart the engine of a car—you done heard it without a single living soul really saying a word. (p. 1842)

But this is also a sociology that understands, here at the end, that when we screen our dreams and our crises on the canvases and through the lenses that the cinematic and electronic society make available to us, we risk becoming storied versions of somebody else's version of who we should be.

Notes

1. The underlying logic of the sports interview is mocked in the following dialogue in Ron Shelton's 1988 film *Bull Durham*. Kevin Costner, who plays an aging pitcher named Crash Davis, says to his protégé, played by Tim Robbins, "Now you are going to the Big Show. You have to learn how to talk to interviewers. When they ask you how it feels to be pitching in Yankee Stadium, you say, 'I just thank the good Lord for all his gifts. I owe it all to him. I just take it one game, one pitch at a time.'"

2. These interview formats blur with the three types of relationships Mishler (1986) identifies between interviewers and interviewees: informants and reporters, collaborators, and advocates.

3. Although prejudice crosses color lines in this film, racial intolerance is connected to the psychology of the speaker (e.g., Vito). It is "rendered as the *how* of personal bigotry" (Guerrero, 1993, p. 154). The economic and political features of institutional racism are not taken up. That is, in Lee's film, "the *why* of racism is left unexplored" (p. 154).

References

Altheide, D. (1995). *An ecology of communication.* New York: Aldine.

Altheide, D., & Snow, R. (1991). *Mediaworlds in the era of postjournalism.* New York: Aldine.

Atkinson, P., & Silverman, D. (1997). Kundera's "Immortality": The interview society and the invention of self. *Qualitative Inquiry, 3,* 304-325.

Bakhtin, M. M. (1968). *Rabelais and his world.* Cambridge, MA: MIT Press.

Bakhtin, M. M. (1986). *Speech, genre, and other essays.* Austin: University of Texas Press.

Blumer, H. (1933). *Movies and conduct.* New York: Macmillan.

Bourdieu, P. (1996). Understanding. *Theory, Culture, & Society, 13,* 17-37.

Brissett, D., & Edgley, C. (Eds.). (1990). *Life as theater: A dramaturgical sourcebook* (2nd ed.). New York: Aldine.

Burawoy, M. (1998). The extended case method. *Sociological Theory, 16,* 4-33.

Denzin, N. (1991). *Images of postmodern society: Social theory and contemporary cinema.* London: Sage.

Denzin, N. (1995a). *The cinematic society.* London: Sage.

Denzin, N. (1995b). Information technologies, communicative acts, and the audience: Couch's legacy to communication research. *Symbolic Interaction, 18,* 247-268.

Denzin, N. (1996). *Interpretive ethnography*. Thousand Oaks, CA: Sage.

Denzin, N. (2000). The cinematic society and the reflexive interview. In J. F. Gubrium & J. A. Holstein (Eds.), *The handbook of interview research* (pp. 833-848). Thousand Oaks, CA: Sage.

Dillard, A. (1982). *Living by fiction*. New York: Harper & Row.

Eason, D. (1984). On journalistic authority: The Janet Cooke scandal. *Critical Studies in Mass Communications, 3,* 429-447.

Eastwood, C. (Director). (1999). *True crime* [Motion picture]. Burbank, CA: Warner Brothers.

Fontana, A., & Frey, J. (1994). The interview: The art of science. In N. K. Denzin & Y. S. Lincoln (Eds.), *Handbook of qualitative research* (pp. 361-376). Thousand Oaks, CA: Sage.

Goffman, E. (1959). *The presentation of self in everyday life*. New York: Doubleday.

Gottschalk, S. (2000). Escape from insanity: "Mental disorder" in the postmodern moment. In D. Fee (Ed.), *Pathology and the postmodern: Mental illness as discourse and experience* (pp. 18-48). Thousand Oaks, CA: Sage.

Gubrium, J., & Holstein, J. (1998). Narrative practice and the coherence of personal stories. *The Sociological Quarterly, 39,* 163-187.

Guerrero, E. (1993). *Framing blackness: The African American image in film*. Philadelphia: Temple University Press.

Hassan, I. (1985). The culture of postmodernism. *Theory, Culture, & Society, 2,* 119-132.

Heyl, B. (2000). Ethnographic interviewing. In S. Delamont, A. Coffey, & P. Atkinson (Eds.), *Handbook of ethnography*. London: Sage.

Holstein, J., & Gubrium, J. (1995). *The active interview*. Thousand Oaks, CA: Sage.

Holstein, H., & Gubrium, J. (2000). *The self that we live by: Narrative identity in the postmodern world*. New York: Oxford University Press.

Jackson, M. (1998). *Minimia ethnographica*. Chicago: University of Chicago Press.

Jameson, F. (1991). *Postmodernism, or the cultural logic of late capitalism*. Durham, NC: Duke University Press.

Kivisto, P. (2004). *Key ideas in sociology* (2nd ed.). Thousand Oaks, CA: Pine Forge Press.

Lopez, A. (1991). Are all Latins from Manhattan? Hollywood, ethnography, and cultural colonialism. In L. D. Friedman (Ed.), *Unspeakable images: Ethnicity and the American cinema* (pp. 404-424). Urbana: University of Illinois Press.

Lyman, S. (1990). *Civilization, culture, discontents, malcontents, and other essays in social theory*. Fayetteville: University of Arkansas Press.

Mishler, E. (1986). *Research interviewing: Context and narrative*. Cambridge, MA: Harvard University Press.

Naylor, G. (1998). Excerpt from "Mamma Day." In P. Hill (Ed.), *Call and response: The Riverside anthology of the African American literary tradition* (pp. 1838-1842). Boston: Houghton Mifflin.

Oudes, B. (1989). *From the president: President Nixon's secret files*. New York: Harper & Row.

Park, R. E. (1950). An autobiographical note. In R. E. Park (Ed.), *Race and culture: Essays in the sociology of contemporary man* (pp. v-ix). New York: Free Press.

Raban, J. (1981). *Old glory: An American voyage*. New York: Simon & Schuster.

Scheurich, J. J. (1995). A postmodernist critique of research interviewing. *Qualitative Studies in Education, 8,* 339-252.

Sports Center. (2000, January 31). Sal Paolantanio interview with Kurt Warner. Bristol, CT: ESPN.

Trinh, T. M. (Director). (1989). *Surname viet given name nam* [Motion picture]. New York: Women Make Movies.

Trinh, T. M. (1991). *When the moon waxes red: Representation, gender, and cultural politics.* New York: Routledge.

Trinh, T. M. (1992). *Framer framed.* New York: Routledge.

Ulmer, G. (1989). *Teletheory: Grammatology in the age of video.* New York: Routledge.

Updike, J. (1984, September 10). Modernist, postmodernist, what will they think of next? *The New Yorker,* 136-138, 140-142.

Vecesy, G. (2000, February 1). Kurt Warner gives hope to others. *New York Times,* p. C29.

Vidich, A., & Lyman, S. (1994). Qualitative methods: Their history in sociology and anthropology. In N. K. Denzin & Y. S. Lincoln (Eds.), *The handbook of qualitative research* (pp. 23-59). Thousand Oaks, CA: Sage.

Weiss, P. (1988, September/October). Party time in Atlanta. *Columbia Journalism Review,* 27-34.

Discussion Questions

1. Offer an overview and a critical evaluation of Denzin's perspective on postmodernism. Compare and contrast his discussion of this concept with the perspective of George Ritzer in Chapter 11.

2. Describe in your own words what Denzin means by "the cinematic society." Connect this concept to the larger idea of postmodernism. Provide an example of the ways that the boundaries between the "real world" and the media-mediated world get blurred.

3. Compare and contrast Denzin's understanding of the postmodern self with the idea of the self that is contained in the thought of Erving Goffman and is discussed in Chapter 10.

CHAPTER 13

Globalization Theory and Religious Fundamentalism

William H. Swatos, Jr.

William H. Swatos, Jr., is Executive Officer of both the Religious Research Association and the Association for the Sociology of Religion. He received his PhD in sociology from the University of Kentucky in 1973 and received the sociology department's distinguished alumni award in 1989. From 1988 to 1994, he was editor of Sociology of Religion: A Quarterly Review. *He has edited, coedited, authored, or coauthored more than 20 books, including* Politics and Religion in Central and Eastern Europe *(1994),* Religious Politics in Global and Comparative Perspective *(1989), and* The Power of Religious Publics *(1999). He is editor-in-chief of* Encyclopedia of Religion and Society *(1998) and with Kevin Christiano and Peter Kivisto he coauthored* Sociology of Religion: Contemporary Developments *(2002), the first entirely new American sociology of religion text to appear in 20 years.*

It is difficult to think of an occurrence that caught Western students of religion more by surprise than the worldwide resurgence of religion—political religion, no less—that occurred with increasing visibility as the 1970s progressed. There had been the appearance of so-called new religious movements, but many of the leading theorists of religion in modernity could accommodate these into an existing secularization paradigm by their very bizarreness. The highly eclectic character of the religious "marketplace" seemed only to confirm the privatization thesis— that religion had become a leisure-time activity, with no social consequences (except for an occasional figure like Charles Manson, who was more good news copy than serious societal assault).

Religious controversies that did reach political proportions were often "explained" (i.e., explained away) by social scientists as merely symbolic expressions of socioeconomic variables (e.g., in Northern Ireland or Israel). The idea that there were concerted groups of people taking religion seriously enough to affect the order of global society gained little credence, in fact, until the appearance of the Ayatollah Khomeini in revolutionary Iran. He meant business, and the "simple" explanation that he was a mere figurehead for those really in power fell into increasingly greater disrepute as the heads of one after another of those "really" in power rolled before the Ayatollah's revolutionary justice.

Standard social-scientific models of change seemed ill equipped to account for a worldwide religious resurgence. The two primary theories of modernization—functionalism's development and Marxism's exploitation—both proceed from the assumption that religious "prejudices" hamper "progress" and are disappearing throughout the world. Secular education, secular armies, secular economics, and secular politics combine to create the modern state. The only real difference between these two models of modernization is whether capitalism is viewed as a friend or a foe to nation-state growth and the good order of the international system of states.

According to either of these theories, religious resurgence represents a deviant occurrence in the broad sweep of history. If, indeed, only an isolated instance of religious resurgence were now to be observed, one could hardly quarrel with such theoretical presuppositions. We have deviants within our own communities, after all, so why not expect the same at the political level in the international system of states? The problem, however, is that the resurgence phenomenon is global in character—so much so that it strains credulity to accept an argument that world-wide religious resurgence represents some form of mass delusion.

Globalization theory provides an approach to the current world situation that addresses these developments. Although rooted in the materialist analyses of Ferdinand Braudel and Immanuel Wallerstein, generally known as world-system theory, globalization has been reshaped by the later work of John Meyer and especially Roland Robertson to include important cultural components, not the least of which is religion.[1] What globalization refers to is most simply conceptualized by Robertson's felicitous phrase that the world is seen as "a single place."[2] As Frank Lechner observes in a survey of the field, "Globalization refers to the worldwide diffusion of practices, expansion of relations across continents, organization of social life on a global scale, and growth of a shared global consciousness." However,

> globalization also recasts the agenda of social theory. . . . Whereas social theory once focused on the rise of individual, state-organized societies, it now must address the implications of change of scale in supraterritorial social relations. While modernization could once be treated as change within a single civilizational area, students of globalization must now examine how world order can arise in the face of civilizational differences.[3]

Globality stands over locality (or localism), but because the local is always within the global, the two are in constant relationship (which may be positive or negative).

The global is universalistic, whereas the local is particularistic. In practice, however, there can be both particularistic universalism and universalistic particularism, giving rise, among other things, to the phenomena of religious resurgence often popularly dubbed fundamentalism.

Strictly speaking, the word *fundamentalism* refers to a specific theological movement that originated in American Protestantism at the beginning of the 20th century. A group of Protestant leaders, concerned about what they considered to be a process of modernism that was shaking the foundations of the Christian religion, set forth five "fundamentals" that they considered essential to the Christian faith. People who subscribed to these were subsequently termed—first by their detractors and later by themselves—*fundamentalists.*[4]

When the worldwide religious resurgence of the 1970s gained attention, however, the term *fundamentalist* was used in a more extensive fashion. It was now extended to all contemporary religious movements that display what Eugen Schoenfeld has demarcated "exclusive militancy."[5] In a definition that rivals Robertson's "seeing the world as a single place" for simplicity, T. K. Oommen has similarly defined fundamentalism as "text without context."[6] This means that religious texts (or scriptures) that were originally written in a specific historical context, and hence social setting, are decontextualized and held to be applicable without regard to local circumstances. At the same time, however, all other competing texts are rejected as having any corresponding claim to truth.

It is important to recognize that all fundamentalisms as they are advanced throughout the world today are specifically modern products and heterodox faith traditions.[7] Of course, this claim is never made by fundamentalists themselves, but it is easily documented by historical surveys of the faith traditions they claim to represent. The majority of those who claim to be Christians do not belong to fundamentalist churches—and never have. The majority of Muslims do not belong to fundamentalist sects of that faith. The historic creeds to which the majority of those who call themselves Christians do assent are not held by most fundamentalists; the central concerns of fundamentalist Muslims are not the essential "Five Pillars" of Islam. Ultraorthodox Jews are more orthodox than the Orthodox, which is in fact a contradiction in terms. All religious fundamentalisms as we know them today were constructed during our own time as responses to the modern world system, which had its beginnings in the 16th century but has come to fruition in the global project that has progressed with increasing certainty since World War II.

Global Culture

If we are to understand the relationship between the seemingly conflicting dynamics of globalization and fundamentalism, we need to reflect on the culture of modernity. World system theorist John Meyer stated the following:

> Modern world culture is more than a simple set of ideals or values diffusing and operating separately in individual sentiments in each society. . . . The power of modern culture—like that of medieval Christendom—lies in the fact

that it is a shared and binding set of rules exogenous to any given society, and located not only in individual sentiments, but also in many world institutions.[8]

These institutions, such as the United Nations or the World Court but also including world financial institutions that make a world economy work, involve an element of faith; that is, they rest on a certain belief that what they do is both right and natural (these two conditions are bound together, for example, in the phrase "human rights").

This worldview (in the double sense) has not characterized human history taken as a whole, even into our own day. Consider the following vignette from social historian Agnes Heller:

> About 30 years ago I became acquainted with the middle-aged owner of a little trattoria in Rome's Campo dei Fiori. After a lively conversation I asked him to advise me about the shortest way to Porta Pia. "I am sorry, but I cannot help you," he answered. "The truth of the matter is I have never ever in my life left the Campo dei Fiori." About one and a half decades later, on board a jumbo jet en route to Australia, I discussed the then current political affairs with my neighbor, a middle-aged woman. It turned out that she was employed by an international trade firm, spoke five languages, and owned three apartments in three different places. Recalling the confession of the trattoria owner, I asked her the obvious question: "Where are you at home?" She was taken aback. After awhile she responded: "Perhaps where my cat lives."
>
> These two people seemingly lived worlds apart. For the first, the earth had a center, it was called Campo dei Fiori, the place where he was born and expected to die. He was deeply committed to the geographic monogamy that wedded him to his tradition. His commitment stretched from the remote past, the past of the Campo, up to a future beyond his own, the future of the Campo. For the second, the earth had no center; she was geographically promiscuous, without pathos. Her whereabouts made no difference to her. My question surprised her because the loaded concept "home" seemingly had no significance for her.
>
> This was confirmed by her unwittingly ironical answer. As long as there is something called home, our cat lives in our home. So when my interlocutor said, in reversing the signs, that "My home is where my cat lives," she had deconstructed the concept "home." Her geographic promiscuity symbolized something uncanny (*unheimlich*), namely the abandonment of, perhaps, the oldest tradition of the Homo sapiens, privileging one, or certain, places against all the others.[9]

Not surprisingly, commentators on the condition of modernity have spoken of both "the homeless mind" and "the absent center."[10]

The illustration by Heller can help us understand particularly well the potential problems of globalization. To move from the worldview of the man of Campo dei Fiori to the woman of the jumbo jet is to move from one way of knowing to another; it is a total shift in *epistemology,* the technical term philosophers apply to systems of knowledge. All ways of knowing, however, rest on systems of beliefs about the universe that are themselves unprovable to observation. One can make logical assertions about evolution, for example, but one can also make logical assertions about the existence of God, as St. Thomas Aquinas did approximately 1,000 years ago. None of us was there to observe either one, however; hence, we ultimately accept one or another account "on faith": The arguments as a whole have a ring of consistency or plausibility that convinces us that they are inherently worthwhile to getting on with life in the present. In short, the worldview of globalization has an essentially religious character in that it requires us to accept beliefs about "the way the world works" that may be in conflict with other beliefs—not only beliefs of the existing formally organized religions, such as Christianity or Islam, but also beliefs of the popular or "implicit" religions on the basis of which people have constructed their lives for centuries.[11]

Globalization particularly flies in the face of the belief in absolute nation-state sovereignty—what Frank Lechner terms *institutionalized societalism*,[12] which, ironically, reached its apex as the very capstone of the globalization process that now threatens its undoing. On the one hand, the globe appears as a union of sovereign states, recognized by world institutions as having transcendent integrity. On the other hand, the sovereignty of these states as political actors is circumscribed by a set of principles—a "higher law"—that in fact rests on beliefs generated by specific world orientations that are themselves metaphysical; that is, the principles of global society are generated by accepting some kinds of faith propositions and not others. In general, these propositions reflect Anglo-American utilitarian-pragmatic philosophy, which lacks absolutes and is thus subject to contradiction as circumstances change.

Before we discuss religious fundamentalism, we examine another formally nonreligious vignette. The nation-state of Iceland has been one of the greatest beneficiaries of the principle of institutionalized societalism; although numbering little more than a quarter of a million people, it has virtually all the privileges in world institutions that are accorded to the United States or Japan and perhaps even more privileges than China. Part of the process of the creation of an independent Iceland, however, was the enshrining of the Icelandic language as the keystone of its claim to distinction—so much so that Icelandic sociologist of religion Pétur Pétursson has described it as characterized by a "language fundamentalism."[13] A manifestation of the Icelandic fascination with Icelandic is a law that all Icelanders must have Icelandic names. One of the by-products of globalization, however, is a world openness that allows the relatively free exchange of peoples and goods across national borders—a relatively fluid view of citizenship (i.e., world citizenship).

Consider the case of "Eternal Peace" Cabrera Hidalgo/Edgarsson. In the late 1980s, Jorge Ricardo Cabrera Hidalgo came to Iceland from Colombia. After he had attended college and worked for some time, he decided to start his own business, upon which he was informed that bureaucratically speaking, it would be much easier for him if he were an Icelandic citizen. Upon being granted Icelandic citizenship in the mid-1990s, however, he was required to take an Icelandic name, which he considered "a violation of basic human rights." To settle the matter temporarily, he chose from the list of authorized names "Eilífur Friður," Eternal Peace, to which was then added the patronymic Edgarsson because Edgar was his father's Christian (first) name. This did not solve his problem, however:

> To complicate matters even further, Eilífur Friður had met an Icelandic woman prior to the citizenship adaptation, with whom he has a daughter, Freyja María Cabrera. Little Freyja María is permitted to keep her name . . . but any sisters or brothers she may subsequently receive will have a surname different from hers: namely Eilífsdóttir [for a girl] or Eilífsson [for a son], which, as Eilífur Friður points out, is sure to raise questions when the family travels abroad, and will be outright rejected in his native country.
>
> "My purpose in choosing the name" [Eternal Peace], he says, "is to call attention to the laws and make people question whether or not they are just. . . . I do not find it just to be forced to change my name."[14]

In this curious case, we see the strange collisions of globalization and localization, of the world system and institutionalized societalism, that on a larger scale can lead to intrasocietal and intersocietal tensions and even to open hostilities. A single dynamic simultaneously facilitates cooperation and conflict. When violence is sanctioned by the transcendent norms of religious belief, it becomes a far more attractive option than the irony of "eternal peace."

Excursus on the History of Religions

Because this book is intended primarily to enhance the study of sociology, a few words need to be said about the historical circumstances that surround the three great Western religious traditions: Christianity, Judaism, and Islam. These are not the only religions to have produced religious fundamentalisms in our time, but a good case can be made that the other fundamentalisms that have emerged have used these religious traditions as the models for their programs (e.g., Hindu fundamentalism is reactive to Islamic fundamentalism and would not otherwise have existed). These three great traditions all find their root in a single place—namely, the call by God of the patriarch Abraham and his response, as detailed in Chapters 12 through 21 of the biblical book of Genesis. Historians of religions thus often call these religions the Abrahamic religions.

Students sometimes ask how it is that three religions and their hundreds of subparts that "worship the same God" can have so much conflict. The answer is that it is really quite easy because each has a different conception of that "same God"; hence, each may perceive the others as perverting the truth. Because each tradition harks back to a common narrative recorded in written form that it considers to be "the word of God," differences of interpretation (or hermeneutics [in Arabic, *ijtihad*]) can become either magnified or reduced through culture contact. This is precisely the problem that globalization highlights in the contrast of universalistic particularism and particularistic universalism. Consider some alternatives that different configurations of religions offer.

Suppose we live in a world in which we think there are many different gods: I have my god, and you have your god. We could fight over whose god is more powerful, and people certainly have done that. Usually, however, when such a conflict occurs, it is relatively localized, and the winners' god displaces the losers' god. We could also, however, agree to disagree, and peace might prevail. I could worship my god; you could worship your god. In many respects, what were once known as the "religions of the Orient" allowed easily for these possibilities, as do other folk religions.[15] We might call them "preglobal," however, in the sense that they do not view the world as a "single place." They are primarily clientelistic as they persist in modernity—from Voodoo to Zen—and represent countermodern tendencies.

The Abrahamic traditions, however, all begin with the assertion of a single, universal God (monotheism). Such is the First Commandment of Judaism, the Summary of the Law given by Jesus of Nazareth, and the first Pillar of Islam. There is only one God over the entire universe, including every human being, and every human being should honor Him.[16] We know, however, that there has been considerable variety within and among the Abrahamic traditions in regard to how God is understood and what fidelity to God means. Again, there are two alternatives. The peaceful alternative allows me to state, in effect, "there is only one God over all the world, but each of us [or each community of us] may come to that God in different ways. We should respect this diversity of approaches." A militant alternative states the following:

> There is only one God over all the world, and there is only one way correctly to come to and live under that God. Anyone who does not conform to this standard must be brought to do so; anyone who persists in acting otherwise is an enemy [both to me and to God].

The first of these alternatives particularizes the universal, whereas the second universalizes the particular. The universalization of the particular at the world level sets the stage for global fundamentalisms.

Until relatively recently, culture contact even within Abrahamic traditions was narrowly circumscribed. Consider, for example, that when the sociologist Émile Durkheim published his famous study on suicide approximately 100 years ago, he was able to compare "racial" differences between the French and the Germans without any real criticisms of his definition of race. Likewise, when Lutherans from various European locales came to North America, they quickly formed congregations for each variation of cultural practice (principally, but not only, language) rather than homogenizing around a common Lutheranism—until the second half of the 20th century. Similarly, the Roman Catholic Church learned at the end of the 19th century that if it did not accommodate ethnic differences by establishing ethnic parishes in North America, the institutional loyalty of its people was not going to hold. These are the parishes the Roman Church is now often being forced to close as specific ethnicities move out of historic neighborhoods and blend into the general Euro-American population. Jews in major urban areas are as likely to refer to synagogues as Russian, German, Sephardic, or Polish as they are to refer to them as Conservative, Reform, or Orthodox.

Globalization and Fundamentalisms

Globalization, however, breaks across cultural barriers through finance, media, and transport. Anglo-America is the preeminent global societal actor. English is the language of air traffic control and the Internet. The dollar, mediated by European bourses, is the measure of world economic value. These technical systems, however, do not speak to the "soul"; that is, the human personality seems to have, at some times and for some people more strongly than others apparently, something we call a "spiritual" dimension. This dynamic is not, however, purely psychological; spirituality involves an element of power. Although each of the Abrahamic traditions contextualizes divine power differently, none fails to assert that the presence of God is the presence of power. In the global setting specifically, the nature of Abrahamic monotheism coupled with the hegemonic position of Anglo-American "know-how" provides a potential resource for confrontation both within our own society and between societies.

We examine three encounters between "the globe" and fundamentalist agendas, none of which can be separated from the joint issues of messiahship and the state of Israel. Although the specifics are different in each case, note that in each, there is a significant commonality in the direction of hostilities, whether rhetorical or corporeal, against national political leaders who favor global peace on the basis of a universal value of human worth. Such hostilities originate with people within their own countries who demand acknowledgment of a particularist view of human action based on transcendent realities. In other words, current religiopolitical crises are not so much based on different ideas about God as they are on different claims about how God expects human beings to behave.

The American Religious Right

"Mixing politics and religion" is not new in the United States or other nations influenced by American thinking. Not only the civil rights and antiwar movements of the recent past but also Prohibition and abolitionism mixed heady doses of politics and religion. In all these cases, social stratification mixed with cultural considerations, including religion. This no more means that economics "causes" religion than that religion causes economics; the two can interact, as can other aspects of human experience, and sometimes these interactions have profound civilizational effects—for example, those that occurred during the Reformation in the 16th century.

One of the differences between some earlier religiopolitical alliances in the United States and the contemporary Religious Right is the global dimension of our experience. Exactly when this began may be debated for generations to come by historians, but we might profitably start with the 1950s and the "Communist Menace." Clearly, some Christian Americans were skeptical of socialism in the 19th century, but others embraced it. After McCarthyism at home and Stalinism abroad, however, "godless communism" became a major foe for Christian combat. Although there was certainly a Catholic anticommunism, fundamentalist Protestants particularly attempted to identify Soviet Marxism with biblical prophecy.

At the center of this religious historiography was the newly founded (or refounded) state of Israel. Marxism was laid over against the restoration of Israel as a nation-state as part of a grand theological plan to herald the end of time (the millennium), the return of Christ, and the judgment of the world. Elaborate explanations, often with increasingly technologically sophisticated visual representations, were constructed to herald a religious end of history. Atomic and hydrogen weaponry only enhanced the cataclysmic drama that would attend Armageddon, the great final battle. Did every Christian American believe this? Certainly not. People did hear enough of the great weapons race of the superpowers, the launching of satellites, and espionage and counterespionage, however, not to dismiss all of it as pure craziness.

The 1967 attack on Israel by a coalition of Muslim Arab states further enhanced the fundamentalist argument. Whether true or not, the Arabs were perceived as working with Soviet backing—both philosophically and materially. The Israeli triumph was enthusiastically received throughout the United States. A sudden alliance of good feeling and mutuality came to prevail among liberals, moderates, and fundamentalists. The victory in Israel was taken as an American victory; it justified American principles and served to give a tentative point of unity to a nation otherwise divided over civil rights issues at home and the Vietnam War abroad. As the years passed, this picture changed. Further military conflict in 1973 and Palestinian problems, the dragging on of a settlement, the rise of militant Islam in Iran, battles in Lebanon, and so on increasingly tried American patience. The fall of the Soviet empire in 1989 without any apparent resolution of the situation in the Holy Land began to make fundamentalist biblical exegesis of prophetic texts less gripping. A new American religious coalition was building over "family values," and a new missionary thrust to the formerly communist countries had more immediate success.

What is often called the Religious Right or (New) Christian Right today emerged in its present form in response to an appeal made by Richard Nixon during his presidency to America's "silent majority." Amid the protests of the Vietnam era, Nixon was sure that a silent majority of Americans (sometimes called the "silent generation") agreed with him and his handling of the situation. Before too many years had passed, a Virginia Independent Baptist pastor with a simply formatted television worship service, Jerry Falwell, had formed a political action group, the Moral Majority, that attempted to move the silent generation at least to send money to allow him to lead the nation to righteousness. The formation of Falwell's group coincided fairly closely with the election of the nation's first bona fide "born again" or evangelical president, Southern Baptist Jimmy Carter, but in fact Falwell's vision was quite different from Carter's. The Moral Majority would support tangentially Christian Ronald Reagan, not Carter, in the 1980 presidential election.

What were the sins of the Carter administration that irked the Religious Right? Clearly, no single act can be designated as the cause of Carter's rejection; his years were ill fated. He followed on, and would not actively work to use his administrative power or legislative influence to alter, the Supreme Court decision in *Roe v. Wade* (1973), which opened the way for legal abortions. The economy fell into deep recession. The Panama Canal was perceived to have been given away. When we examine the global situation, however, two other aspects also emerge. First, Carter and many of his advisers on international affairs had been or were part of a global "think tank" known as the Trilateral Commission. For right-wing activists, the Trilateral Commission represented a form of communist appeasement, on the one hand, and something of a sellout to the Japanese business interests, on the other hand. Carter was labeled as soft on communism while selling out American industry. Carter was perceived as not really "believing" in America. Second, Carter allowed Americans to be taken hostage by an infidel regime in Iran and proved impotent as commander in chief. Carter was perceived as having betrayed Christian America on virtually all fronts, an apostate to our civil religion. His humanism was demonized both at home and abroad. He was also hindered by the fact that his vice president, Walter Mondale, whom Reagan absolutely trounced in 1984, was the half-brother of a signer of the Humanist Manifesto.

Ironically, the Religious Right gained very little of its specifically religious agenda during the administrations of favored sons Ronald Reagan and the elder George Bush. Although both presidents talked the right language on abortion and school prayer, neither was able to effect any significant changes. The fall of the "evil" Soviet empire may have been hastened by the Reagan-Bush line, but it was so entirely unanticipated in the West that this can hardly have been a major factor. Wise investors used these years to internationalize the American economy even further, rather than the reverse, and China first became a significant economic player in American markets. Reagan and Bush proved virtually powerless to resolve Holy Land crises—indeed, the worst single loss of American lives in the Holy Land, the bombing of the Marine barracks in Lebanon, occurred during the Reagan years. Also, the nation was plunged ever further into debt.

One might think, therefore, that a joint slate of Southern Baptists in the persons of Bill Clinton and Al Gore would have rallied the evangelical-fundamentalist cadre. This was hardly the case, however: Lukewarm Episcopalian George Bush was by far their choice. Indeed, a demonization process can again be said to have operated with respect to Clinton-Gore, who found themselves not only in trouble with the Christian Right but also precariously positioned in relation to the traditionally Democrat Jewish constituency, which is currently divided over the "peace process" in Israel. Rather than embrace such men, the Religious Right first put its hopes in 1996 on populist Catholic Republican Pat Buchanan, only to eke out a weak compromise with Bob Dole.

The idea of a Catholic president would have utterly horrified fundamentalists when that movement was founded, but a look at Buchanan's candidacy helps us to see the interplay between globalization and religion for today's American Religious Right. The issues today are not over a "foreign power" (the pope) having control over the United States; rather, the Religious Right wants to assert authority in contradistinction to negotiation. The Religious Right is looking for leadership that will assert "traditional Judeo-Christian" moral principles as unassailably true. What Pat Buchanan offered was an "America first" agenda that was palpably uncompromising. He was, at least then, not a politician, and that has an appeal among a sector that increasingly has come to feel that politics as "the art of compromise" is also an act of betrayal. Buchanan's concerns about foreign influences are directed toward global capital and the might of multinational corporations that owe fealty to no flag.

Why is this so? Again, no single reason accounts for any sociocultural complex; nevertheless, we cannot ignore in the growth of the Religious Right the operation of status variables in social stratification. James D. Davidson and colleagues have shown that mainline American religious groups are overrepresented among American elites, and that among Protestants there has been very little change in this proportion over time.[17] Fundamentalist Christians, for whatever reason, are people who are not getting their fair share of the politicoeconomic pie. Although they may earn a decent living, they are at increasing distance from economic elites, and they perceive themselves to have little political control, even—perhaps especially—in their local communities (e.g., in schools and housing projects). Faceless bureaucracies and court jurisdictions far from their communities mandate systems of action (or prohibit countervailing action) contrary to their perceptions of right and wrong. The more globalization advances, the more a sense of "place" in society recedes. At the same time, other religious groups, most notably Reform Jews and the religiously unaffiliated, advance ahead of the Christian fundamentalists into the political-economic elites. Hence, evangelical-fundamentalist Protestants, traditionalist Catholics, and Orthodox Jews form a loose political alliance that attempts to assert citizen control over local issues. The aim of the "stealth" candidates of the Christian Coalition in the early 1990s, for example, was to place religious conservatives on local boards of education, city councils, and county commissions. It is certainly the case that George W. Bush's embrace of "faith-based" programs and "charitable choice" are especially directed toward this constituency rather than the historical Protestant or Catholic mainstream.

Islamization

Many Muslims would prefer, because of the historically Christian associations of the word *fundamentalist*, that the movement often called Islamic fundamentalism be termed *Islamization* and its adherents *Islamicists*. The movements roots are varied, but they can probably be traced to reactions to the British colonial presence in Egypt and in that part of India now known as Pakistan. Until the Six Day War of 1967, however, these movements had little effect—although for different reasons, they were largely sidelined, as were the United States' Christian fundamentalists. The failure of the Arab alliance to succeed in defeating the Israelis, however, began to give new urgency to Islamic conservatives.

The attack on Israel was the dream of Egyptian (later, United Arab Republic) president Gamal Abdal Nasser, largely a secularist, who enticed other secular Arab leaders to join his plan. When it failed, this began to allow an opening for conservative Muslim preachers to claim that the basis for the defeat was not Jewish military superiority but, rather, the failure of Muslims to immerse themselves adequately in Islam. Human pride rather than submission to Allah was at the heart of the Arab defeat.

The momentum for Islamization built slowly because most secular Arab leaders were reluctant to allow the mullahs opportunities to promulgate their critiques.

Economic pressures often intervened. Again, an increasing disparity between those largely secular Arabs who benefited from the oil trade and the rest of the population sent the disenfranchised looking for alternative explanations for their plight. University students, small-business people, craftsmen, and some members of the old middle class (not least those who provided men with vocations to Muslim ministry) provided fertile soil for the seeds of Islamization. Palestinians who were termed "terrorists" in the West were made heroes in the Muslim world. Nevertheless, such activities remained relatively marginal to the world system until 1978 and 1979, with the rise of the Ayatollah Khomeini in Iran.

Perhaps no more perfect case of both the interaction of and confrontation between globalization and local intransigence could be imagined than Iran; indeed, in some ways, it stretched the imaginations of many social scientists, who gave inadequate weight to the religious dimension when they attempted to predict Iranian outcomes. Mohammed Reza Shah Pahlevi, Iran's ruler for almost four decades prior to the Iranian revolution, who ascended the throne at age 22, was a dedicated modernist. He rejoiced in U.S. political and economic support and enjoyed the Western lifestyle. He saw his vocation as bringing Iran into the forefront of global geopolitics: He claimed that "Iran could be the showcase for all of Asia. America cannot spread its assistance in every country everywhere. Here is the place with the best prospect for a great transformation."[18]

Perhaps the Shah was correct in his analysis, but in hindsight we can see that he made at least three mistakes in implementation: (a) Economically, he placed too much emphasis on oil and did not demand sufficient diversification of U.S. assistance to share the benefits of Iran's oil resources and geopolitical setting adequately throughout the population; (b) socioculturally, he demanded changes that exceeded the prerequisites of the project of modernization (such as not permitting the wearing of the veil by women attending universities, reducing support for the mosques, and implementing policies to displace small shopkeepers); and (c) politically, he created a secret police force (SAVAK) that used extreme cruelty to attack those who disagreed with his policies.

By the late 1970s, spiraling inflation, population pressures in the cities, and a crisis on the world oil market clearly put the Shah in trouble. That was not too much of a surprise to American social scientists savvy in Middle Eastern studies. What was a surprise was the role that came to be played by the Islamicist Ayatollah Ruholla Khomeini in the foundation of the Islamic Republic of Iran. Why? Preeminently this was because secular social science had totally overlooked the persistence of the religious dimension as a possible trajectory for the demonstration of human resentment against oppression—this despite the fact that practically every foundational social theorist, including Karl Marx, had recognized the religious dimension as integrally connected to deprivation, although not merely a reflection of deprivation. The Ayatollah's explanation of his appeal and success was that "we did not want oil, we did not want independence, we wanted Islam."[19]

What did he mean by that? The Shah was a professing Muslim; this was not enough. What the Ayatollah meant was a lifeworld level affirmation of stability, a continuation of "things the way they always ought to have been." Note carefully the use of the word "ought"; it is important to understanding the fundamentalist dynamic because what fundamentalism protests against as much as anything in the internationalist vision of globalization is the relativization of cultural values that seems to be part and parcel of impersonal market "forces" that drive high-technology multinationalist capitalism. Only the most naive fundamentalist would claim that in some past time, "everyone" was religious or moral or both. What the fundamentalist would claim was that in the past there was a religioethical core within sociocultural systems that was generally acknowledged: "Sin was sin," and truth was truth. Ironically, the world of the nation-state, whether in the Arab world or in Christian Europe, provided a buffering device that established cultural pre-rogatives. The Reformation principle of *cuius regio, eius religio* and Muslim princi-ples surrounding the caliphate had a commonsense reality for everyday activity, particularly when language separated major cultural groups. People who "talked different" were different. Every culture knew it was right and others were wrong. Common language and common religion went hand in hand.

Globalization changed this simple worldview; accommodation and compro-mise became the order of the day. When we look at Islamicization efforts, for example, we see that with few exceptions they are directly proportional to involve-ment by a Muslim leader in the ethic (ethos) of globalization—that is, in that "shared and binding set of rules exogenous to any given society" of which John Meyer speaks. The murder of Egyptian president Anwar Sadat in 1981 is an excel-lent but not the sole example. This was similarly the set of values to which the Shah of Iran was at least giving lip service, and it is the basis on which a female leader such as Benazir Bhutto of Pakistan ultimately attempted to sustain her claim to legitimacy. Although Americans often see specific acts of Islamicist terrorism directed against them, the bigger picture clearly shows the primary targets to be Muslim leaders. It is not "the American way of life" that is under attack by Islamicists but, rather, attempts to harmonize Islam with that way of life. Unlike the New Christian Right, most Islamicists are quite willing to let America go to hell if it wants to; what they resist are attempts by the global system of states, of which they see the United States as the principal economic and cultural actor, to alter their life world.

Nowhere do the contradictions between the global system of states and the Islamic life world become more pronounced than in the place given to the state of Israel, particularly by the United States. The state of Israel is an "offense" to Muslims, not merely because the Jews are people of a different religion—because Islam has generally been tolerant toward Jews, indeed in many cases far more so than Christianity. Rather, the state of Israel places into juxtaposition irrational and rational political policies, which themselves result from a unique religious configu-ration in the United States between Jews and the Christian Right. The creation of the state of Israel caused the undermining of the secular ideology of the nation-state in the Muslim world because, in a Western betrayal of its own commitments to the secular state, a religious ideology was used to justify the creation of Israel. The establishment of the state of Israel was clearly a response to the Holocaust, but it was also intimately related to fundamentalist Protestant understandings of the necessity for the reunion of the Jewish peoples at Jerusalem prior to some form of millennial return and reign of Jesus Christ. Inseparable from this is the demographic fact that since World War II, the United States has had the largest Jewish population in the world and the fact that U.S. citizens may hold unique joint citizenship in the United States and Israel, a condition virtually unknown elsewhere in the entire global system.

Muslims thus see a moral fissure in the ethic of globalization along these lines: The state of Israel has been established in the center of the historic Islamic world as an outpost for a new campaign to blot out the Islamic way of life. Like the crusades of old, this effort seeks to impede the practice of Islam through other standards of behavior, to which Muslims will be forced to conform or else by which they will be excluded from the benefits of global citizenship. From the Muslim point of view, in contrast, Islam provides a set of principles for universal world government. Here, then, is the center of the conflict between Islamicization and globalization: As pre-eminently a system of rules, not beliefs, Islam offers an alternative to the dominant model of secular high-technology multinational capitalism that forms the basis for the global system of states in late modernity. Islamicization proposes the universalization of the particular and, in contrast, it views the Western system as doing nothing but the same. That is, Islamicists see the Western system of globalization not as the implementation of "universal" human values but, rather, of specifically Western values. Islamicists might find some support for their position sociologically in Talcott Parsons's claim that the West has not been secularized but, rather, has been so permeated by the core values of the "Judeo-Christian ethic" as to render itself sacralized.[20] Consider simply as one example U.S. postage stamps that carry the message "love."

This observation highlights one of the central propositions of globalization theory, particularly as articulated in the work of Roland Robertson and colleagues; namely the role of ethics (ethoses) in constructing systems of interaction. Derived from the work of both Weber and Parsons, this point of view suggests that systems of valuing, whether or not they originate in material conditions, have an influence, perhaps a determinative influence, on subsequent political and economic relationships. Peoples whose worldview continues to be shaped by Islam, which is founded on a warrior ethic, will be essentially at variance with the core values of globalization.[21] Failure to recognize the depth to which these cultural components structure political organization leads Westerners to think that the assumptions of modern rationalism can provide a basis for "reasonable" compromise, when in fact they cannot. Instead, the warrior ethic sees stand-off as a transcendent scenario in which different "strong men" contend for power. This view "came home" to Americans most dramatically in the events of September 11, 2001, with the al-Qaeda attacks on the World Trade Center: Perhaps no more dramatic symbol of international capitalism could have been chosen for a *Star Wars*–esque scenario wherein the hub of globalization was attacked by the forces of an almost mythical strong man domiciled in one of the most remote parts of the world, governed by the most religiously reactionary regimes.

A fascinating Weberian study of religion and political democracy by James Duke and Barry Johnson takes up a variant of Weber's Protestant ethic thesis to demonstrate that Protestantism has acted causally with respect to the development of political democracy.[22] More to the point, however, is that, using four different indicators of democracy, Islamic nations appear at the bottom of five major religious groups on two of the four indicators and next to the bottom (higher only than tribal religions) on the other two. This is intensified by the fact that whereas in the poorest nations (per capita gross national product [GNP] of less than $399) democracy is weak across the board, states with tribal religions drop out of the picture at the uppermost end of the GNP spectrum but Islamic nations do not. In addition, the undemocratic nature of Islamic regimes is unrelated to whether a previous colonial regime was of a more or less democratically oriented religion (e.g., French Catholicism or English Protestantism).

We might turn this around and say that from the Islamicist viewpoint, Muslim leaders who adopt the ethic of globalization as Meyer summarizes it have already betrayed the faith; that is, the warrior ethic mediates between "upstream" doctrine and day-to-day practice. This dynamic runs through the bulk of Islamic history, although the specific terms have differed across time. Ironically for the West, movements toward democratic pluralism on the global level have actually allowed Islamicist activities to grow in their degree of both local and international influence because the same means of communication, transport, and exchange that provide the infrastructure to globalization can be employed for the deployment of Islamicist values (much the same way, for example, as Christian televangelists in the United States use the very media of which they are hypercritical as the means for propagating their own views). The Ayatollah Khomeini sent audiotape cassettes to Iran while he was a refugee in France, just as bin Laden appears to continue to provoke his adversaries and encourage his followers. Those societies of Muslim heritage that have most intentionally embraced Western democratic models have created the conditions for the growth of Islamicist parties, which in their extremism simply reinforce the tendencies that are already latent in the warrior ethic. This is particularly the case when the fruits of the globalization project are inequitably distributed—for example, in Iran.

Ultraorthodoxy

For approximately the past 25 years, Americans have come to anticipate various forms of Palestinian-Islamicist terrorism in and adjacent to the territory now occupied by the state of Israel. Bus bombings, airplane hijackings, suicide attacks, and so on are recurrent copy for television and newspaper headlines. Thus, it was with no small surprise that Americans learned that the assassin of Israeli prime minister Yitzhak Rabin was not a Muslim, or even a Palestinian sympathizer, but a Jew who proclaimed, "I did this to stop the peace process. . . . We need to be cold-hearted. . . . When you kill in war, it is an act that is allowed."

As the story developed, it became clear that there was an intimate connection between the inspiration of assassin Yigal Amir and Orthodox Jewry in New York City. Specifically, New York rabbi Abraham Hecht, leader of Brooklyn's largest Syrian synagogue, had publicly ruled the previous June that Rabin and his colleague, Shimon Peres, were in a state of *mosher,* of someone who surrenders his people. As *The New Yorker* writer David Remnick recounted,

A Jew who hands over Jewish land or wealth to an alien people, Hecht said, is guilty of a sin worthy of the death penalty. And what is more, he went on, Maimonides, the greatest of all Jewish philosophers, said that if a man kills such a person he has done a good deed.[23]

This most prominent murder among the thousands who have lost their lives in the 20th-century battle for the Holy Land uniquely highlights the intersecting dynamics of globalization and fundamentalism: A local congregational pastor in one part of the world, thousands of miles from a law student elsewhere, inspires the death of a major figure not only in the Middle Eastern "peace process" but also potentially in the entire global system—due to media of communication and transport that brought his remarks into one of the crucial value articulations of globalization, a free press. Indeed, so much was this the case that Israelis immediately after the assassination attempted to formalize laws that would actually restrict the publication of such "opinions" as those of Hecht (who was, in fact, fired by his New York congregation soon after Rabin's murder).

In the assassination of Yitzhak Rabin, the global norms of freedom of religion and freedom of the press, written for example into a whole series of world institutional documents, yielded antiglobal results, enabled by the very technologies that advance the globalization to which, for example, Islamicists object. Indeed, one might argue that from an Islamicist viewpoint, the assassination of Rabin could be taken as evidence that globalization will be its own grave digger.

There is a counterargument, however, to which I have already alluded—namely that the creation of the state of Israel as it was effected by the allies following World War II, and especially by the United States, was in conflict with, and contrary to, the norms of globalization; hence, we should anticipate ongoing actual conflict over that sociopolitical fact. The United States will be especially immediately involved in that conflict because of its violation of the principles of nation-state citizenship rules—because of the unique citizenship privileges that pertain between Israeli citizens of American origin. In other words, the world systemic conflict in and about the state of Israel is the "exception that proves the rule" of globalization theory precisely because the foundation of the state of Israel essentially violates the "value-neutral" or "secular" politics that is the norm of global society.

From the restriction of the papal empire within the walls of the Vatican to the transformation of the Ottoman empire into modern Turkey, the de-deification of the emperor of Japan, and the disestablishment of one state church after another, the entire trend of globalization has been away from the particularizing of politics by intrasocietal cultural norms associated with the historical religions. How could the state of Israel possibly be founded in contradistinction to this trend? The answer is multiplex.

First, the psychodynamics of guilt over the Holocaust must be acknowledged. Although specific numbers may be debated until time immemorial, the genocide inflicted on European Jews by the Nazi regime when the majority of "liberal" politicians of all Western democracies stood largely deaf, dumb, and blind yielded in due time its legitimate emotional remorse. The state of Israel was a global irrational response to an even more overwhelming irrational system of oppression. It flew in the face of the rational politics of the world system, but those political principles were themselves still in the stage of formal institutionalization in such bodies as the United Nations. Not to be forgotten is the fact that the first attempt toward operationalizing these principles in the League of Nations failed, and perhaps one reason that it failed was the lack of membership of the United States, which as a result of the Holocaust had become the nation with the largest Jewish population in the world by 1945.

Second, the Jewish people were disarrayed by the Holocaust; many of the proponents of the idea of a "Jewish homeland" (i.e., the modern state of Israel) articulated the concept in secular terms. In other words, when the state of Israel concept was discussed in political circles, it was advanced not as a religious cause but, rather, as an efficient political solution to a world political problem of refugee peoples and a resolution to colonial control of a portion of the Middle East. In apparent ignorance of the actual population of Palestine, many Western politicians saw the creation of the state of Israel as an act of political self-determination consistent with world societal principles. The British were keen to withdraw from the region and saw American support for the state of Israel as the ideal avenue for their own exit.

Third, the same infrastructural developments that have allowed the Christian Religious Right and Islamicism to move from lifeworld conditions to system actors have allowed the development of a Jewish religious form—ultraorthodoxy—that has been heretofore unknown in Judaism. Whereas ultraist forms of Judaism have previously been privatizations of the spiritual dynamic, the "open market" of globalization has allowed the conditions for the appearance of a public spirituality making political demands. Among the Jews especially, who have traditionally been what Max Weber terms a "pariah people,"[24] only the free conditions of globalization have allowed the politicization of action that could result in the assassination of a world political leader. The great Maimonides may well have said that killing a *mosher* would be doing a good deed and meant it, but that Maimonides ever thought he was saying that killing the prime minister of Israel for participating in the global peace process was a good deed is quite inconceivable. Maimonides was speaking to a global situation in which Jews were a pariah people and not actors in the world system of states.

Conclusion

This final observation brings us to the heart of globalization theory as an explanation and demonstrates its value in understanding the "resurgence of religion" in our time. It is to be found in the simple definition of fundamentalism from T. K. Oommen that I introduced at the outset: text without context. What happened between Maimonides and Yigal Amir was that the context changed. I believe that Maimonides said what he said and that he meant what he said, and, in addition, I believe that in the context in which he was writing—namely that of Jews as a pariah people—he was morally right. I also believe that Rabbi Hecht was absolutely wrong in his application of the text; he was wrong because he chose to discount context, which from a sociological standpoint is utterly stupid and, given the availability of sociological knowledge, morally unjustifiable.

In the previous paragraph, I spoke rather forcefully, perhaps, for a social theorist. I have done so quite intentionally, however, because as a move toward concluding this essay on globalization, I want to make it as clear as I can that I believe that social theory—at least globalization theory, which is my responsibility in this chapter—has clear, practical application, and that by studying sociology one actually does learn something useful. I will make my point as simply as I can: Sociology teaches us that all sociocultural products arise out of sociocultural contexts.

The words of Maimonides are sociocultural products. This does not mean that they are not true. It does mean that all truth is mediated by context. To say this is not the same thing as saying that "everything is relative" but, rather, to assert that sociocultural context is integral to the truthfulness of any proposition about social relations. This is most succinctly epitomized in sociology in the phrase, "definition of the situation," coined by W. I. Thomas. Situations by their very nature have always been historically particular; hence, the universalizing dynamic of globalization creates an inherently perilous setting for misinterpretation when the particular is universalized (i.e., text is taken out of context). This is precisely what led to the death of Yitzhak Rabin. Globalization theory within sociology can make a crucial contribution to human welfare by demonstrating how understanding context is essential to the application of prescriptive texts, religious or otherwise.

The murder of Yitzhak Rabin set in the context not only of the rise of political ultraorthodoxy in Judaism but also in relation to the other movements in Christianity and Islam that we have examined lets us address another important theoretical argument in sociology—namely the secularization controversy, specifically the supposed privatization of religion. Acknowledging that all these terms admit of definitional manipulation, there has nevertheless been a general debate in sociology about whether there has been a process of secularization, or a declining influence of religion, in the world over a period of centuries. This is a complex issue that cannot be solved in a few pages; what I want to indicate, however, is that the process of globalization has created a new publicization of religion (the "resurgence" of religion) that is at variance with the dominant chord of secularization theories. Simultaneously, however, the resurgent forms of at least the Abrahamic traditions that we have examined in this chapter are also new forms of these religions.

Globalization theory can, in this respect, help us out of the quagmire of secularization. That is, secularization theories are, generally speaking, unsociological in the same way that most fundamentalisms are unsociological, in that they tend to minimize context. Secularization theories generally treat religion as fixed rather than flexible. I have argued, in contrast, using the definition-of-the-situation concept, that if we understand that sociologically religions as forms of worship and ethical orientation are cultural products of infinite variability—precisely because they refer to a transcendent realm and hence are not subject to the same constraints as sociocultural systems rooted in material objects—then as sociologists, we should expect religions to change.[25] For example, whereas Jesus Christ may be "the same, yesterday, today, and forever," Christianity is going to change. These changes may be dramatic or gradual, great or small, but they will occur as long as humans practice the religion. Indeed, the only religions that will not change are religions that cease to be practiced.

The global resurgence of religious traditions in new forms is evidence for both the truth of the relation of context to religion, which is inherent to the participation of human beings in religion, and the essential error of the secularization concept. Sociology teaches us that all religion is secular because all religion exists in relation to both system and life world; how specific religions orient and reorient themselves to system and life world will vary as systems and life worlds change. At the same time, however, systems and life worlds will include religious considerations in the total matrix of experience and interpretation that leads to specific action and hence to changes in patterns of action. The very processes that create the sociocultural contexts in and through which globalization theory becomes good theory also create the contexts for the resurgent religious forms that we tend to characterize as fundamentalisms. This dialectic between material and ideal culture is inherent in all sociocultural processes *in sæcula sæculorem*. A complete globalization theory will predict countersystem tendencies by the very nature of the dynamics that create the system. Globalization theory explains both why the systems of religion that are rising are rising and why those that are falling are falling. It also explains why those forms that are rising are probably unlikely to achieve their ultimate goals and why those that may appear to be falling may not experience the "withering" that either their critics or mourners expect.[26]

Notes

1. The different approaches within globalization are discussed profitably at considerable length in Beyer, P. (1994). *Religion and globalization* (pp. 15-44). London: Sage. Readers who wish to pursue at greater length the discussion initiated in this chapter will find Beyer's book an excellent starting point.

2. Robertson, R. (1992). *Globalization*. London: Sage; Robertson, R., & Chirico, J. A. (1985). Humanity, globalization, and worldwide religious resurgence. *Sociological Analysis, 46,* 219-242; Robertson, R., & Lechner, F. (1985). Modernization, globalization, and the problem of culture in world-systems theory. *Theory, Culture and Society, 2,* 103-118.

3. Lechner, F. (2004). Globalization. In G. Ritzer (Ed.), *Encyclopedia of social theory.* Thousand Oaks, CA: Sage.

4. The self-profession of fundamentalists as fundamentalists (or, in other traditions, what may be translated into "pious ones" or "holy ones") is important to a consistent social scientific use of the term that can otherwise become a label for anyone who disagrees with us and maintains his or her position. If one looks in phone books or newspaper church advertising pages, one can usually find Christian churches that openly profess themselves "fundamental" or "fundamentalist." An equivalent process occurs among Jews and Muslims, with the necessary translations being made. Students of sociological theory need to be especially cautious regarding the dangers of using a concept as a label to stigmatize a sector of the population. The self-profession of fundamentalist identity in a positive way (e.g., advertising) legitimates its social scientific employment.

5. Schoenfeld, E. (1987). Militant religion. In W. H. Swatos, Jr. (Ed.), *Religious sociology* (pp. 125-137). New York: Greenwood.

6. Oommen, T. K. (1994). Religious nationalism and democratic polity. *Sociology of Religion, 55,* 455-472.

7. See Lechner, F. J. (1985). Modernity and its discontents. In J. Alexander (Ed.), *Neofunctionalism* (pp. 157-176). Beverly Hills, CA: Sage.

8. Meyer, J. (1980). The world polity and the authority of the nation-state. In A. Bergesen (Ed.), *Studies of the modern world-system* (p. 117). New York: Academic Press.

9. Heller, A. (1995). Where are we at home? *Thesis Eleven, 41,* 1.

10. Berger, P., & Kellner, H. (1974). *The homeless mind.* Garden City, NY: Doubleday; Lemert, C. C. (1975). Social structure and the absent center. *Sociological Analysis, 36,* 95-107.

11. Charles Y. Glock, in his Furfey lecture, "The Ways the World Works" (*Sociological Analysis, 49,* 93-103, 1988), argues that the essential religious question is always most properly understood as one of how the world works, and different answers to this question account for religious differences, both small and great. On the concept of implicit religion, see Bailey, E. (1990). The implicit religion of contemporary society. *Social Compass, 37,* 483-509. In a variety of essays, I have similarly argued that the phenomenon that sociologists have often termed "secularization" is preeminently a shift in epistemologies rather than a move away from "religion"; see especially the introductory chapter in Swatos, W. H., Jr., & Gissurarson, L. R. (1996). *Icelandic spiritualism.* New Brunswick, NJ: Transaction Books.

12. Lechner, F. (1989). Cultural aspects of the modern world-system. In W. H. Swatos, Jr. (Ed.), *Religious politics in global and comparative perspective* (pp. 11-27). New York: Greenwood.

13. Pétursson, P. (1988). The relevance of secularization in Iceland. *Social Compass, 35,* 107-124.

14. "Eternal peace." (1996). *Iceland Reporter, 243,* 2. To complicate matters even further, Icelandic naming laws now also permit children to take or be given their mothers' Christian name to form their last name (matrinymic). This is interesting evidence of the ways in which particularisms and universalisms interact: Iceland has traditionally been relatively gender egalitarian, and this has been enhanced as this norm has been given great positive sanction in world institutions. Hence, the laws are changed to reflect this universalistic norm but correspondingly even more particularized in regard to naming. (Of course, just as anywhere else in the world, in everyday interaction people may use whatever name ["nickname"] they please; at issue is one's legal or citizenship name—hence the right of the nation-state to exercise authority over citizens.)

15. Murvar has indeed pointed out in "Some Tentative Modifications of Weber's Typology" (*Social Forces, 44,* 381-389, 1966) that in concrete instances what has been called the Occidental/Oriental contrast (following Max Weber) among world religions is really a contrast between the Western synthesis and religions of antiquity generally.

16. Although there is now a practice among some contemporary Western Christians that uses a female pronoun for the deity (Her), the universal practice of the Abrahamic traditions, which are formally patriarchal traditions, is to refer to the deity as deity using male forms of address.

17. Davidson, J. D. (1994). Religion among America's elite. *Sociology of Religion, 54,* 419-440; Davidson, J. D., Pyle, R. E., & Reyes, D. V. (1995). Persistence and change in the Protestant establishment. *Social Forces, 74,* 157-175.

18. Quoted in Kimmel, M. S., & Tavakol, R. (1986). Against Satan. In R. M. Glassman & W. H. Swatos, Jr. (Eds.), *Charisma, history, and social structure* (p. 106). New York: Greenwood.

19. Quoted in Kimmel & Tavakol (1986). In *Charisma, history, and social structure,* p. 112.

20. Parsons, T. (1964). Christianity and modern industrial society. In L. Schneider (Ed.), *Religion, culture, and society* (pp. 273-298). New York: John Wiley.

21. The warrior ethic concept derives from the work of Max Weber. I discuss it at length in Swatos, W. H., Jr. (1995). Islam and capitalism. In R. H. Roberts (Ed.), *Religion and the transformations of capitalism* (pp. 47-62). London: Routledge.

22. Duke, J. T., & Johnson, B. L. (1989). Protestantism and the spirit of democracy. In W. H. Swatos, Jr. (Ed.), *Religious politics in global and comparative perspective* (pp. 131-146). New York: Greenwood.

23. Quoted in Remnick, D. (1995, November 20). The Jewish conversation. *The New Yorker*, 37.

24. Weber, M. (1952). *Ancient Judaism.* Glencoe, IL: Free Press. (Original work published 1917-1919)

25. See Swatos, W. H., Jr. (1990). Renewing "religion" for sociology. *Sociological Focus, 23*, 141-153.

26. See Beyer, P. (1994). *Religion and globalization.*

Discussion Questions

1. When you describe a person as a "fundamentalist," or you hear someone described that way, what kinds of behaviors do you associate with that description? Do you view this description as basically positive or negative? Why?

2. In your own usage of the term *fundamentalist*, would you differentiate the label from the label "very religious"? For example, does your understanding of the statement, "Kim is a fundamentalist," differ from your understanding of the statement, "Kim is very religious"? How?

3. Technology, such as in the form of fax and Internet communications, has played a significant role in a number of world-altering events, including the prodemocracy demonstrations in Beijing's Tiananmen Square, the collapse of the Soviet empire with "the fall of the Wall," and the attack on the World Trade Center. Although Americans have tended to celebrate the former, they deplore the latter. What options do you see for ensuring uses of technology that advance global civilization, and who do you think is best situated to determine what constitutes an advance?

Index